ANTIQUE TRADER®

AMERICAN & EUROPEAN

Decorative and

Art Glass

PRICE GUIDE

EDITED BY
Kyle Husfloen
CONTRIBUTING EDITOR
Louis O. St. Aubin, Jr.

© 2000
by Krause Publications

Published by
Antique Trader Books, A Division of

**krause
publications**

700 E. State Street • Iola, WI 54990-0001
Telephone: 715/445-2214
Web: www.krause.com

Please, call or write us for our free catalog of antiques and collectibles publications.
To place an order or receive our free catalog, call 800-258-0929.
For editorial comment and further information,
use our regular business telephone at (715) 445-2214.

Library of Congress Catalog Number: 00-104629
ISBN: 0-87341-896-4

Printed in the United States of America

Introduction

In the spring of 1994 Antique Trader Books began an expanded program of publishing price guides and reference books for collectors. Building on twenty-five years experience in the price guide publishing field, highlighted by our *Annual Antiques & Collectibles Price Guide,* we launched our new efforts with the release of *Antique Trader Books Pottery & Porcelain Ceramics Price Guide,* a comprehensive survey of all types of American and foreign ceramic wares from the 18th century through the 20th. The third edition of this guide was recently released.

This successful release was followed up in Fall 1994 with a book of similar size and format dealing with collectible glassware—*Antique Trader Books American Pressed Glass & Bottles Price Guide.* The book you now hold is a second edition of the sequel to this glass reference and covers all types of American and European decorative and Art glasswares of the 19th and 20th centuries.

Antique Trader Books American & European Decorative & Art Glass Price Guide, 2nd Edition, offers you a truly comprehensive guide to the finest glasswares produced since the mid-19th century. In that era glassmakers in Europe, England and America began to produce very ornate and decorative glass pieces to appeal to the tastes of the 'carriage trade' as well as the increasingly prosperous middle class who wished to emulate the tastes and fashions of the elegant elite. Popular magazines and newspapers of the day helped spread the word about what was new and chic and large international expositions, beginning with England's Crystal Palace exposition of 1851, served as an ideal venue for glass manufacturers to spotlight their newest and most elegant wares. With hundreds of thousands of visitors during the course of such World's Fairs, a great demand was spurred among all levels of society for glasswares (and many other products) which people had seen on display. To help serve this demand some glass companies actually set-up small factories right on the exposition grounds to produce and sell souvenir glass items, a prime example being Gillinder & Sons display at the 1876 Philadelphia Centennial Exposition.

By the last decades of the 19th century every glass factory of any size or pretension was striving to produce new and novel lines of glass to attract a wider buying public. Several American glassmakers led the way in this field by designing and patenting a number of unique and quite expensive glass lines such as Amberina, Burmese and Crown Milano. Today collectors refer to these and related colorful wares as "Art Glass," since they were always meant more for artful show than for everyday use. Although some of these exclusive products were beyond the pocketbooks of average buyers, glassmakers saw to it that less expensive but still colorful and showy wares were available to fit their budgets and yet still provide at least the illusion of taste and style.

The demand for elegant glasswares in colorful Art glass or "Brilliant Period" fine cut glass continued right through the turn of the 20th century. As new styles evolved, like the Art Nouveau movement of the 1890s, designers and tastemakers such as Louis Comfort Tiffany came forward to provide a new range of elegant, exotic and choice glasswares. This Victorian era interest in the elegant seemed to scarcely abate until the hard realities of the first World War made such frivolousness seem outdated and unimportant.

From the 1920s onward for many years there was a strong reaction against all things Victorian, including glassware. Some elegant lines continued to be produced by firms such as Steuben, but the sparkling excess of the 1880-1910 era was over. When the great Depression of the 1930s hit, the production of expensive, elegant glass took another hit and since that era only a handful of makers have attempted to revive the look and style of the 19th century's rarest glasswares. Today there is evolving a

Studio Glass movement where glass artisans design and hand produce fine pieces, some inspired by earlier lines, but many of unique modernist style. Fewer and fewer glassmakers in this country and abroad can afford to develop, produce and market the wonderfully-diverse range of handcrafted glass which was available to our ancestors a century ago. That, of course, is why those increasingly rare and unique Victorian examples are so much in demand today.

I hope you'll find our revised guide to these decorative and Art glasswares of great assistance. We feel we're providing an excellent introduction to this realm of collecting beginning with a special introductory feature by noted writer, appraiser and television personality Bob Rau. We are also most proud to have noted Art glass authority Louis St. Aubin, Jr. serve as our Contributing Editor for this new edition. Mr. St. Aubin is well known for his years of work in the field of American Art glass, especially wares produced in New England. His shop, Brookside Antiques in New Bedford, Massachusetts, is a mecca for all those who love America's finest Art glass.

In addition to our price listings, we provide a brief introductory paragraph about each line we list and, in many instances, we include a copy of the mark or markings which may be found on typical examples. We also are offering a series of sketches which highlight typical forms used in antique Art glass. And to round out our text we are offering a Glossary of Terms, a Selected Bibliography and Appendices covering Clubs for collectors and Museums which feature glass collections.

My staff and I have worked hard to gather a wide range of pricing information from many sources which should provide an accurate and in-depth gauge of current collecting trends. We have also expanded the number of illustrations to show as many unique examples as possible. After all, a picture is worth a thousand words, especially when a unique piece of glass is being considered. A special 16 page color section also highlights this volume.

I hope you'll find our new guide interesting and informative and I'll look forward to hearing your comments. We're always interested in reader input and we strive to meet your needs whenever possible. Let me know what you think after you've had a chance to sit back and peruse the world of colorful and elegant glass encased in the following pages.

—Kyle Husfloen, Editor

Please note: Though listings have been double-checked and every effort has been made to insure the accuracy, neither the compilers, editors nor publisher can assume responsibility for any losses that might be incurred as a result of consulting this guide, or of errors, typographical or otherwise.

Photography Credits

Photographers who have contributed to this issue include: Stanley L. Baker, Minneapolis, Minnesota; Johanna S. Billings, Danielsville, Pennsylvania; Vance Hall, Wichita, Kansas, Robert G. Jason-Ickes, Olympia, Washington and Bill Pitt, New Bedford, Massachusetts.

For other photographs, artwork, data or permission to photograph in their shops, we sincerely express appreciation to the following auctioneers, galleries, museums, individuals and shops:

Albrecht Auction Service, Vassar, Michigan; Antique Publications, Marietta, Ohio; The Burmese Cruet, Montgomeryville, Pennsylvania; The Cedars - Antiques, Aurelia, Iowa; Christie's, New York, New York; Collectors Sales & Services, Pomfret Center, Connecticut; William Doyle Galleries, New York, New York; DuMouchelles Art Galleries Company, Detroit, Michigan; Early's Auction Company, Milford, Ohio; Ruth A. Forsythe, Galena, Ohio; Garth's Auctions, Inc., Delaware, Ohio; Green Valley Auctions, Mt. Crawford, Virginia; Grunewald Antiques, Hillsborough, North Carolina; Vance Hall, A Touch of Glass, Ltd., Wichita, Kansas; Harmer Rooke Galleries, New York, New York; Gene Harris Antique Auction Center, Marshalltown, Iowa; the late William Heacock, Marietta, Ohio; Jackson's Auctions, Cedar Falls, Iowa; James Julia, Fairfield, Maine; Joy Luke Gallery, Bloomington, Illinois; Dr. James Measell, Marietta, Ohio; L.H. Selman, Ltd., Santa Cruz, California; Skinner, Inc., Bolton, Massachusetts; Louis O. St. Aubin, New Bedford, Massachusetts; Sotheby's, New York, New York; Temples Antiques, Eden Prairie, Minnesota; Treadway Gallery, Cincinnati, Ohio; Lee Vines, Hewlett, New York; Web Wilson's Antique Hardware Auctions, Portsmouth, Rhode Island; and Wolf's Fine Arts Auctioneers, Cleveland, Ohio

On the Cover:

Front cover: Left to right - A cut and enameled Legras tall square vase, 8 1/2" h., courtesy of Jackson's Auctioneers, Cedar Falls, Iowa; a lovely Burmese pitcher hand-painted with an ivy vine and inscription from Charles Dickens, private collection; a three-layer English cameo scent bottle with sterling silver collar and cap, 2 3/4" h., courtesy of The Burmese Cruet, Montgomeryville, Pennsylvania. In the background, a partial view of a tall slender Burmese pitcher.

Back cover: A Wheeling Peach Blow cruet, 6 3/4" h., courtesy of The Burmese Cruet, Montgomeryville, Pennsylvania.

Special Feature

The Evolution of Art Glass 1880-1930

• *Bob Rau*

For years crystal clear glass had been the standard for buyers of the best glasswares in Europe and America, but by the mid-nineteenth century the public was growing tired of colorless wares, even those with beautiful cut designs. They wanted color and more flair in design, and these elements became paramount in satisfying the tastes of the glass-buying public.

Glass industry innovations in colored glass began around 1850 in England and elsewhere in Europe and tremendous advances were soon made. Many great glass designers and technicians were centered in England. The first true 'world's fair,' the Great Exhibition of 1851 at the Crystal Palace in London, showed how inventive the major British glasshouses were and the determination to maintain their traditional excellence in deep cut crystal. The British glasshouses also wanted to challenge and excel the famous French and Bohemian makers of colored, cased and enamel-painted products. During the 1850s and 1860s some of the most sophisticated glassware was crystal enhanced by engraving, often done by immigrant Bohemians. In the following decades, Venetian inspired creations (especially ornate table centerpieces) were developed and quickly gave rise to a craving for fancy colors and shapes in glassware.

Some glass firms in Stourbridge, a major English glass center, introduced cameo glass, which required extensive etching and carving through a white glass casing to a dark colored ground. Most designs in English cameo were classically inspired and soon rivaled the Italian shell cameos.

Thomas Webb & Sons signed cameo vase. It features a frosted yellow ground layered with red and white opal and cut and carved with a bouquet of wild geranium blossoms, buds and leaves and linear border above and below. 9" h. Photo courtesy of Skinner, Inc., Bolton, Massachusetts.

By the 1870s and 1880s, names like Thomas Webb and Sons, Stevens and Williams, the Northwood Family, the Richardsons, George Woodall and Joseph Locke were well established as leaders in the production of some of the most exciting glasswares ever developed. Although widely appreciated in this country, you would be fortunate in visiting a museum in England to find many of these pieces on display today.

During the mid-nineteenth century in France, Bohemia, Austria and Germany, glasshouses were producing significant amounts of deep-cut crystal in imitation of English wares and experimental and innovative color products similar to those that were associated with earlier Bohemian artisans. Opaline, often with elaborate painted or gilded decorations, was especially favored by the public. French paperweights with artistic colored designs became famous worldwide, while the large factories of Baccarat and St. Louis moved to satisfy the evergrowing demand for glass artifacts.

Individual French artists, however, rather than the large companies experimented in decorative glass work. Joseph Brocard and Eugene Rousseau were two such glass artists. The most famous, though, was Emile Gallé, a newcomer who arrived on the scene around 1885 and eventually established his own school in Nancy, France.

Gallé soon became a true master of glass, lending his talents to the carving of glass with exotic botanical themes. Although the English had earlier revived the ancient cameo glass technique, it was Gallé who originated a multicolored cameo ware featuring many unique designs and hues. Later, when the Daum Brothers of France became interested in glass, they received help and advice from Gallé. Their combined talents developed new and different techniques for interior and intaglio work on cameo glass. It is not surprising that the finer pieces of Daum rank very close to those of Emile Gallé in desirability and value.

Pâté de verre (literally "paste of glass"), was another glassmaking technique popular with the French. Unlike cameo, with its cut-back layers of various colors, *pâté de verre* involved building up layers of colored glass with a compound that created unique and often life-like designs.

While the French focused on cameo, enameled and *pâté de verre* art glass, the English and Americans continued to develop a broad range of colorful lines in the period from 1885 to 1900.

Some English wares, such as Rainbow, Pull-Up and Silveria, are rarely found on the open market today and may go unrecognized except by a few experts. Many American-made lines are much more readily recognized and available.

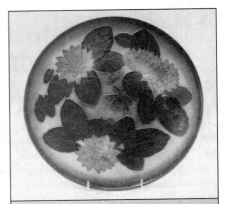

This large 16 1/4" d. charger is a choice example of Gallé's cameo work. It features a slightly opalescent lemon yellow ground shading to amber at the rim and overlaid in amber and rhododendron pink and cut with lotus blossoms, pads and foliage. Ca. 1900. Photo courtesy of Sotheby's, New York, New York.

A cameo inkwell by Daum, Nancy. The squared body and matching lid are in amber overlaid in lavender and cut with a continuous landscape scene. 5" h. Photo courtesy of Wolf's Fine Art Auctioneers, Cleveland, Ohio.

An interesting pâté de verre oval tray molded with a realistic dark green fish on a lighter green ground highlighted with molded seaweeds. Signed "A. Walter Nancy," one of the major French producers of this type of glass. 51/2 x 91/4". Photo courtesy of Skinner, Inc., Bolton, Massachusetts.

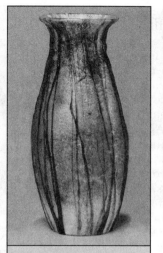

Burmese was another heat-reactive glass patented by the Mount Washington Glass Company. Pieces shade from a deep peach to a pale yellow and some, such as this 7 1/2" h. vase, are decorated with lovely enameled scenes of florals, birds, or fish. The colorful fish in this scene is being snared by a hand-painted heavy gilt enamel net. Photo courtesy of DuMouchelle's, Detroit, Michigan.

This "Silveria" vase is an example of a lesser known line produced by the Stevens and Williams firm early in the 20th century. It features clear glass internally decorated with foil and overlaid with transparent molten glass in spring green, pink, yellow, and cobalt blue and randomly applied with green vertical threading. It features an etched mark "S&W - 107." 11 3/8" h. Photo courtesy of Sotheby's, New York, New York.

One of the most ornate lines produced by the Mount Washington Glass Company was Crown Milano. Pieces featured a creamy or white opal body decorated with florals, scenes, or heavy gilt trim. This 15 1/2" h. vase is highlighted with an elaborate Venetian gondola scene in polychrome enamels and further gilt scrolling frames. It is marked on the base with the "CM" in wreath mark. Photo courtesy of Skinner, Inc., Bolton Massachusetts.

By the middle of the nineteenth century many American glass companies were employing European craftsmen and designers, though the standard glasswares were pressed glass, sometimes in patterns to imitate cut glass. By the time of the Centennial Exhibition in 1876, crystal glass produced in the United States was comparable in quality to most produced overseas. One of the most celebrated companies of the era was the New England Glass Company of East Cambridge, Massachusetts, which later became the Libbey Glass Company and was relocated to Toledo, Ohio. This firm patented several colorful Art glass lines including Amberina, Peach Blow, Pomona, and Agata. Other notable glass companies producing Art glass were the Mt. Washington Glass Company of New Bedford, Massachusetts (Burmese, Crown Milano, Royal Flemish) and Hobbs, Brockunier & Company of Wheeling, West Virginia (Wheeling Peach Blow, pressed Amberina and Opalescent lines.)

In the 1890s one of the greatest proponents of the new style of Art glass was Louis Comfort Tiffany. Tiffany had been born into a notable mercantile family and his father, Charles Tiffany, was a man of considerable wealth and business experience and founder of the premier jewelry firm, Tiffany and Company, of New York City.

Louis Comfort worked long and hard in the jewelry trade while growing up and perhaps it was this experience which developed his interest in art. It must have been a shock to his father, however, when, at age 19, Louis announced his desire to study art rather than attend college. Not only did he study art but he became a leading interior designer of the Gilded Age and then evolved an interest in designing and producing stunning leaded glass windows, lamps, and, of course, unique decorative glasswares. Tiffany's Favrile glass, with its lustrous, shimmering metallic effects in a rainbow of colors, was one of his most startling creations. Most frequently encountered are gold and blue, but there are also impressive examples with brown, green, red and black lustre finishes. A leading designer in the Art Nouveau style of the 1890s (his works were first publicly exhibited in 1893), Tiffany also developed other glass lines with exotic names such as Lava, Tel El Amarna, Agate and Cypriote. These wares are rare and much sought after.

Tiffany's genius guided the development of other glass artists including Kimble, Durand, Nash and many others, some of whom went on to open their own glass firms.

The one glass artist who closely rivaled Tiffany in creativity was the transplanted Englishman, Frederick Carder, who came to

A rare variation of Amberina is Plated Amberina, which is cased glass. It features the same coloring as Amberina but pieces always have molded ribbing around the sides. This lovely pitcher has an applied amber handle.

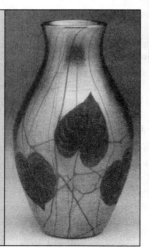

A handsome Tiffany baluster-form vase with a golden amber iridescent finish with green inclusions which are wheel-cut as broad naturalistic leaves. Marked on the base "L.C. Tiffany Favrile - 3403L." 8 5/8" h. Photo courtesy of Skinner, Inc., Bolton, Massachusetts.

One of Louis Tiffany's unique and innovative glass lines was called "Lava." This pitcher in Lava features rough-hewn navy blue iridescent hourglass devices, the interior and applied C-scroll handle also in amber iridescence. It is signed "L.C. Tiffany 4586C." Ca. 1908. 6 7/8" h. Photo courtesy of Sotheby's, New York, New York.

Frederick Carder developed the iridescent Aurene line for Steuben. These baluster- and ring-turned candlesticks feature an overall gold Aurene iridescent finish. One is marked "Aurene 3100," 8 1/4" h. Photo courtesy of Skinner, Inc., Bolton, Massachusetts.

Among the many interesting types of glass developed by Frederick Carder was Jade. This three-prong tree-trunk vase in green Jade features realistic thorns. 3 3/4" d., 6 1/8" h. Photo courtesy of Temples Antiques, Eden Prairie, Minnesota.

this country in 1903 and helped found the Steuben Glass Works in Corning, New York. Over his long career (he lived for nearly a century), Carder developed and promoted iridescent glass as a true art form and built a studio known for its many talented artists.

The many glass creations of Louis Tiffany and Frederick Carder remain as monuments to the vivid imaginations and skills of these glass artists. Both of these men served as a bridge between the ornate and fussy Art glass of the 1880s, the Art Nouveau era of the turn-of-the-century, and the dawning of the modern era of glass design.

Tiffany had his "Favrile" glass and Carder developed a similar line he called "Aurene," but other glassmakers followed their lead and also produced iridized glasswares.

A. Douglas Nash, who had worked for Tiffany for many years, purchased the Tiffany glass furnaces in 1928 and started his own company, producing lines which closely resembled Tiffany's earlier work. He also developed his own unique lines, such as Chintz and Cluthra. In 1931, when his company failed, he went to work for the Libbey Glass Company of Toledo, where he designed the Libbey-Nash line.

Martin Bach, another former employee of Tiffany, established the Quezel Art Glass & Decorating Company, Brooklyn, New York, in 1901. His glasswares are so similar to Tiffany's that they can prove confusing to today's collector. Of course his old master, Tiffany, was both amazed and angered by Bach's overt opportunism in producing rival glass.

The Vineland Flint Glass Works of Vineland, New Jersey, was opened by Victor Durand, Jr. in 1897 and became another well-known glass factory at the turn of the

This Durand vase in the "King Tut" pattern features green walls decorated with iridescent cobalt blue, opaque blue, opaque white and gold pulled and trailed overall designs. 6 1/2" h. Photo courtesy of Wolf's Fine Art Auctioneers, Cleveland, Ohio.

The best known line of glass developed by A. Douglas Nash was Chintz. This tall vase in Chintz features green and blue draped stripes. Ca. 1930. 17 5/8" h. Photo courtesy of Skinner, Inc., Bolton, Massachusetts.

Closely resembling the iridescent wares of Tiffany, this simple Quezal glass vase features blue swirled designs on a gold iridescent ground. It is signed on the bottom. 6 1/2" h. Photo courtesy of Wolf's Fine Art Auctioneers, Cleveland, Ohio.

century. About 1920 Martin Bach developed a gold lustre glass decorated with random threading for the Vineland firm and this line eventually won first prize at the Sesquicentennial International Exposition in Philadelphia in 1926. Most of Durand's glass was signed "V. Durand" or just "Durand."

After his death in 1931, Evan F. Kimble took over the Vineland factory and started the Kimble Glass Company, today best remembered for its version of Cluthra glass. Kimble glass was produced for only a short time, and the few marked pieces today can bring high prices.

The Union Glass Works of Somerville, Massachusetts, established in 1851, today is best known for the production of the Art Nouveau era line of glass called Kew Blas. This iridized glass of the 1890s derives its name from an anagram of the name of the plant manager of that time, W(illiam) S. Blake.

Another type of iridescent glass closely resembling Tiffany is "Kew Blas." This Kew Blas pitcher features a white ground decorated with green and gold iridescent pulled-feather designs. It has a scrolled and ribbed applied gold handle and gold interior. Ca. 1900. 4 1/8" h. Photo courtesy of Skinner, Inc., Bolton, Massachusetts.

This dresser box with an ornate molded square form decorated with large daisies on a dark background is an example of the Kelva line from the C.F. Monroe Company. Photo courtesy of Doris Johnson, Rockford, Illinois.

Scarce white opal wares with colored decoration were also produced by the Handel Glass Decorating Co. This humidor, marked "Tobacco" on the lid, has a drinking scene on the side on a shaded russet to green background with gilt trim. 7 1/2" w., 7 3/4" h. Courtesy of Lee Vines, Hewlett, New York.

Not all turn-of-the-century Art glass was iridized, of course. Several famous lines of decorated white opal glass with molded designs and painted decoration were released by the C.F. Monroe Company of Meriden, Connecticut. Wave Crest ware was their most famous and abundant line, but similar pieces were marked with the names Nakara and Kelva. The Handel Glass Decorating Company, Meriden, Connecticut, famous for their decorative lamps, also

Beautifully decorated with the bust portrait of a Victorian lady, this large round dresser box is an example of the Nakara line from C.F. Monroe. 8" d., 5 1/2" h. Private collection.

An ornate Wave Crest dresser box with gilt-metal hinged rim fittings and base band with scroll feet. The body features black and white banding with delicate hand-painted florals and heavy gilt trim. 6 3/4" w., 6" h. Photo courtesy of Joy Luke Gallery, Bloomington, Illinois.

A selection of American Victorian Art Glass. Left to right: a New England Glass Company Amberina lily-form vase, 7" h.; a New England Amberina angular pitcher in the Inverted Thumbprint pattern, 4 3/4" h.; a New England Amberina finger bowl, 5 1/2" d., 2 1/2" h.; a New England Peach Blow tumbler, a Burmese tumbler, a Green Opaque tumbler and (back) a Coralene-decorated tumbler in the seaweed design.

produced a limited line of decorated white opal wares and a frosted clear line with a chipped ice effect and painted decoration which they called Teroma.

This brief discussion can't possibly cover all the diverse and colorful glasswares of the Art glass era, but you will find many others touched upon in the following pages. We hope this will inspire you to learn all you can about this unique era in glass production. Whatever color or form of glass is your favorite, there is undoubtedly an Art glass ware that will appeal to you. Although the rarest examples can bring astronomical prices, with care, study, and diligence, most collectors can still locate and afford pieces which they can display with pride.

ABOUT THE AUTHOR

Bob Rau is a well-known writer, lecturer and appraiser who is familiar to many antiquers as the former host of popular PBS television series, "The Collectors."

Bob has been a frequent contributor to The Antique Trader Price Guide and authored our 1989 Special Focus feature, 'The Art of Steuben Glass.' In addition he authored the book, "The Collectors," published by the Graphic Arts Center Publishing Company in 1989.

Typical Forms

BASKETS & BOWLS

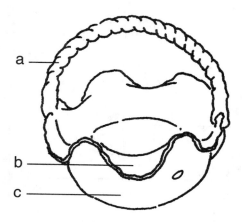

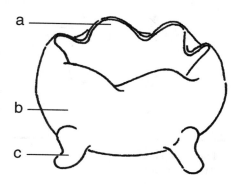

BASKET

a. Applied rope-twist handle
b. Deeply ruffled flaring rim
c. Squatty, bulbous body

BOWL

a. Incurved, ruffled rim
b. Squatty, bulbous body
c. Applied feet

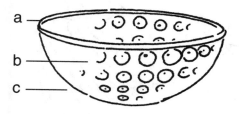

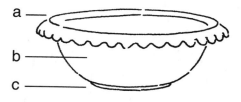

BOWL

a. Flat rim
b. Pressed overall pattern
c. Deep rounded body

BOWL

a. Scalloped, rolled rim
b. Deep rounded body
c. Footing

CRUETS & DECANTERS

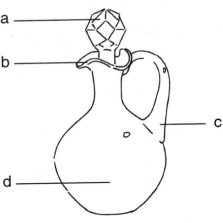

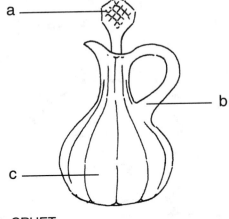

CRUET

a. Facet-cut stopper
b. Tricorner rim
c. Applied handle
d. Bulbous ovoid body

CRUET

a. Facet-molded stopper
b. Pressed handle
c. Paneled squatty bulbous body

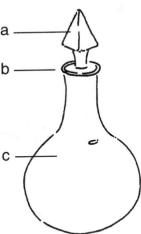

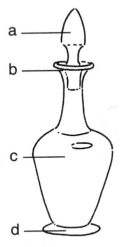

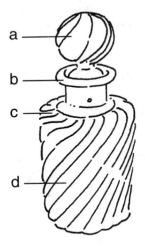

DECANTER

a. Cut, paneled & pointed stopper
b. Cylindrical neck with flat rim
c. Spherical body

DECANTER

a. Pointed teardrop stopper
b. Waisted cylindrical neck with flared rim
c. Tapering ovoid body
d. Applied foot

DECANTER

a. Ball stopper with molded & swirled ribs
b. Short cylindrical neck with rolled rim
c. Flat shoulder
d. Cylindrical body with molded & swirled ribs

PITCHERS & EWERS

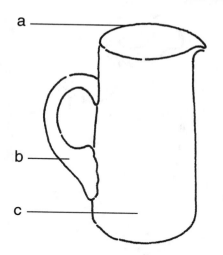

PITCHER

a. Flat rim with pinched spout
b. Applied handle, sometimes "reeded" (ribbed)
c. Tankard-style

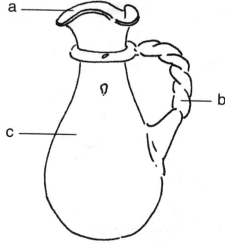

PITCHER

a. Tricorner rim
b. Applied rope-twist (braided) handle & neck ring
c. Tapering ovoid body

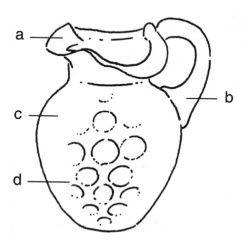

PITCHER

a. Tricorner rim with rolled edges
b. Applied handle
c. Ovoid body
d. Overall pattern molded design

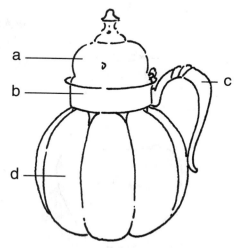

PITCHER

a. Silver plate domed lift-lid with finial
b. Silver plate neck collar
c. Silver plate handle
d. Spherical melon-lobed body

PITCHERS & EWERS

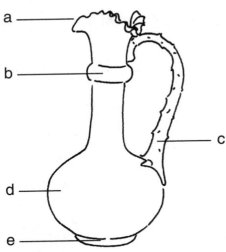

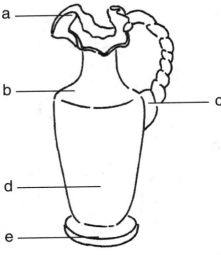

EWER

a. Tricorner crimped & ruffled rim
b. Molded neck ring on tall neck
c. Applied 'thorn' handle
d. Bulbous body
e. Molded footring

EWER

a. Tricorner ruffled rim
b. Tapering shoulder
c. Applied rope-twist (braided) handle
d. Tapering ovoid body
e. Cushion foot

VASES

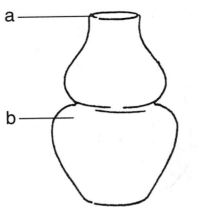

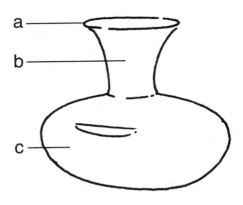

VASE

a. Short cylindrical neck with flat rim
b. Double gourd-form body

VASE

a. Flat rim
b. Trumpet-form neck
c. Squatty bulbous body

VASES

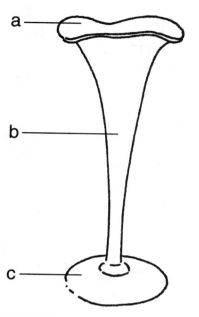

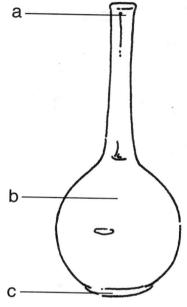

LILY-FORM VASE

a. Widely flaring, lightly ruffled rim
b. Slender trumpet-form body
c. Applied disc-form foot

BOTTLE-FORM VASE

a. Tall slender 'stick' neck with flat rim
b. Spherical body
c. Molded footring

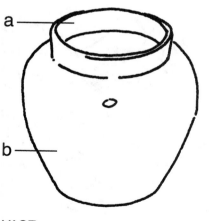

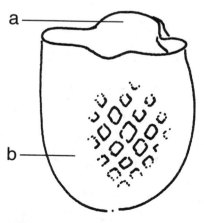

VASE

a. Short, wide cylindrical neck
b. Wide ovoid body

VASE

a. Lobed, flat rim
b. Egg-shaped body with overall
   pattern-molded design

VASES

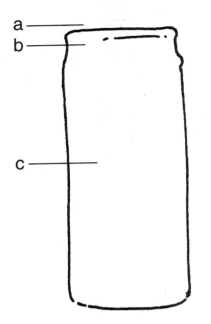

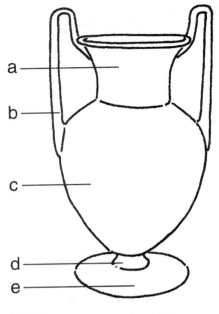

VASE

a. Flat rim
b. Short waisted neck
c. Simple cylindrical body

VASE

a. Flaring cylindrical neck
b. Slender applied angled handle
c. Baluster-shaped, urn-form body
d. Short pedestal
e. Applied disc foot

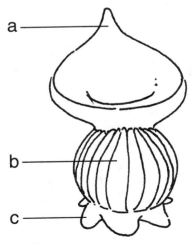

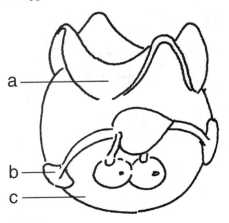

VASE

a. Jack-in-the Pulpit rim
b. Spherical body with molded ribs
c. Applied 'petal' feet

VASE

a. Four-lobed ruffled rim
b. 'Appliqued' decoration of fruit
c. Spherical body

AGATA

Agata was patented by Joseph Locke of the New England Glass Company in 1887. The application of mineral stain left a mottled effect on the surface of the article. It was applied chiefly to the Wild Rose (Peach Blow) line but sometimes was applied as a border on a pale opaque green. In production for a short time, it is scarce. Items listed below are of the Wild Rose line unless otherwise noted.

Bowl, flaring cylindrical sides w/deep ruffling, 5" d., 2 1/2" h. **$770**

Fine Agata Bowl

Bowl, 5 1/4" d., 2 1/2" h., deep gently flaring sides w/a ten-ruffle rim, good color & spotting (ILLUS.) **546**
Bowl, 5 1/2" d., 2 3/4" h., upright deeply ruffled sides... **950**
Celery vase, bulbous base tapering slightly w/a gently flaring rim, green opaque ground decorated w/lacy gold trim on the rim & shoulder, 6 7/8" h.............................. **985**
Celery vase, green opaque............................. **750**
Cruet w/original stopper, green opaque, spherical body tapering to a slender neck w/tricorner rim, applied green handle & facet-cut green stopper.................... **1,650**
Finger bowl, deep round upright ruffled form **550**
Finger bowls & underplates, deep round upright ruffled bowls & matching ruffled underplates, fine mottling, set of 6 .... **7,920**
Juice tumbler, slightly tapering cylindrical body, old Maude Feld sticker, 3 3/4" h. **550**
Lemonade glass, tall slightly tapering form w/small applied pink loop handle near the base **688**
Pitcher, 5 1/4" h., milk, bulbous ovoid body w/a short squared neck, applied handle....... **935**
Pitcher, 7" h., bulbous ovoid body tapering to a short squared neck, applied reeded pink handle, uniform mottling **4,500**

Rare Agata Spooner

Spooner, deeply ruffled lavender rim, 4 1/2" h. (ILLUS.)...................................... **1,250**

Toothpick holder, cylindrical w/square rim, good mottling... **1,100**
Toothpick holder, green opaque, bulbous body tapering gently to a slightly flared rim **990**
Toothpick holder, green opaque, squatty ovoid body tapering to a widely flaring rim, decorated around the rim w/a band of blue mottled stain w/a gold border band, 2 1/4" h... **950**
Toothpick holder, ovoid body tapering to a short cylindrical neck................................ **1,760**
Toothpick holder, squatty ovoid base tapering to a flaring rim, green opaque ground decorated w/lacy gold trim on the rim & shoulder **1,150**
Toothpick holder, tri-cornered rim **2,000**
Toothpick holder, cylindrical w/a tricorner incurved rim, fine mottling, 2" h. **950**

Fine Agata Tumbler

Tumbler, cylindrical, 3 3/4" h. (ILLUS.) **550-750**
Tumbler, cylindrical, dark mottled & gold tracery **800**
Tumbler, cylindrical, deep raspberry shading to creamy pink, decorated w/oily mottling & blue spotting, 2 1/2" d., 3 7/8" h. **750**
Tumbler, cylindrical, heavy overall blue 'oil spotting' on the mottled ground, 3 3/4" h. **550**
Tumbler, cylindrical, scattered blue 'oil spots' on a finely mottled surface, 3 3/4" h. **750**
Tumbler, nicely mottled, sticker of Maude B. Feld, 3 3/4" h. **750**
Tumblers, deep color w/excellent spotting, 3 1/4" h., set of 6 .... **4,000**
Vase, 4 1/2" h., cylindrical body w/squared scalloped rim, fine coloring, ... **880**
Vase, 4 5/8" h., ovoid body w/four deeply dimpled sides tapering to an upright flaring crimped four-point rim, New England .. **1,380**
Vase, 6 1/4" h., green opaque, fourteen-rib gently tapering ovoid body w/flared rim, New England Glass Co. **650**
Vase, 7 3/4" hlily-form w/tricorner rim, glossy finish, ... **1,500**
Vase, 8" h., bottle-form, bulbous ovoid body tapering to a tall slender 'stick' neck, excellent gold & blue spotting, New England.. **1,955**

Vase, 8 1/4" h., bottle-form, ovoid body tapering to a tall slender 'stick' neck, good mottling on the lower half **798**

Rare Agata Water Set

Water set: tankard pitcher & six tumblers; the tall pitcher w/applied handle, fine coloring, tumblers 3 3/4" h., pitcher 8 3/4" h., the set (ILLUS. of part) **9,150**
Whiskey tumbler, cylindrical, fine mottling, 2 1/2" h. **375**

ALEXANDRITE

Inspired by the gemstone of the same name, Alexandrite is a decorative glass shading from yellow-green to rose to blue. It was produced by Thomas Webb & Sons and Stevens & Williams of England in the late 19th century. The Moser firm of Karlsbad, Bohemia made a similar line.

Finger bowl & underplate, rounded bowl w/squared top on a matching underplate, shading from amber to rose w/lovely blue rims, bowl 5" d., plate 6" d., the set **$2,200**
Finger bowl & underplate, the wide stepped bowl w/an upright crimped & swirled rim, shading violet blue to amber, w/matching round crimped underplate, Webb, underplate 6" d., 2 pcs. **1,176**
Goblet, large bell-form bowl w/tiny optic honeycomb design, plain stem & round foot, Thomas Webb & Sons, 4 1/2" h. **950**

Rare Webb Alexandrite Nut Dish

Nut dish, round w/deeply ruffled & flared upright sides, Honeycomb patt., Thomas Webb & Sons, 3" d. (ILLUS.) **750-950**
Punch cup, barrel-shaped w/applied citron handle, 2 1/4" d., 2 3/4" h. **650**
Toothpick holder, a small applied amber foot below the tall cylindrical cupped body w/an optic herringbone design, 3 1/4" h. **1,100**

Small Alexandrite Vase

Vase, 3" h., squatty bulbous base tapering to an upright hexagonal neck, molded Diamond Quilted patt. (ILLUS.) **750**
Vase, 4 1/4" h., Honeycomb patt. **950**
Vase, 4 7/8" h., jack-in-the-pulpit-form, blue foot, possibly Webb **1,073**

Alexandrite Trumpet-form Vase

Vase, 8 1/4" h., trumpet-shaped, round foot, swirl-molded compressed base (ILLUS.) **2,200**
Wine, Optic patt., 4 1/2" h. **950**
Wine glass, deep rounded Diamond Quilted patt. bowl on a slender stem & round foot, 4 1/2" h. **1,200**

AMBERINA

Amberina was developed in the late 1880s by the New England Glass Company and a pressed version was made by Hobbs, Brockunier & Company (under license from the former). A similar ware, called Rose Amber, was made by the Mt. Washington Glass Works. Amberina-Rose Amber shades from amber to deep red or fuchsia and cut and plated (lined with creamy white) examples were also made. The Libbey Glass Company briefly revived blown Amberina, using modern shapes, in 1917.

Amberina Mark

Bar bottle, with original amber facet-cut stopper, Swirled Rib. patt., 8" h.................. **$350**

Basket, footed w/serrated rim, decorated w/h.p pink & blue flowers, applied ruffled amber handle, six applied amber feet, berry pontil **575**

Basket, swirled body w/applied amber ropetwist handle & applied amber feet, finely enameled w/florals, 11" h.................... **440**

Basket, ruffled rim, applied amber feet & handle, New England, 4" d., 9" h. **650**

Large Amberina Basket

Basket, tall flaring 'poke bonnet' form w/swirled Optic Rib patt., applied amber wishbone feet & applied amber rigaree handle, 7" w., 10 3/4" h. (ILLUS.) **395**

Berry set: 9" sq., 2 1/2" h. master bowl & six 5" sq., 1 3/8" h. sauce dishes; pressed Daisy & Button patt., attributed to Hobbs, Brockunier & Co., the set (minor rim chips) **650**

Bonbon, shape No. 3029, Libbey Glass Co., signed... **450**

Small Cylindrical Amberina Bowl

Bowl, 3 3/4" d., 2 3/4" h., cylindrical body w/a deeply ruffled fuchsia rim (ILLUS.) **325**

Bowl, 5" d., ice cream, individual, pressed Daisy & Button patt. **92**

Amberina Footed Bowl

Bowl, 5 3/4" d., 3 3/4" h., squatty bulbous body w/incurved six-crimp rim, Inverted Thumbprint patt., raised on three applied amber scroll feet, decorated around the rim w/gold florals (ILLUS.) **325**

Amberina Bowl & Barrel-shaped Mug

Bowl, 5 3/4" d., 3 3/4" h., squatty bulbous body w/swirled molded ribbing below the deeply ruffled & crimped rim (ILLUS. right) **135**

Bowl, 6 1/2" d., 6 3/4" h., deeply ruffled flaring amber rim, applied amber handles, applied amber base forming feet **350**

Fine Amberina Bowl

Bowl, 8 3/4" d., 4" h., squatty bulbous wide base w/high ruffled & flaring sides, Diamond Quilted patt., ground base pontil (ILLUS.) **475**

Bowl, 10" l., oval, pressed Daisy & Button patt. **350**

Bowl, 10" w., oblong diamond shape, pressed Daisy & Button patt. **400**

Bowl, 10 1/2" l., Reverse Amberina, Diamond Quilted patt. in a rounded heart-form bowl w/a rolled & tightly crimped rim, a curved, looped clear applied thorn handle at one side, late 19th c. **550**

Bowl, 11" d., shape No. 3026, Libbey Glass Co., signed....................................... **650**

Bowl, 6 1/2" x 11 3/4", Swirl patt., footed, applied amber handles, rim edging & feet **325**

Bowl, squatty rounded base w/waisted sides to a widely flaring rim, light vertical molding, Mt. Washington............................ **225**

Bowl-vase, Plated Amberina, waisted cylindrical twelve-ribbed body, New England Glass Co., 3 1/2" h. **4,500**

Bowls, individual berry, 5" sq., pressed Daisy & Button patt., set of 6...................... **500**

Butter dish, cov., Diagonal Block patt. **235**

Butter dish, cov., Inverted Thumbprint patt., 5" h. **220**

Butter dish, cov., round blown cover in Inverted Thumbprint patt., pressed Daisy & Button underplate **275**

Butter pat, petal-shaped, pressed Daisy & Button patt., 3" d. **115**

Butter pat, square, pressed Daisy & Button patt. **125**

Carafe, Reverse Amberina, Inverted Thumbprint patt., 7 1/2" h............................. **275**

Castor set: four bottle w/mustard jar, shaker, oil & vinegar cruets & one stopper; each bottle engraved, in a silver plate frame, the set 985

Celery vase, Diamond Quilted patt., New England Glass Co., 6 1/2" h. 375

Celery vase, pressed Daisy & Button patt., Hobbs, Brockunier & Co............................. 225

Celery vase, scalloped rim, in ornate silver plate frame marked "Pairpoint," 4" d., 6 1/2" h. celery insert w/original Mt. Washington Glass Co. seal, overall 11 1/4" h. 950

Cheese dish, cov., twelve-paneled cover w/cut finial, Optic patt., 9 1/2" d., 7" h. 345

Cheese plate, twelve-paneled, optic design, 9 1/2" d. 315

Cologne bottle, w/original facet-cut stopper, Inverted Thumbprint patt., New England Glass Co., 5" h. 275

Cologne bottle, w/original stopper, bulbous, Swirl patt., 5 1/4" h. 475

Cologne bottle, w/original stopper, shape No. 3040, Libbey Glass Co., signed, 2 oz. 750

Compote, open, ruffled rim, ball connector, flat disk base, shape No. 3016, Libbey Glass Co., signed..................................... 2,800

Compote, open, shape No. 3017, Libbey Glass Co., signed, 6 1/2" d., 8" h. 950

Condiment set: cylindrical salt & pepper shakers w/silver plate lids & an ovoid mustard jar w/silver plate lid all fitted in a silver plate frame w/central handle; each container in the Raindrop patt., frame marked by the Pairpoint Mfg. Co., the set 2,200

Creamer, globular base, slender neck w/flaring rim & pinched lip, applied angular amber handle, Swirl patt., 3 3/8" d., 5" h. 135

Creamer, Inverted Thumbprint patt., 4 3/4" h. 275

Creamer, ovoid body tapering to a short cylindrical neck w/arched spout, applied amber handle, Inverted Thumbprint patt., 5 1/2" h. 187

Cruet w/original stopper, bulbous body supported on a pedestal base, applied amber handle & amber facet-cut stopper, polished pontil 375

Amberina Melon-ribbed Cruet

Cruet w/original stopper, bulbous melon-ribbed body w/molded long leaf designs on alternating ribs, applied amber han-

dle, amber bubble stopper, 6 3/4" (ILLUS.).. 250

Amberina Cruet

Cruet w/original stopper, bulbous ovoid body w/lightly molded optic ribbing, slender cylindrical neck w/tricorner rim, applied amber handle, facet-cut amber stopper, New England Glass Co., 6 1/2" h. (ILLUS.)..................................... 425

Cruet w/original stopper, bulbous tapering Inverted Thumbprint Reverse Amberina body w/a slender neck & arched spout, applied amber reeded handle, amber bubble stopper, 7 1/2" h. 440

Cruet w/original stopper, Plated Amberina, spherical body w/a tall slender neck & a tricorner rim, applied amber handle, facet-cut amber stopper 8,500

Cruet w/original stopper, Plated Amberina spherical body w/a cylindrical neck & tricorner rim, applied amber handle & amber facet-cut stopper, deep ruby above creamy white decorated w/amber ribbing 5,000-6,500

Cruet w/original stopper, squatty bulbous body tapering to a tall slender neck w/tricorner rim, Inverted Thumbprint patt., applied amber handle & facet-cut amber stopper, 6" h. 225

Superb Plated Amberina Cruet

Cruet w/original stopper, Plated Amberina, spherical body w/a tall slender neck & a tricorner rim, applied amber handle, facet-cut amber stopper, superb coloring & wonderful condition, 7" h. (ILLUS.) 8,800

Cruet w/stopper, squatty bulbous body tapering to a slender neck w/arched spout, Inverted Thumbprint patt., decorated w/delicate enameled forget-me-nots, applied amber handle & facet-cut amber stopper **1,210**

Cuspidor, lady's, round squatty bulbous form w/a widely flaring gently ruffled rim, rich colors, 5" d., 2 7/8" h. **330**

Decanter, w/original amber bubble stopper, ovoid body tapering to a cylindrical neck w/pinched spout, applied amber handle, 4" d., 9" h. **275**

Decanter, w/original amber facet-cut stopper, Inverted Thumbprint patt., 10 1/2" h. **395**

Dish, sawtooth rim, diamond-shaped, pressed Daisy & Button patt., Gillinder Glass Co., 4 1/4" w., 6 1/8" l. **375**

Tall Amberina Ewer

Ewer, bulbous ovoid Inverted Thumbprint patt. body tapering to cylindrical neck w/small pinched spout, applied amber angled handle, 5 1/8" d., 10 1/8" h. (ILLUS.) **150**

Finger bowl, deep upright ten-crimp sides, faint optic ribbing, New England Glass Co., 5 1/2" d., 2 1/2" h. **172**

Finger bowl, fluted rim, fine color **375**

Finger bowl, Hobnail patt., squared rim on squatty rounded body, 4 3/8" d., 2 3/4" h. **125**

Finger bowl, square, Hobnail patt., Mt. Washington Glass Co. **225**

Inverted Thumbprint Finger Bowl

Finger bowl, squatty bulbous body w/closed, slightly ruffled rim, Inverted Thumbprint patt., 4 3/8" d., 2" h. (ILLUS.) **250**

Goblet, rose to amber coloring, optic ribbed design, 3 3/8" d., 6 1/8" h. **125**

Ice bucket, Diamond Optic patt., w/cut star on base, tab handles, 6 3/4" d., 5" h. **950**

Ice bucket, slightly flaring sides w/tab handles, decorated overall w/delicate blue & yellow flowers & green foliage, 7 1/4" d., 5 1/2" h. **200**

Ice cream set: master bowl & six plates; pressed Daisy & Button patt., 7 pcs. **1,200**

Lamp globe, 6 1/2" across at widest, 6 1/2" deep, 3" d. fitter **145**

Amberina Hall Lantern

Lantern, hall-type, kerosene, the large teardrop-form shade w/an Inverted Thumbprint design, brass fittings at the top & bottom, 6 3/4" d, 12 1/2" h. (ILLUS.) **500**

Lemonade glass, slightly tapering tall cylindrical body w/a small applied reeded ring handle near the base **175**

Lemonade glass, tall slightly flaring cylindrical form, Plated Amberina, applied amber loop handle near base, 4 3/4" h. ... **4,750**

Lemonade set: 10" h. pitcher & six 4" h. tumblers; pitcher w/cylindrical melon-lobed body over a reverse diamond-quilted design, the angled shoulder centered by a tall square neck, clear applied handle, matching tumblers, the set **385**

Lemonade set: 7" h. pitcher w/square rim & applied reeded handle & five matching 2 1/4" h. punch cups w/applied handles; Inverted Thumbprint patt., 6 pcs. **600**

Liquor bottle, w/original stopper, Ripple patt., 9 1/2" h. **125**

Model of a canoe, hanging-type, pressed Daisy & Button patt. **425**

Mug, barrel-shaped swirled optic-ribbed body on an applied disk foot, amber twisted rope handle w/end curl, heavily decorated w/gold flowers & leaves, 2 3/4" d., 4 5/8" h., (ILLUS. left with bowl)... **150**

Amberina Tall Cylindrical Mug

Mug, tall cylindrical body swelled at the base, wide swirled ribs up the sides to a plain rim, applied amber ropetwist C-form handle, decorated w/gilt stems w/flowers & leaves, 2 1/2" d., 5 1/2" h. (ILLUS.) **165**

Mug, barrel-shaped, swirled optic-ribbed pattern w/applied amber handle, 3" d., 3 3/4" h. 55

Perfume bottle w/stopper, disk foot below the tall slender ovoid body w/a flattened four-lobed rim, large optic ribbed ball stopper, stamped "Libbey Amberina," ca. 1917, 8 1/4" h. 2,530

Pickle castor, cylindrical Amberina insert in the Coin Spot patt., ornate silver plate holder 523

Bulbous Plated Amberina Pitcher

Pitcher, Plated Amberina, bulbous ovoid body tapering to a tricorner mouth, applied ruby handle, creamy white lining (ILLUS.) 10,000

Plated Amberina Tankard Pitcher

Pitcher, Plated Amberina, tankard-type, small pinched spout, applied amber handle (ILLUS.) 12,000

Pitcher, 4 3/4" h., Inverted Thumbprint patt., flaring base below long angled sides to the flaring squared rim, applied reeded amber handle, New England Glass Co. 375

Pitcher, 5" h., bulbous body w/a squared rim & applied amber handle, Inverted Thumbprint patt. 220

Pitcher, 7" h., tankard-type, slightly tapering cylindrical Diamond Quilted patt., applied amber handle.................................. 431

Pitcher, 7 1/2" h., bulbous w/ruffled tip, Inverted Thumbprint patt., applied amber reeded handle 149

Pitcher, 7 3/4" h., bulbous ovoid Diamond Quilted patt. body w/a tall, wide cylindrical neck w/pinched spout, applied angled reeded amber handle (ILLUS. top next column).......................... 380

Pitcher, 7 7/8" h., bulbous ovoid body tapering to a flared square mouth,

Inverted Thumbprint patt., applied reeded amber handle, late 19th c. 275-375

Amberina Diamond Quilted Pitcher

Pitcher, 8 1/2" h., Inverted Thumbprint patt., bulbous ovoid body w/four pinched-in sides below a cylindrical neck w/pinched spout, applied angled clear handle, 19th c. 275

Inverted Thumbprint Amberina Pitcher

Pitcher, 8 1/2" h., 6 1/2" d., Inverted Thumbprint patt., nearly spherical body w/a tall tri-lobed neck, applied amber handle (ILLUS.)..................................... 250

Pitcher & tumbler, pitcher 6 1/2" h., 2 1/2" d., the pitcher w/a footed ovoid body in the Inverted Thumbprint patt. tapering to a cylindrical neck w/a small pinched spout, applied angled amber handle, matching footed 3 3/8" h. tumbler, 2 pcs..................................... 185

Plate, 4 3/4" d., flared rim, Diamond Quilted patt., Mt. Washington Glass Co. 95

Plate, 6 7/8" d., Inverted Thumbprint patt........ 160

Punch cup, Diamond Quilted patt., applied threaded handle, New England Glass Co.,.. 150

Punch cup, eighteen optic ribs, New England Glass Co., 2 1/2" h. 185

Punch Cup, Inverted Thumbprint patt., w/applied amber handle, Mt. Washington Glass Co. 175

Rose bowl, triangular pinched-in rim, applied amber ribbed feet & berry prunt, Inverted Thumbprint patt., 3 3/4" d., 6" h...... 250

Salt dips, elongated oval w/pointed ends, pressed Daisy & Button patt., 4 1/2" l., pr. 248

Salt & pepper shakers, cylindrical optic-ribbed salt & pepper shakers w/original silver-plate tops set in an ornate silver-plate Victorian frame centered by a napkin ring below a tiny trumpet-form bud vase, bead & leaf brackets & pierced scroll feet on stand, the set (ILLUS. top next page) 900

Amberina Shakers in Ornate Frame

Salt & pepper shakers w/original metal lids, cylindrical molded rib design, pr........... **303**

Salt & pepper shakers w/original metal lids, cylindrical, Inverted Thumbprint patt., 3 1/2" h., pr. **275**

Salt shaker w/original two-piece lid, Baby Thumbprint patt., bulging dual mold-blown body, 2 1/2" h............................ **235**

Pressed Amberina Sauce Dish

Sauce dish, pressed Daisy & Button patt., square w/rounded corners, Hobbs, Brockunier & Co., Wheeling, West Virginia, 1880s, 5" w., 1 5/8" h. (ILLUS.) **110**

Spooner, Diamond Quilted patt., New England Glass Co., 4 1/2" h. **235**

Spooner, Inverted Thumbprint patt., 4 3/4" h... **95**

Sugar bowl, cov., pressed Daisy & Button patt., cylindrical bucket-style w/tab rim handles & flattened fitted cover w/knob finial, base in all-amber, 5 1/4" h. (flake on cover) **575**

Sugar bowl, open, Plated Amberina, squatty bulbous base tapering to a wide flat mouth, applied amber loop handles at shoulder, fine coloring, 2" h. **9,500**

Sugar shaker w/original lid, footed squatty bulbous plain body tapering to a swelled neck, Reverse Amberina, 4 1/2" h... **385**

Syrup pitcher w/original silver plate top, ball-shaped, Inverted Thumbprint patt., New England Glass Co. **1,250**

Toothpick holder, cylindrical body w/infolded tricorner rim, Venetian Diamond patt. **275**

Toothpick holder, cylindrical w/rounded bottom raised on a short pedestal foot, Inverted Thumbprint patt. **193**

Toothpick holder, cylindrical w/square rim, Diamond Quilted patt., New England Glass Co. (ILLUS. top column) **275**

Toothpick holder, cylindrical w/tricorner rim, Diamond Quilted patt. **330**

Amberina Toothpick Holder

Toothpick holder, ovoid body tapering to short flared neck, Diamond Quilted patt....... **165**

Toothpick holder, Plated Amberina, squatty bulbous base below the tapering cylindrical sides **11,000**

Diamond Quilted Amberina Tumbler

Tumbler, Diamond Quilted patt., cylindrical, New England Glass Co., 2 1/2" d., 3 5/8" h. (ILLUS.)... **100**

Tumbler, Inverted Thumbprint patt., flat bottom, 2 3/4" d., 3 3/4" h............................... **65**

Tumbler, Optic Rib patt., cylindrical **125**

Tumbler, optic Swirled Coin Spot patt., cylindrical, 3 3/4" h. **94**

Tumbler, Plated Amberina, embossed ribs, New England Glass Co., ca. 1880 3 3/4" h... **2,200**

Tumbler, Reverse Amberina, Inverted Thumbprint patt. **75**

Tumbler, Tiny Inverted Thumbprint patt........... **125**

Tumbler, cylindrical, a plain rim above a body cut overall in the Russian patt., 3 3/4" h. **2,530**

Tumbler, Optic Ribbed patt., cylindrical, attributed to Libbey, ca. 1917, 3 3/4" h. **105**

Tumblers, Diamond Quilted patt., cylindrical, 3 5/8" h., pr. **149**

Tumblers, juice, slightly flaring cylindrical form w/a small applied ribbed ring handle near the base, 3 1/2-3 3/4" h., set of 10 .... **690**

Vase. 3 12" h., miniature, bulbous form w/pinched neck & swirled dimpled body, applied rigaree collar..................................... **495**

Vase, 5" h., 5 3/4" w., jack-in-the-pulpit form, signed "Libbey" **1,200**

Bulbous Decorated Amberina Vase

Vase, 5 1/4" h., 3 5/8" d., bulbous ovoid body w/dimpled sides tapering to a short neck w/a flaring crimped rim, decorated w/enameled white blossoms, blue leaves & gold vines (ILLUS.) **225**

Vase, 6" h., tapering ovoid optic ribbed body on a small amber disk foot, rounded shoulder w/a small rolled neck, applied amber trailing shoulder handles, the sides finely enameled w/colorful floral decoration **715**

Vase, 6 1/4" h., Plated Amberina, waisted cylindrical form w/gently flaring flat rim, New England... **4,025**

Three Amberina Vases

Vase, 6 3/8" h., 4 1/8" d., melon-lobed ovoid body tapering to a widely flaring four-ruffle neck, h.p. dainty white & yellow flowers & green leaves (ILLUS. at left) **250**

Vase, 7" d., trumpet-form, wafer foot................ **550**

Vase, 7" h., lily-form w/tricorner rim, New England Glass Co. **375**

Vase, 7 1/8" h., 3 3/4" d., cylindrical body w/a narrow cushion foot, pattern-molded swirled rib design, h.p. soft pink flowers & green leaves, gilt rim (ILLUS. at right, w/other vases)... **245**

Vase, 8" h., lily-form, set in a silver plate holder w/decorative handles, four raised medallions of a classic warrior & scrolling, holder marked "Meriden" **450**

Vase, 8 1/2" h., 3" d., tall slender cylindrical form w/twisted optic design, applied amber serpent twists around base, on applied amber leaf feet (ILLUS. top next column) **175**

Vase, 10" h., Plated Amberina, lily-form, slender trumpet-form body w/flaring tri-corner rim, applied round amber foot **4,400**

Vase, 10" h., scalloped & ruffled 6" d. flared rim **210**

Amberina Vase with Applied Decor

Vase, 10 3/4" h., bulbous base, flared neck & applied ruffled rim, Swirled Rib patt., ... **300**

Decorated Amberina Vase

Vase, 11" h., baluster-form body on a stepped cushion foot, flaring cylindrical neck w/a deeply crimped & flaring rim, decorated in white enamel in the Mary Gregory style w/a boy & bird in a landscape (ILLUS.) **875**

Vase, 11 3/4" h., stick-form, swirled design from rim down the sides, Libbey, ca. 1917 .... **440**

Vase, 12" h., bud-type, disk foot supporting a very tall, slender slightly swelled cylindrical stem, signed "Libbey Amberina," ca. 1917................................... **770**

Vase, 12" h., cylindrical w/three applied triangular ribbed feet, Swirled Rib patt., polished pontil **250**

Vase, 12" h. 5" d., gladiolus-type, rim decorated w/a wide gold tracery band & the center enameled w/florals, ... **450**

Vase, 12" h., 5 1/2" d., jack-in-the-pulpit-style, tall tapering ovoid body in the Inverted Thumbprint patt., the wide rolled rim w/a fluted edge & a pull-up back peak, on an applied amber foot (ILLUS. at center, previous column)............ **245**

Vase, 13" h., bulbous w/circular foot & folded ruffled rim, Inverted Thumbprint patt. **330**

Vase, 13 1/2" h., 5 1/2" d., blown optic glass w/applied foot, attributed to Libbey.. **1,350**
Vase, 14" h., 6" d., cylindrical form w/fluted rim **425**

Tall Amberina Vases

Vases, 12 1/4" h., 3 1/4" d., lily-form, tall slender tapering scroll-form Optic Ribbed patt. body on a ball knob stem applied to a disk foot, applied amber spiral trim around the lower half, rim coming to a point at the back, pr. (ILLUS.) **295**

Amberina Water Set

Water set: 9 1/2" h., 4" d. tankard pitcher & four 3 3/4" h. tumblers; all in the Inverted Thumbprint patt., the pitcher w/a flat angle-cut rim & applied angled amber handle, the set (ILLUS.) **395**
Water set: pitcher & four tumblers; New England Glass Co., 5 pcs.......................... **1,250**
Water set: pitcher & six tumblers; the bulbous pitcher w/a swirled Coin Spot patt. & applied reeded amber handle, matching tumblers w/optic swirled design, tumblers 3 3/4" h., pitcher 9" h., the set **715**

APPLIQUED

Simply stated, this is an art glass form with applied decoration. Sometimes master glass craftsmen applied stems or branches to an art glass object and then added molded glass flowers or fruit specimens to these branches or stems. At other times a button of molten glass was daubed on the object and a tool pressed over it to form a prunt in the form of a raspberry, rosette or other shape. Always the work of a skilled glassmaker, applied decoration can be found on both cased (two-layer) and single layer glass. The English firm of Stevens and Williams was renowned for the appliqued glass they produced.

Bowl, 6" d., 3 7/8" h., wide cylindrical form w/a swelled bottom, pale blue opaque

w/an overshot background & applied amber rigaree around the rim & applied green leaves on purple stems w/blue & red & white & red applied blossoms (ILLUS. below) **$195**

Appliqued & Overshot Bowl

Bowl, 6 1/4" d., 6 1/4" h., footed, pink opalescent body applied w/a clear leaf & applied clear ribbed feet, late 19th c. **55**
Box w/hinged lid, rounded base in yellowish opalescent fitted w/gilt brass scroll feet & hinged collar fittings w/a wide domed cover applied w/amethyst branches & green leaves w/a red flower & bud, 5 5/8" d., 4 1/4" h. **450**

Small Pink Appliqued Vase

Vase, 3 1/4" h., 3" d., miniature, cylindrical w/flaring crimped & pulled rim in shaded cased pink, clear applied leaves & feet applied in rows, late 19th c. (ILLUS.) **115**

Fan-topped Vase with Acorns

Vase, 7" h., 4 1/2" d., opaque white w/a fanned & crimped rim w/applied amber edging, the spherical footed base applied w/a large amber leaf & acorn cluster (ILLUS.) **135**
Vase, 7" h., 5" d., baluster-form w/a bulbous body tapering to a widely flaring ruffled & crimped rim, white opaque body w/applied crimped amber foot band

& rim band & a large amber leaf & bell-flower around the body................................. **135**

Large Appliqued Vase

Vase, 14 1/4" h., 5 1/4" d., squatty swelled squared base tapering to a tall cylindrical body in pink opalescent, applied w/vaseline opalescent large blossoms & leafy vine (ILLUS.) **425**

ART GLASS BASKETS

Popular novelties in the late Victorian era, these ornate baskets of glass were usually hand-crafted of free-blown or mold-blown glass. They were made in a wide spectrum of colors and shapes. Pieces were highlighted with tall applied handles and often applied feet; however, fancier ones might also carry additional appliqued trim.

Shaded & Enameled Glass Basket

Cased, footed spherical form w/wide mouth crimped down on two sides, the exterior in shaded brown to yellow enamel w/white & pink daisies, gold leaves, branches & scrolled border, applied twisted clear handle, 5 1/2 x 7 1/4", 8" h. (ILLUS.).. **$225**
Cased, white body w/amber rim band, decorated w/red cherries & multicolored leaves, 5" d., 7 1/2" h. **143**
Cased pale blue, the squatty lobed bowl w/an upright crimped & ruffled rim w/applied clear edging, white interior, applied clear angled thorn handle, 6 1/2" w. **110**
Colored swags, a tall slender waisted form w/a widely flaring rim pulled up on two

sides & joined by a high applied clear arched handle, the sides composed of alternating dark green, gold & white swags, iridescent interior, attributed to Imperial, 9 1/2" h. **275**
Light green custard, applied floral decoration & applied green twisted handle **127**
Mother-of-pearl satin, shaded blue Diamond Quilted patt., ruffled rim, applied frosted clear handle, 4 1/2" w., 6" h. **440**
Pink opalescent, ruffled rim & applied clear twisted handle, applied white flowers, glossy finish, 4 1/2" d., 6 3/4" h. **176**

Rubina Honeycomb Basket

Rubina, bulbous nearly spherical form in the Honeycomb patt., the wide ruffled & crimped rim applied w/a high clear angular thorn handle, 5 1/2" d., 9" h. (ILLUS.) **175**
Rubina verde, footed rounded body w/a wide deeply rolled & crimped rim w/two sides pulled up & joined by a high applied light green twisted thorn handle, the body w/applied green leaves & red & white blossoms, 8 1/2" h. **253**

Sapphire Blue Art Glass Basket

Sapphire blue, squatty bulbous optic ribbed body tapering to a flared rim, clear applied petal feet, petal rim band & high twisted handle, 5" d., 9" h. (ILLUS.)...... **175**
Sapphire blue, squatty round bowl w/swirl-molded design continuing to the deeply rolled & crimped rim w/the back edge

pulled up, applied clear handle, 5 1/2" d.,
6" h. **145**

Spangled Art Glass Basket

Spangled, footed spherical body in blue
w/a coral-like silver mica decoration,
white lining, applied clear arched &
pinched handle, 5 3/4" d., 9 1/4" h.
(ILLUS.) **295**

Spangled, gold cased in white body w/a
layer of golden mica flecks, ribbed sides
w/applied clear reeded & pointed han-
dle, 7" d., 7" h. **88**

Spangled, pink w/overall mica flecks, ruffled rim, applied clear handle, 5 1/2" d.,
5" h. **121**

Spatter, deep upright ribbed & fluted bowl
w/spatter exterior in maroon, gold &
blue, white interior, applied clear twisted
thorn handle, 6" d., 7" h. **165**

Egg-shaped Amber Spatter Basket

Spatter, tall ovoid egg-shaped body in
amber w/a Diamond Quilted patt., white
spatter throughout, crimped rim, applied
twisted amber handle, 6" h. (ILLUS.) **200-225**

Spatter, wide rounded bowl w/star-crimped
upright rim, maroon, orange & yellow
spatter cased in white, applied clear
angled thorn handle, 5 7/8" d., 5 1/2" h. **175**

Spatter, squatty bulbous body w/a wide
upright crimped rim, the exterior in yellow, gold & pink spatter, white lining,
applied high clear knobby handle, 5" d.,
6 1/2" h. **165**

BACCARAT

*Baccarat glass has been made by Cristalleries
de Baccarat, France, since 1765. The firm has pro-*
*duced various glassware of excellent quality as well
as paperweights. Baccarat's Rose Teinte is often
referred to as Baccarat's Amberina.*

Box w/hinged cover, square crystal, the
cover incrusted w/a sulphide portrait
medallion of Louis Philippe of France,
the body cut w/overall spiral gadroons,
the ormolu mounts w/cast stiff leaftips,
mid-19th c., 5 1/8" h. **$7,475**

Cologne bottle w/stopper, cylindrical
w/short cylindrical neck w/flared rim,
dark blue Swirl patt., matching Swirl ball
stopper, 2 1/4" d., 5 3/4" h. **85**

"Rose Teinte" Cologne Bottle

Cologne bottle w/stopper, "Rose Teinte,"
cylindrical shouldered form w/short cylindrical neck & flared rim, Pinwheel patt.
w/matching ball stopper, 2 1/2" d.,
6 1/4" h. (ILLUS.) **85**

Baccarat Cruet with Paper Label

Cruet w/stopper, spherical body w/a slender cylindrical neck w/pinched spout,
sapphire blue w/applied clear handle,
clear facet-cut stopper, the sides enameled w/flowering branches, a disc &
reserve in gold, yellow & white, original
paper label, 4 1/2" d., 8 1/2" h. (ILLUS.) **225**

Decanter w/stopper, "Rose Teinte," spherical body molded w/plain swirled bands
alternating w/square hob bands, tall paneled & ringed neck w/a flared rim,
matching original knob stopper, 5" d.,
10 1/4" h. (ILLUS. top next page) **225**

Vase, 12" h., tall waisted cylindrical form,
clear frosted & textured ground enam-

eled in lavender, rust & white w/a large iris & gilded foliage, base marked "Les Vaporisateurs Paris Baccarat," ca. 1900 (wear to gilded rim) **345**

"Rose Teinte" Baccarat Decanter

BOHEMIAN

Numerous types of glass were made in the once-independent country of Bohemia and fine colored, cut and engraved glass was turned out. Flashed and other inexpensive wares also were made; many of these, including amber- and ruby-shaded glass, were exported to the United States during the 19th and 20th centuries. One favorite pattern in the late 19th and early 20th centuries was Deer & Castle. Another was Deer and Pine Tree.

Chalice, barrel-shaped bowl raised on a tall facet-cut & ringed stem on a scallop-cut round foot, clear w/amber flashing, the bowl intricately engraved w/a herd of deer on a forested bluff, late 19th c., 11" h. (minor nicks to facets)...................... **$748**

Fine Bohemian Covered Chalice

Chalice, cov., tall bell-form bowl raised on a tapering panel-cut knopped stem & octagonal foot, clear flashed in deep ruby red & engraved around the bowl w/a scene of a stag & deer in the woods, silver plate chased foliate cover w/tall knopped finial, a grape leaf silver plate band around the foot, ca. 1860, wear, 9 3/4" h. (ILLUS.)... **748**

Console set: 10" d. console bowl & pair of candlesticks; ruby-flashed & cut to clear, the bowl w/a small footring supporting wide deep rounded sides w/a flat rim engraved w/large scrolled cartouches alternating w/leaping stags, a narrow band of scrolls around the rim, the footed baluster-form candlesticks w/flaring sockets w/similar engraving, late 19th to early 20th c., the set......................... **259**

Console set: 12" d. footed bowl & pair 12" h. candlesticks; each amber-colored & etched w/foliate & landscape designs, late 19th - early 20th c., the set................... **230**

Cruet w/stopper, ruby-flashed, footed bulbous body tapering to a curved rim spout & hollow knop stopper, ruby engraved w/a leaping stag design, clear applied smooth handle, late-19th to early-20th c., 5 1/2" h. **110**

Cup & saucer, deep ruby blown widely flaring rounded cup w/applied handle decorated w/an enameled portrait of a woman framed by gilt scrolling & floral swags, dished matching saucer, late 19th c. **75**

Goblet, blue overlay cut to clear, etched w/titled scenes & dated "1857," flowerform foot, third quarter 19th c., 5 7/8" h........ **288**

Goblet, double overlay, pink cut to clear w/white interior, 19th c., 5 3/4" h. **115**

Goblet, a trumpet-form bowl w/a flared rim set on a thick short stem on a round disk foot, clear w/an engraved body w/a layer of vaseline & black stain, the sides w/engraved oval panels w/wheat design borders, one panel showing a girl w/a watering can in a garden, one showing a house w/trees & a third showing a church & trees, black stain w/clear cut panels around the base of the bowl above the black-stained stem w/an engraved diamond design above the black-stained foot cut w/clear rounded petals, ca. 1880-90, 7" h. **1,475**

Rare Bohemian Flashed & Cut Goblet

Goblet, cov., chalice-form, ruby-flashed, the tall flaring panel-cut bowl etched to clear w/a continuous hunt scene, the heavy double-knop facet-cut stem on a deeply cut & paneled round foot, the panel-cut & domed cover w/a notch-cut rim & tall paneled & pointed finial, late 19th c., 20" h. (ILLUS.)............................. **6,325**

Goblets, paneled octagonal body, ruby-flashed cut w/panels & enameled in color w/florals & scrolled foliate designs, 19th c., 6 3/8" h. , pr. (gilt wear) **690**

Jars, cov., tall chalice-form, cut-overlay in yellow cut to clear, late-19th to early 20th c., 13 1/4" h., pr. **288**

Jewelry casket, cov., rectangular, clear molded & cut block design w/green overlay in each block, 5 1/2" l., 4" h. **182**

Lamps, cut-overlay, baluster-form body of ruby overlaid in white & cut w/trellis & oval panels, decorated w/red, orange, blue & green enameled flowers, raised on a chased silvered metal base, ca. 1925, overall 35" h., pr. (replaced lamp fittings)....................... **403**

Vase, 4 3/4" h., ruby red, thick disk foot w/a short knob stem supporting the flaring waisted bowl finely enameled w/a bust portrait of a woman within a gold scrolled cartouche & gilt florals, probably Moser, late 19th c........................ **77**

Enamel-decorated Handled Vase

Vase, 5 1/4" h., footed squatty bulbous body tapering to a trumpet neck flanked by enameled elephant head handles, colorless lightly iridized body w/applied enameled fish decoration trimmed w/blues, greens & white, polished pontil, possibly Harrach, ca. 1890, slight enamel wear (ILLUS.) **345**

Amber-flashed Etched Vase

Vase, 6 1/4" h., amber-flashed, the widely flaring trumpet-form body w/a pointed scallop rim cut to clear w/a continuous deer in forest scene, the lower bulbous body facet-cut above a short pedestal & thick round foot (ILLUS.) **145**

Vase, 8" h., cushion base below the tall cylindrical body, dark blue ornately

enameled w/a colorful figure of a standing Harlequin against a gilt-stenciled garden terrace background, attributed to Rossler, ca. 1920 (ILLUS. below) **250**

Decorated Cylindrical Vase

Vase, 8 3/4" h., tapered ovoid body, clear green ground w/interior texture giving a glitter effect, etched & enameled to depict mauve & yellow iris, gilt trim **518**

Vase, 9 1/2" h., ovoid body w/short flaring neck, burgundy red cased w/opal white, the exterior elaborately decorated in gilded scroll & swag designs trimmed w/glass beads of opal, green & turquoise, late 19th c. **431**

Vase, 9 1/2" h., squatty bulbous base below tall tapering slender body w/flared lip, ambergris decorated w/a zig-zag textured bluish green iridescent surface highlighted w/white streaks, early 20th c...... **173**

Vase, 9 1/2" h., wide flat-bottomed spherical form w/a short, wide flared neck, the satin ground decorated w/a large finely h.p. medallion of colorful roses & leaves, late 19th to early 20th c. **105**

Vase, 9 3/4" h., 4 3/4" d., trumpet-form body w/an eight-scallop rim & a flaring eight-scallop foot, cranberry cut to clear w/eight elongated arches up the sides to below a wide rim band enameled in ivory & gold w/intertwined scrolls, each scallop of the foot w/similar decoration, ca. 1840 .... **1,275**

Unusual Bohemian Iridescent Vase

Vase, 10 1/2" h., a squatty bulbous base issuing four solid slender open buttress handles around the slender center body, short cylindrical neck w/a flattened rim, rose red iridescent finish, polished pontil, late 19th to early 20th c. (ILLUS.).. **489**

Vase, 15" h., bulbous ovoid body tapering to a tall cylindrical neck, deep ruby decorated overall w/silver leaf designs & enameled bird & flower in blue sharkskin, early 20th c. **413**

Vase, 17" h., tall cylindrical form w/wide base & flared ruffled rim, frosted lightly iridized ground shading from blue to green w/gilt & enameled entwining roses, large polished pontil, late 19th c. **374**

Elaborate Persian-style Victorian Vase

Vase, 20" h., Persian-style, a flaring pedestal base supporting a wide squatty compressed body tapering to a tall ringed cylindrical neck, ruby w/blue & white enameled delicate birds & flowers in bands & reserves w/further gilt decoration, inscribed "Bouteille Persane en Verre Epoque Sass Anide," 19th c. (ILLUS.) **3,680**

Vase, 22 1/2" h., squatty bulbous bottom tapering sharply to a very tall slender body w/flared & ruffled rim, clear w/optic ribbing, ornately enameled w/delicate gold, green & blue leafy scrolls up the sides, ground pontil **280**

Fine Cut-overlay Bohemian Vase

Vases, 16 1/2" h., white cut to blue cut-overlay, classic baluster-form, each w/an octagonal flaring neck, the lip suspending spade-form leaves, the sides w/anthemion alternating w/stylized foliage & floral diamonds, the ground gilt overall w/scrolling foliage, on circular bases cut w/overlapping leaves, mid-19th c., pr. (ILLUS. of one) **3,450**

Wine set: decanter w/large bubble stopper & six stemmed wine glasses; dark ruby cut to clear, the decanter w/a small cushion foot below the wide round compressed body centered by a tall slender waisted neck, the edges of the body cut w/oval reserves alternating w/crossed leafy branches & a flowerhead, a panel-cut neck & stopper, matching design on the wines, early-20th c., decanter 11" h., the set **275**

BRIDE'S BASKETS & BOWLS

These berry or fruit bowls were popular late Victorian wedding gifts, hence the name. They were produced in a variety of quality art glasswares and sometimes were fitted in ornate silver plate holders.

Unusual Pressed Glass Basket

Blue bowl, pale blue pressed glass arched rectangular bowl w/a star in block design, bowl swinging in a metal harp above a figural brass base w/two standing cherubs, late 19th c., 5 x 7", 8 1/2" h. (ILLUS.) **$325**

Cased bowl, deep green to golden amber interior w/a deeply fluted & crimped rim, decorated w/pink-trimmed white florals on the interior, white exterior, 11" d. **112**

Large Fancy Bride's Basket

Cased bowl, deep rounded bowl w/deeply fluted & crimped rim, dark blue interior enameled in color w/floral clusters, a butterfly & green leaves, white exterior, in an ornate silver plate footed frame & high arched handle marked by E.G. Webster, 8 1/2" d., 11 1/2" h. (ILLUS.) **435**

Cased bowl, deeply crimped & ruffled upturned sides w/a molded hobnail effect, shaded pink interior, white exterior, mounted on a brass pedestal w/a ringed shaft & domed foot w/embossed scroll band design, 9 1/2" d., 7 3/4" h. (ILLUS. below) **175**

Pink Cased Bowl on Brass Base

Bride's Basket with Figural Silver Base

Cased bowl, pink interior w/deep flaring lobed & crimped rim w/applied frosted clear band, white exterior, the interior enameled w/small maroon sprays & orange buds, ornate resilvered silver plate pedestal stand w/three figural small dolphins above a scroll- and shell-cast three-footed base, 7 1/2" d., 8 1/4" h. (ILLUS.).. **325**

Cased Rich Pink Bride's Bowl

Cased bowl, rich shaded pink interior w/crimped rim applied w/clear band & the front edge turned down, decorated around the interior w/gold & silver sanded flowers & leafy branch decoration, white exterior, 8" d., 3 1/8" h. (ILLUS.)...................................... **165**
Cased bowl, shaded pink interior decorated w/large yellow & white daisy-like blossoms & greenish brown leaves, deeply ruffled & crimped rim pulled into points, white exterior, ornate silver plate frame w/looped & arched handle, 10 3/4" d., 10 3/4" h. (ILLUS. top next column) **395**
Cased bowl, shaded pink interior, white exterior, wide crimped rim pulled into pointed ruffles, in Colonial Silver Co. sil-

ver plate stand w/high serpentine twisted bail handle, 11 3/4" d., 11 1/2" h. **275**

Shaded Pink Decorated Basket

Cased bowl, shaded dark green satin interior relief-molded in a lattice design, ruffled rim, white exterior, 11 1/2" d., 3 5/8" h. **150**

Large Pink Decorated Bride's Bowl

Cased bowl, deep pink shaded to white, eight-lobed & crimped rim w/applied clear band, the interior brightly enameled w/purple & yellow pansies, green leaves & gold scrolls, 12" d. (ILLUS.).......... **225**
Cased bowl, green shading to white interior richly enameled w/florals & scrolls, white exterior, deep rounded sides w/a wide deeply crimped & ruffled rim, silverplate pedestal base supported by two winged cherubs & marked "Meriden," 12" h. **460**
Cased satin, shaded lavender interior enameled w/yellow, white & lavender florals, angular ruffled rim, 10 1/2" d., 4" h. **220**
Cranberry bowl, wide shallow rounded form w/applied scalloped clear rigaree around the rim, set in a fancy silver plate frame w/rams' heads above hoof feet supporting the flattened edge w/engraved leaves & a fixed bail handle, England, late 19th c., 9 1/2" d., 8 1/2" h. **715**

Shaded Pink Decorated Bowl

Pink shading to frosted clear bowl, wide shell-shaped form w/ruffled rim & two turned-in edge sections, decorated w/white & pink scrolling feather-like clusters & small blue & white flowers & tiny gold flowers, gilt edge band, on a resilvered silver plate scroll-footed stand, 10 1/2" d., 4 1/4" h. (ILLUS.) 295

Shaded pink bowl, deeply ruffled & folded rim, glossy finish, ornate silver plate frame w/fruit decoration, bowl 9" d. 440

Spangled bowl, shaded blue to white w/silver mica flecks, ornate silver plate frame 132

BURMESE

Burmese is a single-layer glass that shades from pink to pale yellow. It was patented by Frederick S. Shirley and made by the Mt. Washington Glass Co. A license to produce the glass in England was granted to Thomas Webb & Sons, which called its articles Queen's Burmese. Gundersen Burmese was made briefly about the middle of the 20th century, and the Pairpoint Company is making limited quantities at the present time.

Bell, high body w/flaring base, applied amber handle, glossy finish, Thomas Webb, 6 3/4" h.. **$750**

Bell, high domed bell w/flaring base, tall applied clear handle w/beehive form finial, glossy finish, Thomas Webb, 11 1/2" h... 750

Bowl, 4" d., 2 1/4" h., rounded bottom w/flaring, crimped star-shaped rim, paper label w/"Thomas Webb & Sons - Queen's Burmese," satin finish 413

Bowl, 4" d., 2 1/2" h., squatty bulbous body w/a wide flat rim, raised on a short foot, the sides decorated w/a blue butterfly & reddish blossoms on slender vines trimmed in gold, attributed to Webb 585

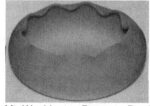

Mt. Washington Burmese Bowl

Bowl, 4 3/4" d., 2 1/8" h., squatty bulbous form w/incurved scalloped rim, satin finish, Mt. Washington Glass Co. (ILLUS.) 350

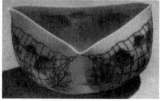

Tricorner Burmese Bowl with Fish Net

Bowl, 5" w., shallow rounded base w/an incurved tricorner rim, enameled around

the sides w/an elaborate fish in net design (ILLUS.) **1,610**

Bowl, 5 1/2" w., 2 1/4" h., rectangular w/slightly folded rim, polished pontil, satin finish 250

Bowl, 5 3/4" d., 2 3/4" h., rounded base below the flaring ruffled star-shaped rim, Mt. Washington, satin finish 303

Bowl, 6 1/4" d., 3 3/4" h., squatty bulbous body on a footring, enameled floral decoration **1,110**

Bowl, 6 1/2" widest d., 2 1/2" h., cylindrical base w/a flaring & folded over elongated oval rim, applied yellow rigaree trim on rim, Mt. Washington Glass Co. 950

Bowl, 7" d., 4 1/2" h., footed squatty bulbous body tapering to a widely flared four-lobed ruffled & crimped turned-down rim, decorated w/enameled stylized flowers, satin finish, attributed to the Mt. Washington Glass Co. 880

Bowl, 8" d., 4 1/4" h., squatty bulbous body tapering to a widely flaring four-lobed rolled & crimped rim, attributed to the Mt. Washington Glass Co. 275

Bowl, 12" d., 3 1/2" h., rounded base below the widely flaring 10-flute rim, glossy finish, late 19th c. 385

Bowls, 5 3/4" d., 3 1/4" h., butterfly rim folds tapering to short cylindrical base, interior decorated w/orange flowers & gold leaves, silver-plated footed frame tapering to twining calla lilies to form handle, calla lily handles on matching spoons, Thos. Webb & Sons Patented, pr. (one bowl slightly darker) **1,675**

Celery vase, footed, fluted rim, Mt. Washington Glass Co., 10" h. 550

Cologne bottle w/original stopper, Mt. Washington Glass Co., 4" d., 5" h. 975

Compote, open, 7" d., 4" h., a wide shallow bowl w/a gently ruffled rim, raised on a baluster-form stem on a round foot, glossy finish,19th c. 330

Condiment set: cylindrical ribbed salt & pepper shakers & barrel-shaped ribbed mustard jar, each w/original silver plate lids, in a fitted silver plate stand w/round ruffled base, support rings & a central handle w/loop top, sterling silver mustard spoon, frame signed by Pairpoint, the set 798

Condiment set: pair of cylindrical ribbed salt & pepper shakers w/original metal tops & a squatty bulbous ribbed cruet tapering to a slender neck & arched spout w/original ribbed pointed stopper, all in a Pairpoint silver plate frame w/a shaker flanking the central cruet, overhead fixed arched handle & tab feet, the set **1,595**

Cracker jar, cov., bulbous tapering ovoid body decorated w/large enameled salmon colored blossoms on brown & green leafy stems, silver plate rim, cover & shaped bail handle, ground pontil, unmarked Webb, 7" h............................... **1,568**

Creamer, footed spherical body w/a wide cylindrical neck w/pinched spout, applied pale yellow handle, glossy finish, Mt. Washington Glass Co., 4" h. **475**

Creamer & open sugar bowl in holder, the wide bulbous ovoid sugar bowl w/a wide upright six-sided mouth, the smaller ovoid creamer w/matching mouth & applied yellow handle, each heavily enameled w/large orangish blossoms & autumnal leaves, fitted into a silver platform w/ring supports & an arched divided central handle, unmarked, overall 7" h., the set **1,568**

Cruet w/original mushroom stopper, melon-ribbed body, Mt. Washington Glass Co., 6 3/4" h. **1,200**

Cruet w/original stopper, enameled white & blue flowers w/green leaves & vines, Mt. Washington **2,950**

Fine Mt. Washington Burmese Cruet

Cruet w/original stopper, squatty bulbous ribbed body tapering to a slender neck w/arched spout, bulbous ribbed & pointed stopper, applied yellow handle, glossy finish, Mt. Washington Glass Co., 7 1/4" h. (ILLUS.) **1,250**

Cruet w/original stopper, squatty bulbous ribbed body w/cylindrical neck, matching ribbed stopper, applied yellow handle, Mt. Washington, 6 3/4" h. **1,045**

Cup & saucer, conical cup w/applied angled handle, satin finish, saucer 4 3/4" d. **550**

Cup & saucer, cylindrical cup w/applied yellow angled handle, wide & deep saucer, glossy finish **550**

Cup & saucer, flaring cylindrical cup w/applied angular yellow handle, deeply dished saucer, saucer w/original Mt. Washington Glass Co. paper label, saucer 4 3/4" d., cup 2" h. **550**

Cup & saucer, deep rounded cylindrical cup w/an applied angular yellow handle, deeply dished saucer, glossy finish, Mt. Washington Glass Co., saucer 5" d., cup 2 1/4" h. **550**

Custard Cup, flared rim, applied yellow handle, glossy finish, Mt. Washington Glass Co., 2 7/8" h. **450**

Dish, ruffled rim, satin finish, 4 3/4" d., 1 1/2" h. **120**

Dish, short cylindrical body w/a widely flaring four-lobed & crimped rim, 5" d. **165**

Dish, short waisted cylindrical form w/crimped flared rim pulled into points, applied leaf on each side, small **413**

Dish, tricornered, satin finish, 5" w. **150**

Ewer, tall ovoid body tapering to a tall, pointed upright spout, an applied loop handle & disk foot, satin finish, Mt. Washington Glass Co., 6" h. **950**

Finger bowl, nine-crimp top, satin finish, Mt. Washington Glass Co., 4 3/8" d., 2 1/4" h. **225**

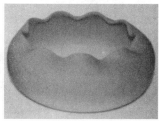

Burmese Finger Bowl

Finger bowl, wide squatty bulbous body w/incurved crimped rim, satin finish, Mt. Washington Glass Co., 4 1/2" d., 2" h. (ILLUS.) **350**

Finger bowl, wide shallow rounded shape w/an incurved crimped rim, satin finish, Mt. Washington Glass Co., 4 1/2" d., 2 1/2" h **325**

Ginger jar, cov., ovoid body tapering to a short cylindrical neck w/a fitted domed cover, decorated w/white enamel clumps of asters on delicate leafy vines w/raised gold berries, Mt. Washington, 5" h. **2,200**

Burmese Lamp with Flying Ibis

Lamp, kerosene table model, a gilt-metal scroll-cast base supporting the wide domed & tapering cylindrical font decorated w/a group of ibis flying over a sunrise scene of pyramids & palm trees, fitted w/a brass shoulder & burner w/wire spider supporting a high domed opentopped matching shade, Burmese glass chimney, ca. 1890s, electrified, shade 10" d., overall 20" h. (ILLUS.) **10,350**

Fine Webb Burmese Lamp

Lamp, kerosene-type, a footed tapering cylindrical base w/a ringed shoulder supporting the burner & shade ring w/a spherical shade w/a crimped rim, shade & base each enameled w/large bands of leafy oak branches w/acorns in browns, greens & yellows, Thomas Webb & Sons Queen's Burmese, late 19th c., 17" h. (ILLUS.) **11,200**

Burmese Lamp with Guba Ducks

Lamp, kerosene-type, a scroll-cast gilt-metal foot supporting a squatty bulbous tapering glass font topped w/a gilt-metal ribbed shoulder & kerosene burner w/spider support for the domed glass shade w/top opening, w/chimney, the base & shade each decorated w/conventionalized flying ducks in bright natural colors painted by Frank Guba, Mt. Washington Glass Co., late 19th c., electrified, shade 10" d., overall 19 1/2" h. (ILLUS.) **11,500**

Mustard pot w/silver plate hinged lid, barrel shaped w/vertical ribbing, silver plate collar & bail handle, Mt. Washington Glass Co., 4 1/2" h. **375**

Oil bottle w/stopper, cylindrical ribbed body, attributed to Mt. Washington Glass Co. **440**

Perfume bottle & stopper, rare partial label on bottom, 5" h. **385**

Pitcher, 4" h., miniature, slender waisted tankard-form, decorated w/enameled & painted flowers on the sides & pink trim bands on the rim & handle, satin finish **1,760**

Pitcher, 5 1/4" h., bulbous body tapering to a ruffled top, Mt. Washington Glass Co. **550**

Pitcher, 5 1/2" h., slightly tapering cylindrical body in the Hobnail patt., applied yellow handle, Mt. Washington Glass Co. **950**

Plate, 8" d., glossy finish **138**

Plate, 9" d., Mt. Washington Glass Co. **250**

Plate, 9" d., satin finish, Mt. Washington Glass Co. **225**

Two Miniature Burmese Rose Bowls

Rose bowl, miniature, spherical body w/an eight-crimp rim, satin finish, unsigned Webb, 2 3/8" d., 2 1/8" h. (ILLUS. right) **225**

Rose bowl, miniature, spherical body enamel-decorated w/green & brown blossoms, leaves & twigs, six-crimp rim, 2 1/4" h. **350**

Miniature Burmese Rose Bowl

Rose bowl, miniature, eight-crimp rim, unsigned Webb, glossy finish, 2 1/4" d., 2 1/4" h. (ILLUS.) **225**

Rose bowl, spherical w/eight-crimp rim, decorated w/pink, green & blue maidenhair fern & outlined in gold, satin finish, unsigned Webb, 2 3/8" d., 2 1/4" h **375**

Rose bowl, miniature, spherical w/an eight-crimp rim, satin finish decorated w/enameled lavender five-petal flowers w/green & brown leaves, attributed to Thomas Webb, 2 3/8" d., 2 3/8" h. (ILLUS. left) **335**

Rose bowl, wide squatty bulbous form w/flat rim, decorated w/h.p. blue butterfly, bittersweet blossoms & gold foliage, Thomas Webb, 4" d., 2 1/2" h. **585**

Rose bowl, ruffled rim, applied molded leaf, 4" d., 2 3/4" h. **700**

Rose bowl, miniature, spherical w/a six-crimp rim, enamel-decorated w/lavender blue flowers, satin finish, 3" h. **275**

Rose bowl, spherical body w/eight-crimp rim, plain undecorated satin finish, unsigned Thomas Webb, 3" d., 3 3/8" h. **210**

Rose bowl, spherical, six-crimp rim, decorated w/bronze & gold-tinted chrysanthemums & leaves all outlined in gold, unsigned Webb, 3 3/8" d., 3 3/8" h. **650**

Floral-decorated Burmese Rose Bowl

Rose bowl, crimped rim, floral decoration & applied glass at rim, marked by Thomas Webb, 6 1/4" d., 3 3/4" h. (ILLUS.) **950**

Salt & pepper shakers w/original metal lids, cylindrical finely ribbed form, satin finish, pr. **413**

Sugar shaker w/original metal top, decorated w/h.p. daisies, Mt. Washington Glass Co., 4 1/4" h. **425**

Sweetmeat jar, cov., compressed globular body, decorated w/enameled flowers & foliage, silver plate rim, cover & overhead handle **375**

Tazza, bowl on short stem joined by a wafer, 7" d., 4 1/2" h. **550**

Toothpick holder, bulbous base w/square top, h.p. pine cone decoration, satin finish, Mt. Washington Glass Co. **375**

Toothpick holder, cylindrical w/folded over tricorner rim, lightly ribbed & enameled w/white & yellow daisies & green stems, Mt. Washington Glass Co. **550**

Toothpick holder, cylindrical w/tricorner rim, Diamond Quilted patt., satin ground decorated w/enameled strawflowers **550**

Toothpick holder, cylindrical w/tricornered rim, Mt. Washington Glass Co. **245**

Toothpick holder, Diamond Quilted patt., satin finish, Mt. Washington Glass Co. . **275-350**

Toothpick holder, footed ovoid body w/a short cylindrical neck, decorated w/lavender blossoms & green & brown leaves, satin finish, attributed to Webb, 2 1/4" d., 3" h. **350**

Toothpick holder, short cylindrical form w/incurved tricorner rim, the body enameled in color w/a spray of berries, Mt. Washington **935**

Toothpick holder, tall cylindrical form w/squared rim, Mt. Washington Glass Co. **220**

Toothpick holder, waisted cylindrical form, polished pontil, satin finish, 2 1/2" h. **250**

Toothpick holder, model of a hat, fine blue glass threading on the brim, glossy finish, 2 1/8" h. **275**

Toothpick holder, bulbous ovoid body tapering to a short six-sided neck, satin finish, 2 1/2" d., 2 1/2" h. **195**

Toothpick holder, bulbous squatty base w/a flaring squared neck, decorated w/lavender blossoms & green & brown leaves, satin finish, attributed to Webb, 2 1/2" d., 2 7/8" h. **325**

Toothpick holder, spherical body w/a short hexagonal neck, undecorated, 2 1/2" h. **237**

Toothpick holder, bulbous body w/six-sided collared rim, polished pontil, satin finish, 3" h. **275**

Tumbler, cylindrical, enameled yellow roses, Mt. Washington Glass Co., 3 3/4" h. **550**

Mt. Washington Burmese Tumbler

Tumbler, cylindrical, satin finish, Mt. Washington Glass Co., 3 7/8" h. (ILLUS.) **250**

Tumbler, lemonade-type, tall slightly tapering cylindrical form w/a small applied loop handle at the base, 4 7/8" h. (broken interior blister) **138**

Tumbler, cylindrical, decorated around the body in the Queen's patt. w/yellow or white dotted enamel daisies & green leaves, enhanced w/raised gold grasses, Mt. Washington Glass Co., 3 3/4" h. **1,750**

Tumbler, cylindrical, glossy finish, Mt. Washington Glass Co., 3 3/4" h. **325**

Vase, 2 1/4" h., miniature, rounded bottom below a widely flaring crimped & ruffled rim, satin finish, Mt. Washington Glass Co. **193**

Vase, 2 1/2" h., miniature, bulbous body w/a six-sided top **165**

Vase, 2 1/2" h., miniature, squatty bulbous body w/Diamond Quilted patt. **150**

Vase, 2 1/2" h., 2" d., miniature, bulbous body w/collared hexagonal top, decorated w/flowers, leaves & branches **295**

Vase, 2 1/2" h., 2 1/2" d., miniature, scalloped rim, glossy finish, marked by Webb **525**

Vase, 2 1/2" h., 3 1/2" d., miniature, squatty body below a hexagonal rim, decorated w/flowers & leaves, satin finish **225**

Vase, 2 3/4" h., miniature, a spherical base below the squared & gently flaring upright neck, enamel-decorated around the neck w/a band of reddish brown blossoms & green leaves **330**

Vase, 2 3/4" h., miniature, spherical body w/a short hexagonal neck, enameled w/floral clusters, satin finish **413**

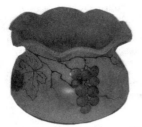

Decorated Miniature Burmese Vase

Vase, 2 3/4" h., 3 1/2" d., miniature, squatty bulbous body tapering to a widely flared ruffled rim, enameled w/yellow & green leaves & clusters of orange & pink berries, satin finish, Thomas Webb & Sons (ILLUS.) 435

Vase, 3" h., miniature, footed squatty bulbous body tapering to an upward flaring, ruffled neck, enamel-decorated w/variegated green ivy vine, satin finish, signed "Thomas Webb & Sons - Queen's Burmese" 319

Vase, 3" h., miniature, spherical body below a widely flaring crimped & flattened rim, enamel-decorated w/fall leaves & red berries, satin finish, Thomas Webb 240

Vase, 3" h., miniature, squatty bulbous base tapering to a flaring, incurved star-shaped rim, decorated w/finely enameled lavender blue flowers & fall foliage, stamped mark "Queen's Burmese - Thomas Webb & Sons" 330

Vase, 3 1/8" h., 3 1/8" d., miniature, ovoid body tapering to a flattened ruffled rim, satin finish, unsigned Webb 200

Vase, 3 1/4" h., miniature, bulbous body w/a six-sided crimped rim, satin finish, decorated w/flowers & leaves, Thomas Webb 358

Vase, 3 1/4" h., miniature, cylindrical w/five-point crimped rim, marked "Thomas Webb and Sons" 303

Vase, 3 1/4" h., miniature, ruffled top, decorated w/wild roses, glossy finish, signed Webb 375

Vase, 3 1/4" h., miniature, spherical body tapering to an upturned tricorner rim, satin finish, attributed to Thomas Webb 193

Vase, 3 1/4" h., miniature, tapering cylindrical body w/a wide flaring & ruffled rim, satin finish, attributed to Libbey Glass Co. 295

Vase, 3 1/4" h., 3 1/2" d., miniature, a footed squatty bulbous body tapering to a narrow neck below a widely flaring fluted rim w/pointed fluting, decorated w/enameled oak leaves & acorns, satin finish 325

Vase, 3 1/2" h., 3" d., miniature, bulbous ovoid body tapering to a short cylindrical neck, decorated w/narrow black bands flanking a band of small blue flowers w/red centers & green leaves, glossy finish, Thomas Webb & Sons, unsigned (ILLUS. top next column) 350

Decorated Webb Burmese Vase

Vase, 3 5/8" h., miniature, bulbous base tapering to cylindrical vertically ribbed sides w/a tricorner rim 330

Small Webb Burmese Vase

Vase, 3 5/8" h., 2 3/8" d., miniature, squatty spherical base below a tall cylindrical six-sided neck, Thomas Webb, glossy finish (ILLUS.) 195

Vase, 3 5/8" h., 3" d., miniature, squatty bulbous base w/a slightly flaring tall cylindrical neck topped by a fluted & crimped rim, glossy finish, unsigned Webb 195

Vase, 3 3/4" h., 2 5/8" d., bulbous base tapering to a cylindrical neck w/flaring & crimped rim, enameled w/lavender five-petal flowers & green & brown leaves, satin finish, unsigned Webb 350

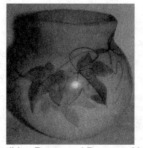

Small Ivy-Decorated Burmese Vase

Vase, 3 3/4" h., 3 1/4" d., spherical body tapering to a short hexagonal neck, the sides enameled w/green, yellow & brown ivy leaves, satin finish, attributed to Thomas Webb (ILLUS.) 395

Vase, 3 3/4" h., 4 1/4" d., eight deep lobed sections continue to the flaring rim, decorated w/ivy in shades of green 480

Small Ruffled Rim Burmese Vase

Vase, 3 7/8" h., 2 7/8" d., squatty bulbous base below a cylindrical neck w/widely flaring ruffled & crimped rim, satin finish, Thomas Webb & Sons, unsigned (ILLUS.)...... 250

Vase, 4" h., 2 3/4" d., bulbous body tapering to a flaring neck w/crimped rim, decorated w/blue & white flowers & brown leaves, satin finish, unsigned Webb............ 375

Vase, 4" h., 2 7/8" d., conical body w/flaring ruffled rim, satin finish w/peach striped effect in glass, unsigned Webb.................... 250

Burmese Vase Attributed to Webb

Vase, 4" h, 2 7/8" d., squatty bulbous base tapering to flared rim w/folded over ruffles, unsigned Webb (ILLUS.)...................... 225

Vase, 4" h., 2 7/8" d., waisted cylindrical body w/folded-over star-shaped rim, satin finish, unsigned Webb......................... 250

Vase, 4 1/8" h., small baluster-form, enameled in color w/bittersweet berries & leaves......................... 275

Vase, 4 1/8" h., tapering cylindrical slightly rounded form w/narrow short neck below the widely flaring crimped rim, the body decorated w/colored enamel florals............ 358

Vase, 4 1/4" h., ribbed baluster-form w/scalloped flaring rim, glossy finish (ILLUS. top next column)............................ 475

Vase, 4 1/4" h., short body w/ruffled rim & applied ruffled foot, satin finish................ 220

Vase, 4 1/4" h., 2 1/2" d., ovoid body w/a four-petal shaped rim, enameled w/coral flower buds & green leaves, satin finish, unsigned Webb......................... 425

Vase, 4 1/2" h., footed baluster-form w/deeply ruffled rim, decorated w/flowers & foliage................. 300

Baluster-Shaped Burmese Vase

Vase, 4 1/2" h., lightly ribbed squatty bulbous bag-form body tapering to a widely flaring, lightly ruffled neck, the neck applied w/a yellow rigaree band w/a button & tassels at the front, Mt. Washington Glass Co. 2,090

Vase, 5" h., bud, bottle-form, footed spherical body w/a tall slender 'stick' neck, the body enameled w/dotted daisy-like blossoms & leaves w/gilt trim, the branches & tracery encircling the body, Mt. Washington Glass Co.......................... 2,860

Vase, 5" h., bulbous ovoid body w/a short cylindrical neck, finely enameled w/clusters of daisies................ 715

Vase, 5" h., urn-form w/applied handles, Mt. Washington Glass Co. 350

Vase, 5 3/4" h., footed spherical body w/a tall slender 'stick' neck, decorated w/yellow-centered white blossoms & green leaves around the body & up the neck, attributed to Mt. Washington Glass Co. 546

Vase, 6" h., bud-type, a small disk foot & slender short pedestal supporting a slender tall cylindrical body w/a ruffled rim, decorated down the sides w/delicate colorful foliage, satin finish............... 495

Vase, 6" h., footed ovoid lower body w/four pinched indentations below the tall slender neck, satin finish 193

Vase, 6 1/4" h., ovoid swirled rib body, satin finish 413

Vase, 6 1/2" h., double-gourd form, a spherical bottom below a small ovoid section at the base of the slender 'stick' neck, enamel-decorated around the base & neck w/a leafy vine of red trumpet flowers, acid-stamped "Thomas Webb & Sons Queen's Burmese".............. 880

Vase, 6 1/2" h., lily-form, round foot & tricorner flaring rim, Mt. Washington Glass Co., satin finish 275

Vase, 6 1/2" h., lily-form w/jack-in-the-pulpit rim, Gundersen-Pairpoint........................... 250

Vase, 6 3/4" h., jack-in-the-pulpit-form, round foot under slender gently flaring cylindrical body w/a crimped & rolled rim 230

Vase, 7" h., classical urn-form w/high arched angled handles from rim to shoulder, short pedestal base, attributed to Mt. Washington Glass Co., No. 153 770

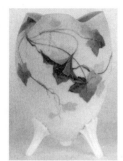

Webb Egg-shaped Burmese Vase

Vase, 7" h., tapering egg-shaped body w/three-lobed rim, raised on three ribbed & pointed legs, enameled around the sides w/large ivy leaves & vines, signed by Thomas Webb & Sons (ILLUS.) **1,250**

Vase, 7 1/4" h., ovoid body, Japanesque style decoration on the 'white burmese' body w/pink at the top, decorated overall w/delicate Oriental scenes in sepia tones, Thomas Webb, England **345**

Webb Burmese Vase with Butterfly

Vase, 8" h., simple ovoid body tapering to a short, wide cylindrical neck, a variegated enameled green vine cascades across the body w/a single large blue clematis blossom & several buds, satin finish, attributed to Webb **1,540**

Decorated Burmese Lily Vase

Vase, 8" h., spherical body below a tall slender 'stick' neck swelled at the base, decorated w/enameled blue & white forget-me-nots, Mt. Washington Glass Co. **575**

Vase, 8 1/8" h., 3 7/8" d., ovoid body tapering to a cylindrical neck, decorated w/coral flower buds w/green & tan foliage, satin finish, unsigned Webb **850**

Burmese Jack-in-the-Pulpit Vase

Vase, 7 1/4" h., 3 1/2" d., jack-in-the-pulpit style, crimped & upturned rim on a slender trumpet-form body on a disk foot, satin finish, Mt. Washington Glass Co. (ILLUS.) **375**

Vase, 7 1/2" h., footed bulbous body w/four pinched indentations, tapering to a tall slender cylindrical neck, enameled in greens, browns & pink w/leafy flower branches, satin finish **743**

Vase, 7 3/4" h., bottle-form, bulbous ovoid body tapering to a slender 'stick' neck, delicately enameled w/tiny red blossoms on green stems & a butterfly, Thomas Webb & Sons (ILLUS. top next column) ... **1,100**

Vase, 7 3/4" h., lily-form on round foot **303**

Vase, 8" h., double gourd-shaped, decorated w/peach-colored roses & turquoise-colored forget-me-not blossoms, Mt. Washington Glass Co. **1,250**

Vase, 8" h., lily-type, tall slender body w/flaring tri-lobed rim, round disk foot, the sides enameled w/delicate forget-me-nots, satin finish, Mt. Washington Glass Co. (ILLUS. center next column)..... **1,200**

Floral-Decorated Vase by Webb

Vase, 8 1/8" h., 3 7/8" d., bulbous body on short foot tapering to thin cylindrical neck w/flat rim, decorated w/coral-colored flower buds w/green & tan foliage, unsigned Webb (ILLUS.)................................ 750

Vase, 8 1/4" h., h.p. floral decoration, in silver plate handled frame, Thomas Webb & Sons.. 515

Vase, 8 1/4" h., trumpet-form w/large ruffled rim, fitted w/metal handles & base, creamy background decorated w/flowers, attributed to Thomas Webb 515

Vase, 8 3/4" h., cylindrical slightly waisted form w/a flaring ruffled rim, glossy finish 385

Vase, 9 1/4" h., trumpet-form w/jack-in-the-pulpit crimped rim, Mt. Washington Glass Co. 316

Vase, 10" h., bottle-form, bulbous ovoid base tapering to a tall slender cylindrical neck, the sides enameled w/a large delicate pale yellow chrysanthemum on a green leafy stem.. 1,100

Vase, 10" h., cushion foot, expanding cylinder w/short narrow flaring cyllindrical neck, decorated w/florals filled w/intricate lines in red, green, blue & gold, heavy gold outlining, Mt. Washington Glass Co. 1,500

Vase, 10" h., lily-form, tri-corner rim, Mt. Washington Glass Co. 750

Fine Decorated Burmese Vase

Vase, 10 1/4" h., 5" d., spherical base centered by a tall slender 'stick' neck w/slightly flared rim, decorated around the body & neck w/green & brown ivy vines, satin finish, impressed Thomas Webb Queen's Burmese base mark (ILLUS.).. 895

Vase, 10 1/2" h., tall simple ovoid form w/a small closed mouth, finely enameled overall w/brown & green leaves & branches & yellow raised flowers & twin songbirds, marked "Queen's Burmese - Thomas Webb & Sons".......................... 3,575

Vase, 11 1/2" h., a tiny round foot supporting a tall ovoid body tapering to a small mouth, enamel-decorated w/an Egyptian desert scene w/pyramids & ibis in flight, gilt trim, Mt. Washington Glass Co., satin finish, late 19th c. (ILLUS. top next column).. 2,530

Vase, 12" h., decorated w/a scene of pyramids, sacred ibis & desert oasis, Mt. Washington Glass Co. 4,500

Vase, 12" h., trumpet-form w/crimped jack-in-the-pulpit rim, overall finely painted pointillist-style large flowers in gold on

slender leafy vining stems down the sides & around the foot, Thomas Webb's Queen's Burmese 2,750

Burmese Vase with Egyptian Scene

Vase, 12 1/2" h., bulbous base w/long 'stick' neck, clear applied handles at the base of the neck, decorated overall w/dainty blossoms, shadow foliage & fragile gold branches................................ 2,500

Vase, 12 1/2" h., lily-form, tricorner rim, satin finish, Mt. Washington Glass Co. (base slightly out of round) 550

Vase, 12 1/2" h., slender trumpet-form w/jack-in-the-pulpit rim, satin finish 750

Vase, 14 1/2" h., a tall trumpet-form glossy vase set in a foliate-pierced cylindrical brass mount w/a raised round foot (repair to mount).. 345

Vases, 6 1/2" h., two-handled, footed rare ginkgo leaf decoration, Mt. Washington Glass Co., pr. 2,100

Vases, 12" h., swelled cylindrical form w/flaring neck & footring, decorated w/flowering vines & two small birds on each, pr. 5,030

Whiskey taster, satin finish, probably Webb, 2 1/2" d., 2 7/8" h. 150

Whiskey tumbler, cylindrical body w/squared rim, Diamond Quilted patt., glossy finish, Mt. Washington Glass Co., 2 1/2" h. 275

Whiskey tumbler, cylindrical w/squared rim, satin finish, 2 1/2" h. 193

CASTORS & CASTOR SETS

Castor bottles were made to hold condiments for table use. Some were produced in sets of several bottles housed in silver plated frames. The word also is sometimes spelled "Caster."

Castor set, a silver plated frame w/central handle & pedestal base w/three clear cordial decanters etched w/grapevines, stand marked by Pairpoint, late 19th c., 10 1/2" h. $374

Pickle castor, amber pressed glass Daisy & Button patt. insert, ornate silver plate footed holder w/warrior face feet supporting a flaring holder base w/a high arched handle & tongs at the side, holder marked by Webster & Sons Plating Co., late 19th c., 9 3/4" h. (ILLUS. top next page) 395

Daisy & Button Pickle Castor

Bohemian Ruby Pickle Castor

Pickle castor, Bohemian ruby-stained & leaf-etched insert, clear pleated base, in silver plate holder w/plain round foot & tall arched & scroll-pierced handle, tongs at the side, late 19th c. (ILLUS.).................. **700**

Decorated Cobalt Blue Pickle Castor

Pickle castor, cobalt blue mold-blown glass insert, squatty bulbous shape w/Inverted Thumbprint patt. & dotted blossom enameling, in a footed silver plate holder w/high arched handle & tongs at the side, late 19th c. (ILLUS.)......... **800**

Cranberry Glass Pickle Castor

Pickle castor, cranberry Inverted Thumbprint waisted cylindrical insert, silver plate holder w/round lacy scalloped base rim, tall conforming arched handle w/scrolled top & cover w/tall flame-form finial, tongs at the side, late 19th c. (ILLUS.)...................................... **525**

Pickle castor, cranberry pear-shaped Inverted Thumbprint patt. insert decorated w/a cluster of blue & white blossoms, in an ornate silver plate frame w/high arched handle, silver plate lid added, 9 1/2" h. **460**

Pickle castor, cylindrical ribbed cranberry insert w/enameled bellflowers & other blossoms, ornate silver plate frame **440**

Mother-of-Pearl Satin Pickle Castor

Pickle castor, mother-of-pearl satin glass Raindrop patt. cylindrical insert, ornate silver plate holder w/square base raised on four pierced tab feet, tall squared handle w/a pointed pierced arch finial, a pair of tongs on each side, late 19th c., overall 13 1/2" h. (ILLUS.) 750

Pickle castor, Rubina glass insert w/swelled base tapering to tall cylindrical sides decorated w/enameled blue daisies & white & orange florals, in an ornate silver plate Rockford Silver Plate Co. frame w/pierced bow-form finial on the arched handle, swelled cylindrical base & original tongs at the side, overall 11 1/2" h. 625

Pickle castor, Rubina mold-blown glass Inverted Thumbprint waisted cylindrical insert decorated w/ornate enameled blue flowering vines w/green leaves, in an ornate silver plate domed & footed frame w/arched overhead handle decorated w/a pierced design of a round fan & small owl, w/pickle fork, Derby marked frame, 11 3/4" h. 546

Vaseline Glass Pickle Castor

Pickle castor, vaseline mold-blown squatty flaring glass insert, silver plate holder w/high scrolled legs, high incurved handles w/an angled finial, tongs at the side, late 19th c. (ILLUS.) 625

CHOCOLATE

This glass is often called Caramel Slag. It was made by the Indiana Tumbler and Goblet Company of Greentown, Indiana, and other glasshouses, beginning at the turn of the 20th century. Various patterns were produced, highly popular among them being Cactus and Leaf Bracket.

Greentown Cat on Hamper Dish

Animal covered dish, Cat on Hamper, Greentown (ILLUS.) **$425**

Animal covered dish, Hen on Nest, Greentown.. 725

Bowl, three-footed, Vintage patt., Fenton 250

Butter dish, cov., Dewey patt., Greentown, 4" d. **200-250**

Cactus Pattern Jelly Compote

Compote, jelly, Cactus patt., Greentown (ILLUS.) 225

Compote, open, Chrysanthemum Leaf patt., 4 3/4" h., 4 1/2" d. 230

Compote, open, Cactus patt., Greentown, 5 1/2" h., 5" d.. 160

Creamer, Shuttle patt., Greentown, 6" h. 45

Cruet w/original stopper, Chrysanthemum Leaf patt. **1,200-1,275**

Cruet w/original stopper, Geneva patt., Greentown.. 850

Cruet w/original stopper, Leaf Bracket patt., Greentown... 265

Dresser bottle w/original stopper, tall ovoid body w/short bulbed neck & tall-stemmed stopper w/mushroom-form top, Venetian patt., early 20th c. 495

Lamp, kerosene table-model, chocolate Wild Rose patt. pedestal base, clear Festoon patt. font 660

Outdoor Drinking Scene Mug

Mug, Outdoor Drinking Scene, Greentown (ILLUS.) 155

Mug, Serenade (or Troubadour) patt., McKee/Greentown, 4 3/4" h. (minor mold roughness on interior rim) 80

Pitcher, water, 8" h., Cactus patt., Greentown (small flake on lip, small chip on edge of foot) 190

Sauce dish, Cactus patt.................................... 50

Sauce dish, Leaf Bracket patt., Greentown 45

Spooner, Cactus patt., Greentown..................... 50

Sugar bowl, cov., Cactus patt., Greentown, 4" d., 6" h. (chip on corner of finial)..... 100

Syrup pitcher w/original lid, Cord Drapery patt. 325

Tall Cactus Pattern Tumbler

Tumbler, iced tea or lemonade, Cactus patt., Greentown (ILLUS.) 63
Tumbler, Leaf Bracket patt., Greentown 75
Vase, 6" h., Scalloped Flange patt., Greentown.. 40

CHRYSANTHEMUM SPRIG, BLUE

The Chrysanthemum Sprig pattern, originally called "Pagoda," was one of several patterns produced by the Northwood Glass Company at the turn-of-the-century in their creamy white Custard glass (which see). A limited amount of this pattern was also produced in a blue opaque color, sometimes erroneously called 'blue custard.'

Blue Sprig Master Berry Bowl

The following prices are for pieces that have 85% of total gold, with no problems in the glass: chips, nicks or cracks. These pieces must also have excellent fire due to the homogeneous factor of the glass mixture.

Bowl, master berry (ILLUS.)......................... $675
Butter dish, cov. 1,375
Celery dish 1,650
Compote, jelly 550
Creamer 425
Cruet w/original stopper, 6 1/2" h. 1,550
Pitcher 1,475

Blue Sprig Salt & Pepper Shakers

Salt & pepper shakers w/original metal tops (ILLUS.) 625

Sauce dish 255
Spooner 365
Tumbler 235
Tumbler, excellent gold trim............................ 275

CORALENE

Coralene is a method of decorating glass, usually satin glass, with the use of beaded-type decoration customarily applied to the glass with the use of enamels, which were melted. Coralene decoration has been faked with the use of glue.

Basket, cased pink mother-of-pearl satin Diamond Quilted patt. w/fine yellow coralene beading, applied frosted clear loop thorn handle (small heat check under one foot) $650
Bowl, 8 1/4" d., footed deep rolled sides, cased satin w/a deep rose shading to white interior w/an applied crimped amber rim & interior decoration of a band of coralene beaded blue flowers & green leaves, white exterior, signed by Thomas Webb 385
Ewer, bulbous body tapering to a tall slender cylindrical neck w/an upright arched spout, shaded lavender satin body & applied frosted lavender handle, body decorated overall w/yellow "seaweed" coralene beading, 8 1/2" h. 248
Ewer, ovoid body w/a thin neck & tricorner rim, decorated w/coralene beaded leaves & flowers, white enamel trim, round applied foot, applied strap crystal handle, 16 1/4" h. 920
Pitcher, 6 1/2" h., bulbous body w/tricorner mouth, pink & white "seaweed" coralene beading, rose interior, applied amber handle 495

Fine Coralene Tankard Pitcher

Pitcher, 12" h., tankard-type, tall slender tapering cylindrical form in shaded pink mother-of-pearl satin Diamond Quilted patt., decorated w/yellow "seaweed" coralene beading (ILLUS.) 1,200-1,500
Powder box, cov., decorated overall w/coralene beaded green leaves w/gold & white water lilies 165
Rose bowl, squatty bulbous shaded pink mother-of-pearl satin Snowflake patt. bowl w/eight-crimp rim, decorated w/yellow "wheat" design coralene beading, raised on applied frosted clear slender feet, 5" d., 3 3/4" h.. 695

Tumbler, shaded rose red satin ground decorated w/overall yellow "seaweed" coralene beading, white lining 248
Tumbler, shaded deep pink to white satin ground decorated w/yellow "seaweed" coralene beading, 3 3/4" h. 358

Small Amber Coralene Vase

Vase, 3 1/2" h., 2 1/4" d., flaring cylindrical body w/angled shoulder to a cupped rim, honey amber w/green & white coralene leaves around the neck & multicolored coralene flowers & leaves around the body (ILLUS.) 135
Vase, 3 7/8" h., footed spherical body w/a short, wide cylindrical neck, shaded blue to white satin ground decorated overall w/yellow "seaweed" coralene beading, 19th c. 193
Vase, 4" h., footed spherical body w/a wide short cylindrical neck, shaded red to white mother-of-pearl satin Diamond Quilted patt., decorated overall w/yellow "seaweed" coralene beading, 19th c. 320
Vase, 4 1/4" h., bulbous ovoid body w/a wide short cylindrical neck, red shaded to white mother-of-pearl Diamond Quilted patt., decorated overall w/yellow "seaweed" coralene beading, 19th c. 330
Vase, 6" h., 7" w., large spherical fiery opalescent body w/wide flat mouth, decorated w/a wide swirled red band & overall colored coralene beaded decoration of a large pear on twigs w/green leaves, on four curved applied amber branch legs, two continuing up the sides to form thorn bands, 19th c. 1,265
Vase, 6 5/8" h., footed spherical lower body w/a slender waist below the swelled cupped neck, shaded blue mother-of-pearl satin Diamond Quilted patt., decorated overall w/pink "seaweed" coralene beading, frosted clear applied snake around the central neck, 19th c. 385
Vase, 7" h., double gourd-form w/cylindrical upper neck, shaded pink to white satin ground decorated w/yellow "seaweed" coralene beading 715
Vase, 7 1/2" h., bulbous ovoid body w/a short flaring flat neck, yellow mother-of-pearl satin Herringbone patt. decorated w/an overall beaded fern leaf decoration, white lining (ILLUS. top next column) 1,055

Satin Glass Coralene Vase

Vase, 8 1/2" h., simple ovoid body w/a small mouth, yellow shaded to pale pink cased satin exterior decorated w/an overall diamond & cross yellow beaded coralene design, gold rim, opal white lining (slight bead loss) 173
Vases, 7 1/4" h., swelled cylindrical melon-lobed body tapering to a short trumpet neck, rainbow satin ground in pink, green, blue, yellow & white decorated w/yellow "seaweed" coralene beading, 19th c., pr. 275

CRACKLE

This type of glassware has been made for centuries by submersing hot glass in cold water, reheating it and then blowing it to produce a crackled or fine spider web effect throughout the body of the piece. Another glass sometimes called "Craquelle" is produced by a different technique and is listed under "Overshot" glass.

Pitcher, 7" h., bulbous, cranberry.................. $245

Olive Green Crackle Glass Pitcher

Pitcher, cov., 8" h., 6" d., spherical body w/a cylindrical neck, olive green w/applied green handle, hinged flat pewter cover w/thumbrest (ILLUS.) 145
Vase, 5 1/4" h., mold-blown pinched fish-bowl sphere of faint opal w/cracked finish, enamel-painted w/fish, water lilies & aquatic plants, Bohemia, late 19th c. 345

CRANBERRY

Gold was added to glass batches to give this glass its color on reheating. It has been made by numerous glasshouses for years and is currently being reproduced. Both blown and molded articles were produced. A less expensive type of cranberry was made with the substitution of copper for gold.

Bell, cranberry bell w/applied clear handle, England, late 19th c., 11" h. **$94**

Bell, cranberry body w/applied crystal handle & original cranberry clapper, 13 1/4" h. **248**

Decorated Cranberry Bottle

Bottle w/stopper, ovoid body tapering to a slender cylindrical neck w/a flared rim, enameled w/white dots & gold bands, clear facet-cut stopper w/white dots, 2 1/2" d., 8 1/2" h. (ILLUS.) **165**

Bottle w/stopper, wide slightly tapering cylindrical shouldered body tapering to a tall cylindrical neck w/flared rim, the exterior w/an overall craquelle finish, worn gold trim bands, clear facet-cut stopper, 4" d., 9 3/4" h. **145**

Bowl, 4 1/2" d., decorated w/heavy gold enameling & multicolored florals in pinks, blues, yellow, greens & pink opalescent, several applied jewels, gold feet...... **248**

Bowl, 8" d., 4 1/2" h., deep flaring four-lobed form w/clear applied wishbone feet & clear applied drops around the rim, the interior enameled w/blue, pink, yellow & white flowers **175**

Cranberry Glass Box

Box, cov., round optic-ribbed base w/wide neck ring w/applied clear shell rigaree,

the inset domed cover w/applied clear flame finial, 6" d., 6" h. (ILLUS.) **210**

Celery vase, cylindrical tapered sides, Inverted Thumbprint patt., enameled w/forget-me-nots, 7" h. **110**

Celery vase, w/floral enamel decoration, attributed to Mt. Washington **250**

Claret jug, cov., tall tapering cylindrical body w/overall fine exterior threading, wide brass collar w/rim spout & flat hinged cover, long pointed angled handle down the side, 5" d., 9 1/2" h. **225**

Cordial set, decanter w/stopper, four cordials & a square tray, late 19th c., the set..... **330**

Cracker jar, cov., cylindrical w/rounded base & shoulder, Inverted Thumbprint patt. w/large enameled blue & white blossoms on green leafy stems, silver plate rim, domed cover & bail handle, 11" h. **280**

Cruet w/original stopper, an oval medallion encircling the body w/gold stain, surrounded by enameled decoration, applied clear handle **138**

Cruet w/stopper, optic ribbed body w/an applied clear handle & stopper, 9" h. **135**

Cruet w/stopper, squatty bulbous body tapering to a slender neck w/arched spout, Inverted Thumbprint patt., decorated overall w/enameled brown floral pods joined by slender stems, applied clear reeded handle, clear bubble stopper, 6 1/2" h. **341**

Decanter w/clear facet-cut stopper, flared cylindrical body w/rounded shoulder & slender cylindrical neck w/flattened, flared rim, wide optic rib design, the shoulder decorated w/a wide gold band & white enamel dots, 2 7/8" d., 8 5/8" h. (ILLUS. below) **135**

Decorated Cranberry Decanter

Decanter w/original stopper, ovoid body tapering to a tall slender neck w/a tricorner rim, the front panel decorated w/two ducks partially hidden among rushes, applied angled clear handle, clear facet-cut stopper, 12 1/4" h. **210**

Dresser box w/hinged cover, cylindrical w/flat top & brass fittings, ring handles & footed ring base, the top decorated w/an ornate white enamel floral cluster & bird, a delicate band of white enamel florals around the sides, late 19th c., 4" h.............. 242

Finger bowl, ruffled rim w/clear applied rigaree around the base, Inverted Thumbprint patt., decorated w/multicolored enameled flowers, England, late 19th c., 4 1/2" d. 66

Loving cup, handled, applied threading & gilt decoration, applied clear foot, 11 1/4" h. 88

Gilt-decorated Cranberry Perfume

Perfume bottle w/facet-cut clear stopper, cylindrical body w/rounded shoulder & short cylindrical neck w/flared rim, the body decorated w/a wide band of squiggle-work between lines, gold-trimmed rim, 1 3/4" d., 4 1/2" h. (ILLUS.) 135

Pickle castor, cylindrical Inverted Thumbprint insert enameled w/delicate flowers, in an ornate footed silver plate frame w/domed cover, upright handle & tongs....... 495

Bulbous Cranberry Pitcher

Pitcher, 6 1/8" h., 4 1/2" d., bulbous spherical body tapering to a wide cylindrical neck w/a pinched spout, rippled optic design, applied clear angled handle (ILLUS.)... 110

Pitcher, water, 7" h., bulbous body in Inverted Thumbprint patt., applied clear reeded handle 88

Cranberry Optic-Ribbed Pitcher

Pitcher, 4 1/2" d., 7 1/2" h., footed wide ovoid optic-ribbed body w/a wide cylindrical neck & pinched spout, applied clear reeded handle (ILLUS.) 135

Pitcher, 7 3/4" h., ribbed bulbous body w/squared top, applied clear rope handle..... 160

Pitcher, 11 1/4" h., 5 1/2" d., tall tapering ovoid tankard-form w/tricorner rim, ice bladder at the back, overall frosted ice finish on the exterior, applied clear handle 195

Salt & pepper shakers, ovoid body w/optic design & enameled w/dainty white daisies, in a fitted silver plate footed stand w/upright central handle w/loop finial, late 19th c., 6" h............................... 220

Sugar shaker w/metal lid, bulbous base 195

Sugar shaker w/metal lid, Parian mold.......... 295

Sugar shaker w/metal lid, ring neck mold, optic rib design 195

Sugar shaker w/metal lid, Venetian Diamond patt. 195

Tumbler, squared ovoid form w/Inverted Thumbprint design & pinched-in sides, overall enameled dainty flowers, 4" h.......... 286

Vases, 10 1/2" h., optic ribbed body tapering to a small neck decorated w/enameled white & pink blossoms, applied enameled buds, attributed to Moser, pr. 330

Vases, 16" h., 7" d., tall slender waisted form w/central raised ring, optic ribbed design, enameled w/large soft yellow flowers & small white flowers & green leaves, pr. 450

CROWN MILANO

This glass, produced by Mt. Washington Glass Company late in the 19th century, is opal glass decorated by painting and enameling. It appears identical to a ware termed Albertine, also made by Mt. Washington.

Printed Crown Milano Mark

Atomizer, swirled body, trumpet vine decoration, 6 1/2" h. $595

Bowl, 9 1/2" w., 3 1/4" h., tricorner-form w/rolled-under sides, yellowish green ground decorated w/pansies, roses &

forget-me-nots, purple "CM" & crown
mark (some interior stain) **1,200**

Stunning Crown Milano Bride's Bowl

Bride's bowl, deep rounded triangular
form w/a crimped tricorner rim, the sides
decorated w/large yellow & purple pansies & gilt edging, set on an ornate Pairpoint silver plate stand w/a round
knopped pedestal above a domed triangular base w/embossed grapevines
raised on three pierced & pointed floral-
decorated feet, signed, 11 1/2" h.
(ILLUS.).. **3,750**
Cracker jar, cov., barrel-shaped, creamy
Burmese-colored decorated w/a cluster
of large exotic blossoms on a branch, all
trimmed in gilt, silver plate cover, rim &
swing bail handle, silver impressed
"MW," "CM" crown mark on base,
7 1/4" h. **1,200**

Crown Milano Cracker Jar

Cracker jar, cov., cylindrical, decorated
w/pastel pansies outlined w/gold &
round panels of swirled spiderwebbing in
gold on a creamy white ground, low
domed silver plate cover molded in relief
w/embossed florals & a figural butterfly
finial, marked w/Crown Milano logo &
"534," 4 1/4" d., 5" h. (ILLUS.) **950**
Cracker jar, cov., peach shaded to cream
body decorated w/gold flowers & leaves
overall, ornate silver plate rim, bail han-
dle & cover marked "Pairpoint".................... **950**
Cracker jar, cov., squatty bulbous body
decorated w/gold & orange roses &
leaves on a white ground, ornate silver
plate rim w/ruffled edge, shaped bail
handle & cover w/figural turtle finial
(ILLUS. top next column) **1,200**

Fine Crown Milano Cracker Jar

Creamer, square, applied ribbed handle,
gold enameled flowers, berries & leaves **275**
Creamer & cov. sugar bowl, each of
squatty bulbous form tapering to a narrow neck, the sugar bowl w/small loop
shoulder handles & a bulbous domed
cover w/knob finial, the creamer w/a high
curved spout & applied handle, each
decorated w/sprays of blue cornflowers,
purple asters, pink & yellow roses & red
wild roses on a soft beige ground
w/heavy gilt trim, sugar 4 3/4" h.,
creamer, 4 1/4" h., pr. (hairline in base of
sugar) **1,250**
Creamer & cov. sugar bowl, each of
squatty bulbous form, the creamer w/sil-
ver plate rim & high curved metal spout,
the sugar bowl w/small loop silver plate
handles, knop finial & marked "M.W.
2039" on lid, each decorated w/blue
flowers on pale pinkish yellow back-
ground, pr. **800**

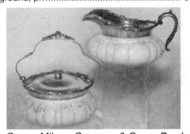

Crown Milano Creamer & Sugar Bowl

Creamer & cov. sugar bowl, squatty bulbous ribbed bodies decorated w/molded
scrolls & florals trimmed w/gilt, silver
plate scroll-edged rim & handle on
creamer & scroll-edged rim, cover & bail
handle on sugar, sugar lid incised "M.W.
2040," sugar 6" h., pr. (ILLUS.) **450**
Creamer & open sugar bowl, white satin
ground decorated w/blush pink around
the edge, lavender violets & gold trim,
w/paper label, sugar bowl 4 1/4" d.,
creamer 3 1/2" h., pr................................. **1,250**
Dish, triangular w/two rolled-in edges, decorated w/multicolored flowers & heavy
gold trim, signed **475**
Ewer, tall ovoid body tapering to a small
neck w/narrow upright spout, gold

arched ropetwist shoulder handle, the sides decorated w/a color vignette of a young couple in 18th c. attire, framed by a heavy gilt scrolling, wreath mark & "#1019," 16" h... **5,775**

Crown Milano Ewer

Ewer, wide squatty bulbous body tapering to a small short neck w/an upright curved spout, slender serpent handle down the shoulder, gold lotus blossoms & green & gold pods outlined in raised gold on a light green ground, gold handle, spout w/aqua & scrolled leaves, No. 0567, ca. 1894, 8" d., 8" h. (ILLUS.) **2,000**

Ewer, tall ovoid body tapering to a short cylindrical neck w/a cupped rim w/a pinched spout, rope-wrapped neck continuing to form rope handle, beige, tan & rust ornately decorated w/jeweled shadow flowers outlined in heavy gold scrolls, ca. 1893, 10 1/2" h. **1,500**

Fine Crown Milano Covered Jar

Jar, cov., bulbous ovoid body tapering to a small domed cover w/a ribbed & pointed finial, creamy white ground ornately decorated w/ivy leaves & vine in heavy green & brown enamel outlined in gold w/light brown scrolls outlined in gold around the base & cover, unmarked, 10 1/2" h. (ILLUS.)................................. **2,750**

Jar, cov., wide low squatty footed body tapering to a tiny cover w/knob finial, the sides applied w/two small reeded scrolled gold handles, decorated w/four open roses, blossoms & colorful tulips & overall heavy gilt trim, marked "1013," 9" d., 5 3/4" h... **2,200**

Jar, cov., wide squatty bulbous base centered by a wide, short cylindrical neck supporting a domed cover w/knob finial,

the neck flanked by small ribbed gold ring handles, the border of the cover & neck decorated w/heavy dark gold, the central cover & lower body in creamy white decorated overall w/scattered colorful enameled floral clusters, knob finial in gold, signed "53".................................... **1,430**

Jardiniere, bulbous body decorated w/ten pansies w/ten medallions in violet, yellow & tan, heavy gold trim around the neck, signed on the bottom, 9 1/4" d., 7" h. **1,250**

Pickle castor, cylindrical insert in creamy yellow decorated w/a large rose red & cream caladium leaf, ornate silver plate frame, cover & tongs, silver marked by Tufts **1,155**

Rose bowl, decorated overall w/h.p. daisies & roses on a soft ivory ground, 3 1/2 x 4 1/2" **350**

Rose bowl, spherical, decorated w/ten pansies h.p. in pastel shades of purple, blue, brown & white & highlighted w/delicate gold foliage, three gold blossoms & randomly placed gold embellishments, 5 1/8" d.. **675**

Rose bowl, spherical, eight-crimp rim, yellow beige satin ground decorated w/blue & lavender pansies, purple crown mark, 5" h... **750**

Crown Milano Rose Bowl with Orchid

Rose bowl, eight-crimp rim, pale blue shaded to white satin ground, h.p. shaded maroon orchid w/long green & yellow leaves, unsigned, 4" d. (ILLUS.).. **250-300**

Salt dip, master size, enameled w/pink & mauve floral decoration **150**

Spooner, embossed diamond quilted body decorated w/chrysanthemums & gold trim **550**

Sweetmeat jar, cov., creamy satin ground decorated w/enameled gold designs, silver plate rim, cover & bail handle, cover marked "M.W." & numbered........................ **450**

Sweetmeat jar, cov., melon-ribbed body, pink shaded to opaque white body decorated w/ornate gold scrolling on upper portion & multicolored flowers on the lower sections, ornate silver plate cover, rim & bail handle, marked, 5 1/4" d., 4" h. **950**

Sweetmeat jar, cov., squatty bulbous body w/lightly molded raised white ribbon swirls alternating w/bands of pastel pink, decorated w/encrusted gold thistle & leaves, ornate silver plate rim, bail handle & inset cover w/a small figural turtle, cover marked "MW4416," base marked "527" **1,485**

Sweetmeat jar, cov., barrel-shaped w/an embossed overall swirled diamond quilted design, decorated w/a biscuit-colored ground enameled w/earthtone holly leaves outlined in raised gold & enhanced by clumps of ruby-jeweled berries & tan shadow coiled designs, original paper label, silver plated domed cover w/twig handle & embossed floral design, 4" h. **1,100**

Fine Crown Milano Syrup Pitcher

Syrup pitcher w/original top, melon-ribbed body, decorated w/enameled gold flowers & leaves & hundreds of blue, white, black, coral & turquoise enamel dottings on a soft butter cream ground, embossed silver plate rim, hinged domed cover & arched twisted handle (ILLUS.).. **1,500**

Syrup pitcher w/original top, white ground shaded to deep orange, decorated w/a blue daisy, green leaves & foliage & a large gold butterfly above the flower, dated "1884," 7 1/2" h. **650**

Table set: creamer, open sugar bowl & cov. jam jar; slightly globular lobed form, shaded pink decorated w/gold chrysanthemums, ormolu mounts, signed, 3 pcs... **1,500**

Tumbler, cylindrical, decorated w/heavy gold garlands, flowers, ribbons & bows on a semi-glossy white ground, marked w/red crown & wreath, 2 7/8" d., 3 7/8" h. **550**

Vase, 4 1/2" h., wide squatty bulbous body w/the top centered by a short small cylindrical neck, almond brown ground decorated overall w/scattered heavy gilt spider mum blossoms & light brown shadow blossoms **825**

Vase, 4 3/4" h., squatty bulbous body tapering to a short rolled neck flanked by small loop handles, decorated w/gilded wild roses over a peach & amber leafy ground, folded gold rim handles, unsigned Mt. Washington (ILLUS. right, top next column)... **750**

Vase, 5" h., footed bulbous ovoid body tapering to a tiny short neck w/a flared four-ruffle rim, creamy ground decorated w/gold ferns & shadow leaves trimmed w/gold... **440**

Two Decorated Crown Milano Vases

Vase, 5" h., footed squatty bulbous ovoid body w/lightly molded swirled ribs up the sharply tapering sides to small neck w/a four-lobed upturned rim, decorated w/tan shadow ferns overlaid w/gold fern fronds outlined w/raised gold, gold-trimmed rim, unmarked **770**

Bulbous Crown Milano Vase

Vase, 6" h., 5 3/4" d., footed bulbous body lightly molded w/narrow swirled ribs tapering to a short small neck w/four-crimp rim, decorated w/clusters of tiny white & blue flowers on the yellow shaded to creamy white ground, logo signature (ILLUS.) **1,100**

Vase, 7" h., baluster-form body w/a narrow neck & widely flaring flattened rim, the body lightly molded w/swirled ribs & decorated w/large white blossoms & buds outlined in gold against a ground of blue scrolls, label on base reads "M & W G Co. Crown Milano" **1,100**

Floral-decorated Crown Milano Vase

Vase, 7" h., 6 3/4" d., squatty bulbous swirl-molded body tapering to a short neck flaring into four fluted lobes, decorated w/dahlia flowers in yellow & burgundy, the leaves & stems w/heavy gold trim, tan shadow leaves in the background, gold trim on foot & rim, unmarked (ILLUS.) **1,750**

Vase, 7 1/2" h., footed squatty bulbous base tapering sharply to a very tall slightly flaring slender cylindrical neck, sepia wash decorated w/gold grape leaves & vines, unsigned **728**

Vase, 7 1/2" h., 3 3/4" d., cylindrical w/blue wash & overlapping heavy gold floral decoration in original Pairpoint silver plated holder **750**

Vase, 8" h., bulbous wide four-sided body tapering to a short cylindrical neck w/a flared rim flanked by two almond applied pointed arch shoulder handles, the body lavishly decorated w/peach & yellow shadow foliage overlaid w/raised gold branches of wild roses w/jewel stamens, buds & leaves, unmarked **650**

Vase, 8" h., squared bulbous spherical body w/a short cylindrical neck w/rolled rim flanked by ribbed S-scroll handles, decorated w/gold enameled oak leaves & acorns over a shadowy amber patterned background, stamped mark in blue (ILLUS. left w/small vase) **1,500**

Scenic Crown Milano Vase

Vase, 8" h., tall cylindrical body w/flat rim, decorated in pastel coloring w/a distant desert city, palm trees & birches in foreground, dotted & gold rim border, unsigned, some dots missing (ILLUS.) **900**

Vase, 8" h., wide ovoid body tapering sharply to a small flat mouth, decorated w/large branches of gold & silver enamel apple blossoms & leaves w/applied bead 'jewels' in the blossom centers, against a pastel yellow & pink floral background, unsigned (gilt worn at rim) **950**

Vase, 9 1/2" h., bulbed satin white body w/flared elongated neck split at rim in four decorative points, delicate pink blossoms w/gold leaves & tracery overall, base marked "(Crown)CM" in purple **863**

Vase, 10" h., footed large spherical body centered by a ring below the slightly flaring cylindrical neck, shadow background blending blue, green, turquoise, opal & lavender creating an ocean wave effect, decorated w/raised gold, multi-jeweled

starfish, finely painted w/two swimming fish & nautilus w/heavy gold trim, original paper label from the C.E. Selzer Store **7,975**

Vase, cov., 10 1/2" h., wide ovoid body w/a small high, domed cover w/a ribbed & pointed finial, the body decorated w/large green & brown ivy leaves & vines w/lighter tan swirled designs on the cover & around the base all on a creamy white ground, unmarked **2,285**

Vase, 11" h., tall slender ovoid body w/pulled-out loop handles from the small mouth & attached to the shoulder, gold decorated scrolling borders enclosing a h.p. scene of a dancing couple in 18th c. attire, glossy finish, base w/red crown-in-wreath mark & "1001" (some gild rim wear) **1,250**

Vase, 12" h., wide squatty bulbous base centered by a tall slender & slightly swelled 'stick' neck, creamy white ground finely decorated w/large stylized enameled flowers highlighted w/jewels & shadow work, signed **1,595**

Vase, 12 1/4" h., bulbous ovoid body tapering to a short flared neck flanked by three small loop handles, decorated w/Egyptian landscape scenes w/an Arab man w/camel & on the reverse a scene of riders & camels in front of pyramids, elaborate gilt borders of Mideastern scroll designs, marked "Albertine" on base, gilt wear (ILLUS. below) **6,900**

Rare "Albertine" Crown Milano Vase

Vase, 12 1/4" h., satin finish on creamy white bulbous body w/graceful elongated neck, decorated by beaded gold & bronze shaded rose blossoms, buds, & thorny branches, purple crown "CM" mark over "565" on base **920**

Vase, 14" h., tall slender ovoid body w/a very slender & slightly flaring tall neck, decorated w/lilacs highlighted w/heavy matte gold scrolls & a cross design on the neck.. **2,800**

Vase, 15" h., wide squatty bulbous base centered by a very tall slender slightly flaring cylindrical neck w/a deeply forked rim w/notched edges, completely covered w/raised gold overlapped fern fronds in exceptional detail, painted tan shadow leaves, paper label marked "Mt. Washington, Crown Milano" **1,500**

CRUETS

Amber, bulbous body w/applied runny white overlay covering the sides, applied reeded amber handle, hollow amber stopper, 7 3/4" h. **$165**

Amber, bulbous optic ribbed body, applied blue handle & blue stopper, 7 3/4" h. **110**

Blue, bulbous optic ribbed body w/applied clear reeded handle & clear facet-cut stopper, 7 1/4" h. **110**

Decorated Lime Green Cruet

Lime green, footed tapering cylindrical body w/optic ribbing, shouldered cylindrical neck w/pinched spout, applied green handle, tall green teardrop stopper, enameled w/large pink & white blossoms & blue leafy sprigs, 3 1/2" d., 9 3/4" h. (ILLUS.)... **145**

Sapphire Blue Decorated Cruet

Sapphire blue, barrel-shaped w/three raised body bands around optic ribbed form tapering to a short cylindrical neck w/a wide arched spout, applied blue handle, bulbous beehive stopper, the body decorated w/bands of white blossoms & leaf swags, 2 3/4" d., 6" h. (ILLUS.).. **125**

Satin glass, shaded blue mother-of-pearl Diamond Quilted patt., squatty bulbous body tapering to a slender neck w/tricorner rim, applied frosted clear reeded handle & frosted clear ovoid stopper, finely enameled w/a bird, 7 1/4" h. **330**

Satin glass, shaded blue mother-of-pearl Herringbone patt., squatty bulbous body

tapering to a slender neck w/wide tricorner rim, applied frosted clear handle, frosted clear optic ribbed teardrop stopper, 6" h.. **550**

Satin glass, shaded butterscotch mother-of-pearl Diamond Quilted patt., ovoid body tapering to a flat base, slender neck w/arched spout, clear frosted applied thorn handle, clear frosted facet-cut stopper, 6 1/2" h. **605**

Satin glass, shaded pink mother-of-pearl Diamond Quilted patt., bulbous body w/applied frosted clear reeded handle & frosted clear stopper, 7 1/2" h. **770**

CUSTARD

This ware takes its name from its color and is a variant of milk white glass. It was produced largely between 1890 and 1915 by the Northwood Glass Co., Heisey Glass Company, Fenton Art Glass Co., Jefferson Glass Co., and a few others. There are 21 major patterns and a number of minor ones. The prime patterns are considered Argonaut Shell, Chrysanthemum Sprig, Inverted Fan and Feather, Louis XV and Winged Scroll. Most custard glass patterns are enhanced with gold and some have additional enameled decoration or stained highlights. Unless otherwise noted, items in this listing are fully decorated.

Northwood Script Mark

ARGONAUT SHELL (NORTHWOOD)
Berry set, master bowl & 6 sauce dishes, 7 pcs... **$575**
Butter dish, cov., decorated **395**
Compote, jelly, 5" d., 5" h................................ **132**
Cruet w/original stopper **850-895**

Argonaut Shell Pitcher

Pitcher, water (ILLUS.) **400-495**
Salt & pepper shakers w/original tops, pr. **325-350**
Sauce dish, gold trim, decorated **65**
Sugar bowl, cov. **204**
Table set: cov. butter dish, cov. sugar bowl, creamer & spooner; 4 pcs................. **550**
Toothpick holder **365**
Tumbler **110**
Water set, pitcher & 6 tumblers, 7 pcs. **900**

BEADED CIRCLE (NORTHWOOD)
Berry set, master bowl & 5 sauce dishes, 6 pcs.. **495**

Bowl, master berry or fruit................................ **185**

Beaded Circle Jelly Compote

Compote, jelly (ILLUS.)................................... **350**
Salt & pepper shakers w/original tops,
  pr. **255**
Sauce dish **55**
Water set, pitcher & 4 tumblers, 5 pcs. **850**

BEADED SWAG (HEISEY)

Beaded Swag Pickle Dish

Pickle dish (ILLUS.)...................................... **250**
Spooner **40-60**
Toothpick holder, ruby-stained........................ **45**
Wine, w/advertising **75**

CARNELIAN - SEE EVERGLADES PATTERN

CHERRY & SCALE OR FENTONIA (FENTON)
Berry set, master bowl & 4 sauce dishes,
  5 pcs.. **280**
Creamer **95**
Cruet w/original stopper, decorated **120**
Pitcher, water... **325**

Cherry & Scale Sugar Bowl

Sugar bowl, cov. (ILLUS.) **125**
Water set, pitcher & 6 tumblers, 7 pcs. **600**

CHRYSANTHEMUM SPRIG (NORTHWOOD'S PAGODA)
Berry set, master bowl & 4 sauce dishes, 5
  pcs.. **375**
Bowl, master berry or fruit, 10 1/2" oval,
  decorated **70**
Celery vase (ILLUS. top next column) **803**
Condiment set, four-footed tray, salt &
  pepper shakers w/original tops, & toothpick holder, 4 pcs. **945**

Chrysanthemum Sprig Celery Vase

Pitcher, water, decorated................................. **476**
Pitcher, water, undecorated............................. **225**
Salt & pepper shakers w/original tops,
  pr. **150-200**
Sauce dish **50-75**
Sauce dishes, oval, gold trim & paint, set
  of 6 .... **250**
Sugar bowl, cov., decorated.......................... **220**
Sugar bowl, cov., undecorated................. **150-180**
Table set, cov. sugar bowl, creamer, cov.
  butter dish & spooner, 4 pcs. **740**
Toothpick holder, gold trim & paint,
  signed.. **283**
Tumbler **82**
Water set, pitcher & 6 tumblers, 7 pcs. **725**

DIAMOND WITH PEG (JEFFERSON)
Berry set, master bowl & 6 sauce dishes, 7
  pcs.. **600**

Diamond with Peg Master Berry Bowl

Bowl, master berry or fruit (ILLUS.)................ **225**
Butter dish, cov. **265**
Creamer, individual size, souvenir **45**
Mug, rose decoration **45**
Napkin ring,. souvenir **145**
Pitcher, tankard... **375**
Pitcher, tankard (wear on gold)...................... **200**
Punch cup **60**
Salt & pepper shakers w/original tops,
  souvenir, pr. **90**
Sauce dish **35**
Sugar bowl, cov., souvenir **105**
Sugar bowl, open **95**
Tumbler, souvenir **39**
Vase, 6" h., souvenir...................................... **50**
Vase, 8" h. **85**
Water set, pitcher & 6 tumblers, 7 pcs. **475-525**
Whiskey shot glass **45**
Wine **38**

EVERGLADES OR CARNELIAN (NORTHWOOD)
Berry set, master bowl & 6 sauce dishes, 7
  pcs.. **725**
Butter dish, cov. **370**

Everglades Cruet

Cruet w/original stopper (ILLUS.) 275
Pitcher, water.. 650
Salt & pepper shakers w/original tops,
   pr. 450
Salt shaker w/original top 150

FAN (DUGAN)
Berry set, master bowl & 6 sauce dishes, 7
   pcs.. 395
Butter dish, cov. 215
Ice cream set, master bowl & 6 individual
   ice cream dishes, 7 pcs............................ 500

Fan Sugar Bowl

Sugar bowl, cov. (ILLUS.) 95
Table set, cov. butter dish, cov. sugar bowl
   & spooner, 3 pcs. 350-450
Tumblers, set of 6....................................... 400
Water set, pitcher & 6 tumblers, 7 pcs. 550-650

FLUTED SCROLLS OR KLONDYKE (NORTHWOOD)
Pitcher, water, footed.................................. 250
Salt & pepper shakers w/original tops,
   pr. 95
Salt shaker w/original top 40
Sauce dish 43
Sugar bowl, cov. 135
Tumbler 35
Water set, pitcher & 6 tumblers, 7 pcs. 475

GENEVA
Banana boat, four-footed, 11" oval 95-125
Berry set, oval master bowl & 6 sauce
   dishes, 7 pcs. 318
Bowl, master berry or fruit, 8 1/2'" d., three-
   footed 135
Butter dish, cov. 160
Compote, jelly 75
Compote, jelly, green stain 45
Creamer 80-100
Cruet w/original stopper 250-350
Pitcher, water... 223
Salt & pepper shakers w/original tops,
   pr. 241
Sauce dish, oval 38-48

Sauce dish, round.. 40
Sugar bowl, cov. 125-150

Geneva Syrup Pitcher

Syrup pitcher w/original top (ILLUS.) 275
Table set, creamer, cov. sugar & spooner,
   3 pcs... 330
Toothpick holder, decorated......................... 125
Tumbler, decorated...................................... 47
Tumbler, w/green 38
Water set, pitcher & 6 tumblers, 7 pcs. 425

GEORGIA GEM OR LITTLE GEM (TARENTUM)
Berry set, master bowl & 6 sauce dishes, 7
   pcs.. 275
Bowl, master berry or fruit, decorated....... 100-125
Celery vase 132
Creamer & cov. sugar bowl, pr. 60
Pitcher, water, decorated............................. 310
Salt & pepper shakers w/original tops,
   pr. 75

Georgia Gem Tumbler

Tumbler (ILLUS.) 50
Water set, pitcher & 4 tumbler, 5 pcs. 435

GRAPE & GOTHIC ARCHES (NORTHWOOD)
Berry set, master bowl & 6 sauce dishes,
   7 pcs... 550
Bowl, master berry or fruit............................. 125
Creamer 90
Pitcher, water... 285
Sauce dish 38

Grape & Gothic Arches Spooner

Spooner (ILLUS.).. 50-75
Sugar bowl, cov... 195
Water set, pitcher & 6 tumblers, 7 pcs. 550-650

INTAGLIO (NORTHWOOD)
Berry set: 7" d. master bowl & six sauce
    dishes, green & gold decoration, 7 pcs. 395

Intaglio Large Fruit Compote

Bowl, fruit, 9" d., footed compote (ILLUS.)....... 325
Butter dish, gold & blue decoration 196
Creamer & cov. sugar bowl, pr. 275
Cruet w/original stopper 310
Pitcher, water..................................... 373
Salt & pepper shakers w/original tops,
    pr. 203
Sauce dish, green decoration........................... 60
Spooner 105
Tumblers, blue & gold trim, set of 4................ 225
Water set, pitcher & 6 tumblers, blue &
    gold trim, 7 pcs..................................... 475

INVERTED FAN & FEATHER (NORTH-WOOD)
Berry set, master bowl & 4 sauce dishes, 5
    pcs.. 570

Inverted Fan & Feather Master Berry Bowl

Bowl, master berry (ILLUS.)............................. 303
Cruet w/original stopper 865
Punch bowl, footed....................................... 2,500
Salt shaker w/original top 168
Table set, cov. butter dish, creamer &
    spooner, 3 pcs... 695
Water set, pitcher & 6 tumblers, 7 pcs. 895

JACKSON OR FLUTED SCROLLS WITH FLOWER BAND (NORTHWOOD)
Bowl, master berry or fruit................................. 85
Creamer (ILLUS. top next column) 85
Pitcher, water, undecorated........................... 275
Salt & pepper shakers w/original tops,
    pr. 135
Salt shaker w/original top, undecorated 58
Tumbler 44
Water set, pitcher & 4 tumblers, 5 pcs. 365-385

Jackson Creamer

LOUIS XV (NORTHWOOD)
Berry set, master bowl & 6 sauce dishes, 7
    pcs.. 500-525
Bowl, master berry w/gold............................... 295
Butter dish, cov. 145
Creamer 80
Cruet w/original stopper 450
Glove box, cov.. 110
Pitcher, water.. 234
Salt shaker w/original top 80
Sauce dish, 5" oval, w/gold trim....................... 38
Spooner 80

Louis XV Sugar Bowl

Sugar bowl, cov. (ILLUS.)............................... 123
Table set, cov. butter, sugar, creamer,
    spooner, 4 pcs... 300
Tumbler 65
Water set, pitcher & 4 tumblers, 5 pcs. 325-425
Water set, pitcher & 6 tumblers, 7 pcs. 800

MAPLE LEAF (NORTHWOOD)
Berry set, master bowl & 6 sauce dishes,
    7 pcs.. 800
Bowl, master berry or fruit............................... 265

Maple Leaf Cruet

Cruet w/original stopper (ILLUS.) 1,100
Salt & pepper shakers w/original tops,
    pr. 500
Table set, creamer, cov. butter dish &
    spooner, 3 pcs... 485
Water set, pitcher & 6 tumblers, 7 pcs. 750

NORTHWOOD GRAPE, GRAPE & CABLE OR GRAPE & THUMBPRINT

Banana boat 325
Berry set, master bowl & 6 sauce dishes, 7
    pcs.. 300
Butter dish, cov. 250
Cologne bottle w/original stopper 538

Northwood Grape Cracker Jar

Cracker jar, cov., two-handled (ILLUS.) 600
Creamer, nutmeg trim 100
Dresser tray 300
Fernery, footed, 7 1/2" d., 4 1/2" h. 150
Hatpin holder 450
Nappy, two-handled 48
Pin dish 165
Pitcher, water.................................... 385
Plate, 8" d....................................... 55
Plate, 8" w., six-sided 65
Punch bowl & base, 2 pcs. 800
Spooner 135
Sugar bowl, cov. 150
Table set, cov. butter dish, cov. sugar bowl
    & creamer, 3 pcs. 475
Tumbler 47
Water set, pitcher & 6 tumblers, 7 pcs. 1,250

PRAYER RUG (IMPERIAL)

Nappy, two-handled, ruffled, 6" d. 55
Plate, 7 1/2" d..................................... 60
Tumbler 80
Tumbler, nutmeg stain 70
Vase 50

PUNTY BAND (HEISEY)

Salt & pepper shaker w/original tops,
    souvenir, pr. 80
Vase, 5 1/2" h., souvenir........................... 75
Wine, souvenir.................................... 50

RIBBED DRAPE (JEFFERSON)

Ribbed Drape Butter Dish

Butter dish, cov. (ILLUS.) 265
Cruet w/original stopper 250
Salt & pepper shakers w/original tops,
    pr. 110
Table set, 4 pcs. (open sugar) 575
Toothpick holder 95

Toothpick holder, rose decoration 273

RING BAND (HEISEY)

Bowl, master berry or fruit, decorated............. 278
Celery Vase 300
Condiment set, condiment tray, jelly com-
    pote, toothpick holder & salt & pepper
    shakers, 5 pcs. 429

Ring Band Creamer

Creamer (ILLUS.)................................. 80
Creamer & cov. sugar bowl, pr. 235
Cruet w/clear stopper, h.p. wild rose dec-
    oration 193
Cruet w/original stopper 300
Pitcher, water, enameled floral decoration...... 450
Salt & pepper shakers w/original tops,
    pr. 100
Salt & pepper shakers w/original tops,
    souvenir, pr. 115
Table set, 4 pcs.................................. 513
Water set, pitcher & 6 tumblers, 7 pcs. 550
Whimsey, hat shape (from tumbler mold)........ 295

VICTORIA (TARENTUM)

Berry set, master bowl & 6 sauce dishes,
    undecorated, 7 pcs............................. 275
Berry set, master bowl & 6 sauce dishes,
    undecorated, green, 7 pcs. 395
Bowl, master berry or fruit...................... 165
Creamer 85

Victoria Water Pitcher

Pitcher, water (ILLUS.) 275
Sauce dish 50
Sugar bowl, cov.................................. 165
Tumbler 60
Water set, pitcher & 4 tumblers, 5 pcs. 380

WINGED SCROLL (HEISEY)

Berry set, master bowl & 6 sauce dishes,
    decorated, 7 pcs.............................. 320
Bowl, master berry 165
Butter dish, cov. 167
Creamer 91
Pitcher, water, 9" h., bulbous 230

Salt & pepper shakers w/original tops,
pr. **150**

Winged Scroll Sugar Bowl

Sugar bowl, cov., decorated (ILLUS.) **195**
Toothpick holder **129**
Tumbler **69**
Water set, tankard pitcher & 6 tumblers, 7
pcs. **725**

MISCELLANEOUS PATTERNS

DELAWARE
Bowl, 5 1/2" (hat-shaped) **45**
Sauce dish, w/blue decoration **45**

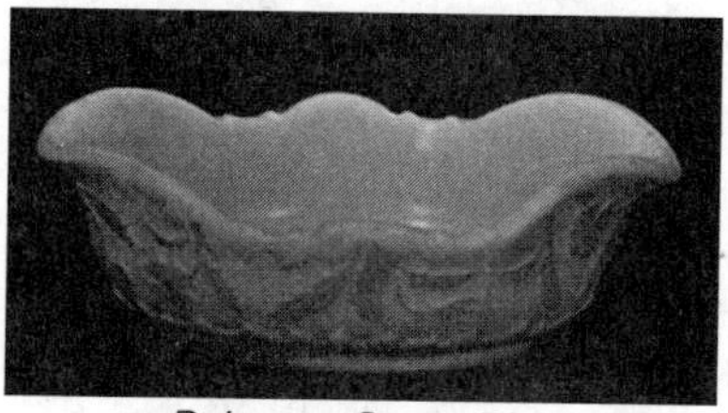

Delaware Sauce Dish

Sauce dish, w/rose stain (ILLUS.) **40-65**

HEART WITH THUMBPRINT
Creamer **40**
Creamer & sugar bowl, individual size, pr. **125**
Finger lamp, w/green decoration **263**
Sugar bowl, open, individual size, w/green
decoration **55**

Heart with Thumbprint Wine

Wine (ILLUS.) **125**

VERMONT

Vermont Card Basket

Card basket, 7 1/2" d. (ILLUS.) **95**
Pickle tray **30**
Pitcher, w/blue trim & enameled decoration **373**
Table set, cov. butter, creamer & spooner,
3 pcs. **195**
Tumbler **75-100**
Vase **25**

WILD BOUQUET
Cruet w/original stopper, undecorated **300**

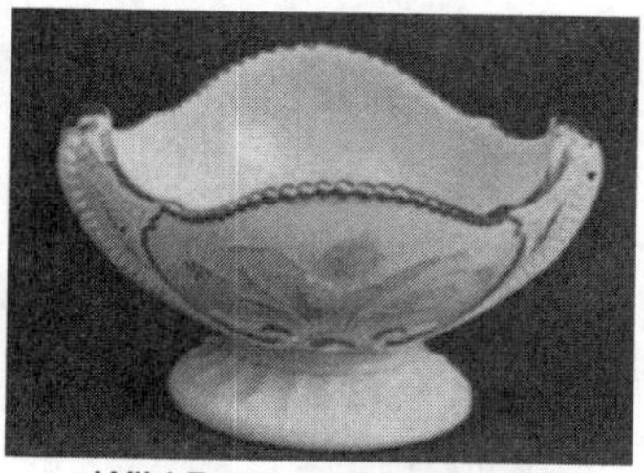

Wild Bouquet Sauce Dish

Sauce dish (ILLUS.) **50**

OTHER MISCELLANEOUS PIECES
Bowl, master berry, Tiny Thumbprint patt. **259**

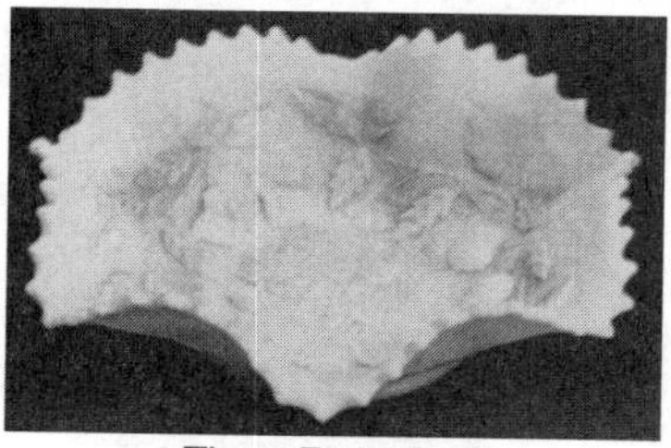

Three Fruits Bowl

Bowl, 7 1/4" d., Three Fruits patt., ruffled
rim, nutmeg stain (ILLUS.) **40**
Lamp, kerosene-type, Sunset patt. **270**
Lamp, kerosene, finger-type, greenish
color w/embossed tulip design, applied
handle complete w/burner & chimney,
3 3/4" to top of collar **185**
Pitcher, tankard, Tiny Thumbprint patt. **369**
Salt & pepper shakers w/original tops,
Tiny Thumbprint patt., pr. **225**
Sauce dish, Tiny Thumbprint patt. **59**
Spooner, Tiny Thumbprint patt. **129**

Sugar bowl, cov., Tiny Thumbprint patt. **165**
Tumbler, Royal Oak, patt. w/green stain **45**

CUT

Cut glass most eagerly sought by collectors is American glass produced during the so-called "Brilliant Period" from 1880 to about 1915. Pieces listed below are by type of article in alphabetical order.

Hawkes, Hoare, Libbey and Straus Marks

BASKETS

Meriden Cut Glass Basket

Meriden-signed, wide shallow form w/two sides turned-up, hobstars, large stars & fans, heavy applied rope twist handle (ILLUS.) **$895**

BOTTLES

Hawkes' Venetian Pattern Cologne

Cologne, Hawkes' Venetian patt., cut diamonds, fans & vesicas, facet-cut stopper, 3 1/2" d., 6 1/2" h. (ILLUS.) **345**
Cologne, hobstars alternating w/notched prisms, facet-cut stopper (ILLUS. top next column) **350**

Cologne with Hobstars & Prism Cuts

BOWLS

Large Centerpiece Fruit Bowl

Centerpiece fruit bowl, Meriden-signed, oblong form cut w/panels of cane design alternating w/large & small hobstars & fans, scalloped & notched rim, 10 1/2" l. (ILLUS.) **1,250**

Clark's Jubilee Pattern Bowl

Clark's Jubilee patt., large hobstars alternating w/fans & diamonds around the rim above plain panels & almond cuts, 9 1/2" d. (ILLUS.) **375**

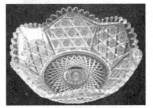

Bowl with Clusters of Hobstars

Clusters of hobstars, six-sided form w/each side cut w/clusters of small hobstars, large hobstar in the bottom, 9 1/4" d. (ILLUS.).. **475**

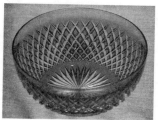

Large Bowl Attributed to Dorflinger

Dorflinger-attributed, wide form w/pointed & arched notched rim, four large hobstars alternating w/small hobstars above fan-cut panels, hobstar in bottom, 12" d. (ILLUS.).. **575**

Dorflinger Ruby to Clear Finger Bowl

Finger bowl, Dorflinger, ruby cut to clear w/overall small diamonds, star-cut bottom, 5" d., 2 1/2" h. (ILLUS.) **345**

Libbey-signed Fruit Bowl

Fruit bowl, Libbey-signed, hobstars alternating w/stars & panels of crosshatched cutting w/a large square of crosshatch cutting in the bottom, 10" d., 4" h. (ILLUS.).. **570**

Handled Long Hawkes' Centauri Bowl

Hawkes' Centauri patt., wide shallow flaring form w/notched loop end handles, cut across the center w/hobstars & fans w/large central hobstar, 12 3/4" l. (ILLUS.).. **1,250**

Fine Hawkes' Kensington Bowl

Hawkes' Kensington patt., large hobstars above triangular panels w/smaller hobstars & buttons, scalloped & notched rims, 9" d. (ILLUS.).................................... **1,000**

Rare Hawkes' Nautilus Bowl

Hawkes' Nautilus patt., three large zippercut shell forms alternating w/pointed arches & hobstars at the rim, 10" d. (ILLUS.).. **3,250**

Hawkes-signed, cut w/four large hobstars separated by large pointed panels w/smaller hobstars & a strawberry diamond panel forming a rim point, crosscutting forms triangles in the design surrounding a large hobstar in the bottom, 10" d., 3 1/4" h. (small rim flakes)................ **413**

Hoare-signed, cut w/three large sunbursts alternating w/cane-cut panels surrounded by deep cross cuts, notched rim, 8 1/4" d., 3 1/2" h. (edge flakes)............ **220**

Hoare Marquis Pattern Bowl

Hoare-signed, Marquis patt., Napoleon's hat form, band of hobstars above cane band & triangles w/cane cutting (ILLUS.).. **1,550**

Hoare-signed, shallow round form, cut overall w/small detailed hobstars w/some forming a large cross across the center, 9" d., 2 1/4" h.................................... **330**

Hobstar & Tusk Cut bowl

Hobstars, large hobstars around the scalloped rim above alternating hobstar clusters & plain tusk designs, hobstar in bottom, 9 1/4" d., 4" h. (ILLUS.) **385**

Footed Bowl with Hobstars

Hobstars, three large hobstars separated w/heavy cross banding w/smaller hobs & buttons, shallow wide bowl on three feet, 8" (ILLUS.).. **175**

Squared Cut Glass Bowl

Hobstars & cane cutting, squared shape w/deeply notched & lobed rim, pointed fan cuts at each corner, 10 1/2" w. (ILLUS.).. **485**

Cut Bowl with Sterling Silver Rim

Hobstars & diamonds, wide deep sides cut w/large hobstars alternating w/diamond & hobstar vesica panels, rolled & pierced applied Gorham sterling silver rim, 11" d., 4" h. (ILLUS.) **1,350**

Hunt's Royal Pattern Bowl

Hunt's Royal patt., wide shallow form w/notched & scalloped rim, 8" d. (ILLUS.)... **395**

Libbey's Florence Pattern Serving Bowl

Libbey's Florence patt., serving-type w/wide shallow unusual form w/upturned sides, two sides w/points & fans rims, large flashed hobstar in bottom, 10" w., 3 1/4" h. (ILLUS.)... **485**

Sylph Pattern Bowl

Monroe's Sylph patt., oblong w/flared zipper-cut sides above a large central hobstar surrounded by eight smaller hobstars, 7 1/2 x 10 1/2", 3 1/4" h. (ILLUS.)... **375**

Wheeler Pattern Bowl

Orange bowl, Mt. Washington's Wheeler patt., large oval boat-shaped from, cut w/bands of strawberry diamond & crosshatching w/fans around the rim, 8" l., 4 1/2" h. (ILLUS.)... **385**

Bowl with Zipper-cut Bands

Zipper-cut bands, shallow form w/long curved bands w/rows of zipper cutting alternating w/small panels of block cutting, fans around the rim, 9" d. (ILLUS.)....... **395**

BOXES

C.F. Monroe Cut Dresser Box

Dresser box, hinged glass cover, round flattened top & tapering cylindrical low sides cut w/hobstars alternating w/zipper cutting, C.F. Monroe Co., 6 1/2" d., 4 1/4" h. (ILLUS.)... **585**

Zipper-cut Dresser Box

Dresser box, spherical w/overall zipper-cut bands, sterling silver domed cover, 5" d. (ILLUS.)... **125**
Dresser box, hinged cover, Hawkes signed, hobstars, crosshatching & fans, 6 1/2" d. **395**

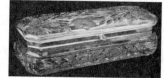

Floral-etched Glove Box

Glove box w/hinged cover, long narrow rectangular form w/notched corners, the

top w/etched floral designs, the base cut w/hobstars, crosshatching & fans (ILLUS.)... **1,350**

Finely Cut Jewelry Box

Jewelry box, rectangular w/rounded corners, hinged flat top w/silver plate mountings, cut overall w/large hobstars alternating w/zipper-cut panels & fans (ILLUS.)... **2,450**

BUTTER DISHES & TUBS

Propeller Pattern Butter Dish

Covered dish, Propeller patt., cut w/hobstars framed by cane cutting & divided by almond-shaped vesicas, facet-cut finial (ILLUS.) **565**

CANDLESTICKS & CANDLEHOLDERS

Bergen's Colonial Pattern Candlestick

Bergen's Colonial patt., tall standard cut w/paneled central stem flanked by facet-cut knobs, hexagonal foot, paneled tulip-form socket, 10 3/4" h., each (ILLUS.) **310**

Russian & Swirl Pattern Candlesticks

Hawkes-signed, baluster-form swirl design stem w/an ovoid Russian cut socket & disk foot, 10" h., pr. (ILLUS.) **2,150**

Hawkes-signed Candlesticks

Hawkes-signed, round disk foot w/a swelled stem resting on a knob & cut w/plain panels below bold diamond cuts, paneled socket w/flattened rim, 10" h., pr. (ILLUS.) **595**

Unusual Cut Glass Chamberstick

Hobstars, strawberry diamonds & fans, chamberstick w/a round shallow dished cut base w/scalloped & notched rim & applied loop handle, plain tulip-form socket w/metal insert, 5" d. (ILLUS.) **875**

CHAMPAGNES, CORDIALS, GOBLETS & WINES

Clark's San Mateo patt., goblet, deep bowl cut w/hobstars alternating w/blocked diamonds, paneled zipper-cut stem, 5 7/8" h. (ILLUS. left, top next column) **75**

Two Cut Glass Goblets

Cross-cut diamonds, goblet, deep bowl w/overall cutting, paneled zipper-cut stem, 6" h. (ILLUS. right) **60**

Dorflinger's No. 28 Champagne

Dorflinger's No. 28 patt., Continental-style flute champagne, tall tapering bowl cut overall w/strawberry diamonds & cross-hatched diamonds w/fans around the top, facet-cut knobbed stem on thick cut disk foot (ILLUS.) **195**

Flutes & Diamonds Cut Wine

Hawkes' Flutes & Diamonds patt., wine, ruby-flashed bowl cut w/rounded flutes above overall diamonds, tapering paneled & zipper-cut stem, 2 3/4" d., 4 3/4" h. (ILLUS.) **320**

Russian Cut Goblet

Russian cut, goblets, knopped facet-cut stem, Russian cut foot, set of 12 (ILLUS. of one) **2,200**

CHEESE DISHES

North Star Pattern Cheese Dish

Clark-signed, North Star patt., diamond-shaped hobstar panels alternating w/large blazing stars & small cane panels, facet-cut finial, 8 1/2" d., 7" h. (ILLUS.).. **695**

CREAMERS & SUGAR BOWLS

Hobstar-cut Creamer & Sugar Bowl

Hobstars & fans, low pedestal foot, notched applied handles, 3 1/4" h., pr. (ILLUS.).. **320**

Harvard Pattern Creamer & Sugar

Libbey-signed, Harvard patt., square form cut w/panels of strawberry diamond & crosshatching w/fans around the rim, angled handle on creamer, pr. (ILLUS.)....... **350**

Heart Pattern Creamer & Sugar

Parsche's Heart patt., sides cut w/blaze-cut heart, large hobstars under creamer spout, notched applied handles, 3 1/4" h., pr. (ILLUS.) **350**

DECANTERS

Columbia & Wheat Pattern Decanters

Bergen's Columbia patt., applied foot, ovoid body w/diamond blocks & vesicas below the paneled zipper-cut neck w/flattened rim, facet-cut ball stopper, 12 1/4" h. (ILLUS. right)................................ **895**

Clark's Orloff Pattern Decanter

Clark's Orloff patt., squatty bulbous body w/large cut rings framed by ornate cutting, tall paneled neck & flattened rim, facet-cut ball stopper, 6 1/4" d., 11" h. (ILLUS.).. **2,175**
Clark-signed, ruby cut to clear, tapering conical body cut w/alternating clear & ruby graduated rings, ringed neck w/spout, matching ringed knob stopper, applied notch-cut handle, 5 1/2" d., 8" h. (ILLUS. top next page) **1,650**
Cross-cut diamonds & fans, flattened round body w/a panel-cut shoulder & slender zipper-cut neck, facet-cut applied handle, facet-cut ball stopper, 4 x 6", 9 1/2" h. (ILLUS. center next page) **320**

Rare Ruby Cut to Clear Decanter

Hoare's Wheat patt., spherical body w/swirled alternating cut panels below the tall facet-cut neck w/flaring flattened rim, facet-cut ball stopper, 12 1/4" h. (ILLUS. left previous page) **1,450**

Nicely Cut Handled Decanter

Hobstars, cane, fans & strawberry diamonds, wide tapering shouldered body w/a short paneled & ringed neck, applied angled handle, facet-cut knob stopper, 9 1/4" h. (ILLUS. top next column) **595**

Decanter with Rounded Body

Ornately Cut Straus Decanter

Straus-signed, wide rounded body deeply cut w/hobstars in squares & cross-cut squares alternating w/rib-cut panels & fans, stepped shoulder & heavy cut ring below ring-cut neck w/silver rim & bulbous floral-embossed silver knob stopper, 11 1/2" h. (ILLUS.) **1,610**

DISHES, MISCELLANEOUS

Wheat Pattern Bonbon Dish

Hobstar-cut Decanter

Hobstars, tapering conical body cut w/a wide band of hobstars around the bottom below the panel-cut shoulder & neck, notch-cut applied handle & facet-cut stopper, 10" h. (ILLUS.).......................... **425**

Bonbon, Wheat patt. by J. Hoare, round swirled design w/Russian cut panels alternating w/wheat head panels, 6" d. (ILLUS.) **325**

Diamond Dish from a Bridge Set

Bridge dish, Newark Cut Glass Co., diamond-shaped, cut w/hobstars in pointed reserves centered by a cane-cut center, one of a set of four (ILLUS.) **115**

Unusual Peru Pattern Candy Dish

Candy dish, Peru patt. by Pairpoint, barbell-shaped w/a narrow center & deep oblong ends cut w/alternating vesicas & fan panels, small hobstars around the rim, 8 3/4" l. (ILLUS.) **650**

Straus-signed Cheese Dish

Cheese, cov., Straus-signed, tall octagonal cover cut w/diamonds & fans, flat top w/facet-cut knob, conforming dished base (ILLUS.) **895**

Cut Glass Mint Dish

Mint, shallow bowl on short pedestal base, hobstars alternating w/cane-cut almond-form panels, star-cut foot, 6" d., 4" h. (ILLUS.) **225**

Cut Individual Nut Dish

Nut, rectangular w/shallow upright sides, hobstar cut in the bottom, diamond-cut deeply notched sides, 2 1/2 x 3 1/4" (ILLUS.) **25**

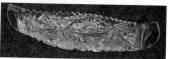

Canoe-shaped Cut Relish Dish

Relish, Pitkin & Brooks' Plaza patt., model of a canoe w/hobstars, triangles & fans around the sides, 3 1/2 x 9" (ILLUS.) **240**

Hawkes-signed Serving Dish

Serving dish, Hawkes-signed, blown-out blank w/eight-petal pinwheel form, alternating petals of hobstars & fans & zipper cutting, 10" d. (ILLUS.) **1,285**

Strawberry Diamond Serving Dish

Serving dish, round w/overall strawberry diamond cutting, hobstar in the center, two applied notched handles, 8 1/4" d. plus handles (ILLUS.) **385**

FLOWER CENTERS

Empress patt. by Libbey, the body cut w/hobstars above cross-cutting alternating w/strawberry diamond panels, facet-cut ringed neck w/diamond-cut rim, 10" d. (ILLUS. top next page) **1,100**

Hobstars & fans, squatty bulbous body cut w/large hobstars alternating w/large fans below the ring-cut shoulder & short neck w/flared & scalloped rim (ILLUS. center next page) **495**

Empress Pattern Flower Center

Flower Center with Hobstars & Fans

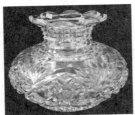

Flower Center with Varied Motifs

Hobstars, fans, cane & strawberry diamonds, squatty bulbous base cut w/large hobstars & fans combined w/other motifs, short flaring ring-cut neck w/notched & scalloped rim, 7 1/2" d., 6 1/4" h. (ILLUS.).. **465**

ICE TUBS & BUCKETS

Diamond-cut Ice Bucket

Diamonds & fans, footed swelled cylindrical form cut w/large diamonds alternating w/fans around the scalloped & notched rim, facet-cut applied handles, 5" h. (ILLUS.).. **385**

Hawkes' Chrysanthemum patt., deep rounded form cut w/large hobstars & cane & cross-hatch cut petals, silver rim band & bail handle, 6 1/2" d. (ILLUS. below).. **545**

Hawkes' Chrysanthemum Ice Bucket

Venetian Pattern Ice Tub

Hawkes-signed, Venetian patt., bulbous form cut w/large hobstars in diamonds alternating w/fans, large blossom-form cutting in the bottom, silver plate rim & bail handle (ILLUS.) **475**

Ice Tub with Hobstar Design

Hobstars, round w/tab handles, large hobstars alternating w/angular cut panels, tab handles w/blazing stars (ILLUS.) **350**

Straus Cut Ice Bucket

Straus-signed, widely flaring bowl w/tab handles & scalloped fan-cut rim above diamonds w/hobstars alternating w/zipper-cut bands, 10 3/4" d. (ILLUS.)................ **795**

JARS

Greek Key Pattern Tobacco Jar

Tobacco, Greek Key patt. by Meriden, vertical bands of hobstars alternating w/cane-cut bands below the Greek Key cut shoulder, 9 1/2" h. (ILLUS.)................ **4,650**

Two Marlboro Pattern Humidors

Tobacco, Marlboro patt. by Dorflinger, overall cutting w/small hobstars, fans & diamonds w/crosshatching (ILLUS. left).... **1,250**
Tobacco, Marlboro patt. by Dorflinger, overall cutting w/small hobstars, fans & diamonds w/crosshatching (ILLUS. right)... **1,450**

KNIFE RESTS

Hobstar & Fan-cut Knife Rest

Barbell-shaped, cut w/hobstar rings & swirled fans, 5 1/4" l. (ILLUS.)...................... **115**

Prism & Strawberry Diamond Rest

Barbell-shaped, notched center ring, notched prism & strawberry diamond cutting, 5" l. (ILLUS.) **170**

Notched Prism-cut Knife Rest

Barbell-shaped, notched prism-cut knob ends, zipper cut crossbar, 5" l. (ILLUS.)......... **55**

Strawberry Diamond-cut Knife Rest

Barbell-shaped, overall strawberry diamond cutting, 4 1/4" l. (ILLUS.) **80**

Knife Rest with Pointed Knob Ends

Barbell-shaped, pointed knob ends cut w/strawberry diamond & pointed bands, zipper-cut crossbar, 5" l. (ILLUS.) **100**

LAMPS

Boudoir lamp, a clear domed shade cut w/strawberry diamond & an outer vertically ribbed band, a large domed hobstar at the top center, raised on a slender waisted faceted standard on a domed foot w/a strawberry diamond band around an outer vertically ribbed band, in the Hawkes - Sinclaire manner, silvered metal two-socket electrical fittings, early 20th c., overall 13 1/2" h. **$690**

Elaborate Dorflinger Lamp

Boudoir lamp, Dorflinger-signed, tall slender inverted trumpet-form base cut w/fans along the base, strawberry diamonds & panels below the connector to the bulbous strawberry diamond-cut font w/metal collar, burner & open-topped

ovoid strawberry diamond-cut shade
(ILLUS.)... **4,650**

Table, 11 1/2" d. domed & pointed shade
cut w/large Hobstars alternating w/fan-
cut panels, on a ring suspending cut
prisms, raised on a tall slender baluster-
form base cut around the top w/Hobstars
alternating w/fan cutting over long cut
panels & a domed foot w/further bands
of Hobstar & fan cutting, electrified, over-
all 29 1/2" h. (minor chips)........................ **3,680**

Table, a 12" d. pointed deep domical
shaped cut & etched w/swirled leaves &
daises on a shade ring hung w/spear-
point prisms, raised on a baluster-form
base w/a matching design & scalloped
sawtooth rim, overall 25" h. **1,150**

El Tova Pattern Lamp by Clark

Table, Clark's El Tova patt., mushroom
shade cut w/large hobstars & narrow
almond panels, shade ring suspending
facet-cut prisms, baluster-form matching base w/domed foot, two-light electric
fitting, 20" h. (ILLUS.) **4,850**

Lamp with Pointed Domed Shade

Table, pointed domical shade cut w/wide
cane panels & diamond point vesicas,
panel-cut lower rim on metal ring, raised
on a trumpet-form matching base, chips
to base, w/prisms, 27" h. (ILLUS.)............. **1,150**

Tall Cut Lamp with Hobstars

Table, teardrop-form shade cut w/zipper
bands at the top above large hobstars
alternating w/spearpoint panels, fitted
into matching all-glass electrified base,
16" h. (ILLUS.)... **3,450**

Fine Early Cut Electric Lamp

Table lamp, by Everett Stage, the large
pointed domical shade cut w/alternating
wide bands of panels & strawberry diamonds, fitted on a matching baluster-
form standard w/cupped top & a wide
domed foot, electrified, 20" h. (ILLUS.) **3,950**

MISCELLANEOUS ITEMS

Bell, panel-cut shoulder, emerald green
w/clear facet-cut stem & knob, probably
Hawkes **295**

Hobstar & Vine Butter Pat

Butter pat, round w/scalloped & notched rim, four hobstars divided by a wide cross engraved w/leafy vines, 2 1/4" d. (ILLUS.) **35**

Sinclaire-engraved Clock

Clock, table model, Sinclaire-engraved, Gothic arch-form case w/rectangular base, the round dial surrounded by finely engraved leafy floral vines & scrolls, a floral vine around the base, 8" h. (ILLUS.) **1,250**

Large Bishop's Hat-form Compote

Compote, bishop's hat-form, the bowl cut w/large hobstars & triangles, the widely rolled rim cut w/fans, hobstars & strawberry diamond-cut panels, star-cut foot, large, 12" d., 8 3/4" h. (ILLUS.) **2,450**

Dorflinger-attributed Cut Compote

Compote, ruby-cut-to-clear, wide shallow bowl cut w/a band of petals enclosing crosshatching, panel-cut stem on star-cut foot, attributed to Dorflinger, 8 1/4" d., 4 1/4" h. (ILLUS.) **510**

Cut Glass Cup & Saucer

Cup & saucer, cut w/hobstars & fans, applied handle on cup, saucer 4 3/4" d., cup 2 3/4" d., 2 1/4" h. (ILLUS.) **235**

Cut & Engraved Lady's Cuspidor

Cuspidor, lady's, Sinclaire-signed, wide ovoid form w/widely rolled finely cut rim, delicate floral engraving around the body, 8" d., 6 1/2" h. (ILLUS.) **395**

Unusual Cut Glass Door Knob

Door knobs, round, florette-style cut design w/small center hobstars & pointed fans, on brass shank, ca. 1900, pr. (ILLUS. of one) **880**

Rare Hawkes Epergne

Epergne, St. Regis patt. by Hawkes, four-lily, the wide dished conical base w/fan-cut upturned edges, metal top fitting supports a tall central trumpet surrounded by three curved smaller lilies all cut w/starbusts & fans, 18 1/2" h. (ILLUS.) **5,850**

Russian Cut Juice Set

Juice set, pitcher & four tumblers, bulbous pitcher w/overall Russian cut design & panel-cut neck, applied notched handle, four matching tapering cylindrical tumblers, the set (ILLUS. bottom previous page) **850**

Loving Cup Cut with Hobstars

Loving cup, ovoid body tapering to flaring notched & scalloped rim, three applied facet-cut handles, large hobstars below the zipper-cut neck, 5" h. (ILLUS.) **495**

Sterling-rimmed Loving Cup

Loving cup, wide swelled cylindrical body tapering to an applied sterling silver rim w/a raised grapevine design, the sides cut w/deep panels & zipper bands, applied notch-cut handles, 3 3/4" h. (ILLUS.) **395**

Brunswick Rose Bowl by Hawkes

Rose bowl, Brunswick patt. by Hawkes, pedestal base below large spherical bowl cut w/long ribbon and zipper-cut bands w/bands of small hobstars around the rim & bottom, 6" h. (ILLUS.) **1,095**

Mercedes Pattern Rose Bowl by Clark

Rose bowl, Clark's Mercedes patt., wide squatty bulbous form tapering to scalloped & notched mouth, cut w/large hobstars below swags of small hobstars & fans (ILLUS.) **1,850**

Navarre Pattern Rose Bowl

Rose bowl, Navarre patt. by Hawkes, spherical, cut w/hobstars & punties alternating w/wide zipper-cut bands & fans, 6" d. (ILLUS.) **475**

Cut Glass Spooner with Hobstars

Spooner, slightly waisted cylindrical form w/notched & lightly scalloped rim, cut w/hobstars, fans & single stars, 3 1/4" d., 4 1/4" h. (ILLUS.) **70**

Sugar shaker, breakfast, Strawbery & Diamond patt. **165**

NAPPIES

Prism Pattern by Bergen Nappy

Bergen's Prism patt., low cylindrical sides & wide flat bottom, large hobstar in bottom, notched applied ring handle, 5 3/4" d. (ILLUS.)... **145**

Fine Rex Variation Pattern Nappy

Rex Variation patt., round shallow form cut w/a band of small hobstars centered by a large blossom-form design, applied notched rim handle, 6 1/2" d. (ILLUS.)......... **425**

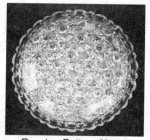

Russian Pattern Nappy

Russian patt., shallow round form w/upturned notched rim, 6" d. (ILLUS.)........ **115**

PITCHERS

Pedestal-based, Hoare-signed, the very tall slender cylindrical body cut w/long panels of zipper cutting framed by diamond plaid panels below the high arched panel-cut spout, long notch-cut applied handle, paneled pedestal base w/star-cut bottom (ILLUS. top next column)... **3,250**

Tankard, cut w/large hobstars alternating w/fanned rays, applied notched handle, 9 1/2" h.. **144**

Fine Pedestaled Hoare-signed Pitcher

Tankard Pitcher with Tiffany Silver Rim

Tankard, flared base below tall cylindrical sides, cut w/bands of large hobstars in zippered diamonds & fans around the base & top w/zipper-cut bands in the center, applied Tiffany sterling silver rim w/raised band of shells & scrolls, 5 1/2" d., 12 1/4" h. (ILLUS.) **1,235**

Tankard, Hawkes' Easter patt., tall tapering cylindrical form w/small rim spout, applied notched handle, cut w/narrow stripes of small hobstars & starbursts alternating w/stripes of small diamonds & plain bands, 12" h. (ILLUS. top next page).. **1,150**

Tankard, slightly tapering body gently flared at the notched rim, cut w/large hobstars in diamond reserves alternating w/large fan-cut panels, applied notched handle, 11 1/2" h. **805**

Easter Pattern Pitcher by Hawkes

Pitcher Cut with Hobstar Bands

Tankard, tall tapering cylindrical form w/a high arched spout, applied notched handle, cut w/long graduated bands of hobstars alternating w/almond-shaped cane & starburst panels, 14" h. (ILLUS.)............ **1,350**

PLATES

Mt. Washington Cut Plate

6 1/2" d., Mt. Washington Glass Co., a large hobstar in center framed by panel cutting & hobstars & fans, smooth rim (ILLUS.).. **110**

Arcadia Plate by Sterling

7" d., Arcadia patt. by Sterling, large hobstars alternating w/crosshatched panels around the rim, inner band of small hobstars enclosing another band of hobstars & a large central hobstar (ILLUS.)............... **250**

Fans & Hobstar Plate

7" d., fans & hobstar, scalloped & notched rim w/large fans surrounding spearpoints & a central large hobstar (ILLUS.)............... **175**

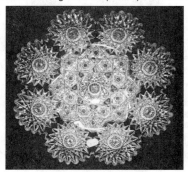

Festoon Variation Plate

7" d. , Festoon Variation patt., eight large hobstar scallops around the border centering clusters of small hobstars w/a larger center hobstar (ILLUS.)...................... **450**

Hawkes' Centauri Pattern Plate

7" d., Hawkes' Centauri patt., central large star within a star-form w/small hobstars framed by fan-cut small panels & diamond-form reserves cut w/alternating sizes of hobstars, notched & scalloped rim (ILLUS.).. **210**

New Panel Pattern Plate by Hawkes

7" d., Hawkes' New Panel patt., a narrow border band of small stars, ring of cut bars around central starburst, signed (ILLUS.).. **125**

Hawkes-signed Plate

7" d., Hawkes-signed, elaborate design of hobstars in diamond panels alternating

w/crosshatched panels & centered by a large star (ILLUS.).. **165**

Plate with Hobstars & Prism Cutting

7" d., hobstars alternating w/wide panels of prism cutting, crossed diamond panels centering a large hobstar in the middle (ILLUS.).. **210**

Plate with Large Hobstars

7" d., hobstars within teardrop panels separated by six rayed cut arms (ILLUS.).......... **225**

Libbey's Azora Pattern Plate

7" d., Libbey's Azora patt., lobed panels cut w/cane & small fans around a central hobstar framed by rays, scalloped & notched rim w/fan-cut sections (ILLUS.) **425**

Colonna Pattern Plate by Libbey

7" **d.,** Libbey's Colonna patt., squared notched rim, florette design w/panels of hobstars, signed (ILLUS.) **185**

7" **d.,** Libbey's Kenmore patt., a central eight-point star motif composed of points w/hobstars & vesicas around a central hobstar, starburst-cut scallops around the rim **295**

Middlesex Variation Pattern Plate

7" **d.,** Middlesex Variation patt., notched rim w/fans alternating w/notched diamonds enclosing hobstars, large starburst in center (ILLUS.) **125**

Neola Pattern Plate by Libbey

7" **d.,** Neola patt. by Libbey, hobstars alternating w/blazing crosses w/a large star in the center (ILLUS.) **415**

Stars & Pillars Plate by Sinclaire

7" **d.,** Sinclaire's Stars & Pillars patt., cut around the border w/large hobstars in diamonds, inner band of pillar-cutting surrounding a central hobstar (ILLUS.) **450**

PUNCH BOWLS, CUPS & SETS

Hawkes' Brazilian Pattern Punch Bowl

Punch bowl, Hawkes' Brazilian patt., a central hobstar framed by ornate fan, crossed-block & crosshatched panels framed by a fan-cut rim, 12 1/2" d., 6 1/2" h. (ILLUS.) **1,575**

Punch or egg nog bowl, the bowl cut w/large hobstars alternating w/fans & cane cutting, the flaring base w/a facet-cut rim above a design matching the bowl, 10" d. **795**

Egginton's Arabian Pattern Punch Bowl

Punch set: bowl, base & eight cups; Egginton's Arabian patt., curved cut bands intersecting large clusters of hobstars on the bowl & base, cups 3" d., 3 1/4" h., bowl 14 1/2" d., 12" h., the set (ILLUS. of bowl) **11,750**

SALT DIPS

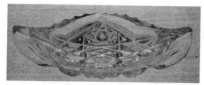

Canoe-shaped Salt Dip

Canoe-shaped, cut w/small hobstars & fans, 1 1/2" l. (ILLUS.) **45**

Cut Glass Salt Dip

Round, deep form cut w/diamond panels, 1 1/4" d. (ILLUS.) **35**

Two Round Salt Dips

Round, diamonds w/crosshatching alternating w/pointed panels, 1 1/4" d. (ILLUS. right) **35**
Round, Pine Tree patt., slash-cut paneled sides, 1" d. (ILLUS. left) **20**

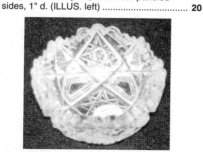

Salt Dip with Hobstars & Panels

Round, small hobstars alternating w/pointed cut panels, hobstar in bottom, 1 1/2" d. (ILLUS.) **35**

TRAYS

Sultana Asparagus Tray

Asparagus, Libbey's Sultana patt., oblong, large hobstars at each end w/a cluster of hobstars & diamonds centering the middle hobstar, 12" l. (ILLUS.) **445**

Libbey's Wedgemere Celery Tray

Celery, Libbey's Wedgemere patt., pointed oblong form cut w/central radiating zipper-cut bands framing strawberry diamond panels & graduated hobstars w/a large hobstar at each end, 11 1/2" l. (ILLUS.) **1,050**

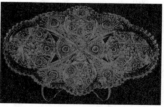

Hunt's Aldine Pattern Tray

Hunt's Aldine patt., oblong, cut w/large round clusters of small hobstars alternating w/larger hobstars, 14" l. (ILLUS.) **475**

Ice Cream Tray with Hobstars

Ice cream, rectangular w/scalloped & notched rim, large hobstars at ends w/panels of hobstars & fans cut around the center, 14" l. (ILLUS.) **950**

Rex Variation Ice Cream Tray

Ice cream, Rex Variation patt., almond-shaped w/pointed ends, scalloped & notched rim w/outer border of hobstars around large central blossom-form starburst, 18" l. (ILLUS.)................................. **2,950**

Hawkes' Centauri Serving Tray

Serving, Hawkes' Centauri patt., a large central cut star framed by small hobstars & comet-cut panels w/an outer border of large hobstars in pointed panels, 12" d. (ILLUS.).. **1,295**

Large Tray with Hobstars & Cane

Serving, round w/notched rim w/scallops & points, large hobstars alternating w/six points & panels of fine cane cutting, six-point star in center, 14" d. (ILLUS.)........... **2,850**

TUMBLERS

Star & Diamond Tumbler by Clark

Clark's Star & Diamond patt., large block-cut diamonds w/fan-cut borders, 3" d., 4" h. (ILLUS.)... **65**

Double-Shot Tumbler with Hobstars

Hobstars & fans, double-shot size, cylindrical, 2 1/4" d., 2 1/2" h. (ILLUS.)................. **45**

Jewel Pattern Tumbler by Libbey

Libbey's Jewel patt., slightly flared cylindrical form cut w/hobstars below fans alternating w/cut spearpoints, signed, 3" d., 3 3/4" h. (ILLUS.) **60**

New Brilliant Pattern Shot Glass

Libbey's New Brilliant patt., shot-size, slightly flaring cylindrical form w/arched fans over hobstars alternating w/zipper-cut bands, 2" d., 2 1/4" h. (ILLUS.)................. **55**

VASES

No. 50 Pattern Vase by Dorflinger

Dorflinger's No. 50 patt., tapering ovoid body on a paneled stem w/star-cut notched round foot, the upper body cut w/hobstars & strawberry diamond above plain cut swirled ribs, 10 1/2" h. (ILLUS.) **895**

Hawke's Brunswick patt., trumpet-form, 14" h. **550**

Brazilian Pattern Vase by Hawkes

Hawkes' Brazilian patt., tall waisted cylindrical form w/notched & scalloped rim, cut w/hobstars, bands of strawberry diamond & fans, 5 3/4" d., 11" h. (ILLUS.) **550**

Hawkes' Queens patt., tall slender trumpet-form w/a four-lobed notched rim, diamond-form panels of graduated hobstars down the sides, notch-cut stem on star-cut foot, 12" h. (ILLUS. top next column) .. **1,250**

Hawkes-signed, tall cylindrical body w/iridized clear finish cut & etched w/flowers, swags & tassels, topped by an applied band of sterling silver w/a repeating swag & oval design, glass stamped "Hawkes" on base, silver marked

"Hawkes Sterling 2262," 3 3/4" d., 9 3/4" h. **460**

Hawkes' Queens Pattern Vase

Large Urn-form Vase

Hobstars, large ovoid urn-form body cut w/overall hobstars, cane-cut panels & crosshatched blocks, paneled & prism-cut neck flanked by applied notched angled handles (ILLUS.) **1,550**

Vase in Jewel's Aberdeen Pattern

Jewel's Aberdeen patt., campana-form, the wide flaring urn-form bowl w/an upright cut rim band above panel-cut sides above a lower hobstar-cut border, raised on a plain applied pedestal & square foot, 12" h. (ILLUS.) **3,950**

Ellsmere Variation Pattern Vase

Libbey's Ellsmere Variation patt., tall baluster-form w/flaring notched rim, large zipper-cut bars around the neck above hobstars & starbursts over further panels of zipper cutting & large hobstars around the base, signed, 6" d., 12" h. (ILLUS.)..... **1,585**

C.F. Monroe Sylph Pattern Vase

Monroe's Sylph patt., footed squatty bulbous lower body below a tall gently flaring neck, scalloped & notched fan-cut rim, cut rings & zipper-cut panels down the neck, a band of hobstars & strawberry diamond above the heavy zipper-cut ribs around the bottom, 7 1/2" d., 9 3/4" h. (ILLUS.).. **685**

Pairpoint-signed, Buckingham patt., tall slender baluster-form body w/a widely flaring trumpet neck mounted on a patinated metal pedestal foot on a square white onyx base raised on a metal rim w/paw feet, impressed "Pairpoint C1517," 15 1/4" h., pr. (abrasions to stone base) **1,840**

Trophy-form, flattened ovoid tapering sides w/wide flared mouth, slender stem on wide round star-cut foot, long D-form applied notch-cut handles, the sides cut w/large starbursts in diamond panels w/fan-cutting at corners, 10 1/4" h............. **1,380**

Trumpet-form, widely flaring bowl cut w/varied designs of graduated hobstars & fan cutting, paneled pedestal & star-cut foot, 8" d., 9" h. (ILLUS.) **565**

Wide Trumpet-form Vase

Trumpet-shaped, tall slender cylindrical body w/flared & ruffled notch-cut rim, diamond panels over large Buzzstars above zipper-cut panels & fan- and star-cutting down to the flaring panel-cut foot w/zipper-cut edge, 14 1/4" h. (rim chips)...... **460**

Ungers Brothers' Hobart patt., tall waisted cylindrical form, detailed cutting w/stripes of small hobstars alternating w/zipper cutting, large hobstars in diamonds around the base & fan-cut rim, 12" h. **650**

Finely Cut Urn-form Vase

Urn-form, wide flaring bowl w/plain scalloped rim, ring-cut sides above squatty bulbous lower body cut w/hobstars, raised on a panel-cut pedestal on a square foot, 9 1/2" d., 7 1/2" h. (ILLUS.) ... **1,825**

Large Ornate Cut Glass Vase

Urn-form, the baluster-form body on a tapering pedestal & thick disk foot, the finely reeded neck below a widely flared cupped rim, the rim & body cut overall w/hobstars divided by arched deep grooves separated by diamond point cutting, panel-cut stem & star-cut foot, rim chips, 16" h (ILLUS.) **1,725**

WATER SETS

Water set: 10 1/2" h. waisted tankard pitcher w/high arched spout & applied notched handle & five matching tumblers; Hawkes signed, the pitcher w/a wide center band w/large hobstars within diamonds alternating w/fan over geometric cutting, wide bands of strawberry diamond cutting at the base & rim, each piece signed, tumblers, 3 5/8" h., the set **550**

CUT VELVET

This mold-blown, two-layer glassware is usually lined in white with a colored exterior with a molded pattern. Pieces have a satiny finish, giving them a 'velvety' appearance. The Mt. Washington Glass Company was one of several firms which produced this glass.

Lovely Cut Velvet Cracker Jar

Cracker jar, cov., cylindrical, pink Diamond Quilted patt., silver plate ring, cover & bail handle, Mount Washington Glass Co., 9" h. (ILLUS.) **$1,000-1,500**

Table lamp, kerosene-type, a stepped & embossed brass foot & short stem supporting a melon-lobed ovoid cut velvet font in dark rose shading to white in the Diamond Quilted patt., a brass shoulder ring & burner fitted w/a frosted & finely ribbed clear ball shade & clear chimney, overall 17" h. **495**

Vase, 6 1/4" h., ovoid w/ruffled fold-over top, pink Swirl patt. **121**

Vase, 8 1/2" h., double gourd-form w/a large ovoid body & bulbed lower neck tapering to a cylindrical upper section, blue Diamond Quilted patt. **275**

Vase, 9" h., ruffled rim, pale yellow Diamond Quilted patt. **138**

Vase, 9 1/4" h., ruffled rim, pale yellow Diamond Quilted patt. **110**

CZECHOSLOVAKIAN GLASS

At the close of World War I, Czechoslovakia was declared an independent republic and immediately developed a large export industry. Czechoslovakian glass factories produced a wide variety of colored and hand-painted glasswares from about 1918 until 1939, when the country was occupied by Germany at the outset of World War II. Between the wars, fine quality blown glasswares were produced along with a deluge of cheaper, vividly colored spatterwares for the American market. Subsequent production was primarily limited to cut crystal or Bohemian-type etched wares for the American market. Although it was marked, much Czechoslovakian glass is mistaken for the work of Tiffany, Loetz, or other glass artisans it imitates. It is often misrepresented and overpriced.

With the recent break-up of Czechoslovakia into two republics, such wares should gain added collector appeal.

Basket, black w/black handle, silver mica flecks, blue lining, 8" h. **$350**

Basket, red & yellow w/crystal twisted handle, 7" h. **220**

Beverage set, amber decanter w/six amber glasses, decanter 9" h., glasses 2 1/2" h., set. **250**

Place Card Holder

Place card holder, blue dancers w/brass footed base, 1 1/2" h. (ILLUS.) **45**

Place card holder, clear w/yellow flowers, 2" h. **8**

Vase with Metal Flower Arranger

Vase, varicolored w/metal flower arranger, 4 1/4" h. (ILLUS.) **100**

Vase, mottled colors w/black edge petal top, 6" h. **110**

Vase, opaque white w/rim & floral trim, 6 1/4" h. **65**

Warrior Vase with Black Handles

Vase, orange w/black handles & painted warriors, 7 1/2" h. (ILLUS.) **175**

Vase with King Tut Decoration

Vase, pink w/blue luster, King Tut decoration, 7 1/2" h. (ILLUS.) **2,800**

Glass Fan Vase

Vase, fan-shaped, orange w/yellow overlay, 8" h. (ILLUS.) **200**
Vase, opaque white w/crystal rim & handles, 8" h. **85**

Spiderweb-type Vase

Vase, orange & green spiderweb-type, 8" h. (ILLUS. top next column) **150**
Vase, bud-type, mottled colors, 8 1/4" h. **75**
Vase, three-handled, green w/blue handles, Powolny, 8 1/4" h. **900**
Vase, blue w/black struts, 9" h. **125**

Perfume Items

Bottle, brass & green jeweled stopper w/dangles, 2 1/2" h. **150**
Bottle, clear w/frosted cranes in stopper, 7 1/4" h. **650**
Bottle, clear w/frosted troubadour in stopper, 5 1/2" h. **325**
Bottle, clear w/pink fan stopper, 6" h. **350**
Bottle, frosted & clear w/opaque black stopper, 3 1/2" h. **125**
Bottle, frosted & clear, w/red stopper, 5" h. **325**
Bottle, green w/some frosting, stopper same, 5" h. **175**
Bottle, heather, heather stopper, rare color, 5" h. **400**
Bottle, opaque blue, opaque blue stopper, 6 1/2" h. **1,800**

Jeweled Perfume Bottle

Bottle, purple, purple stopper w/cupids, jeweled, 5 1/2" h. (ILLUS.) **2,200**
Bottle, purple w/purple peacock stopper, 4 1/2" h. **450**
Bottle, purse-type, topaz w/jewels in brass, screw-top, 2" h. **275**
Bottle, turquoise, turquoise stopper, rare color, 7 1/2" h. **450**
Mirror, hand-type, perfume stopper handle, 6 1/2" h. **100**
Powder box, cov., pink cut glass, 4 1/2" h. **300**
Toilet bottles, enameled decoration of people, set of 3, 4 1/2" h., each.................... **250**

D'ARGENTAL

Glass known by this name is co-called after its producer, who fashioned fine cameo pieces in St. Louis, France late 19th century and up to 1918.

D'Argental Mark

Cameo box, cov., egg-shaped, yellow overlaid w/crimson, the base carved w/azaleas, the cover w/butterflies, signed in cameo, ca. 1910, 6" h. (ILLUS. top next page) **$1,150**

D'Argental Egg-shaped Box

Cameo lamp, table model, a 10 1/2" d. pointed wide mushroom shade & matching tall slender ovoid body on a wide disk foot, both in grey infused w/ochre-yellow & overlaid in deep crimson, cut w/an overall pattern of ripe blackberries, leafage & thorny branches, w/a three-arm bronze mount, base signed in cameo "D'Argental," ca. 1915, overall 22" h. **6,325**

D'Argental Cameo Powder Box

Cameo powder jar, cov., squatty bulbous form w/applied knob finial, yellow overlaid w/russet & dark purple, the cover cut w/flowers, buds & leaves on thorny stems, the base w/a border of leaves on short stems, signed in cameo, ca. 1900, 6 3/4" d. (ILLUS.)..................................... **1,150**

Cameo vase, 9 3/4" h., tall ovoid body tapering to a flat rim, fiery amber overlaid in maroon brown & cameo-cut w/blossoming trumpet vine pendent after signature "D'Argental" at the lower side (some interior bubbles) **1,035**

Cameo vase, 6 1/4" h., tall slender ovoid form w/a small flared rim, yellow overlaid w/orange & cameo-cut w/a continuous river landscape w/tall trees in the foreground, signed **460**

Cameo vase, 8" h., simple ovoid body tapering to a tiny neck, lime green overlaid w/dark brown & cut overall w/large clusters of berries on leafy vines, cameo signature **990**

Cameo vase, 8" h., swelled cylindrical form w/a short tapering neck & flat rim, yellow overlaid in maroon & cut w/a Mediterranean village landscape, signed in cameo "D'Argental".. **345**

Cameo vase, 10 1/2" h., 4 1/2" d., tall tapering cylindrical body w/a short tapering neck, yellow overlaid in dark brown cut to tan w/a forested mountainside scene w/a castle in the distance, signed (ILLUS. top next column) **1,500**

Cameo vase, 13" h., tall very slender swelled cylindrical body w/a flared rim & cushion foot, frosted shaded dark to light purple ground overlaid in dark purple & cut w/detailed wisteria blossoms down the sides, cameo signature **1,320**

D'Argental Mountainous Scenic Vase

Cameo vase, 13 3/4" h., tall ovoid body tapering to a short cylindrical neck, grey overlaid w/amethyst & shades of light blue & cut w/a romantic view of an ocean sunset framed w/oak foliage, signed on the side.. **3,696**

D'Argental Tropical Scene Vase

Cameo vase, 13 3/4" h., tall slender ovoid body w/a rounded shoulder to a short flaring neck, amber overlaid w/brown & cut w/a continuous scene of palm trees & mountains by water, ca. 1910, signed in cameo (ILLUS.) **1,495**

DAUM NANCY

This fine glass, much of it cameo, was made by Auguste and Antonin Daum, who founded a factory in 1875 in Nancy, France. Most of their cameo and enameled glass was made from the 1890s into the early 20th century.

Daum Nancy Marks

Daum Cut & Enameled Small Bowl

Bowl, 4 1/4" h., pointed cup-form bowl raised on three deep purple loop feet, the bowl in grey mottled w/white shading to deep purple, cut w/violets & leaves & finely enameled in purple & green trimmed w/gilt, signed, ca. 1900 (ILLUS.) **$5,570**

Bowl, 7 3/4" d., 3" h., rounded incurved low sides w/a pinched rim, mottled white, pink, purple & yellow etched & intricately enameled w/Coreopsis daisies in shades of yellow w/green foliage, signed in enamel on the side, ca. 1910 (interior burst bubble) **2,070**

Enameled Daum Nancy Bowl

Bowl, 8" w., the quatrefoil body in grey tinted w/apple green, cut & enameled in green, brown & black w/a spring landscape, signed in enamel, ca. 1910 (ILLUS.) **1,380**

Etched & Enameled Daum Box

Box, cov., squatty bulbous tapering form w/a wide shoulder centered by a fitted domed cover, rose etched & enameled in pastel tones to depict floral sprays w/gilt accents, the cover w/a butterfly & dragonfly, gilt signature, 2 1/8" h. (ILLUS.) **3,680**

Box, cov., three short pad feet below a swelled ring base below the short cylindrical sides, fitted nearly flat cover, grey shading to rich violet at the base, internally streaked w/frosty white cut w/stalks of wheat, leafage & pinwheels, enameled in green, amber & cream, the whole trimmed in gilt, all reserved against a textured ground, unsigned, ca. 1900, 7" d. **6,900**

Cameo bowl, 3 7/8" h., cushion foot below the squatty bulbous body w/a four-lobed rim, cream mottled w/yellow & overlaid in dark green, wheel-carved w/a design of berried leafy branches, signed, ca. 1900 .... **4,600**

Cameo bowl, 8 1/2" d., wide disk foot supporting a deep rounded bowl w/flat rim, clear overlaid w/green & cut w/a morning glory vine w/gilt trim, reserved on an acid-textured ground, mounted w/a silver gadrooned foot rim & a floral vine rim at the lip possibly added later & damaged, faintly inscribed, ca. 1900 (ILLUS. top next column) **2,300**

Daum Nancy Cameo Bowl

Cameo bowl-vase, squatty bulbous oblong form tapering to a wide flat rim, mottled frosted white ground overlaid w/green & maroon & cut w/rose blossoms on leafy stems, ca. 1910, 4 1/4" h. **6,900**

Cameo lamp, table model, the 16" d. cameo shade in a disk form w/a wide angled border centered by an inset dome, in swirled & mottled amber & yellow overlaid w/mottled brown & black & cut w/large horse chestnut leaves, raised on a Louis Majorelle gilt-bronze base w/pierced scrolling arms & a ribbed vine-like standard w/inwardly scrolling loops at the base, signed in cameo, ca. 1900, overall 26" h. **25,300**

Cameo pitcher, 7 1/2" h., flattened round form w/applied handle, grey cased & internally decorated w/yellow & orange powders, inscribed "DAUM NANCY" w/cross of Lorraine, ca. 1920s **345**

Cameo vase, 6 3/8" h., cushion foot & shoulder pedestal base supporting a bulbous ovoid body tapering to a short wide flared neck, frosted white ground overlaid w/mottled rust, brown & green & cut w/leafy stems, signed in intaglio, ca. 1910 .... **4,600**

Cameo vase, 7 1/4" h., tall square form, clear cased to a yellow interior & cameo-etched & engraved as wild roses, gold enamel highlights & borders, base signed in gold enamel **805**

Daum Nancy Dandelions Cameo Vase

Cameo vase, 7 5/8" h., tapering shouldered body w/a flat front & back & w/a short cylindrical neck, grey overlaid in turquoise & green, cut w/dandelions, signed in cameo & w/retailer's label, ca. 1900 (ILLUS.) **1,840**

Cameo vase, 8 1/4" h., bulbous baluster-form w/flared short neck & cushion foot, mottled grey & purple rising to yellow, layered in vitrified colors of red, purple & green & etched w/grapes on the vine, highlighted by an applied glass snail & etched signature in the polished pontil (ground spot at loss of second snail) **2,875**

Cameo vase, 9" h., Martelé-type, elongated bell-form w/a slender & bulbed neck, pink overlaid in grass green, carved & etched w/a flowering thistle on a martelé ground, base signed, ca. 1900.. **1,610**

Rare Martelé Cameo Daum Vase

Cameo vase, 9 1/4" h., four-sided baluster-form w/flared neck & applied foot, martelé (hammered) clear ground overlaid in white & carved from the base upward w/slender thorny blossom branches supporting a spiderweb, signed in intaglio, ca. 1900 (ILLUS.)...................... **11,500**

Cameo vase, 11 1/4" h., bottle-form, nearly spherical base below a very tall slender 'stick' neck w/flared rim, pale aquamarine blue overlaid in deep crimson red, cut w/cyclamen blossoms & undulating leafage, all finely wheel-carved, signed in gilt intaglio "DAUM - NANCY" w/cross of Lorraine, ca. 1900 .... **6,900**

Cameo vase, 11 1/4" h., tall swelled cylindrical form w/a narrow shoulder & short flaring neck, shaded dark blue to white to mottled orange to dark purple ground, overlaid & blown-out w/thick dark purple plant stems w/blossomheads around the shoulder, signed in gilt intaglio **13,800**

Daum Cameo Vase with Roses

Cameo vase, 13 1/2" h., thick cushion foot below the tall slender swelled cylindrical body tapering to a cupped rim, mottled white, pink & clear overlaid in shades of green & rose & etched w/branching roses, signed, staining (ILLUS.) **11,500**

Cameo vase, 15 3/4" h., tall slender ovoid body w/flared rim raised on a double knop stem on a disk foot, grey internally mottled w/pale lavender, shading to ochre yellow & deepest purple at the base, overlaid in mottled olive green & cut w/poppy leafage, the blossoms w/applied burnt orange & purple finely delineated w/wheel carving, signed in intaglio "DAUM - NANCY" w/a cross of Lorraine, ca. 1900 .... **11,500**

Cameo vase, 18 1/2" h., a cushion foot below a slender pedestal continuing to a bulbous lower body tapering to a very tall, slender & slightly flaring neck, three applied loop handles around the lower body, shaded from mottled white to yellow & overlaid w/mottled green to light rose & cut w/a slender blossom stem rising from green foliage at the base, signed in intaglio, ca. 1904...................... **14,950**

Large Cameo Vase with Leaves

Cameo vase, 19 3/4" h., cushion foot below the tall slightly flaring cylindrical body w/a bulbed rim, mottled white & blue overlaid w/streaked reddish orange & cut w/leaf & nut clusters, signed, ca. 1900 (ILLUS.) **4,600**

Cameo vase, 23 1/2" h., footed bulbous base tapering to a very tall cylindrical neck w/molded rim, mottled blue & white neck shading to mottled purple at the base & overlaid in mottled green, yellow & purple & cut w/flying dragonflies around the sides & base w/ranunculus leaves & blossoms around the base, signed in cameo, ca. 1904 .... **26,450**

Center bowl, Ice patt., heavy walled crystal square form, molded decoration of ice formations at base, inscribed on base, 3 3/8" h. **173**

Cordials, cylindrical, various background colors, each etched w/a different landscape & enameled w/naturalistic colors, signed, w/original silk-lined presentation box, each 1 7/8" h., set of 6...................... **8,050**

Fine Daum Nancy Creamer

Creamer, wide ovoid body tapering to a wide mouth w/pinched spout, applied frosted amber handle, the speckled rose body shading to mint green, etched & enameled w/a meadow landscape dotted w/wild flowers, tree-bordered pond & distant village *en grisaille*, gilt trim & signature, 5 3/4" h. (ILLUS.) **8,050**

Ewer, bulbous ovoid body w/a short slightly flaring neck w/small pinched spout, applied C-form handle, grey cut w/delicate bell-form flowers w/long narrow leaves, a dragonfly & a butterfly, inscribed signature in gilt, ca. 1900, 4 1/4" h. **862**

Miniature Daum Nancy Pitcher

Pitcher, 3 1/2" h., miniature, footed spherical body flattened on the front & back, short flaring neck & applied loop handle, opalescent grey cut w/clover blossoms & leaves on an acid-textured ground, the neck w/a beaded gilt band & scrolling vine, enameled in pink, grey, black & gold, signed, some wear to rim gilt, ca. 1900 (ILLUS.) **2,415**

Miniature Daum Landscape Vases

Vase, 1 5/8" h., miniature, flattened ovoid form, grey tinted w/yellow shading to amber, cut w/leafless brown trees in a snowy field, signed, ca. 1900 (ILLUS. left) **1,265**

Vase, 2 5/8" h., miniature, footed bulbous baluster-form, grey mottled w/white & specks of blue, cut w/a river landscape w/pine trees & trees w/falling leaves, enameled in yellow, red, green & brown, signed, ca. 1900 (ILLUS. right) **1,265**

Vase, 4 1/4" h., bulbous ovoid body w/thick D-form handles flanking the rim, light green & pale red etched & enameled w/a Japanese-style scene of herons & water plants & gilded trailing vines, mounted w/finely cast & chased silver mounts w/roses & foliage around the rim & raised round foot, French hallmarks for 925 fine, etched & gilt signature, ca. 1894 .... **3,105**

Vase, 4 7/8" h., wide flattened ovoid form w/a flat rim, mottled blue & pumpkin orange ground etched & enameled to depict a snowy Dutch winter landscape scene w/windmills, in white, brown & *grisaille*, signed **3,450**

Vase, 5" h., slightly swelled cylindrical form, grey shaded w/purple at the base, cut w/branches of bleeding heart blossoms & enameled in pink, purple & green, incised signature, ca. 1900 .... **1,610**

Vase, 8" h., baluster-form w/short flared neck, grey mottled w/yellow shading to ochre, cut w/an orchid-type flower growing among grasses, enameled in shades of green & russet, incised signature "DAUM - NANCY" w/cross of Lorraine **1,840**

Vase, 8" h., the lower body round & gently flaring below the very irregular rim which is high & arched on one side w/a sharp drop to the stepped lower half, clear frosted ground w/an enameled landscape in pale green & lavender w/a very large leafy green tree on the tall half, signed in enamel **6,900**

Vase, 8" h., "verre parlant," wide squatty bulbous ovoid body w/the wide rounded shoulder centered by a short tapered cylindrical neck w/molded rim, frosted aqua ground enameled in gold around the neck w/dragonflies, the body enameled in light rose & pale green w/water lilies & lily pads w/a gilt enameled inscription in French "Et des roses sortaient des eaux - Et des esprits sortaient des roses. - V. Hugo," signed in gilt, ca. 1895 .... **6,900**

Daum Acid-etched Vase

Vase, 8 1/4" h., bulbous ovoid body w/a flat molded rim, light blue deeply etched w/three rows of rectangles separated by horizontal bands, signed, drilled near base & filled, ca. 1925 (ILLUS.) **1,380**

Vase, 8 1/2" h., coupe-form, small pedestal foot below the deep cup-form body w/applied dark loop rim handles, mottled dark brown, orange, pale yellow & amber w/gold foil inclusions, signed, ca. 1925 .... **4,600**

Rare Vitrified Enamel Daum Vase

Vase, 9" h., simple baluster-form w/a flaring neck & molded rim, mottled blue to greenish amber ground enameled w/a vitrified spring landscape of styliized greenish brown trees w/reddish brown leafage, dark greenish black foot, signed in intaglio, ca. 1906 (ILLUS.) **11,500**

Daum Vases with Molded Designs

Vase, 10 1/2" h., footed wide campana-form w/wide flared rim, mottled cranberry, molded w/a circle & wave design, signed (ILLUS. right) **2,415**

Vase, 10 1/2" h., gently swelled cylindrical form tapering slightly at the shoulder to a short neck w/a closed rim, grey mottled w/tangerine & raspberry, cut w/branches of apple blossoms & enameled w/white, pink & yellow flowers on brown stems w/green leaves, incised & enameled signature, ca. 1900................................... **3,737**

Vase, 11 1/2" h., flat wide rim on cylindrical sides tapering in at base above thick domed cushion foot, grey internally mottled w/yellow & orange, cut w/a barren winter landscape enameled in charcoal & frosty white, signed in enamel "DAUM - NANCY" w/cross of Lorraine, ca. 1910 ... **4,025**

Vase, 11 1/2" h., flat-bottomed ovoid body w/a short neck & flattened rim, aquamarine, the lower half molded w/overlapping pointed stylized leaves below a textured upper ground, signed (ILLUS. left) **1,840**

Tall Daum Vase with Fuchsias

Vase, 13 1/8" h., a cushion foot below a bulbed stem continuing to a tall slender trumpet-form body, frosted milky white shading to violet etched w/delicate fuchsia blossoms & foliage, enameled in magenta, lavender & green w/gilt accent, cameo signature (ILLUS.)............. **6,325**

Fine Acid-etched Daum Vase

Vase, 13 1/4" h., bulbous ovoid body w/a short slightly flaring cylindrical neck, textured clear ground etched w/a stylized jungle scene w/a large gazelle all enameled in black, signed, ca. 1925 (ILLUS.)... **11,500**

Vase, 13 5/8" h., simple cylindrical form, shaded mottled yellow to dark brown ground, etched w/slender leafy stems up the sides & enameled w/reddish orange blossoms, etched gilt-trimmed scrolls around the base, signed in gilt **5,175**

Vase, 15 1/4" h., acid-etched, a tall trumpet-form body on a thick square foot w/notched corners, the body in clear cut w/four rows of vertical small rectangles, inscribed "Daum Nancy - France" w/a cross of Lorraine, ca. 1925....................... **2,875**

Large Rare Enameled Daum Vase

Vase, 15 7/8" h., disk foot w/double-knop stem in frosted white, the tall baluster-form body in mottled frosted pale blue etched & enameled w/a winter landscape of large snow-covered trees & blackbirds, signed in intaglio, ca. 1910 (ILLUS.) **19,550**

Vase, 16 5/8" h., a tall slender cylindrical body w/a small bulb above the wide cushion foot, a large bulbed top tapering to a small flared mouth, grey mottled w/ochre yellow shading to crimson & moss green, cut w/a pattern of prunus blossoms & leafage enameled in shades of white, grey, brown & green, signed in enameled cameo "DAUM - NANCY FRANCE," w/a cross of Lorraine, ca. 1900 .... **4,025**

Vase, 17 1/2", a cushion foot tapering to a tall slender trumpet-form body, salmon & yellow streaked ground etched & enameled w/thistles & foliage w/gilt accents, etched mark **3,220**

Vase, 21 7/8" h., wide cushion foot supporting a tall cylindrical body w/a slightly flared rim, mottled white to purple ground, the foot & lower body etched & highlighted in gilt w/angular bands & scrolls w/panels of insects & leafage, the body enameled in dark green w/large violet leaves & tall slender stems w/purple violet blossoms, signed in intaglio **23,000**

Vase, 25 1/2" h., spreading square form in mottled blue, purple & green **1,955**

Wine glasses, ovoid bowl on a slender stem on a disk foot, opalescent & frosted sea green, etched & enameled w/violets in pale rose & green, gilded rims, base inscribed & enameled "Daum Nancy Rube 62 B2 Haussmann Paris," pr. (light wear) **2,185**

DE LATTE

Andre de Latte of Nancy, France, produced a range of opaque and cameo glass after 1921. His company also produced light fixtures but his cameo wares are most collectible today.

DeLatte Marks

Cameo vase, 8" h., ovoid double-gourd form, orange overlaid in dark amethyst & cut w/a continuous design of leaves & berries, signed in cameo "Delatte Nancy" **$600**

De Latte Cameo Landscape Vase

Cameo vase, 15" h., very slender ovoid body w/a short neck & wide flattened rim, raised on a round cushion foot, light blue overlaid w/green & dark blue, w/peacocks & trees in the foreground, a lake in the middle ground & architectural ruins & trees in the distance, inscribed "ADELATTTE - NANCY," ca. 1925 (ILLUS.) **1,150**

Vase, 6 1/8" h., flared cylindrical form, frosted colorless enameled in brown & etched w/a tree-lined shore & rocky outcropping & distant hills, raised on a gilt-metal pedestal w/raised leaf design, signed "A. Delatte Nancy," on lower side, ca. 1920 .... **518**

Vase, 18" h., ovoid body w/spreading round foot, two-handled, in shades of pink & blue w/silver foil inclusions, signed **1,955**

DEVEZ & DEGUÉ

The Saint-Hilaire, Touvier, de Varreaux and Company of Pantin, France used the name De Vez on their cameo glass earlier this century. Some of their examples were marked "Degué," after one of their master glassmakers. Officially the company was named "Cristallerie de Pantin."

DeVez and Degué Marks

Cameo perfume bottle w/stopper, slender teardrop-form, pink cased to clear & layered in cobalt blue & etched as waterfowl in a marsh scene, signed "DeVez" in cameo, base marked "Mignon Paris," partial metal mount, 7 1/2" h. (loss to metal mount) **$374**

Scenic DeVez Cameo Vase

Cameo vase, 5" h., 2 1/2" d., deeply waisted ovoid form tapering to a small flat mouth, frosted clear overlaid in dark blue & gold & cut w/a landscape of an island, house, trees & water w/mountains in the background & leafy branches in the foreground, signed "DeVez" (ILLUS.) **645**

Cameo vase, 5 1/2" h., cylindrical w/a tapered raised rim, mottled shades of frosted orange layered in dark brown, etched w/a desert oasis scene w/camels & palm trees, signed on the side "Degué," early 20th c. (small chip inside rim, small scratch) **748**

Cameo vase, 6 1/4" h., footed bulbous ovoid body tapering to a slender trumpet neck, white frosted ground overlaid in butterscotch & cut w/an overall design of flowers & leafy stems, signed in cameo "de Vez".. **230**

Cameo vase, 6 1/4" h., footed ovoid body tapering to a slender trumpet neck, opaque cream overlaid in rose red & maroon & cameo-cut w/detailed poppy blossoms, seed pods & leafy stems, signed "DeVez" on lower edge **1,380**

Cameo vase, 8 1/4" h., slender ovoid body tapering to a tall slender neck, pale lavender overlaid in dark purple & cut w/a lakeside scene w/leafy branches & grasses in the foreground & a sailboat in the background, signed in cameo "de Vez"... **805**

Cameo vase, 10" h., elongated ovoid form, frosted colorless cased in amber, olive & deep blue, cameo-etched silhouetted trees overlooking water w/distant village & mountains, signed "de Vez" on lower side.. **1,150**

Cameo vase, 13 1/4" h., ovoid body w/a short flaring rim, grey mottled w/traces of ochre, overlaid w/purple shading to reddish orange & cut w/morning glory vines, signed "Degué," ca. 1925 (ILLUS. left, top next column)...................................... **2,300**

Degué Cameo Vases

Cameo vase, 13 1/2" h., thick disk foot below the slender ovoid body w/a heavy molded ring mouth, grey overlaid w/orange powdered glass cut w/a long zig-zag design against an acid-treated ground, signed in cameo "Degué," ca. 1920s **805**

Cameo vase, 15 1/2" h., double-gourd form w/flaring neck, blue & grey mottled ground overlaid w/tangerine shading to dark purple & cut w/stylized bellflowers on thin stems w/spade-form leaves, signed "Degué - France," ca. 1925 (ILLUS. right)... **1,610**

Degué Cameo Vase

Cameo vase, 17" h., ovoid body w/wide flattened rim & cushion foot, frosted grey overlaid w/lavender mottled w/white & cut w/stylized petals around the neck, signed in cameo "Degué," ca. 1925 (ILLUS.)... **690**

Cameo vase, 18" h., tall gently swelled ovoid form w/a flaring rim, acid-etched clear overlaid in mottled green & cameo-etched w/large barred Art Deco-style triangles, signed on side "Degué" (interior stain) **920**

Vase, 6" h., ovoid body in maroon & fiery amber, etched w/cottages & a mother & child under tall trees, polished rim, signed "deVez" at side **863**

Vase, 9 1/2" h., cylindrical, Art Deco style, grey infused w/blue & acid-etched w/stylized scrolls, signed "Degué," ca. 1920-30 .... **690**

Vase, 10 1/4" h., ovoid body molded w/stylized vines, the interior applied w/metallic decoration, acid-etched "Degué," ca. 1925 .... **287**

Vase, 17 h., monumental form, Art Deco style, black base, the sides in varied colors w/prominent blues w/yellows, greens & various other tones, signed "Degué"........ **990**

DURAND

Fine decorative glass similar to that made by Tiffany and other outstanding glasshouses of its day was made by the Vineland Flint Glass Works Co. in Vineland, New Jersey, first headed by Victor Durand, Sr., and subsequently by his son Victor Durand, Jr., in the 1920s.

Boudoir lamps, a tapering ovoid body in deep orange w/pinkish silver iridescent "King Tut" patt. fitted on a brass connector to a matching cylindrical glass pedestal on a flaring ringed brass foot, brass collar & electric socket w/a clear & frosted glass chimney fitted w/a wide conical pierced filigree silver plate Gorham shade, early 20th c., glass unmarked, 15" h., pr. **$1,750**

Bowl, 4 1/4" d., 2" h., wide squatty lower body tapering slightly to an upright smooth rim, overall blue iridescence w/white heart & vine decoration, base marked in silver "V Durand #3" **575**

Bowl, 6" d., shallow cased bowl w/a wide flattened & gently ruffled rim, overall gold iridescence, signed "V. Durand".................. **450**

Bowl, footed, 6 1/2" d., 4 1/4" h., wide bulbous acorn-form body w/closed rim in iridescent cobalt blue decorated w/iridescent blue leaves & entwined vines, raised on a short ambergris pedestal & round foot **1,870**

Box, cov., footed squatty round form w/flattened round fitted cover, "King Tut" patt., "Lady Gay Rose" color w/gold interior, applied ambergris disk foot, cover starcut at center top pontil mark, unsigned, 4 1/2" d., 3 1/4" h.,..................................... **1,610**

Center bowl, blue iridescence, signed, 14" w. **1,500**

Center bowl, low wide flat-bottomed form w/a wide rolled rim, overall butterscotch iridescence, signed & numbered 2605, 14" d., 2 1/2" h... **385**

Center bowl, ruffled rim, red crackle iridescent exterior, stretch iridescent interior, 11" d. **650**

Durand Charger & Small Vase

Charger, large transparent blue disk centered by five colorless & lighter blue & grey pulled feathers, numerous bubbles, 14 1/4" d. (ILLUS. right) **747**

Compote, cov., 10 1/2" h., "Bridgeton Rose" design, a round disk foot below a short knopped stem supporting a tall inverted pear-form body w/a short rim fitted w/a tall bell-form cover w/a knob finial, Spanish yellow cased body

w/etched & wheel-cut floral sprig decoration cut to clear, matching cover, marked w/Durand in "V" mark, possibly added (ILLUS. below)................................... **450**

Durand "Bridgeton Rose" Compote

Ginger jar, cov., wide ovoid body fitted w/a domed cover, overall dark blue iridescence decorated w/overall dark blue random threading, a small yellow reeded florette finial on the cover, 8 1/4" d., 9" h. (slight threading loss) **1,650**

Ginger jar, cov., wide ovoid shouldered body w/a domed cover fitted w/an amber button finial, the body & cover w/an overall golden iridescent "King Tut" design on a dark ground, mounted as a lamp on a round bronze base raised on eight pawform feet, overall 11 1/2" h. **2,035**

Ice bucket, cut-overlay, cylindrical form in blue cut to clear w/a design of honeycomb vesicas connected by crosshatched diamonds, silver plate rim & bail handle, 6" h. (short crack in base)............... **248**

Unusual Durand Jar

Jar, cov., wide sharply tapering ovoid body w/a domed fitted cover, green w/iridized "King Tut" decoration, applied amber button on cover, 7 1/4" h. (ILLUS.)............ **3,105**

Lamp base, bulbous squatty base below a tall slender trumpet-form neck, decorated overall w/green & iridescent "King-Tut" swirled design, fitted on a silvered metal round foot & w/an electric socket cap fitting, shape No. 1730, glass 6 1/2" h. (ILLUS. top next page).................. **690**

Lamp base, "King Tut" patt., simple ovoid body tapering to a trumpet neck, mounted on an octagonal gilt-metal base, gilt-metal electric fittings at the top w/two sockets, the body of golden orange iridescence w/dark olive green pulled coils & swirls, glass 12" h., overall 20" h. **750**

Durand Lamp Base

Parfait, ribbed footed base & ribbed bowl w/fluted top, deep shiny rose pink, by Emil Larsen, 5 3/4" h. **165**

Plate, 8" d., round w/turned-up rim, the center w/a wide circle of opalescent white "King Tut" pulled swirl design w/lightly iridized finish, the opalescent yellow wide border band w/spaced stripes of blue pulled design **1,320**

Rose bowl, short pedestal base below the spherical bowl, iridescent yellowish amber w/the exterior etched overall w/a design of fern wreath & fringed blossoms, early 20th c., signed, 4 3/4" h. **1,100**

Sherbet, wide deep round orangish gold iridescent bowl wrapped w/golden threading, raised on a short stem & disk foot in bluish green iridescence, 4 1/4" d., 3" h. **385**

Sherbet & underplate, footed emerald green sherbet w/widely flaring optic-ribbed bowl w/a gently ruffled rim trimmed w/an applied white band, matching underplate w/white rim, underplate 6 1/4" d., sherbet 2 1/2" h., the set **193**

Egyptian Crackle Durand Torcheres

Torcheres, tall slender trumpet-form in green & white striated design w/iridescent gold "Egyptian crackle" decoration, mounted in a bronze acanthus leaf electrified base, ca. 1926, overall 15 1/2" h., pr. (ILLUS.) **1,725**

Vase, 4" h., nearly spherical form, colorless w/controlled bubble interior decoration, base signed "V. Durand 1995-4" (ILLUS. left, w/charger) **288**

Vase, 4" h., overall gold iridescence, Shape No. 1710, signed in script **330**

Vase, 4 1/4" h., oviform w/tapering base & flared extended rim, exterior decorated w/pulled & hooked designs in bluish green overall, gold lustre interior, base signed "Durand 1710-4" **1,150**

Vase, 5 3/4" h., footed squatty bulbous base centered by a tall trumpet neck, overall gold iridescent interior & exterior, signed "V. Durand 1990 6" **518**

Threaded & Plain Durand Vases

Vase, 6" h., large ovoid body tapering to a widely flaring short neck, opal ground w/greenish gold leaves & silvery gold threading, gold iridescent interior, signed "V Durand 1812-6," some thread loss (ILLUS. left) **633**

Vase, 6" h., slender ovoid body w/a short cylindrical neck, overall blue iridescence, signed "Durand 1722 1/2 - 6" (ILLUS. right) **431**

Vase, 6" h., wide ovoid body tapering to a wide mouth w/a low rolled rim, overall iridescent blue decorated around the body w/random white opal webbed vines & scattered heart-shaped leaves, signed "V. Durand 1968-6" **990**

Vase, 6" h., wide ovoid body w/the rounded shoulder tapering to a short widely flaring flattened neck, overall ambergris gold iridescence, signed "V. Durand 1710-6" **374**

Durand "King Tut" Pattern Vase

Vase, 6 1/4" h., bulbous baluster-form w/wide flaring neck, overall "King Tut" design in iridescent green swirls & coils on a warm orange ground cased in white w/lustered orange interior, Larson foot (ILLUS.) **600-800**

Vase, 6 3/16" h., ovoid, amber iridescence decorated w/heart-shaped leaves & random trailing in pale green, inscribed "Durand - 1968-6," ca. 1920 .... **650**

Vase, 6 3/8" h., broad ovoid shouldered body w/a wide short flaring neck, ambergris w/a peachy gold iridized finish & applied overall random gold threading, cased w/a white-flashed gold interior, polished pontil (minor loss to threading) **460**

Vase, 6 3/4" h., footed ovoid body w/a short widely flaring flattened neck, gold iridescent exterior, cased in white, inscribed "Durand" in script across a Larson white pontil.. **403**

Leaf-decorated Durand Vase

Vase, 6 7/8" h., ovoid body w/everted rim, amber iridescence decorated w/heart-shaped leafage & trailings in green, inscribed "Durand - 1710-9," ca. 1920 (ILLUS.).. **1,200**

Two Durand "King Tut" Vases

Vase, 7" h., baluster-form body w/a flaring trumpet neck, "King Tut" patt., white pulled & hooked design over the iridescent blue ground, unsigned (ILLUS. left)... **1,200**

Vase, 7 1/2" h., simple ovoid body tapering to a short, wide flaring neck, overall dark blue iridescence decorated w/random white opal entwined vines w/scattered heart-shaped leaves, signed "Durand #1812-7".. **1,100**

Vase, 7 1/2" h., simple ovoid body w/a short wide flaring neck, grey & yellow w/peach iridescence & green trailing vines w/heart-shaped leaves, signed "DURAND - 1812 - 7" w/a "V," 1920s (ILLUS. right w/large vase).......................... **977**

Vase, 7 3/4" h., squatty bulbous base tapering to a trumpet-form neck, brilliant silvery blue iridescence, signed "Durand - 1986 - 8," ca. 1925 (ILLUS. top next column) **900**

Blue Iridescent Durand Vase

Vase, 8" h., the wide squatty base centered by a widely flaring trumpet neck, lightly molded ribbing, ambergris w/bright blue iridescent finish highlighted by purplish green, base signed in silver "V. Durand 1986-8"... **950**

Vase, 8" h., wide cylindrical form rounded at the base & shoulder w/a short, wide rim, overall strong blue iridescence, polished pontil signed "Durand 1968-8" **805**

Vase, 8 1/4" h., "King Tut" patt., wide footed baluster-form body w/a wide short cylindrical neck w/flaring flattened rim, cased amber to opal w/gold iridescent interior, swirling green hooked & coiled decoration on the exterior, unsigned......... **1,500**

Vase, 8 1/4" h., wide bulbous baluster-form w/flattened flaring rim, "King Tut" patt., iridescent green hooked & pulled swirls on a golden orange cased to opal ground, signed "Durand" across the pontil (ILLUS. right, previous column) **1,750**

Graceful Blue Durand Vase

Vase, 8 1/2" h., footed tall ovoid body w/a wide flaring short neck, body in overall dark blue iridescence, disk foot w/golden iridescence (ILLUS.)................................... **1,000**

Decorated Durand Vase

Vase, 8 1/2" h., simple ovoid form w/a short flaring neck, white ground decorated w/pulled feather design in blue & yellow w/applied random threading in gold iridescence, unsigned, ca. 1910 (ILLUS.) **546**

Threaded Durand Vase

Vase, 8 1/2" h., swelled cylindrical body w/a rounded shoulder to the short trumpet neck, ambergris body w/overall lustrous blue iridescent random threading, unsigned (ILLUS.) **650**

Vase, 9" h., cut-overlay, large ovoid body w/a small, short cylindrical neck, deep ruby cut to clear w/a design of large punties & crossed petals, panel-cut around the base **2,475**

Vase, 9 3/4" h., gently swelled ovoid body tapering to a short flaring trumpet neck, "Lady Gay Rose," orange lining cased w/white decorated w/a rose red surface covered w/a swirled "King Tut" iridescent design in gold & silver **1,750**

Vase, 9 3/4" h., tall wide waisted cylindrical form swelled at the base & w/a wide stepped shoulder to the wide flat mouth, golden iridescent ground decorated overall w/cascading dark blue iridescent vines & heart-shaped leaves, signed "Durand - 1969-10".................................. **1,375**

Vase, 10" h., green on gold "King Tut" design, broad shouldered cased glass oval body w/strong green pulled & coiled decoration on lustrous iridescent gold surface, gold interior over opal, base inscribed "Durand 1964-10" **2,415**

Vase, 10" h., tall slender waisted form w/a swelled top w/closed mouth tapering to a gently flaring base, overall pale green & gold "King Tut" design, Shape No. 1717 ... **1,540**

Vase, 12" h., "Moorish" type crackle glass, cushion foot tapering to a trumpet-form body w/ten molded ribs & overall crackled finish, ambergris w/gold iridescence, silver mark "V. Durand" on base **1,500**

Tall Decorated Durand Vase

Vase, 12 1/8" h., tall ovoid body w/waisted neck & flaring lip, brilliant amber-orange iridescence decorated w/green heart-shaped leafage & trailings, inscribed "Durand - 2011 - 12," ca. 1925 (ILLUS.) ... **1,200**

Large & Smaller Durand Vases

Vase, 12 1/4" h., cushion base below the widely flaring trumpet-form body w/an angled shoulder to the wide trumpet neck, grey w/orange, yellow & silver iridescence, signed "DURAND - 20139-12," ca. 1920s (ILLUS. left) **977**

Vase, 12 1/4" h., footed slender trumpet-form body, shaded purplish blue iridescence w/overall gold heart & vine design & an applied gold pedestal foot, marked "Durand 20120-12" **1,950**

Vase, 12 3/8" h., shouldered ovoid body, brilliant amber iridescence decorated w/opalescent striated feathering edge in blue iridescence, inscribed "Durand," ca. 1925 .... **1,200**

Large Decorated Durand Vase

Vase, 12 1/2" h., cushion foot below the wide squatty bulbous body w/a wide rounded shoulder tapering to a tall cylindrical neck w/flared rim, rose pink w/coiled iridescence, yellowish white interior, silver enameled mark on pontil "Durand" (ILLUS.)..................................... **2,875**

Vase, 13" h., bulbous ovoid body w/a stepped shoulder w/a small mouth, amber w/gold iridescence, polished pontil, unsigned, minor surface wear, Shape No. 1978, ca. 1925 (ILLUS. top next page) **920**

Durand Vase with Stepped Shoulder

Vase, 14" h., tall slender trumpet-form, the sides decorated w/a tall pulled feather design on the creamy ground, on a purplish amber applied round foot, model No. 1724.. **935**

Vase, 16 1/4" h., globular body tapering to a tall trumpet neck, brilliant blue shading to purple iridescence, signed "Durand - 1716.16," ca. 1900 .... **1,750**

Vase, 17" h., large spherical body topped by a tall flaring trumpet neck, the emerald green exterior covered in the "King Tut" design w/iridescent silvery & golden banding, iridescent gold interior, silver company signature w/"#1716-167 1/2" h."... **3,795**

Vases, 4 1/4" h., ovoid body w/an everted rim, the iridescent gold ground decorated w/an iridescent silvery green wave design, signed, each drilled, pr. **300**

FINDLAY ONYX & FLORADINE

In January, 1889, the glass firm of Dalzell, Gilmore & Leighton Co. of Findlay, Ohio began production of these scarce glass lines. Onyx ware was a white-lined glass produced mainly in onyx (creamy yellowish white) but also in bronze and ruby shades sometimes called cinnamon, rose or raspberry. Pieces featured raised flowers and leaves that are silver-colored or, less often, bronze. By contrast the Floradine line was produced in ruby and autumn leaf (gold) with opalescent flowers and leaves. It is not lined.

Celery vase, creamy white w/silver flowers & leaves **$495**

Findlay Onyx Creamer

Creamer, bulbous ovoid body w/an upright ribbed neck, applied handle, creamy white w/silver flowers & leaves, 3" h. (ILLUS.) **485**

Extremely Rare Findlay Onyx Lamp

Lamp, kerosene table model, black opaque glass base w/flaring ruffled foot & wide short cylindrical shaft supporting the squatty bulbous Findlay Onyx font w/brass collar, burner & chimney, piece of base rim reglued, overall to burner 7 1/4" h. (ILLUS.)...................................... **7,150**

Findlay Onyx Spooner

Spooner, bulbous tapering to an upright ribbed neck, creamy white w/silver blossoms & leaves, 4 1/4" h. (ILLUS.) **375**

Floradine Sugar Bowl

Sugar shaker w/original lid, Floradine, cranberry (ILLUS.).. **800**

Tumbler, barrel-shaped, creamy ground w/deep orangish red blossoms & golden yellow leaves & stems (slight line between the layers).................................. **2,530**

FRANCES WARE

The "Frances" decoration was developed by Hobbs, Brockunier & Co., Wheeling, West Virginia, in the 1880s. It is frosted glass with stained amber tops or rims and was both mold-blown and pressed. It was used on several glass patterns including their Hobnail and Swirl lines.

Berry set: 7 1/2" d. master bowl & five 4" square sauce dishes; frosted hobnail w/amber rim, the set.................................. **$200**
Butter dish, cov., frosted swirl w/amber rim..... **175**
Celery dish, frosted swirl w/amber rim **75**

Frances Ware Hobnail Creamer

Creamer, frosted hobnail w/amber rim (ILLUS.)... **95**
Cruet w/stopper, spherical frosted Hobnail body w/an amber ringed neck & clear pointed facet-cut stopper, applied frosted handle, 8" h. **193**
Ice cream set: master bowl & 6 serving dishes; frosted hobnail w/amber rim, 7 pcs... **395**
Pitcher, milk, frosted swirl w/amber rim **125**
Pitcher, water, 7" h., Hobnail patt., spherical body w/a squared neck, applied frosted to clear handle................................. **193**
Sugar shaker w/original top, frosted swirl w/amber rim **335**
Toothpick holder, frosted hobnail w/amber rim **53**

GALLÉ

Gallé glass was made in Nancy, France, by Emile Gallé, a founder of the Nancy School and a leader in the Art Nouveau movement in France. Much of his glass, both enameled and cameo, is decorated with naturalistic motifs. The finest pieces were made in the last two decades of the 19th century and the opening years of the 20th.

Pieces marked with a star preceding the name were made between 1904, the year of Gallé's death, and 1914.

Various Gallé Marks

Bottle w/stopper, footed bulbous squared ovoid lobed body w/a tiny cylindrical neck w/mushroom stopper, clear enameled in mauve, maroon, teal, chartreuse, black, white & gilt w/a dragonfly among delicate sprigs of flowers, inscribed "E. Gallé - Nancy," ca. 1895, 5 1/2" h., ... **$1,092**

Silver-mounted Gallé Box

Box, cov., upright square form in mottled burnt orange, ochre, white & lemon yellow, lightly acid-etched & enameled w/a design of wildflowers & grasses, the hinged cover matching, w/foliate pierced leafy & berry silver mounts around the rim & forming the footed base, glass inscribed "Emile Gallé - à Nancy - Modéle et décors déposés," silver hallmarked, ca. 1900, 6 1/4" h. (ILLUS.) ... **7,475**
Cameo atomizer, bulbous spherical base tapering to a tall, slender trumpet neck fitted w/an atomizer, frosted & shaded yellow to pale purple to green ground overlaid in dark purple & cut w/a continuous landscape w/large trees in the foreground & mountains in the distance, cameo signature, 7" h. **880**
Cameo box, cov., circular cushion-form, grey shaded yellow, overlaid w/brown, the base carved w/leaves, the cover w/a landscape, signed in cameo, ca. 1900, 4 1/2" d.. **1,610**
Cameo box, cov., flattened diamond form in opalescent grey infused w/pale pink & overlaid w/purplish red, the cover cut w/a rowboat by a wooded shore, the base w/falling leaves, cover & base signed, ca. 1900, 7 3/4" l............................ **2,300**
Cameo flower bowl, pale pink footed bowl w/four pulled points, overlaid in light yellowish green & amber & etched w/clusters of blossoms on leafy branches, signed w/a star & signature among the leaves, ca. 1904, 7 3/4" d., 4 1/4" h. (several bubble bursts, wear to interior)....... **690**
Cameo lamp, table model, 10 1/2" d. domical shade in golden amber overlay w/deep maroon & cut w/large stylized leaves & blossoms, supported on bronze spider arms above the slender balusterform matching base cut w/a matching design, base & shade signed, ca.1900, overall 20 1/2" h. **16,100**

Fine Gallé Cameo Table Lamp

Cameo lamp, table model, 7 1/2" w. domed squared shade in deep golden amber overlaid in deep maroon & cut w/large leafy branches of fuchsia blossoms, supported above a matching ovoid base, shade & base signed in cameo, overall 11" h. (ILLUS.) **12,650**

Cameo vase, 2 3/4" h., miniature, shouldered ovoid body in rose & white overlaid w/green & cut w/flowers, signed **863**

Cameo vase, 5 3/4" h., spherical body tapering to a tiny neck w/wide deep cupped rim, yellow ground overlaid in pale blue, sea green & aubergine & etched w/a wooded lake scene featuring fir trees & mountains in the distance, signed **3,450**

Cameo vase, 6 1/4" h., swelled cylindrical body w/a narrow shoulder centered by a short cylindrical neck, clear & frosted golden amber layered in amber & cameo-etched w/hydrangea blossoms over leafy branches, signed on reverse "Gallé" **863**

Cameo vase, 6 3/4" h., bottle-form, bulbous ovoid base tapering to a tall, slightly flaring 'stick' neck, frosted grey overlaid in brown, cut w/stylized flowers & leaves, signed in cameo **575**

Gallé Cameo Vase with Bellflowers

Cameo vase, 7" h., wide ovoid body w/a wide flaring rim, yellow overlaid in blue & cut w/a design of large bellflowers, signed (ILLUS.) **3,162**

Cameo vase, 7 1/2" h., footed shaped & tapering cylindrical form w/flat rim, rose ground overlaid in amber & cameo-etched w/flowers & foliage, signed **977**

Cameo vase, 8" h., bulbous base w/a tall slender neck, grey w/pink streaks, lay-

ered in periwinkle & green, acid-etched w/a stalk of stylized flowers, signed near base **863**

Cameo vase, 8" h., bulbous tapering ovoid body w/a slender trumpet neck, light blue overlaid w/dark blue & cut w/morning glories & vines, fire polished, signed .. **1,610**

Cameo vase, 9" h., trumpet foot supporting a nearly spherical body below a trumpet neck, grey shaded pale yellow, overlaid in yellow & brown & cut w/Chinese lanterns & leafage, signed in cameo, ca. 1900 .... **2,875**

Cameo vase, 10" h., baluster-form, yellow cased in deep rose & maroon & cameo-carved around the body w/large branches of wild roses, signed **4,235**

Mold-blown Gallé Cameo Vase

Cameo vase, 10" h., mold-blown footed swelled cylindrical body w/a short cylindrical neck, frosted colorless shaded to teal ground, overlaid & molded w/lime green, brown & white, etched & carved as water lilies among lily pads, signed at lower edge, small rim chip (ILLUS.) **12,650**

Cameo vase, 11" h., spherical body w/a small trumpet neck, shaded light amber & clear frosted ground overlaid w/dark brown down the neck & shoulders & cut w/pendent grapevine suspending 'blown-out' golden grape clusters, signed in cameo **5,750**

Cameo vase, 11 1/4" h., tall slender barbell-form on a cushion foot, grey shaded w/green, overlaid w/brown & cut w/ferns, signed in cameo, ca. 1900 .... **1,265**

Gallé Vase with Apples

Top Row: Fine Agata tumbler with great color, 3 3/4" h. $550-750. Courtesy of Brookside Antiques, New Bedford, Massachusetts, Photo by Bill Pitt; Rare Webb Alexandrite nut dish, 3" d. $750-950. Courtesy of Brookside Antiques, New Bedford, Massachusetts, Photo by Bill Pitt.

Bottom Row: Rare Agata spooner, 4 1/2" h. $1,250. Courtesy of The Cedars - Antiques, Aurelia, Iowa; Large Amberina basket, 10 3/4" h. $395. Courtesy of Temples Antiques, Eden Prairie, Minnesota; Amberina cruet in the Inverted Thumbprint pattern, 6" h. $250-275. Courtesy of Temples Antiques, Eden Prairie, Minnesota.

Top Row: Enamel-decorated Bohemian vase, attributed to Rossler, 8" h. $250. Courtesy of Johanna S. Billings, Danielsville, Pennsylvania; Pink cased satin glass bride's bowl on an ornate silver plate stand, 8 1/4" h. $325. Courtesy of Temples Antiques, Eden Prairie, Minnesota.

Center: Tall Amberina vase with a jack-in-the-pulpit rim, 12" h. $225. Courtesy of Temples Antiques, Eden Prairie, Minnesota.

Bottom Row: Rare Plated Amberina cruet $5,000-6,500. Courtesy of Brookside Antiques, New Bedford, Massachusetts, Photo by Bill Pitt; Lovely decorated Burmese vase, attributed to Thomas Webb, 8 1/8" h. $750. Courtesy of Temples Antiques, Eden Prairie, Minnesota

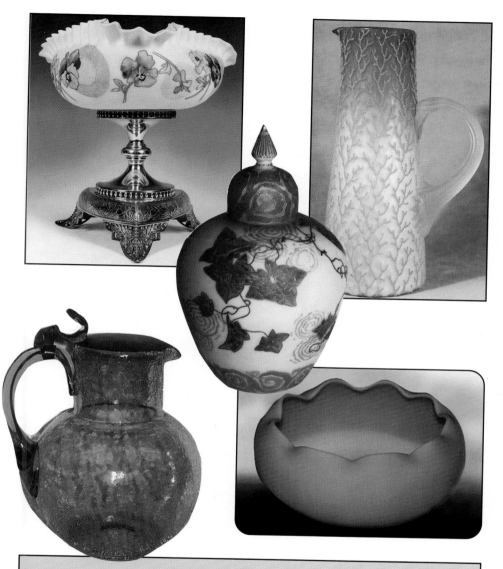

Top Row: Very fine Crown Milano bride's bowl on silver plate stand, 11 1/2" h. $3,750. Courtesy of Jackson's Auctioneers, Cedar Falls, Iowa; Fine Coralene tankard pitcher, 12" h. $1,200 to 1,500. Courtesy of Brookside Antiques, New Bedford, Massachusetts, Photo by Bill Pitt

Center: Ornately decorated Crown Milano covered jar, 10 1/2" h. $2,750. Courtesy of The Cedars - Antiques, Aurelia, Iowa

Bottom Row: Olive green crackle glass pitcher with metal cover, 8" h. $145. Courtesy of Temples Antiques, Eden Prairie, Minnesota; Mt. Washington Burmese finger bowl, 4 1/2" d. $325. Courtesy of Temples Antiques, Eden Prairie, Minnesota

Top Row: Two sizes of Dorflinger's cut Marlboro pattern tobacco jar. Left, $1,250, right, $1,450. Courtesy of Vance Hall, A Touch of Glass, Wichita, Kansas; Covered cut glass cheese dish in Clark's North Star pattern, 7" h. $695. Courtesy of Vance Hall, A Touch of Glass, Wichita, Kansas.

Center: Cut Sultana pattern asparagus tray signed by Libbey, 12" l. $445. Courtesy of Vance Hall, A Touch of Glass, Wichita, Kansas.

Bottom Row: A cut glass serving dish in the Strawberry Diamond pattern, 8 1/4" d. without the handles $385. Courtesy of Vance Hall, A Touch of Glass, Wichita, Kansas; Hawkes' Brunswick pattern footed cut glass rose bowl, 6" h. $1,095. Courtesy of Vance Hall, A Touch of Glass, Wichita, Kansas.

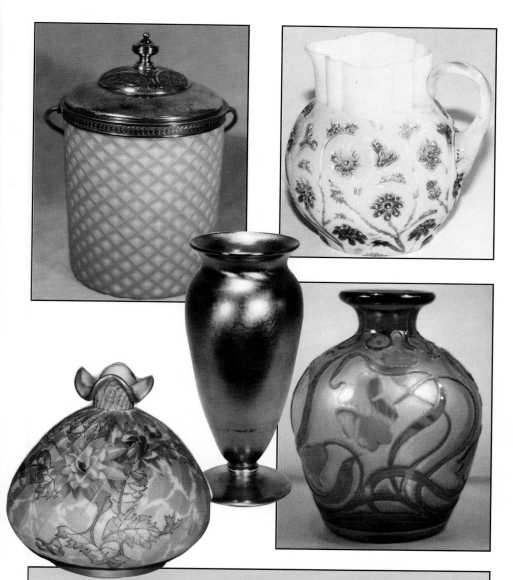

Top Row: Pink Cut Velvet cracker jar with silver plate fittings, 9" h. $1,000-1,500. Courtesy of Brookside Antiques, New Bedford, Massachusetts, Photo by Bill Pitt; Findlay Onyx creamer, 4 1/2" h. $485. Courtesy of Robert G. Jason-Ickes, Olympia, Washington.

Center: Durand iridescent vase in blue with an amber foot, 8 1/2" h. $1,000. Courtesy of DuMouchelles, Detroit, Michigan.

Bottom Row: Floral-decorated squatty Crown Milano vase, 7" h. $1,750. Courtesy of The Cedars - Antiques, Aurelia, Iowa; Rare Honesdale cameo vase with floral decoration, 6 1/2" h. $900-1,200. Courtesy of Brookside Antiques, New Bedford, Massachusetts, Photo by Bill Pitt.

Top Row: Lovely Kelva box in rose red with white flowers, 4 1/2" d., 2 1/2" h. $550. Courtesy of Temples Antiques, Eden Prairie, Minnesota; Lalique "Baies" pattern vase with black enamel trim, 10 1/2" h. $13,800. Courtesy of William Doyle Galleries, New York, New York.

Bottom Row: Spatter glass footed jack-in-the-pulpit vase, 8" h. $150. Courtesy of Temples Antiques, Eden Prairie, Minnesota; Lalique "Ronces" pattern vase with green stain, 9 1/4" h. $2,415. Courtesy of William Doyle Galleries, New York, New York; Pink overlay jack-in-the-pulpit vase with enameled decoration, 7 1/2" h. $175. Courtesy of Temples Antiques, Eden Prairie, Minnesota.

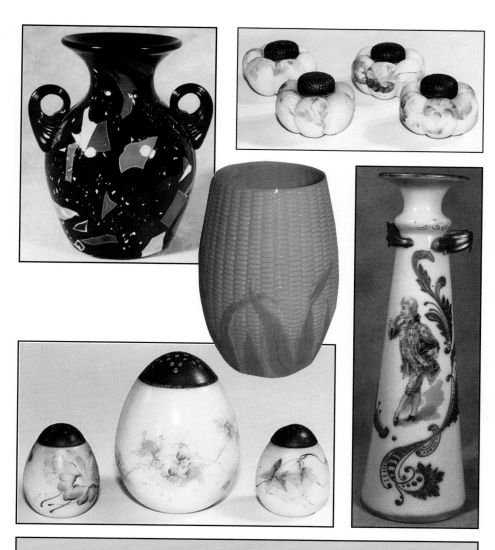

Top Row: Mt. Washington "Lava" glass vase, 6" h. $2,000-2,800. Courtesy of Brookside Antiques, New Bedford, Massachusetts, Photo by Bill Pitt; A set of four tomato-shaped salt & pepper shakers from The Mt. Washington Glass Company, each 2" h. $400 the set. Courtesy of Robert G. Jason-Ickes, Olympia, Washington.

Center: Libbey "Maize" pattern celery vase, 6 1/2" h. $225. Courtesy of Temples Antiques, Eden Prairie, Minnesota.

Bottom Row: A decorated Mt. Washington egg-shaped sugar shaker flanked by matching salt & pepper shakers. The sugar shaker, $375, the salt & pepper shakers, $325 the pair. Courtesy of Robert G. Jason-Ickes, Olympia, Washington; Tall Mt. Washington "Colonial Ware" vase, 12" h. $1,000-1,500. Courtesy of Brookside Antiques, New Bedford, Massachusetts, Photo by Bill Pitt.

Top Row: Pairpoint "Flambo" console set with silver overlay $3,500- 5,000. Courtesy of Brookside Antiques, New Bedford, Massachusetts, Photo by Bill Pitt; Elegant Nakara vase by C.F. Monroe, 15 3/4" h. $2,000. Courtesy of The Cedars - Antiques, Aurelia, Iowa.

Center: Floral-decorated Nakara jewelry box, 3 1/4" w., 3" h. $375. Courtesy of Johanna S. Billings, Danielsville, Pennsylvania.

Bottom Row: Cranberry overshot glass tankard pitcher with metal cover, 9 1/4" h. $175. Courtesy of Temples Antiques, Eden Prairie, Minnesota; Large Nakara Crown mold footed box with pink roses, 8" d., 6 1/4" h. $2,500. Courtesy of The Cedars - Antiques, Aurelia, Iowa.

Top Row: Pairpoint 'Tavern line' vase, 6" h. early 20th century $325. Courtesy of The Burmese Cruet, Montgomeryville, Pennsylvania; Wheeling Peach Blow "Morgan Vase" with satin finish, 8" h. $2,200-2,800. Courtesy of Brookside Antiques, New Bedford, Massachusetts, Photo by Bill Pitt.

Bottom Row: Gold Ruby Gundersen - Pairpoint vase $400-600. Courtesy of Brookside Antiques, New Bedford, Massachusetts, Photo by Bill Pitt; Wheeling Peach Blow bottle-form vase with 'stick' neck, 9 1/4" h. $985. Courtesy of The Burmese Cruet, Montgomeryville, Pennsylvania; Gundersen Peach Blow footed decanter with satin finish $750-1,000. Courtesy of Brookside Antiques, New Bedford, Massachusetts, Photo by Bill Pitt.

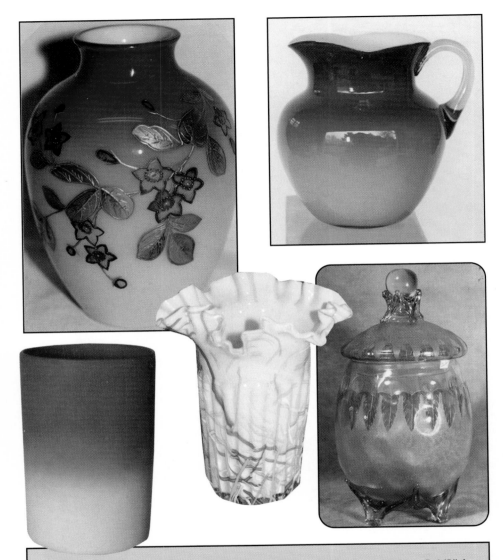

Top Row: Webb Peach Blow vase with silver and gold decoration, 5 1/8" h. $295. Courtesy of Temples Antiques, Eden Prairie, Minnesota; Small Wheeling Peach Blow creamer, 4 1/4" h. $785. Courtesy of The Burmese Cruet, Montgomeryville, Pennsylvania.

Bottom Row: New England Peach Blow tumbler, 3 3/4" h. $425-475. Courtesy of The Burmese Cruet, Montgomeryville, Pennsylvania; Peloton ribbed vase with ruffled rim, 4 1/2" h. $225. Courtesy of Temples Antiques, Eden Prairie, Minnesota; Pomona 1st patent cracker jar with acanthus leaf decoration $1,200-1,500. Courtesy of Brookside Antiques, New Bedford, Massachusetts, Photo by Bill Pitt.

Top Row: Mother-of-pearl Rainbow satin glass ewer in the Herringbone pattern, 10 1/2" h. $1,500-2,000. Courtesy of Brookside Antiques, New Bedford, Massachusetts, Photo by Bill Pitt; Royal Flemish cracker jar with the Roman Coin decoration $1,800-2,200. Courtesy of Brookside Antiques, New Bedford, Massachusetts, Photo by Bill Pitt.

Bottom Row: Two Pomona glass tumblers with blue cornflower decoration, 2nd patent, 3 5/8" h. each $135. Courtesy of Temples Antiques, Eden Prairie, Minnesota; Mother-of-pearl satin glass decorated vase in the Herringbone pattern, 6 1/2" h. $225. Courtesy of Temples Antiques, Eden Prairie, Minnesota; Mother-of-pearl satin glass decorated vase in the Diamond Quilted pattern, 7 3/4" h. $225. Courtesy of Temples Antiques, Eden Prairie, Minnesota.

Top Row: Rare signed Smith Brothers canteen-form vase, 8 1/2" h. $2,000-2,500. Courtesy of Brookside Antiques, New Bedford, Massachusetts, Photo by Bill Pitt; A pair of Smith Brothers cylindrical vases with storks, 4 1/4" h. pair $200. Courtesy of Johanna S. Billings, Danielsville, Pennsylvania.

Bottom Row: Fine Art Nouveau style silver deposit vase, 12 1/2" h. $700. Courtesy of Robert G. Jason-Ickes, Olympia, Washington; Silver overlay lobed perfume bottle dated 1913, 4 3/4" h. $305. Courtesy of Robert G. Jason-Ickes, Olympia, Washington; Maroon and white enamel-decorated spatter glass cruet, 5 1/2" h. $245. Courtesy of Temples Antiques, Eden Prairie, Minnesota.

Top Row: Portion of a signed Tiffany Favrile wine set; decanter and six wine glasses. The set $3,000-4,000. Courtesy of Brookside Antiques, New Bedford, Massachusetts, Photo by Bill Pitt; Unusual Stevens & Williams appliqued glass bottle with peacock stopper finial, 11" h. $500. Courtesy of Temples Antiques, Eden Prairie, Minnesota; A Steuben "Ivrene" glass jack-in-the-pulpit vase, 12 1/2" h. $1,200. Courtesy of Robert G. Jason-Ickes, Olympia, Washington.

Bottom Row: A fine Stevens & Williams Pompeian Swirl shaded mother-of-pearl satin glass vase, 5 1/4" d., 5 3/8" h. $750. Courtesy of Temples Antiques, Eden Prairie, Minnesota; A heavy Steuben etched 'Lion' vase in smoky amber, 12 1/2" h. $2,750. Courtesy of DuMouchelles, Detroit, Michigan.

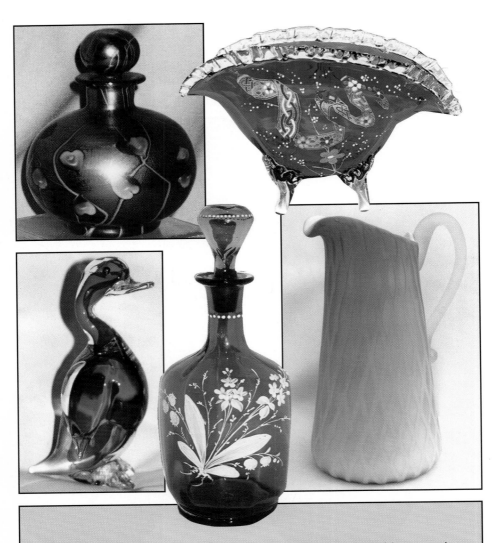

Top Row: Tiffany Favrile perfume bottle in iridescent blue with green vines and leaves, 5 1/4" h. $2,900. Courtesy of DuMouchelles, Detroit, Michigan; Ornately enameled Victorian colored glass fanned bowl on feet, 12" w., 8" h. $275. Courtesy of Temples Antiques, Eden Prairie, Minnesota.

Bottom Row: Venetian blown glass model of a duck in ruby cased in clear, 20th century, 6" h. $100. Courtesy of Johanna S. Billings, Danielsville, Pennsylvania; Victorian colored glass bottle and stopper with white enameled decoration, 9 1/4" h. $135. Courtesy of Temples Antiques, Eden Prairie, Minnesota; Venetian reproduction mother-of-pearl satin glass pitcher in the Diamond Quilted pattern, mid-20th century, 9" h. $90. Courtesy of Johanna S. Billings, Danielsville, Pennsylvania.

Top Row: Lovely tall Wave Crest vase, 11 1/2" h. $1,500-2,000. Courtesy of Brookside Antiques, New Bedford, Massachusetts, Photo by Bill Pitt; An unmarked Wave Crest humidor with brass cover. Decorated with three bulldogs titled "Three Guardsmen," 6 1/2" h. $525. Courtesy of Temples Antiques, Eden Prairie, Minnesota.

Center: Wave Crest Baroque Shell mold box with floral decoration and pink trim, 7" d., 4" h. $750. Courtesy of Temples Antiques, Eden Prairie, Minnesota.

Bottom Row: Lobed Victorian colored glass purple vase with fine enamel decoration, 8 1/4" h. $245. Courtesy of Temples Antiques, Eden Prairie, Minnesota; A large Wave Crest Egg Crate mold box with floral decoration and gilt-metal mounts, 6 3/4" w., 6 1/2" h. $1,750. Courtesy of The Cedars - Antiques, Aurelia, Iowa; Large dark amethyst Victorian colored vase with a large bouquet of flowers and a butterfly, 10 3/4" h. $225. Courtesy of Temples Antiques, Eden Prairie, Minnesota.

Top Row: Fabulous Thomas Webb & Sons "Gem Cameo" bowl, 7 x 9" $28,000. Courtesy of Jackson's Auctioneers, Cedar Falls, Iowa; A reproduction Maize pattern rose bowl in amber cased glass, 7 1/2" d., 4 1/2" h. $85-125. Courtesy of Johanna S. Billings, Danielsville, Pennsylvania.

Center Row: Satin glass "Floral Embossed" pattern rose bowl in shaded pink, 3 1/2" h. $125-175. Courtesy of Johanna S. Billings, Danielsville, Pennsylvania; Shaded blue mother-of-pearl satin rose bowl in the Diamond Quilted pattern, 3 3/4" h. $275-325. Courtesy of Johanna S. Billings, Danielsville, Pennsylvania.

Bottom Row: Cased satin glass box-pleated rose bowl in brown shaded to creamy white, 4 3/4" h. $200-250. Courtesy of Johanna S. Billings, Danielsville, Pennsylvania; Souvenir satin glass rose bowl, 3 1/2" h. $125-175. Courtesy of Johanna S. Billings, Danielsville, Pennsylvania.

Cameo vase, 11 5/8" h., ovoid body w/a wide flat mouth, grey infused w/yellow, overlaid w/lime green & deep amber & molded in medium- and low-relief w/branches laden w/ripening apples, signed in cameo (ILLUS.) **9,775**

Cameo vase, 11 5/8" h., simple ovoid body tapering to a short neck w/a flattened rim, shaded light to dark golden yellow overlaid w/deep rose & maroon & cut w/branches of fuchsia dropping from the rim, signed, ca. 1925 .... **8,625**

Cameo vase, 13" h., footed slender flattened ovoid body tapering to a small flared rim, pink shading to white & overlaid in dark blue, cut w/a landscape of tall trees in the foreground & a fence & shorter trees near a river in the distance... **2,990**

Cameo vase, 13" h., footed tall slender ovoid body tapering to a flattened flared cylindrical neck, amber & frosted clear layered in light green & olive green & etched as leafy Japanese maple branches, signed near base **920**

Cameo vase, 13 5/8" h., slender ovoid body w/a spreading round foot, grey overlaid w/white & caramel, cut w/flowering blossoms on long stems, incised on bottom "Galle deposé" w/leaf, "EG" & a cross of Lorraine, partial original paper label, ca. 1900 .... **2,300**

Cameo vase, 13 3/4" h., footed low flared disk base tapering to a tall slender cylindrical body w/a flared rim, grey shaded w/bands of lemon yellow, overlaid in purple & brown & cut w/a mountainous landscape w/pine trees, signed in cameo, ca. 1900 .... **5,175**

Cameo vase, 14" h., slender ovoid body tapering to a short trumpet neck, grey shaded lemon yellow overlaid in red, amber & green & cut w/hibiscus blossoms & leafage, signed in cameo, ca. 1900 .... **11,500**

Gallé Cameo Vase with Clematis

Cameo vase, 14 1/4" h., footed large spherical body w/a short cylindrical neck, grey opalescent mottled w/lemon yellow & overlaid in blue & purple, cut w/clematis blossoms, buds & trailing foliage, signed in cameo (ILLUS.) **12,650**

Cameo vase, 14 1/2" h., wide squatty bulbous body w/angled low shoulder tapering sharply up to the short flared & flattened neck, mottled golden yellow & orange overlaid in dark reddish orange &

maroon & cameo cut around the sides w/large swirled calla lily blossoms & leafage, signed, ca. 1925 .... **74,000**

Gallé Cameo Vase with Branches

Cameo vase, 15" h., flat-bottomed ovoid form tapering to a slender trumpet neck w/lobed rim, pink shading to white, overlaid in yellow & green & cut w/leafy branches, signed (ILLUS.) **1,840**

Cameo vase, 15" h., yellow ground overlaid & mold-blown in very dark green, cut w/large stylized palm trees & molded w/a parade of walking elephants around the middle, signed in cameo, ca. 1925 .... **57,500**

Two Tall Gallé Cameo Vases

Cameo vase, 15 1/2" h., elongated & flared neck on an ovoid body, pale transparent smoky amber layered in opaque pink & etched w/hanging vines of wisteria over clouds, signed among the clouds, large polished pontil (ILLUS. right) **1,380**

Cameo vase, 15 5/8" h., tall footed ovoid form w/the shoulder tapering to a short cylindrical neck, golden yellow overlaid in dark green, cameo cut w/dark green leafy branches w/mold-blown pale blue plums, signed, ca. 1900 .... **6,900**

Cameo vase, 15 3/4" h., footed tall flaring cylindrical form w/a tapering shoulder to the cylindrical neck, yellow ground overlaid w/deep purple & 'blown-out' clusters of pendent plums & cut leafy vines, signed in cameo, ca. 1925 .... **16,100**

Cameo vase, 17 3/4" h., flaring cushion foot below the tall slender slightly tapering cylindrical body w/a flared rim, grey infused w/palest pink, overlaid in lime green & cut w/thistle blossoms & leafage, signed in cameo w/name & a star, post-1904 .... **2,070**

Cameo vase, 19 3/4" h., baluster-form, thick waisted foot below the slender ovoid body tapering to a tall slender neck w/flared rim, opalescent grey infused w/pale pink, overlaid in white, lavender & moss green & cut w/hydrangea blossoms & leafage, signed in cameo, ca. 1900.................................... **4,600**

Cameo vase, 19 7/8" h., footed slender ovoid body tapering to a flat trumpet neck, yellow overlaid w/maroon & cameo cut w/trumpet vine & blossoms pendent from the upper rim, signed, ca. 1900 .... **11,500**

Cameo vase, 20 1/8" h., tall ovoid body w/angled shoulder centered by a short widely flaring trumpet neck, mottled golden yellow & orange overlaid w/blue & dark greenish brown, cameo cut w/upright clusters of blue trumpet-form blossoms on leafy branches, signed, ca. 1900 .... **10,925**

Gallé Scenic Cameo Vase

Cameo vase, 21" h., tall slender baluster form, grey opalescent overlaid w/lime green & deep umber, cut w/a verdant spring landscape w/leafy trees & waving grasses surrounding a tranquil pond, signed in intaglio, ca. 1900 (ILLUS.) **7,475**

Cameo vase, 23 1/2" h., cylindrical w/swollen base, grey & rose layered in chartreuse & leaf greens, etched w/leafy branches & suspended chains of florettes, cameo-signed w/a star, ca. 1904 (ILLUS. left) **2,070**

Cameo vase, 24 3/4" h., tall baluster-form body w/short trumpet neck, mottled golden yellow overlaid w/dark green & blue, cameo cut w/large pendent clusters of blue wisteria & leafy branches, signed, ca. 1900 .... **28,750**

Cameo veilleuse (night light), footed squatty bulbous form w/a short neck supporting a metal umbrella-form cover cast w/ferns & a berry finial, the body in grey overlaid w/russet & cut w/ferns, signed in cameo, ca. 1900, 4" h. **2,415**

Finely Decorated Gallé Center Bowl

Center bowl, wide shallow form w/tri-lobed upturned & incurved sides, decorated w/internal decorations, applied, enameled & wheel-carved designs on the clear frosted & mottled amber ground, decorated w/slender leafy stems w/large rounded blossoms, signed in enamel "Emile Gallé - fecit," ca.1900, 9 3/4" w., 3 1/4" h. (ILLUS.)..................................... **5,750**

Rare Small Gallé Flacon

Flacon, cov., footed ovoid body tapering to a short cylindrical neck w/low-domed fitted cap, optic-ribbed, the neck in deep lavender shading to pale amethyst & deep amethyst at the base, applied shell-form appliques on the shoulder, the body enameled w/stylized stems, leaves & blossoms in light brown & green, enameled in intaglio "E. Gallé - déposé," 5 1/4" h. (ILLUS.)..................................... **5,750**

Scent bottle w/stopper, footed ovoid form w/a tiny cylindrical neck w/mushroom stopper, pale lavender w/each side applied w/oval bosses, one showing a landscape, the body cut w/leaves & berries enameled in shades of yellow, ochre, pale blue & orange, the whole trimmed w/gilt, signed in gilt cameo, w/original retailer's paper label, ca. 1880, 6 1/4" h. **6,900**

Tazza, a trefoil dish in amber applied & enameled w/pink & green thistles, the underside acid-etched w/leaves, on a pedestal silver foot chased w/thistles, signed in enamel "Cristallerie - d'Emile Gallé - à Nancy," ca. 1900, 5 1/8" d. **1,380**

Vase, 6 1/8" h., Islamic-style, round foot below the squatty bulbous tapering body below the tall conical neck, clear ground ornately enameled around the neck w/gilt florets enclosing different animals & around the body w/gilt horses & riders, a finely enameled background of arabesques & scrolling lines in black & gold, signed, ca. 1890 .... **16,100**

Rare Gallé Exposition Vase

Vase, 6 1/2" h., classic wide baluster-form, clear swirled w/dark blue & golden amber internally decorated, faceted & enameled on the exterior w/a large exotic bird & Oriental-style white & gold blossoms around the sides, designed for the Exposition Universelle, Paris, 1889, signed in gilt intaglio "Emile Gallé - Nancy - Paris Exposition 1889" (ILLUS.)... **48,875**

Vase, 8 1/2" h., barrel-form in transparent topaz etched & enameled as grains of barley in naturalistic colors, signed near base, ca. 1890 (some enamel wear)............ **863**

Vase, 13 3/8" h., thick wide disk foot below the gently tapering tall cylindrical body, grey shaded pale aubergine & cut w/squash, blossoms & leaves & enameled in shades of grass & lime green, mustard yellow, cream, rust & pink, the whole trimmed w/gilt, signed in enameled cameo, ca. 1900 (signature worn)..... **5,175**

HANDEL

Lamps, shades and other types of glass by Handel & Co., which subsequently became The Handel Co., Inc., were produced in Meriden, Connecticut, from 1893 to 1941.

Handel Mark

Ashtray, circular shallow glass base decorated w/h.p. owl perched on a branch, a metal collar w/applied foliate cigarette rests, base marked in black "Handelware," early 20th c., 4 3/4" d. (metal corrosion) **$173**

Opalware Pug Dog Tray

Tray, metal-mounted opalware glass dish handpainted w/red collared pug dog, signed by artist "Bauer," mounted on base, "4091/S" w/partial Handel Ware shield mark, 4 3/4" h. (ILLUS.) **633**

Vase, 8" h., Teroma, slightly swelled cylindrical form w/a waisted short flaring neck, exterior "chipped ice" finish, reverse-painted w/a continuous mountainous landscape w/a pair of birch trees by a lake, natural shades of green, blue, yellow & purple, signed "Broggi," marked on base "Teroma Handel 4210," ca. 1925 .... **920**

HOBBS, BROCKUNIER & CO.

The Hobbs Company originated about 1845 in Wheeling, West Virginia with the founding of Hobbs, Barnes & Co. by John L. Hobbs and James B. Barnes, both former employees of the New England Glass Company. Their sons eventually joined the firm and in 1863 the company became Hobbs, Brockunier & Co. when John L. and John H. Hobbs and Charles Brockunier took over. That year they hired William Leighton, Sr., former superintendent of the New England Glass Company. Leighton took charge of production and in 1864 he revolutionized the American glass industry by devising a formula for soda lime glass, a cheaper method of producing clear glass which didn't require lead oxide. By the 1880s Hobbs was producing a number of decorative glassware lines including Peach Blow, Spangled, pressed Amberina and various opalescent patterns. The plant closed in the 1890s. Also see OPALESCENT GLASS.

Relish tray, Crystallina patt., frosted clear w/amber trim **$60**

Sugar shaker, w/original top, Polka Dot No. 398, cranberry **325**

Syrup pitcher w/original metal lid, Leaf & Flower patt., amber-stained **275**

HOLLY AMBER

Holly Amber, originally marketed under the name "Golden Agate," was produced for only a few months in 1903 by the Indiana Tumbler and Goblet Company of Greentown, Indiana. When this factory burned in June 1903 all production of this ware ceased, making it very rare today. The same "Holly" pressed pattern was also produced in clear glass by the Greentown factory. Collectors should note that the St. Clair Glass Company has reproduced some Holly Amber pieces.

Bowl, 7 1/4" d., low sides **$495**
Plate, 7 3/4" d. **578**
Relish dish, oval, 7 1/2" l. **440**

HONESDALE

The Honesdale Decorating Company, Honesdale, Pennsylvania, was originally founded to decorate glass for the C. Dorflinger & Sons firm. Purchased in 1918 by C.F. Prosch, the firm then bought other glass blanks which they etched and decorated. The factory closed in 1932.

Rare Honesdale Cameo Vase

Cameo vase, 6 1/2" h., broad ovoid body tapering to a short, thick flared neck, crystal overlaid w/deep amber & yellow & cameo cut w/vining flowers & leaves w/gold trim, signed (ILLUS.) **$900-1,200**
Cameo vase, 9 3/4" h., tall waisted body w/a bulbous shoulder below the widely flaring rim, clear layered in chartreuse & orange, cameo-etched as leafy chrysanthemums on a textured ground, gilt enamel highlights, polished pontil signed in gold (gilt wear, nick on base) **489**
Vase, 10" h., flared crystal cylinder w/gold amber etched foliate design enhanced by gold accents, "Honesdale" base mark **403**

IMPERIAL

MISCELLANEOUS PATTERNS & LINES

Bowl-vase, Free-Hand ware, a wide waisted cylindrical body w/a widely flaring six-ruffle rim, marigold iridescent exterior decorated w/light blue vines & heart-shaped leaves, blue rim band, marigold iridescent interior, original Imperial Free-Hand label, 7 1/4" d., 5" h. **$1,320**
Vase, 6 1/2" h., Free-Hand ware, wide ovoid body w/a short trumpet neck, overall marigold iridescence on interior & exterior **138**
Vase, 7 1/2" h., Free-Hand ware, bulbous ovoid body tapering to a widely flaring trumpet neck, white opal ground decorated w/wide dark blue swagged bands, orange iridescent interior **935**
Vase, 8 3/4" h., Free-Hand ware, tall slender cylindrical form w/a slightly flared base & rim, white opal exterior decorated w/looped green heart & vine decoration, gold iridescent interior **495**
Vase, 10 3/4" h., Free-Hand ware, tall slender baluster-form w/cushion foot & short flared neck, cobalt blue ground decorated w/overall light blue looping vines & large opal white heart-shaped leaves **1,595**
Vase, 11 1/2" h., Free-Hand ware, a tall slender baluster-form body w/a bulbed neck flared at the top & pulled into three downward curled loops attaching to the upper neck, iridescent opal surface decorated overall w/light blue entwining vines & heart-shaped leaves, iridescent marigold interior **1,595**

JACK-IN-THE-PULPIT VASES

Glass vases in varying sizes and resembling in appearance the flower of this name have been popular with collectors since the 19th century. They were produced in various solid colors and in shaded wares.

Black Amethyst Vase

Black amethyst, widely flaring oversized top w/shallow opening, raised on a slender baluster-form stem on a round foot, 6" h. (ILLUS.) **$40**

Blue Opalescent Jack-in-the-Pulpit

Blue opalescent, round blue foot below slender body & widely flaring opalescent rim, probably English, ca. 1880, 7" h. (ILLUS.).. **65-75**

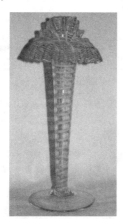

Stevens & Williams "Gingham" Vase

Blue, white & clear, swirled stripes of blue & white in clear, Gingham patt., attributed to Stevens & Williams, England, 12" h. (ILLUS.)... **250**

Cased Deep Rose Jack-in-the-Pulpit

Cased, deep rose pink interior w/an applied clear crimped rim & a small enameled floral cluster, the white exterior enameled w/delicate blue & gold blossoms, cushion foot, 5 1/2" d., 7 1/2" h. (ILLUS.)..... **175**

Cased Jack-in-the-Pulpit Vase

Cased, satin white exterior, yellow interior, spherical body w/a short neck to the widely flaring & scalloped rim, 19th c., 7" h. (ILLUS.)... **50-75**

Cranberry Shaded Jack-in-the-Pulpit

Cranberry shaded to pink, squatty bulbous base below the tall cylindrical body w/a crimped & ruffled rim, applied clear rim, 4 1/2" d., 7 3/4" h. (ILLUS.) **165**

Cranberry shaded to pink, the squatty bulbous base in pink centered by a wide tall cylindrical neck shading to deep cranberry scattered w/bits of goldstone, flaring rolled & ruffled rim w/applied clear edge band & upturned back, 4 1/2" d., 7 3/4" h. **165**

Green, cushion foot w/a slender flaring body below the wide rolled rim, satiny ground decorated w/bold gold flowers &

leaves trimmed w/white, Bohemia, ca. 1900, 9" h. (ILLUS. below) 150

Green Decorated Jack-in-the-Pulpit

Westmoreland Jack-in-the-Pulpits

Green satin, hexagonal foot below the plain flaring sides & wide gently scalloped rim, original Westmoreland Glass Company sticker on the foot, 7" h. (ILLUS. left) **25-50**

Iridescent Jack-in-the-Pulpit

Iridescent, squatty bulbous base tapering to a cylindrical body w/wide rolled rim,

purple & green streaked iridescent highlights w/stretched effect at rim, Glasform, Blackpool, England, designed by John Ditchfield, modern, 9" h. (ILLUS.) **175-200**

Maroon & Opalescent Vase

Maroon shading to white opalescent, widely flaring rolled & crimped top w/Hobnail design & back pulled into a point, tapering squatty bulbous body w/overall tiny Diamond Quilted patt. (ILLUS.) **110**
Pigeon blood, hexagonal foot below the plain flaring sides & wide gently scalloped rim, Westmoreland Glass Company, 7" h. (ILLUS. right) **25-50**

Fenton White Jack-in-the-Pulpit

White opaque, flared base tapering to a tall slender waisted body below the widely flaring & ruffled rim, marked w/Fenton logo, post-1970, 15" h. (ILLUS.) **25-50**

KELVA

Kelva was made early in the 20th century by the C.F. Monroe Co., Meriden, Connecticut, and was a type of decorated opal glass very like the same company's Wave Crest and Nakara wares. This type of glass was produced until about the time of the first World War. Also see NAKARA and WAVE CREST.

Box, cov., Crown mold, decorated w/blue, grey & white flowers on pinkish rose ground, 6 1/4" d., 4 1/4" h. **$1,225**

Fine Blue Kelva Box

Box w/hinged cover, round mold, bright blue ground w/pink daisies, 6" d. (ILLUS.) 850

Box w/hinged lid, pink flowers on blue ground, 6" d., 3 1/2" h. 775

Kelva Hexagonal Box

Box w/hinged lid, Hexagonal mold, lid decorated w/a molded yellow rose on a mottled green ground, 3 3/4" d., 2 1/2" h. (ILLUS.)... 750

Box w/hinged lid, Octagonal mold, lid enameled w/pink & white flowers on a mottled green ground, 4" w., 3 3/4" h. 350

Box w/hinged lid, round, lid decorated w/pink flowers on a mottled bluish grey ground, mirror inside the lid, 4 1/2" d. 750

Kelva Rose Ground Box

Box w/hinged lid, round, lid decorated w/white flowers & green leaves on a mottled rose ground, 4 1/2" d., 2 1/2" h. (ILLUS.)... 550

Box w/hinged lid, heavy gold floral decoration on a dark green ground, 5 1/2" d., 5" h.. 475

Box w/hinged lid, round, bluish grey flowers on a red ground, 6" d., 3 1/2" h. 750

Dish, open-handled, green ground, 6" h. 575

Dresser box w/hinged cover, round, the cover & base decorated w/pink floral bouquets on a mottled slate grey ground, marked, 6" d., 3" h. 770

Fernery, oblong, decorated in dark green w/pink florals, original metal liner, signed, 6 1/2 x 7 1/2"..................................... 440

Humidor w/hinged cover, mottled blue ground, "Cigars" in gold across the front, 5" d.. 900

Jewelry dish, dainty pink flowers on a mottled green ground, ornate ormolu handles & rim, signed, overall 4 1/2" w. 200

Planter w/original liner, embossed borders, green ground w/large pink flowers around body, 8 1/2" l. 875

Vase, 7 3/4" h., short cylindrical neck on swelled cylindrical body w/white & pink flowers w/brown stems & green leaves on a bluish ground, beige beaded pastel ribbon around lower russet-colored base set on a round four-footed gilt-metal base 725

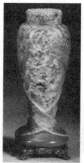

Lovely Kelva Vase on Base

Vase, 8 1/2" h., slender baluster-form body raised on an ornate scroll-cast silver plate foot, the body w/a mottled blue background of pink blossoms & gold scrolls, marked "Kelva Trade - Mark" (ILLUS.)... 650

Vase, 11" h., tall ovoid body tapering slightly to a wide flat mouth w/a silver plate rim band, raised on a silver plate three-footed holder, a dark green mottled ground decorated w/soft pink roses, red 1904 mark 1,750

Vase, 13 1/2" h., footed, green mottled ground w/pink flowers 795

Watch box, cov., green mottled ground w/dusty rose floral & beige ribbon, heavy beading on cover, ornate ormolu fittings (one bead missing)..................................... 600

KEW BLAS

In the 1890s the Union Glass Works, Somerville, Massachusetts, produced a line of iridescent glasswares closely resembling Louis Tiffany's wares. The name was derived from an anagram of the name of the factory's manager, William S. Blake.

Candlestick, cylindrical socket w/flattened wide rim raised on a swirled baluster-form shaft on a round foot, overall gold iridescence, inscribed mark, 8 1/4" h. (ILLUS. top next page) $450

Compote, open, 4 1/2" d., 3 1/2" h., wide round domed foot below a short baluster-form stem supporting a wide squatty bulbous bowl w/a widely flaring rim, overall gold iridescence, signed "Kew Blas" on base 550

Kew Blas Candlestick

Console set: compote & pair of candlesticks; Alexandrite wide shallow bowl on compote on matching stem, matching baluster-form candlesticks w/tall candle sockets, each piece on a clear "bubble" base knob on an Alexandrite foot, the heat reactive glass in red shaded to blue w/'chocolate' shading, experimental color, compote 6 3/4" h., candlesticks 10" h., the set 1,265

Cordial, inverted pear-shaped bowl w/a widely flaring rim, raised on a slender swelled stem & round foot, overall reddish gold iridescence, signed, 5" h. 358

Finger bowl, rounded ribbed form, overall bright gold iridescence, signed 220

Goblet, overall gold iridescence, 7 1/2" h........ 165

Pitcher, 3" h., squatty bulbous base w/short wide cylindrical neck & wide arched spout, applied gold lustre handle, the gold lustre body w/an overall pulled green lustre decoration, signed "Kew Blas" on polished pontil 575

Rose bowl, spherical form w/a closed lightly scalloped rim, cased, the exterior in green w/vertical "zipper" stripes alternating w/orange stripes, orange iridescent interior, base inscribed "Kew Blas," 4" h. 750

Tumbler, cylindrical pinch-sided form, overall gold iridescence, 3 1/4" h. 303

Tumbler, swelled cylindrical body w/flaring rim & large dimples around the sides, overall gold iridescence, signed, 3" h. 375

Vase, 3 1/4" h., miniature, white body w/gold iridescent floral roping from top to bottom, gold iridescent interior 990

Vase, 4 1/4" h., 5 1/4" d., simple flared ribbed trumpet form in amber w/pulled emerald green internal decoration, engraved mark on base 805

Vase, 7" h., elongated ovoid w/flaring rim, gold iridescent & green diagonally striped large fishscale design, engraved mark 900

Vase, 7" h., simple ovoid body tapering to a short cylindrical neck, cased ambergris w/gold iridescent pulled feather design on an opal ground, folded gold iridescent rim, signed "Kew-Blas" on base (ILLUS. top next column)...................................... 1,100

Fine Kew Blas Vase

Vase, 8" h., 3 3/4" d., elongated double gourd-form w/a tiny cylindrical neck, iridescent gold ground decorated w/dark gold pulled feather decoration, signed 990

Vase, 9" h., waisted cylindrical body w/scalloped rim, overall gold iridescence w/carved bees 950

Vase, 10" h., cylindrical w/flared base, rim w/alternating peaks & lower scallops, iridescent gold body w/repeating green pulled leaf decoration, inscribed mark......... 750

Vase, 10" h., tooled spiked top rim on flared amber cylinder w/green pulled feather decoration & iridescent lustre overall, "Kew Blas" inscribed on base....................... 518

Vase, 10" h., waisted tall form w/a four-petal top, caramel color w/green iridescent swirled stems from top to bottom, signed.. 660

Vase, 12" h., lightly fluted trumpet form raised on a bulbed applied disk foot, amber w/strong exterior gold iridescence, interior w/stretched gold iridescence, polished pontil signed "Kew Blas"..... 863

KIMBLE

Evan K. Kimble took over the Vineland Flint Glass Works, Vineland, New Jersey in 1931, after the death of Victor Durand, Jr. Most art glass production ceased except for a line of Cluthra-style wares featuring various colors and embedded air bubbles.

Vase, 8 1/2" h., Cluthra, tall slender ovoid body w/a swelled shoulder tapering to a short flaring neck, mottled & swirled bittersweet orange & opalescent white on a clear round foot, No. 2011-8 .... $330

Vase, 8 1/2" h., footed slender ovoid form tapering to a short flared neck, overall Cluthra design w/swirled deep orange & opal, on a clear foot, signed "2011 - 18k - Dec 7" 303

Vase, 12" h., 5 1/2" d., cylindrical, Cluthra, mottled orange & yellowish brown, No. 1998-13 688

Vase, 14 1/4" h., Cluthra, spherical body centered by a tall slightly flaring cylindrical neck, mottled opal white, yellow & tangerine, marked "#20167-14 - Dec. 31" 550

Vase, 15" h., Cluthra, a bulbous ovoid body tapering to a very tall trumpet neck, reddish orange mixed in white & colorless & raised on a thick disk foot, signed "K Dec. 7 - 20169 - 15" 230

Vase, 16" h., Cluthra, tall form w/bulbed body, mottled tans & streaks of olive green w/a sponged design on the bulbous portion, marked "14-16 Dec. 49" **248**

Vases, 4" h., Cluthra, bulbous nearly spherical body w/a small flat mouth, cased clear w/light blue powder & internal bubble decoration, polished pontils, one inscribed & silver-enameled "K 1995-4 Dee-8," the other "Dee 8," pr........... **230**

Vases, 11 3/4" h., Cluthra, footed tall slender ovoid body w/a rounded shoulder tapering to a short wide flaring rim, mottled tangerine, mocha brown & opal on a clear foot, marked, pr. **660**

KOSTA

The Kosta Glassworks were founded in the Smaland region of Sweden in 1742 and have grown over the past two centuries to become one of that country's leading makers of fine glassware. Originally their products were utilitarian but by the 19th century they were producing decorative and tablewares. In the 20th century they produced fine crystal wares in modern designs by noted glass artists. In 1970 they merged with several other Swedish glasshouses and continue to produce high quality cut glass and tableware.

Bowl, 5 3/8" d., swirled glass-type, colorless half-round internally decorated by opaque white horizontal threading, base inscribed "LH 1004," stamped "Kosta/Lind/Strand" **$230**

Paperweight, mushroom-shaped crystal w/bubbled core, bluish green looping inclusions in base, by Ann or Goran Warff, base signed "Kosta 97070 Warff," 5 1/2" h. **259**

Paperweight, mushroom-type, colorless cap revealing internal bubbles above amber-colored stem, base inscribed "Kosta 97323/Warff," designed by Ann Warff, 3 3/4" h. **288**

Sculpture, aquamarine glass iceberg w/etched elk at center, base edge inscribed "Kosta V. Lindstrand W.L. 90002," 6" h. **201**

Tray, square, clear decorated below w/various symbols centered by a stylized blue face in the square foot, highlighted w/a metal figure of a man & applied red glass arc, base inscribed "Kosta Boda B. Vallien 79365," ca. 1965, 8 1/2" sq. **201**

Vase, 6 3/4" h., Trad I-type, heavy walled flattened colorless oval internally decorated by dark tree forms w/multicolored leaves around base & falling above, labeled at side & inscribed "Kosta 41753 Lindstrand," designed by Vicke Lindstrand **1,265**

Vase, 5 1/2" h., heavy thick-walled flattened ovoid form, colorless internally decorated w/delicate aubergine spiral lines, base signed "Kosta LH 1384," attributed to Vicke Lindstrand, ca. 1955 (annealing flaw within base)........................ **460**

Vase, 7" h., "Trad I Autumn," thick-walled simple ovoid body w/flat rim in colorless crystal internally decorated w/stylized blackish brown trees w/multicolored

leaves falling & below in yellow, red & orange, designed by Vicke Lindstrand, signed on the base "Kosta LU 2011" (shallow scratch on side)........................... **2,645**

Vase, 7 1/8" h., crystal thick cylinder internally decorated by teal blue amorphous element enhanced by cut & polished surface ovals, designed by Vicke Lindstrand, signed "Kosta 46693 V. Lindstrand" **518**

Engraved Kosta Vase

Vase, 12 1/4" h., tall trumpet-form on a small base, colorless body engraved w/stylized trees w/occasional small birds among the polished leaves, designed by Vicke Lindstrand, engraved on base "Kosta LG2268" (ILLUS.) **1,093**

Vase, 13" h., slender double-gourd form, tall swelled & waisted form w/a sheared angled mouth, clear w/slender internal canes of alternating white & black, designed by V. Lindstrand, engraved "Kosta LH 1258," ca. 1950s (scratches)....... **330**

LALIQUE

Fine glass, which includes numerous extraordinary molded articles, has been made by the glasshouse established by René Lalique early in the 20th century in France. The firm was carried on by his son, Marc, until his death in 1977 and is now headed by Marc's daughter, Marie-Claude. All Lalique glass is marked, usually on, or near, the bottom with either an engraved or molded signature. Unless otherwise noted, we list only those pieces marked "R. Lalique" produced before the death of René Lalique in 1945.

R. Lalique France N=3152

R L A L I Q U E   **R.LALIQUE**

FRANCE   **FRANCE**

Lalique Marks

Ashtray, "Dindon," circular dish centering a molded turkey, smoky brown, inscribed "R. Lalique - France - No. 287," ca. 1925, 3" h. **$690**

Ashtray, "Faune," a shallow round clear dish centered by a vertical round clear & frosted disk molded w/a dancing satyr, grey stain, introduced in 1931, 4 1/8" d., 3 3/4" h. **1,035**

Ashtray, "Sirènes," a clear & frosted round dish w/raised sides & a wide central knob molded at the top w/two intertwined female figures, blue stain, introduced in 1920, 4 1/2" d. **863**

Bowl, 8" d., "Ondes," round opalescent form w/deep sides molded in low-relief w/diminishing elliptical disks, introduced in 1935 .... **488**

Bowl, 9 3/8" d., "Poissons No. 1," deep rounded sides w/wide flat rim, clear opalescent w/molded spiral design of stylized slender fish, introduced in 1921 .... **1,035**

Lalique Perruches Bowl

Bowl, 9 3/4" d., "Perruches," round w/upright gently curved sides, clear & frosted opalescent molded w/a band of large parakeets, green stain, introduced in 1931 (ILLUS.) **3,220**

Bowl, 10" d., "Bulbes," a wide shallow round form in opalescent molded w/a central flower & radiating bulb design, extended flared rim, stamped "R. Lalique" **575**

Box, cov., "Enfants," cylindrical base in grey molded in relief w/a continuous band of infants supporting tiers of roses on the domed cover, coral patina, acid-stamped "R. LALIQUE - FRANCE," introduced in 1931, 3 1/4" h. **1,265**

Box, cov., "Figurines et Voiles," cylindrical w/flat molded cover, clear & frosted molded on top & base w/bands of diaphanously clad maidens, blue stain, introduced 1929, 4 1/4" d., 2 5/8" h. **2,070**

Box, cov., "Georgette," round shallow form in opalescent w/the interior of the cover molded in relief w/three dragonflies & molded "R. LALIQUE" & acid-etched "France No. 51," the base acid-stamped "R. LALIQUE - FRANCE," ca. 1922, 8 1/8" d. (two tiny rim chips on cover) **1,265**

Candy Box with Molded Roses

Candy box, cov., "Roses en Relief," low wide oblong base w/a wide low domed cover, frosted pink patina, molded across the cover & down the sides w/bands of molded rose blossoms & vines, base molded "Lalique," introduced in 1914, 7" l., 1 3/4" h. (ILLUS.) **13,800**

Carafe w/original stopper, "Sainte-Odile," No. P.736, rectilinear body w/chamfered edges, ring-molded neck, raspberry-form stopper & decorated w/molded profile medallion of Ste. Odile, traces of sepia patina, introduced in 1927, "R. LALIQUE" molded under medallion, bottom molded "CLOS STE. ODILE - OBERNAI - PIERRE WEISSEN-BURGER," 7 1/2" h. (ILLUS. below) **805**

Lalique "Sainte-Odile" Carafe

Champagne glasses, "Strasbourg," clear & frosted, each stem molded w/two male grape pressers, introduced in 1926, set of 6 .... **1,035**

Clock, desk-type, "Papillons," large round frosted disk molded around the face in low-relief w/overlapping butterflies, upright on a round disk foot, the Arabic numerals enameled in black, pale blue patina, acid-stamped "R. LALIQUE - FRANCE," introduced in 1931, 9 1/8" h. ... **6,325**

Lalique "Hirondelles" Clock

Clock, "Hirondelles," No. 761, flattened rectangular case molded w/five swallows w/blue enamel trim, on a molded foot, clock dial at the center, introduced in 1920, molded "R. LALIQUE" & inscribed "R. Lalique - France," 5 7/8" h. (ILLUS.).... **2,875**

Lalique "Inséparables" Clock

Clock, "Inséparables," No. 765, square grey & frosted glass molded in medium-relief w/two pairs of love birds perched on flowering branches flanking the circular clock face, introduced in 1926, molded "R. LALIQUE" & inscribed "Lalique France," 4 3/8" h. (ILLUS.) **1,725**

Clock, "Quatre Perruches," table model, thin upright rectangular plaque on a narrow molded foot, frosted grey molded in low-relief w/perching birds below leafy branches, a round clock in the center, glass molded "R. LALIQUE," introduced in 1920, 5 3/4" h. **1,380**

Clock, table model, "Deux Figurines," an upright rounded flat colorless sheet etched w/two classical maidens wrapping a wreath of flowers around the central round clock dial, raised in a flaring rectangular metal base w/gilt leafy scroll design & raised on small knob feet, the base lighted, ca. 1926, 13 1/2" l., 13 1/2" h. (slight wear & abrasions to base).......... **6,900**

Clock, table model, "Quatre Moineaux du Japon," square flattened frosted clear base w/a round central dial surrounded by four molded plump birds amid dogwood blossoms, wheel-cut "R.Lalique France," the clock dial signed "ATO" & engraved "Made in France," together w/a rectangular metal stand, introduced in 1928, 7 1/4" h. **2,300**

Cruet set: flaring cylindrical pair of bottles w/tall stoppers all fitted in an oval holder; "Bourgueil," clear, the lower half molded w/tiered bands of triangles, introduced in 1933, 5 1/2" h., the set **230**

Decanter w/stopper, "Nippon" patt., clear footed tall flaring cylindrical form w/a tapering shoulder to a small flaring neck, graduated bands of beads around the base of the body & on the acorn-form stopper, introduced in 1930, 9 3/4" h. **809**

Decanter w/stopper, "Reine Marguerite," large rounded base w/two flattened sides molded as large flowerheads, tapering plain neck fitted w/a wide low domed stopper, clear & frosted w/brown enamel detail & stain, 10 3/4" h................. **2,300**

"L'Air du Temps" Display Bottle

Display bottle w/stopper, "L'Air du Temps," ovoid spiral-ribbed clear bottle supporting a stopper w/a pair of large flying doves in frosted clear w/polished highlights, model created in 1947, overall 12 1/4" h. (ILLUS.)................................. **403**

Figure group, two dancing female nudes in frosted clear standing close together on a textured clear round base, inscribed "Lalique France," 10" h................................ **546**

Figure of a woman, "Thais," opalescent form of a nude female shown dancing & holding up a large diaphanous drapery, inscribed "R. Lalique - France," introduced in 1925, 8 1/4" h. (right hand recarved) **5,175**

Hood ornament, "Libellule," grey molded full-relief stylized dragonfly, mounted on a chrome radiator cap, glass molded "LALIQUE," & inscribed "R. Lalique," mount cast "The Stant Mfg. Co. Connersville, Ind.," introduced in 1928, 9" h. (chip to tail)... **4,600**

Hood ornament, "Longchamps," frosted clear model in full-relief of a horse head, molded "R. Lalique," introduced in 1929, 5" h. (polished chip on one ear) **2,530**

Hood ornament, "Victoire," frosted smokey grey molded in full-relief w/the head of a female w/stylized pointed-back windblown hair, molded "R. LALIQUE - FRANCE," introduced in 1928, 10" l......... **8,050**

Lalique Hood Ornament

Hood ornament, "Cinq Chevaux," No. 1122, grey glass molded in high-relief w/five rearing steeds, set within a chromed-metal mount, introduced in 1925, molded "R. LALIQUE," 5 1/8" h. (ILLUS.) **9,200**

Luminaire, "Gros Poisson," grey glass full-relief model of a freshwater fish, resting on a cast bronze round base pierce-cast w/seaweed, glass molded "R. Lalique," base inscribed "R.Lalique," introduced in 1922, 17" w., overall 15 1/8" h................... **6,900**

Luminaire, "Groupe de six moineaux," rectangular nickled-metal light box base supporting a clear frosted row of small birds in various positions, introduced in 1933, acid-stamped "R. Lalique - France," 11 3/4" l., 2 pcs. **10,925**

Lalique Model of a Cat

Model of a cat, "Chat Assis," No. 1208, molded clear & frosted seated cat, introduced in 1932, inscribed "Lalique - France," 8 1/8" h. (ILLUS.) **1,725**

Oil lamp, "Artichaut," small bulbous body in grey molded in full-relief w/bands of artichoke leaves, pierced conical metal cap, molded "R. LALIQUE - LAMP HYGIENIQUE BERGER - MADE IN FRANCE," introduced in 1927, 3 1/2" h. **1,380**

Lalique Rooster Paperweight

Paperweight, "Coq Nain," No. 1135, molded clear chicken, head lowered & tall tail raised, square base, introduced in 1928, molded "R. LALIQUE - FRANCE," inconspicuous chip to tail, 7 3/4" h. (ILLUS.) **1,380**

Pendant, "Guepes," oval green disk molded w/rows of wasps & two apertures for hanging cord & tassel, inscribed "Lalique," hung w/a green silk tassel, introduced in 1920, 2 1/4" l. **1,035**

Perfume bottle & stopper, "Au Coeur des Calices," for Coty, tapering domical frosted pale blue base molded w/tiered flower petals, the small molded mouth fitted w/a figural bee stopper, signed "Lalique," 2 5/8" h. **5,175**

Perfume bottle & stopper, "Bouchon Figurines," upright flattened square bottle in grey & frosted, centered w/an oval reserve w/two back-to-back nude figures holding up & separated by flowering branches, the small cylindrical neck fitted w/an openwork stopper cast as two nude females leaning back & holding up

floral garlands, signed "R. Lalique - No. 490," introduced in 1912, 5 1/4" h. **8,050**

Perfume flacon w/stopper, slightly swelled tall cylindrical shouldered form w/short neck & flattened rim, knobbed stopper, frosted w/a design of overall overlapping leaves, blue patina, inscribed "R. Lalique France 478," 1 3/4" d., 4 1/4" h. **1,035**

Lalique Perfume Flacon

Perfume flacon w/stopper, "Bouchon Fleurs de Pommier," clear barrel-shaped body w/green patina in scalloped ridges, molded tiara stopper w/matching patina on blossom motif, base inscribed "R. Lalique France No. 493," 5 1/2" h. (ILLUS.) **10,063**

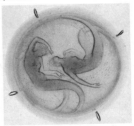

Rare Lalique Plafonnier

Plafonnier, "Deux Sirenes," round shaded reddish amber molded w/two large swirling sirens, molded "R. Lalique," introduced in 1921, 15 1/2" d. (ILLUS.) **24,150**

Plate, 11" d., "Ondines," round opalescent form molded in medium-relief w/floating female nudes, inscribed "R. LALIQUE - FRANCE," introduced in 1929.................. **1,725**

Platter, 14 1/2" d., "Pivoines," round & slightly dished grey form molded w/a large swirled branch of stylized rounded peony-like blossoms & slender leaves all enameled in dark blue, signed in intaglio "R. Lalique," introduced in 1920 (minor rim chip) **9,200**

Platter, 14 3/4" d., "Deux Pigeons," flat round clear disk enameled in black w/two large pigeons perched among curved branches of tiny blossoms, signed, ca. 1920 (ILLUS. top next page)... **4,887**

Lalique Two Pigeons Platter

Powder box, cov., round, the flattened cover molded w/an outer band of elongated running rabbits surrounding an inner design of tiny birds & leafy vines, clear w/brown patina, molded "R. Lalique," 3 1/2" d., 1 1/2" h............... **633**

Serving set: ten 7 3/4" d. plates & an 11" d. tray; Black Alga, each in black satin polished crystal w/molded aquatic plant designs, bases signed "Lalique France," designed by Marc Lalique, ca. 1950, the set **633**

Vase, 4 1/2" h., "Grenade," footed spherical body tapering to a short rolled neck, clear & frosted, molded w/overall bands of stylized rounded flower petals, blue stain, introduced in 1930 .... **1,380**

Lalique Dahlias Vase

Vase, 4 7/8" h., "Dahlias," No. 938, compressed spherical clear & frosted body decorated w/dahlia blossoms w/black enameled centers, brown patina, introduced in 1923, inscribed "R. Lalique - France No. 938" (ILLUS.)...................... **1,295**

Vase, 5" h., "Moissac," short widely flaring inverted conical form in opalescent molded in high-relief w/overlapping leaves, traces of blue patina, molded "R. LALIQUE - FRANCE," introduced in 1927 .... **1,380**

Vase, 5 1/4" h., "Canards," tapering ovoid body w/flared neck, clear & frosted decorated w/spiraling bands of stylized ducks up around the sides, black enamel detail, introduced in 1931 .... **1,610**

Vase, 5 3/4" h., "Fontaines," No. 906, bulbous body w/short narrow cylindrical neck, blue frosted molded in low-relief w/an abstract pattern resembling flames or water, introduced in 1912, inscribed "Lalique" (ILLUS. top next column) **1,092**

Vase, 6" h., "Fougères," bulbous frosted blue form tapering to a small flared neck, molded w/tiered rows of stylized long

leaves w/molded knob buds, white stain, introduced in 1912...................................... **5,750**

Lalique "Fontaines" Vase

Vase, 6 1/8" h., "Esterel," sharply tapering wide ovoid body w/a wide shoulder centered by a short cylindrical neck, deep amber molded w/large heavily veined leaves in clear & frosted, introduced in 1923 .... **2,300**

Vase, 6 1/4" h., cire perdure type, "Poivre Graines en Relief, Feuilles en Creux," simple ovoid body w/a wide, flat rim, grey molded in low- and medium-relief w/pendent clusters of peppercorns interspersed w/rows of leafage, inscribed "R. LALIQUE 194-20," dated 1920............... **36,800**

Vase, 6 3/4" h., "Bagatelles," small cylindrical foot below the wide swelled cylindrical body w/a wide short cylindrical neck, the clear & frosted sides molded in bold relief w/plump birds among foliage, blue stain, introduced in 1939 .... **1,955**

Vase, 7" h., "Danaides," footed swelled cylindrical body w/a wide flat rim, smokey grey frosted molded in low relief w/female nudes emptying urns of water, molded "R. LALIQUE - France," introduced in 1926... **2,415**

Vase, 7 1/8" h., "Danaides," footed swelled cylindrical form, opalescent, molded in low-relief w/a band of stylized maidens emptying vessels of water, signed "R. Lalique - France - No. 972," introduced in 1926 .... **3,737**

Lalique "Danaides" Vase

Vase, 7 1/8" h., "Danaides," molded foot below the wide gently flaring cylindrical body w/a wide flat mouth, clear & frosted opalescent molded w/full-length figures of female nudes pouring cascades of water from jugs on their shoulders, introduced in 1926 (ILLUS.) **5,750**

Lalique "Courges" Vase

Vase, 7 1/2" h., "Courges," No. 900, bulbous base tapering to short narrow cylindrical neck, molded & frosted deep turquoise blue w/low-relief-molded pear-shaped gourds pendent from swirling vines, introduced in 1914 & molded "LALIQUE" (ILLUS.) **13,800**

Vase, 8 1/4" h., "Domrémy," wide ovoid green body tapering to a short wide rolled neck, molded in relief w/large round thistle heads & molded tall thistle stems, white stain, introduced in 1926 ...... **6,038**

Vase, 8 1/4" h., "Tulipes," bulbous ovoid body in grey & frosted molded in high relief overall w/large undulating stems & rounded tulip blossoms, molded "R. LALIQUE," introduced in 1927 .... **2,875**

Vase, 8 1/2" h., "Domrémy," tapering ovoid opalescent body molded in relief w/thistles, inscribed "R. Lalique - France," introduced in 1926 .... **1,495**

Lalique "Languedoc" Vase

Vase, 8 3/4" h., "Languedoc," No. 1021, bulbous body w/short wide cylindrical neck, molded w/overlapping rows of spiky serrated leaves, frosted deep emerald green, introduced in 1929, inscribed "R. Lalique France No. 1021" (ILLUS.) **31,625**

Vase, 9" h., "Malesherbes," bulbous ovoid body tapering to a small neck w/flattened flared rim, opalescent molded in medium-relief w/overlapping pointed leaves, inscribed "R. LALIQUE" **1,495**

Vase, 9 1/4" h., "Ronces," footed tall slender swelled cylindrical body w/a tiny cylindrical neck, clear & frosted molded overall in bold relief w/thorny branches, green stain, introduced in 1921 (ILLUS. top next column) **2,415**

Vase, 9 1/2" h., "Aras," footed widely swelled squatty bulbous form w/a small short tapering neck at the top, rich wintergreen molded overall w/large exotic birds perched on entwined berried vines, original white patina, inscribed "R. Lalique France No. 919," introduced in 1924 .... **11,500**

Vase, 9 1/2" h., "Poivre," frosted & clear bulbous ovoid body w/a rounded shoulder centering a small, short cylindrical neck, two sides molded w/dense clusters of berries, faintly molded "LALIQUE," ca. 1921 .... **1,265**

Green-stained "Ronces" Lalique Vase

Vase, 10 1/4" h., "Sophora," large wide spherical body w/a wide shoulder centered by a short trumpet neck w/flattened rim, clear & frosted molded w/vertical bands of stylized leafy branches, green stain, introduced in 1926 .... **4,600**

Fine Lalique "Baies" Vase

Vase, 10 1/2" h., "Baies," spherical body w/a small short cylindrical neck, clear & frosted molded overall w/interlacing budding thorny branches, black enamel trim, introduced in 1924 (ILLUS.) **13,800**

Vase, 10 1/2" h., "Tortues," footed bulbous ovoid body w/a short cylindrical neck & flattened rim, deep amber molded overall in medium-relief w/overlapping tortoiseshells, molded "R. LALIQUE," inscribed "France," introduced in 1926.... **20,700**

Vase, 11" h., "Davos," swelled wide cylindrical body w/a short cylindrical wide mouth, clear plum brown molded overall w/variously sized bubble-like scales forming a geometric design, introduced in 1932 .... **5,463**

Vase, 11 1/8" h., "Acanthes," No. 902, shouldered bulbous ovoid body w/narrow molded rim, molded in low-relief w/acanthus leaves, frosted red, original white patina, introduced in 1921, inscribed "Lalique," (ILLUS. top next page) **16,100**

Vase, 11 1/4" h., "Acanthes," large ovoid body tapering to a tiny flared mouth, cased deep amber orange, molded w/an overall design of acanthus leaves, signed, introduced in 1921 .... **18,400**

Vase, 13" h., "Nanking," spherical form composed of overall facets of molded concentric triangles, clear & frosted w/green stain, introduced in 1925 .... **8,050**

Lalique "Acanthes" Vase

Vase, 13 3/4" h., "Grande Boule Lierre," footed spherical form w/a small, short clear neck, the body in gray molded in low-relief overall w/trailing ivy vines & leaves, inscribed "R. LALIQUE" & acid-etched "R.LALIQUE - FRANCE," introduced in 1919.. **14,375**

Vases, 16" h., "Palestre," flat-bottomed ovoid body w/a short, wide flared rim, molded around the sides w/standing & walking nude males in various poses, frosted clear, unsigned, drilled for use as lamps, introduced in 1928, pr................. **17,250**

Wine rinser, "Ricquewihr," slightly flaring wide cylindrical body w/three thick bands decorated w/delicate trailing grapevines, clear w/teal patina, inscribed "R. LALIQUE - FRANCE," ca. 1938, 5" h.......... **517**

LE VERRE FRANCAIS

Glassware carrying this marking was produced at the French glass factory founded by Charles Schneider in 1908. A great deal of cameo glass was exported to the United States early in the 20th century and much of it was marketed through Ovingtons in New York City.

Various Le Verre Francais Marks

Cameo ewer, bulbous cylindrical lower body tapering to a tall slender neck w/bulbed top & upright pointed spout, D-form applied purple handle from rim to center of neck, mottled yellow & flame orange overlaid w/brown & cut w/a frieze of cats in various positions, abstract brickwork cut around the neck & shoulder, signed in intaglio "Le Verre Francais," ca. 1920-22, 11 1/2" h. **$3,737**

Le Verre Francais Cameo Ewer

Cameo ewer, ovoid body tapering to a bulbed neck w/a tall upright pointed spout, applied pointed angular handle, shaded pink overlaid in lavender & cut w/stylized flowers & leaves, signed, 12 1/2" h. (ILLUS.).. **1,150**

Le Verre Francais Jar & Lamp

Cameo jar, cov., bulbous ovoid ginger jar-form w/fitted domed cover, mottled pink overlaid w/purple & cut w/five stylized dahlias alternating w/spade-form leaves, signed, 14" h. (ILLUS. left) **3,737**

Cameo lamp table model, the tapering cylindrical base w/a cushion foot mounted w/three wrought-iron arms ending in leaves supporting the mushroom-form shade, all in grey internally shaded w/light blue & yellow, overlaid in purple mottled w/orange & cut w/stylized thistles & leaves, signed, ca. 1925-27, 19" h. (ILLUS. right)................................... **4,025**

Le Verre Francais Cameo Vase

Cameo vase, 4 1/8" h., squatty spherical body tapering to a short wide rolled neck, mottled yellow & peach ground overlaid in mottled aubergine & etched around the shoulder w/a band of cats at play above a geometric lower band, engraved signature (ILLUS.) **1,955**

Cameo vase, 5 1/2" h., cushion foot on a wide swelled cylindrical body w/a wide flared rim flanked by tiny loop handles, yellow overlaid w/mottled & shaded purple to orange & cut w/a geometric Art Deco design w/vines & berries around the top & stepped rectangular blocks down the center, signed on the bottom "Le Verre Francais" **690**

Cameo vase, 8" h., Art Deco style, baluster-form w/cushion foot, mottled golden orange ground overlaid w/bright orange shaded down to dark blue & cameo cut w/stylized balloon-form blossoms on scrolling trees **715**

Cameo vase, 8 1/4" h., thick waisted cushion pedestal base supporting a slender ovoid body w/a small flaring neck, grey internally mottled w/white & cobalt blue, overlaid w/mottled sea foam green & cut w/two luxuriating mermaids blowing bubbles among fish & sea grass, the foot cut w/scales, signed in intaglio, ca. 1928........ **4,600**

Le Verre Francais Cameo Vase

Cameo vase, 10 1/2" h., ovoid tapering body w/flaring lip in purple & pink mot-

tled w/touches of yellow & green, overlaid w/purple & cut w/festoons, signed in cameo "Charder," engraved "Le Verre Francais" & acid-etched "France," ca. 1925 (ILLUS.)... **1,035**

Cameo vase, 11 1/2" h., a cushion foot below a slender stem flaring to a large bulbous top w/a closed rim, grey mottled w/yellow & light blue, overlaid w/reddish orange shading to purple, cut w/three orchids on leafy stems, inscribed "Le Verre Francais," ca. 1925-27 .... **1,840**

Cameo vase, 12 1/4" h., flared trumpet-form, yellow shaded to reddish orange overlaid in mottled green & brown, cameo-etched & cut as cascading flowers, pedestal foot signed "Le Verre Francais" & "Ovington New York" on base **978**

Cameo vase, 14 1/4" h., bulbous triangular base tapering sharply to a very tall slender slightly flaring neck, mottled red, orange & yellow overlaid in brown & cut w/clusters of stylized leafy flowers, the neck w/a honeycomb border, signed in cameo "Charder," inscribed "Le Verre Francais - FRANCE," ca. 1928 .... **1,955**

Cameo vase, 15" h., slender baluster-form body w/a flared neck & cushion foot, grey mottled w/yellow overlaid w/reddish orange shading to purplish brown & cut w/three orchids on leafy stems, signed, ca. 1925-27................................. **1,725**

Three Le Verre Francais Vases

Cameo vase, 15 3/4" h., tall slender inverted pear-form body w/a wide flat rim, raised on a thick cushion foot, mottled orange, red & yellow, overlaid in glossy maroon cameo-etched w/trailing vines of stylized grape clusters, foot signed (ILLUS. left) **1,495**

Cameo vase, 17" h., cushion foot w/narrow short stem supporting the bulbous ovoid body tapering to a tall slender neck w/flaring top, mottled white overlaid in tortoiseshell amber & browns shaded to orange, cameo etched w/an abstract design of twisting ribbons & dots, signed on the foot (ILLUS. right).............................. **920**

Cameo vase, 18 1/2" h., round cushion foot supporting the tall ovoid body tapering to a small flared rim, grey internally decorated w/yellow & overlaid w/dark purple shading to red, cut w/six stems of stylized poppy buds growing from a border of tiles around the foot, inscribed "Le Verre Francais," ca. 1925........................... **2,530**

Cameo vase, 19" h., 13 1/2" d., very large trumpet-form body on a thick cushion foot, yellow overlaid in deep cobalt blue w/a variegated orange band cameo etched w/stylized hollyhocks, signed (ILLUS. center).. **3,738**

Cameo vase, 20 1/4" h., cushion foot supporting a tall tapering cylindrical body rounded at the bottom & w/a short flaring neck, mottled orange ground w/"chipped ice" finish overlaid in mottled orange, pink & green & cut w/an Art Deco geometric honeycomb design around the base, the neck & upper half **1,800**

Cameo vase, 20 1/4" h., tall swelled trumpet-form bowl on a bulbous knopped stem & cushion foot, clear w/mottled pink & white layered in striated maroon rising to orange, acid-etched w/stylized foxglove, signed "Charder - Le Verre Francais" (light abrasions)...................... **2,300**

Three Tall Le Verre Francais Vases

Cameo vase, 23 3/8" h., cushion foot tapering to a tall slender ovoid body w/a flat mouth, mottled yellow & orange overlaid w/orange shading to brown & cut w/a garden of stylized peonies above a leaftip border, signed in cameo "Charder" & inscribed "Le Verre Francais," ca. 1928 (ILLUS. right) **2,415**

Cameo vase, 24 3/4" h., tall cylindrical body w/a slightly flaring lip & cushion foot, mottled light blue overlaid w/royal blue & cut w/stylized berried branches & a lower border of brickwork, inscribed "Le Verre Francais - France," ca. 1925 ..... **1,840**

Cameo vase, 25" h., cushion foot supporting a bulbous lower body tapering sharply to a tall slender slightly waisted cyindrical neck w/flared rim, grey mottled w/pink & overlaid w/purple & cut w/stylized dahlias, signed, ca. 1925-27 (ILLUS. center)...................................... **2,760**

Cameo vase, 26 1/2" h., thick cushion foot tapering to a knopped stem below the tall slender ovoid body tapering to a small flared rim, grey overlaid w/tangerine shading to red & traces of violet & cut w/four vertical bands each decorated w/six stylized flowerheads, signed in cameo "Charder," inscribed "Le Verre Francais," ca. 1928 (ILLUS. left) **2,587**

Acid-etched Le Verre Francais Vase

Vase, 11 1/4" h., ovoid body in light blue decorated w/stylized floral vines, on a dark purple round foot, engraved "Charder - Le Verre Francais," ca. 1925 (ILLUS.)... **805**

Veilleuse (night light), a mushroom-shaped glass shade in grey mottled w/white & blue, overlaid w/mottled brick red & cobalt blue & cut w/stylized fuchsia blossoms, on a round metal base w/three arched leaf-form feet, shade inscribed "Le Verre Francais," ca. 1925, 6" h. **920**

LEGRAS

Cameo and enameled glass somewhat similar to that made by Gallé, Daum Nancy and other factories of the period was made at the Legras works in Saint Denis, France, late last century and until the outbreak of World War I.

Bowl, 10" d., 3 3/4" h., Art Deco style, broad round form of olive green, heavily etched & engraved w/a swag & drapery design, polished to enhanced design, acid-etched near base "Legras," ca. 1925 .... **$805**

Cameo vase, 6" h., nearly spherical w/a tri-lobed rim, clear cased in mottled white & cameo-etched & enameled w/a wide band of stylized grapevine w/leaves & grape clusters, side signed "Legras" **288**

Cameo vase, 7" h., simple ovoid shouldered body w/a short rounded neck w/closed rim, frosted bluish ground overlaid in deep red & pink & cut w/a design of pheasants flying among the drooping branches of trees **880**

Cameo vase, 10" h., a footed compressed cushion-form base below tall sharply tapering conical sides w/a small mouth, carnelian ground overlaid dark green & cut overall w/a delicate scene of aquatic plants.. **605**

Cameo vase, 11 1/2" h., ovoid body, a cameo-carved zigzag band of Art Deco style fans on a cased white ground mottled w/brown **825**

Cameo vase, 13 3/4" h., tall slender cylindrical body tapering slightly to a bulbed neck w/flat rim, grey w/citrine shading & internal blue & green mottling overlaid in powder blue opalescent & cut w/apple blossoms & branches enameled in light green, brown & amber, signed in cameo .. **2,016**

Cameo vase, 15 3/4" h., tall simple ovoid body w/a flaring mouth, acid-cut purple enameled flowers on a pink 'chipped ice' ground, signed in cameo **1,600**

Legras Enameled Lamps

Lamps, tall cylindrical form w/flared base, enameled overall w/winter landscape scenes at sunset, mounted in a pierced wood base w/metal lamp fittings, signed in enamel, damage to wood bases, wear to metal, 13 1/2" h., pr. (ILLUS.) **1,495**

Rose bowl, spherical w/six-crimp rim, deep orangish amber ground enameled w/a winter landscape w/bare trees, snow & birds in flight, signed **550**

Vase, 4 3/4" h., spherical body w/quatre-form rim, colorless body enameled w/a scene of bare trees in snow at sunset, signed near base **403**

Vase, 5 5/8" h., wide waisted ovoid form w/a pinched four-lobed rim, colorless etched & enameled w/dark fuchsia ivy on a textured & frosted surface, signed on the side, ca. 1920 (light scratches to enamel) **345**

Vase, 7 1/4" h., dimpled ovoid body, etched & painted w/sea fauna, signed **460**

Vase, 11 1/4" h., tall slightly waisted cylindrical body w/a squared mouth, shaded pink ground enameled w/a landscape scene w/green trees in the foreground & a sailboat on a lake beyond **311**

Decorated Legras Vase

Vase, 12 3/8" h., tall slender ovoid body tapering to a slightly swelled neck, grey acid-etched & painted w/a scene of a sailboat on a lake in brown, orange, yel-

low, blue & white, signed in enamel, ca. 1900 (ILLUS.) **1,092**

Vase, 13" h., bottle-form, squatty bulbous base below a tall slender 'stick' neck w/a bulbed top & small flared rim, orangish red top shading to a mottled cream & tan body enamel-decorated w/autumn leaves in shades of brown & tan w/blue berries **358**

Vase, 14 1/2" h., baluster-form, grey infused w/yellow & enameled w/leafage in blue & green, enameled signature **460**

LIBBEY

In 1878, William L. Libbey obtained a lease on the New England Glass Company of Cambridge, Massachusetts, changing the name to the New England Glass Works, W.L. Libbey and Son, Proprietors. After his death in 1883, his son, Edward D. Libbey, continued to operate the company at Cambridge until 1888 when the factory was closed. Edward Libbey moved to Toledo, Ohio, and set up the company subsequently known as Libbey Glass Co. During the 1880s, the firm's master technician, Joseph Locke, developed the now much desired colored art glass lines of Agata, Amberina, Peach Blow and Pomona. Renowned for its Cut Glass of the Brilliant Period (see CUT GLASS), the company continues in operation today as Libbey Glassware, a division of Owens-Illinois, Inc.

Bowl, 5 1/2" d., 2 1/2" h., Amberina, bulbous base w/rectangular rim, ribbed pattern **$300**

Bowl, 6" d., Peking patt., pink, scalloped edge, Libbey-Nash series **125**

Bowl, 6" d., 4" h., Amberina, paneled optic design w/ruffled rim, signed **595**

Bowl, 7" d., clear shallow sides etched w/satin holly leaves & berries forming a large snowflake, flared rim cut w/satin icicles, signed **250**

Bowl, 9" d., experimental, clear w/internal bubble design & pale green powders, designed by Nash, stamped on base "Libbey" **86**

Candlesticks, pedestal foot supporting a bulbous base tapering to a tall cylindrical neck, intaglio-cut floral design, 12" h., pr **550**

Champagne, Silhouette patt., clear bowl, opalescent figural squirrel stem **163**

Claret, Silhouette patt., clear bowl, opalescent figural bear stem, Libby-Nash series **225**

Cocktail, Silhouette patt., clear bowl, frosted figural bear stem **95**

Cocktail, Silhouette patt., clear bowl, opalescent figural kangaroo stem, signed, 6" h. **100-125**

Cocktail, Silhouette patt., clear bowl, opalescent figural squirrel stem, signed, 6" h. **95**

Compote, open, 7 1/2" d., 3 1/4" h., Amberina, a flattened & widely flaring rim on a rounded bowl raised on a short knop stem w/a round foot, marked "Amberina" & "Libbey" in a circle, ca. 1917 .... **550**

Libbey Silhouette Elephant Compote

Compote, open, 11" d., 7 1/2" h., Silhouette patt., wide crystal bowl on an opalescent figural elephant stem, signed (ILLUS.)...... 750

Console set: 12" d. center bowl & four matching candleholders; wide shallow crystal bowl on a wafer & thick square foot, half-round crystal candleholder on a thick square foot, stamped mark on base, 1939-42, candleholders 3 3/4" h., the set...... 288

Console set: bowl & 12" h., candlesticks; cobalt blue over clear, polished pontils, 3 pcs...... 750

Cordial, Silhouette patt., clear bowl, opalescent figural greyhound stem...... 175

Cordial, Silhouette patt., figural kangaroo stem...... 110

Cordial, Silhouette patt., figural monkey stem...... 150

Engraved Libbey Decanter

Decanter w/pointed teardrop stopper, the clear footed inverted pear-form body tapering to a slender panel-cut neck w/flared rim, the body engraved w/a design of long-stemmed wheat & grain grasses w/an elaborate monogram, the stopper also engraved, signed, 13" h. (ILLUS.)...... 650

Dinner bell, etched "1893 World's Fair" & molded w/"1893 World's Columbian Xposition (sic)," frosted glass handle & metal clapper, 5 3/4" h...... 285

Goblet, Silhouette patt., clear bowl, opalescent figural monkey stem...... 175

Goblet, water, Silhouette patt., clear bowl, opalescent figural cat stem...... 225

Maize Celery Vase

Maize celery vase, clear w/amber iridescent kernels & blue husks (ILLUS.)...... 225

Maize Celery with Yellow Husks

Maize celery vase, creamy white ground w/yellow husks, 6 1/2" h. (ILLUS.)...... 225

Maize salt shaker, original top, condiment size, creamy opaque...... 125

Maize sugar shaker w/original lid, creamy opaque w/green husks...... 325-375

Maize sugar shaker w/original top, creamy opaque w/blue husks...... 325

Maize sugar shaker w/original top, creamy opaque w/yellow husks & gold trim...... 300-350

Libbey Maize Tumbler

Maize tumbler, creamy opaque w/blue husks (ILLUS.)...... 225

Maize tumbler, creamy opaque w/green husks trimmed in gold...... 150

Model of a shoe, embossed florals on the toe, peach shoe w/black heel...... 175

Punch cup, pressed clear petal-form marked "World's Fair 1893," impressed "Libbey Glass Co., Toledo, Ohio - World's Fair" inside...... 75

Rose bowl, round w/eight-crimp rim, pink w/light ribbing in white, glossy finish, probably produced at the 1893 Columbian Exposition...... 330

Sherbet, low, Silhouette patt., clear bowl, opalescent figural rabbit stem, Libby-Nash series **75-100**

Sherbet, Silhouette patt., clear bowl, black figural squirrel stem, signed, 4" h. **145**

Sherbet, Silhouette patt., clear bowl, opalescent figural squirrel stem, 4" h. **110**

Libbey Silhouette Sherry

Sherry, Silhouette patt., clear bowl, opalescent figural monkey stem (ILLUS.) **95-125**

Stemware set: two champagnes, nine red wines, a water goblet, eight white wines, seven highballs & one liqueur; Art Deco design, clear w/a drawn ovoid bowl, fluted rectangular stem & circular foot, etched Libbey mark, the group................. **2,645**

Sugar shaker w/original metal lid, Maize patt., yellow leaves, 5 3/4" h........................ **413**

Table service: six wine goblets w/polar bear stems, four candlesticks w/camel stems, one compote w/giraffe stem; Silhouette patt., opalescent stems on colorless glassware, each piece stamped "Libbey," designed by Nash, compote 7" h., the group... **2,300**

Tumblers, Currier & Ives Classics Collection, 12 oz.., set of 4, mint in original box....... **75**

Vase, 8" h., clear pedestal base, white opal ground w/pink pulled feather design, signed in pontil **750**

Vase, 8 3/4" h., tall waisted cylindrical form w/scalloped rim, clear w/eight faceted side panels deeply intaglio engraved w/frosted foliate designs, signed "Libbey" in a circle, late 19th - early 20th c. **633**

Vase, 9" h., two applied handles, fuchsia flower etching on a clear ground, signed **150**

Vase, 10" h., turquoise zipper pattern on a clear ground, signed.................................... **475**

Vase, 11" h., Amberina, #3304, ca. 1917 .... **750**

Vase, 12" h., cushion base tapering to a tall trumpet-form body, colorless crystal w/seafoam green "zipper" decoration, designed by Nash, catalog No. K523 (ILLUS. top next column) **345**

Vase, 14" h., 'Talisman' patt., optic ribbed flared oval of colorless glass w/spiraled green internal thread, raised on applied colorless foot, base marked "Libbey," designed by Nash **230**

Vase, 15" h., lily-shaped, Amberina, signed, ca. 1917...................................... **1,200**

Libbey-Nash "Zipper" Vase

Wine, Silhouette patt., black figural polar bear stem, signed, 6" h. **125**

Wine, Silhouette patt., opalescent figural kangaroo stem, signed, 6" h........................ **135**

Wine, Silhouette patt., opalescent figural monkey stem, signed, 6" h. **125**

LOETZ

Iridescent glass, some of it somewhat resembling that of Tiffany and other contemporary glasshouses, was produced by the Bohemian firm of J. Loetz Witwe of Klostermule and is referred to as Loetz. Some cameo pieces were also made. Not all pieces are marked.

Loetz Mark

Bowl, 6 3/4" d., 2 1/2" h., ruffled sides, blue oil spotting on a gold iridescent ground, blue iridescent interior **$275**

Loetz Bowl-Vase

Bowl-vase, globular body w/four large dimples around the sides below the wide flattened mouth, green w/gold-striped iridescent pink pulled feather design, bears partial paper label, ca. 1900, 5" d. (ILLUS.)... **1,265**

Cameo bowl, 5" d., 3" h., a deep wide cupped form raised on three ball feet, white cased in amethyst & cut vining leaf & blossom design around the sides **660**

Rare Loetz Cameo Vase

Cameo vase, 10 1/4" h., swelled cylindrical form w/lightly flared rim, yellow overlaid in grey & etched w/vertical bands w/panels of stylized leafy vines above diamond & dot designs, designed by Josef Hoffmann, Model 8127, ca. 1912, unsigned (ILLUS.) **9,200**

Loetz Signed Ewer

Ewer, tall hexagonal baluster-form body w/a cylindrical neck, cupped rim & long angled rim spout, applied loop handle from rim to shoulder, opalescent ground w/amber feathering & silvery blue iridescence, signed, ca. 1900, 10 1/4" h. (ILLUS.).. **1,955**

Simple Loetz Iridescent Vase

Vase, slightly tapering cylindrical body w/a widely flaring six-ruffle rim, dark golden iridescence w/blue highlights, signed (ILLUS.) **275**
Vase, 1 3/4" h., 1 3/4" d., miniature, small spherical body w/a small flared neck, loop handles from rim to shoulder, overall gold iridescence w/oil spotting................. **468**

Vase, 2" h., miniature, footed simple ovoid body w/a short flared neck, overall golden iridescence w/bluish highlights & oil spotting **303**

Miniature Silver Overlaid Loetz Vase

Vase, 3" h., miniature, spherical form w/wide slightly flared mouth, light blue & green iridescent ground w/six dollops of silver applied around the shoulder & silver leafy scrolls around the body, ca. 1900, signed (ILLUS.) **1,150**
Vase, 3 3/4" h., miniature, a squatty bulbous base centering a wide cylindrical neck w/flared rim, iridescent green decorated overall w/heavy sterling silver overlay in vining leaf & blossom design **770**
Vase, 3 3/4" h., wide squatty bulbous body raised on a tapering base, the wide shoulder centering a short flaring neck, rich amber shaded w/bands of salmon at the neck & purple around the base, decorated w/iridescent silvery blue waves, designed by Franz Hofstatter, signed "Loetz - Austria," ca. 1900......................... **4,887**

Two Fine Loetz Vases

Vase, 4 1/8" h., bulbous ovoid form w/deeply pinched-in sides below the wide flaring mouth, amber ground decorated w/iridescent silver sweeping swirls, engraved "Loetz Austria" (ILLUS. right) **920**
Vase, 4 3/4" h., bulbous ovoid body tapering to a wide upright scrolled & crimped rim, golden amber decorated w/swirling trailings in silvery blue & pink iridescence, signed "Loetz - Austria" **2,300**
Vase, 4 3/4" h., "Lava," ovoid body, cobalt blue, the surface of bubbled decoration w/bluish green iridescence, polished pontil (rim imperfection)............................... **518**
Vase, 5" h., simple ovoid body w/three-lobed rim, orange ground decorated w/iridescent green & blue & cased in clear, overlaid w/overall pierced silver scrolling leafy vine decoration, small chip to base, ca. 1900, unsigned (ILLUS. top next page) **1,380**

Loetz Vase with Ornate Silver Overlay

Vase, 5 1/8" h., footed spherical body w/a flaring cylindrical neck, applied scrolled loop handles from side of neck to shoulder, iridescent pale green ground decorated w/an iridescent blue oil spot design, silver overlay cast in a scrolling foliate design in bands down the sides & the handles encased in silver (ILLUS. left, previous page)..................................... **2,530**

Vase, 5 1/8" h., tapering rounded rectangular form in pale yellow w/amber iridescent oil spotting, overlaid w/a stylized silver web applied w/two turquoise glass 'jewels,' unsigned, ca. 1900 .... **862**

Vase, 5 1/4" h., bulbous ovoid body tapering to a widely flaring crimped & folded rim, greenish amber decorated in silvery blue wavy oil spots, signed, early 1900s **287**

Vase, 5 3/4" h., a wide squatty bulbous base w/a flattened shoulder centering a wide swelled cylindrical neck w/flared rim, yellow iridescent ground w/overall King Tut looping design w/silvery blue iridescence.. **1,430**

Loetz Vase with Floral Silver Overlay

Vase, 6 1/2" h., sharply tapering cylindrical form, swirled iridescent green rising to pearly blue, silver overlay Art Nouveau looping vines & blossoms, polished pontil, rubbed marks on silver, ca. 1905 (ILLUS.).. **748**

Vase, 6 3/4" h., ovoid body w/slightly everted lip, amber w/pink iridescent trailings & heart-form leaves, unsigned, ca. 1900 .... **1,610**

Vase, 7 1/8" h., bulbous ovoid body tapering to a small foot, the wide flat shoulder centered by a short cylindrical flared neck, deep red decorated w/overall silvery blue wavy concentric trailings, signed, ca. 1900 .... **2,875**

Vase, 8" h., squatty bulbous base tapering sharply to a tall slender cylindrical neck w/a widely flaring & flattened rim, pale green ground w/a band of heavy blue threading wrapped around the neck & blue applied disks around the lower body, overall pale purple & green iridescence.. **358**

Vase, 9 1/4" h., ovoid double-gourd form w/a tapering neck, amber w/silvery blue iridescence & oil spotting, overlaid w/silver flowering whiplash decoration, ca. 1900 .... **2,070**

Vase, 9 1/2" h., trumpet-form w/a bulbous neck & a flaring rim, iridescent bluish gold base & gold top **275**

Thistle Silver Overlay on Loetz Vase

Vase, 10" h., gently swelled cylindrical form w/flat rim, gold spot decoration & iridescent lustre ground applied overall w/a delicate silver thistle design (ILLUS.) **2,185**

Vase, 10 1/2" h., ovoid bottle-form w/deeply dimpled bottom & tall neck w/rounded knob below the flattened, flared rim, pale amber opalescent decorated w/pulled trailings in silvery iridescence, signed, ca. 1900 .... **2,875**

Loetz Vase with Looped Trailings

Vase, 11 3/8" h., squatty bulbous base tapering to a tall cylindrical neck w/applied chain of looping trailings, colorless shaded w/amber & finished w/pink & blue iridescence, erroneously signed "LCT," ca. 1901 (ILLUS.) **1,725**

Vase, 11 1/2" h., baluster-form w/a short crimped & flared rim, citrine shaded w/cranberry mottling & pulled green leaves under an iridescent finish, ground pontil, unmarked...................................... **1,232**

Vase, 18" h., squatty bulbous wide base centered by a tall slender & slightly flaring neck w/a flared & crimped rim, green iridescent ground decorated w/a blue papillon finish of iridescent oil spots......... **3,850**

Vase, 18 1/2" h., bottle-form, spherical dimpled bottom tapering to a tall slender & slightly tapering neck w/flattened flaring rim, grey cased in peach & decorated overall w/concentric trailings of golden iridescence, further decorated w/four applied prunts around the lower body w/slender straight tails running up the neck, ca. 1901, signed "Loetz - Austria".. **11,500**

LUSTRES

Lustres were Victorian glass vase-like decorative objects often hung around the rim with prisms. They were generally sold as matched pairs to be displayed on fireplace mantels. A wide range of colored glasswares were used in producing lustres and pieces were often highlighted with colored enameled decoration.

Fine Bristol Glass Decorated Lustre

Bristol, milky white w/a wide squatty bulbous top bowl w/a high four-lobed rolled & crimped rim & a ringed base raised on a slender ringed pedestal above the stepped cushion foot, the top bowl finely enameled w/delicate florals, the base of the bowl hung w/two rows of long facet-cut triangular prisms in two sizes, 16 1/2" h., pr. (ILLUS. of one,) **$1,320**

Cut overlay, cranberry cut to clear, the wide round bowl-form top w/ruffled, flared rim cut w/a leafy vine design, raised on a slender slightly tapering standard on a round domed foot with further cut panels & gilt band trim, hung w/large triangular cut spearpoint prisms, 13" h. **550**

Cut overlay, opaque white cut to cranberry, the wide shallow bowl cut w/short arched panels around the sides, raised on a baluster-form standard on a panel-cut foot, decorated overall w/colored floral enameling & gilt trim, long facet-cut triangular prisms, 13" h., pr. (wear &

edge flakes, prisms mismatched & w/some chips) **715**

Deep Green Mantel Lustre

Deep green, the wide paneled socket-form top w/flared rim above a shallow round mid drip pan raised on a ringed paneled shaft w/a ringed botton on the paneled foot, the pan hung w/clear facet-cut prisms, 10" h., pr. (ILLUS. of one) **518**

Ruby, a squatty bulbous round top bowl w/a high flared & crown-cut top rim, raised on a slender baluster-form pedestal & round stepped foot, the bowl enameled in white w/daisy-like blossoms & leaves, white dot trim, long facet-cut triangular prisms suspended from base of bowl, deep color, 10 1/2" h., pr..................... **420**

Ruby, the top w/a wide cupped & notch-cut rim above the wide squatty cylindrical bowl raised on a tall slender ringed pedestal on a round foot, decorated around the rim & bowl w/ornate polychrome & gold enameling, long facet-cut triangular prisms hung from the bowl, 14 1/4" h., pr. **468**

MARY GREGORY

Glass enameled in white with silhouette-type figures, primarily of children, is now termed "Mary Gergory" and was attributed to the Boston and Sandwich Glass Company. However, recent research has proven conclusively that this was not decorated by Mary Gregory, nor was it made at the Sandwich plant. Miss Gregory was employed by Boston and Sandwich Glass Company as a decorator; however, records show her assignment was the painting of naturalistic landscape scenes on larger items such as lamps and shades, but never the charming children for which her name has become synonymous. Further, in the inspection of fragments from the factory site, no paintings of children were found.

It is now known that all wares collectors call "Mary Gregory" originated in Bohemia beginning in the late 19th century and were extensively exported to England and the United States well into this century.

For further information, see The Glass Industry in Sandwich, Volume #4, *by Raymond E. Barlow and Joan E. Kaiser, and the book,* Mary Gregory Glassware, 1880-1900, *by R. & D. Truitt.*

Cake basket, a silver-plate frame w/tall tapering legs supporting a round dished bowl w/a wide reeded border framing a central round blue glass disk enameled in white w/a figure of a girl feeding a bird, an overhead swing strap handle, frame by the Middletown Silver Co., late 19th c., 9 1/2" d., 10" h. **$550**

Cologne bottle w/stopper, footed optic ribbed ovoid body w/a ringed short cylindrical neck w/flared rim, amber w/white enameled figure of a young lady in a garden, clear bubbled stopper, 3" d., 8" h. **175**

Cranberry Mary Gregory Decanter

Decanter w/original clear facet-cut stopper, cranberry, the footed tapering cylindrical & ring-molded body w/an optic rib design & wide shoulder, tall cylindrical neck w/flared rim, decorated w/white enameled winged cupid batting at a heart, white lily-of-the-valley trim, gilt banding, 4" d., 10" h. (ILLUS.) **185**

Decanter w/stopper, slightly flaring cylindrical optic ribbed body w/a wide tapering shoulder centering a tall cylindrical neck w/flared rim, sapphire blue w/a white enameled figure of a young girl walking in a garden, 3 1/2" d., 8 1/2" h. **195**

Blue Mary Gregory Decanter

Decanter w/tall ringed & tapering blown stopper, sapphire blue, the footed flaring cylindrical body w/a stepped shoulder & tall cylindrical neck, optic rib design, white enamel decoration of a young boy in a garden, 3 1/4" d., 10 1/4" h. (ILLUS.) **195**

Mary Gregory Jewel Box

Jewel box w/hinged cover, round squatty bulbous optic ribbed form, amber w/a white enameled figure on the cover of a boy walking & holding up a bird, 3 1/2" d., 3 1/4" h. (ILLUS. top next page) **225**

Mary Gregory Lemonade Set

Lemonade set: tall waisted tankard pitcher w/applied handle & two tall tapering cylindrical tumblers; lime green w/optic ribbing, the pitcher w/a white enameled scene of a man on a bicycle w/color-painted face & hands, one tumbler w/a man on a bicycle, the other w/a lady on a bicycle, late 19th - early 20th c., pitcher 13" h., the set (ILLUS.) **435**

Mug, cranberry, cylindrical w/an applied clear handle, white enameled young girl walking on tiptoes through a garden, engraved "Dora" on one side, 2 3/8" d., 3 5/8" h. (ILLUS. top next page) **95**

Perfume atomizer, white enameled scene of little girl **345**

Mary Gregory Cranberry Mug

Plates, 9 3/8" d., cobalt blue, one w/a white enameled figure of a young woman in long dress holding a fan in a garden, the other w/a young man in armor & shield, pr. **350**

Pocket watch - ring tray, a brass round ring around a shallow light blue glass dish flanked by decorated upright tall legs joined by a top arch & braces to a round metal pocket watch holder, the dish decorated w/a white enameled figure of a young boy holding a balloon on a string, 5 1/4" w., 6 1/4" h. **297**

Tumbler, sapphire blue, white enameled girl in garden **50**

Slender Mary Gregory Vase with Trim

Vase, 7" h., 2 7/8" d., cobalt blue, footed tall slender waisted cylindrical body w/clear applied shell rigaree trim down each side, white enamel young boy standing among lily-of-the-valley blossoms & leaves (ILLUS.) **145**

Vase, 11 1/8" h., 4" d., baluster-form, green opaque Bristol glass body w/cushion foot, ringed stem, tall swelled cylindrical body w/a multiple ring shoulder below the wide cylindrical neck w/a crimped rim, white enamel figure of a boy carrying a tray of flowers **225**

Large Mary Gregory Vase with Figures

Vase, 13 1/2" h., 5 3/4" d., olive green, wide baluster-form body w/cushion foot & white ringed & cupped rim, optic ribbing, decorated w/white enamel figures of a woman & man in 18th-c. costume standing near a rail fence (ILLUS.) **395**

Vases, 8 3/4" h., footed simple slender ovoid body w/a short cylindrical neck, dark lavender blue, one decorated w/a white enameled girl holding a flower, the other w/a boy holding a basket of flowers, pr. **231**

Vases, 10 1/4" h., baluster-form w/cushion foot & short cylindrical neck w/deeply ruffled & crimped rolled rim, dark blue, one w/a white enameled figure of a girl, another w/a facing figure of a boy, pr. **523**

Vases, 10 3/4" h., tall waisted cylindrical form w/a wide ringed shoulder below the slightly flaring short neck, applied clear rigaree down each side, dark green w/white enameled figure of a youth on one & a maiden on the other, each w/colored enamel faces, pr. (pinpoint flakes) **358**

MONT JOYE

Cameo and enameled glass bearing this mark was made in Pantin, France, by the same works that produced pieces signed De Vez.

Bowl, 8" d., a low round foot below the wide rounded & lobed bowl in colorless heavily etched & enameled w/chestnuts on leafy branches in ochre, olive green & rust on an ice finished ground w/gilt enamel foliate border, base w/worn gold enamel signature "Mont Joye L.C.," ca. 1910 (wear to enamel) **$518**

Ewer, green satin textured ground decorated w/pink wild roses w/gold leaves **495**

Vase, 6 1/2" h., tall upright rectangular form w/gently rounded sides, thickly enameled iris & gilt leaves on a textured chipped ice clear ground w/icicle rim, signed in gilt (minor blemish on one side) **448**

Vase, 7 1/2" h., frosted clear textured ground enameled in color w/violets & a gold collar & gold tint on the base, unsigned... **303**

Vase, 7 1/2" h., swollen cylindrical form, textured, frosted clear ground enameled as fading white & pink chrysanthemums w/gold enamel foliage, gold enamel spiked border, ca. 1900.............................. **374**

Vase, 7 3/4" h., ovoid body w/a rounded shoulder to the cylindrical neck, optic ribbed frosted clear ground thickly enameled w/spider mums & gilt leaves, icicle rim, signed in gilt **560**

Vase, 13" h., bulbous lower body tapering sharply to a tall cylindrical neck, frosted ground decorated w/large purple & lavender irises w/golden green leaves & stems, signed **935**

MOSER

Ludwig Moser opened his first glass shop in 1857 in Karlsbad, Bohemia (now Karlovy Vary, in the former Czechoslovakia). Here he engraved and decorated fine glasswares especially to appeal to rich visitors to the local health spa. Later other shops were opened in various cities and throughout the 19th and early 20th century lovely, colorful glasswares, many beautifully enameled, were produced by Moser's shops and reached a wide market in Europe and America. Ludwig died in 1916 and the firm continued under his sons. They were forced to merge with the Meyer's Nephews glass factory after World War I. The glassworks were sold out of the Moser family in 1933.

Bowl, 7 1/2" d., 5" h., rounded w/a fold-over top edge, decorated in enameled colorful flowers on a blue ground on the orange body, applied amber feet **$330**

Cameo vase, 8" h., 7" d., wide bulbous ovoid body tapering slightly to the wide flared rim, deep amethyst cut to deep amber & decorated w/a continuous tropical landscape of elephants feeding among palm trees, trimmed w/white & gold enameling, gold lines around the rim & base, signed in raised gold "Moser - Karlsbad" & "R.W." as well as a script signature on the base.............................. **3,575**

Cruet w/original blue facet-cut stopper, squatty bulbous blue body tapering to a cylindrical neck w/arched spout, applied blue handle, enamel-decorated overall w/white lily-of-the-valley w/gold leaves **358**

Cruet w/original gilt ball stopper, miniature, cranberry, footed spherical body w/a slender neck & pinched rim spout, applied gilt handle from rim to shoulder, heavy gilt band around top of neck & the shoulder w/overall ornate gilt scrolling & dainty flowers **440**

Cruet w/original stopper, footed dark blue bulbous body tapering to a slender neck w/cupped rim w/spout, applied amber handle, blue teardrop stopper, fancy overall enameled gold scrolling & numerous enameled flowers **195**

Cruet w/original teardrop stopper, blue, pedestal base w/stepped foot supporting a flattened spherical body tapering to a tall cylindrical neck w/arched spout, applied blue handle, tall stopper, neck & shoulder decorated w/wide gold bands w/jewels & gold stylized flowers **1,210**

Cruet w/stopper, bulbous amethyst body shading to clear, decorated w/multicolored enameled flowers, applied handle, 7 3/4" h. **550**

Cup & saucer, cranberry, tall cylindrical cup w/rounded base, heavy wide gilt band around the rim & applied gilt handle, overall ornate gilt flowers & vines, on a matching saucer w/a light scalloped rim, decorated w/a wide undulating gilt rim band & dainty gilt flowers in the center **385**

Ewers, bulbous cobalt blue body trimmed in gold & encrusted w/gold & white enameled flowers, 13 1/2" h., pr.................. **385**

Moser Flashed Finger Bowl & Plate

Finger bowl & underplate, dark green flashed on clear, a deep rounded bowl w/scalloped rim on a matching underplate, each etched w/paneled scenes of pairs of birds in clear between etched green trees & ground, bowl 4 1/2" d., plate 7" d., pr. (ILLUS.).................................. **400**

Goblet, marriage-type, cranberry, a tall cup-form bowl raised on a wide figural stem on a notch-cut round foot, the bowl ornately engraved & trimmed w/a wide gold rim band, gilt trim on stem & foot, 19th c. **550**

Goblet, Middle Eastern-style decoration enameled in blues, reds, green & yellow on a white ground w/gold borders, 5 3/4" h. **385**

Liqueur set: two tall footed decanters w/stoppers & twelve cordial glasses; the decanters w/a slender conical amber body raised on an applied medium blue pedestal & round foot, the sides tapering to a tall slender neck w/arched spout & the sides enameled w/two bluebirds in flight among enameled flowers & vines, an applied blue handle & a tall-stemmed pointed blue stopper, each cordial w/a tapering enameled amber bowl & a blue stem & foot, the set **770**

Mug, cylindrical, cranberry w/applied amber handle, the sides ornately enameled overall w/raised acorns & multicolored leaves... **495**

Patch box w/hinged lid, cranberry, squatty bulbous base w/white enameled bead band, the cover ornately enameled w/dainty vining florals around a large central blossomhead **303**

Perfume bottles w/original stoppers, heavily enameled w/applied colorful fish against an enameled aquatic background, pr. **385**

Pitcher, 8 3/4" h., tankard, ribbed amber body enameled overall w/flowers, some outlined in black **165**

Plates, 8" d., cranberry w/gilt grapevine decoration, set of 6 (some w/slight wear)..... **594**

Powder box w/hinged lid, round w/molded ribs, cranberry w/overall floral enameled decoration in yellow & white, gilt-metal base band w/leaf feet, 4 1/2" d., 5" h. **385**

Acid-etched Moser Rose Bowl

Rose bowl, spherical, Art Deco design in smoky ground heavily acid-etched w/a design of stylized deer in a garden, signed on the polished pontil, ca. 1920s, 5 1/2" d., 4 1/4" h. (ILLUS.) **403**

Sherbets & underplates, the sherbet w/a wide rounded bowl w/upright tightly crimped rim, on a clear stem & round foot, green shaded to clear decorated w/heavy gold decoration, matching plate, two prs. **285**

Moser Cranberry & Clear Stemware

Stemware set: six wines, six tumblers & four cordials; the wines w/deep rounded ruby bowls ornately enameled in gilt & raised on a finely ringed trumpet stem, slender slightly tapering cylindrical ruby tumblers w/ornate enameling & four ruby-bowled cordials on clear stems w/ornate enameling, the set (ILLUS.)........... **500**

Vase, 7 1/2" h., footed, clear w/a double gold ring at the top, body covered overall w/stylized enameled flowers in various colors........................ **220**

Moser Portrait Vase

Vase, 14" h., urn-form, wide ovoid body w/a short wide cylindrical neck & flanged rim, raised on a small short pedestal & thick disk foot, emerald green ground decorated w/a large round reserve w/a bust portrait of a woman wearing a lacy shawl, outlined in scrolling gold & w/overall lacy gilt vines (ILLUS.) **2,800**

Lovely Moser Portrait Vases

Vases, tall slender baluster-form w/a cushion foot & short ringed stem supporting the long ovoid body w/a tall trumpet neck, emerald green, each decorated w/a large oval medallion enclosing a bust portrait in color of a Victorian woman, scrolling white medallion border & leafy gold vine background decoration, late 19th c., unsigned, pr. (ILLUS.) **500**

Vases, tall swelled cylindrical & optic-ribbed body in dark purple shading to clear, deeply engraved w/large tulip blossoms on leafy stems, signed, early 20th c., pr. (ILLUS. of one, top next page)... **1,800**

Vases, 12" h., amber ribbed body decorated w/a bright bouquet of spring wildflowers w/an applied metal bee nearby, pr. **330**

Finely Engraved Moser Vase

Wine glass, amethyst cut to crystal bowl w/a floral diamond design, tall pedestal base, signed **193**

MT. WASHINGTON

A wide diversity of glass was made by the Mt. Washington Glass Company of New Bedford, Massachusetts, between 1869 and 1900. It was succeeded in 1900 by the Pairpoint Corporation. Miscellaneous types are listed below.

Rare "Lava" Glass Kerosene Lamp

Banquet lamp, kerosene-type, "Lava," the square black glass foot w/a brass connector to the Lava glass waisted cylindrical pedestal w/a flared neck supporting a brass cap & short connector below the squatty bulbous clear frosted kerosene font cut w/a band of punties in diamonds w/fans, late 19th c. (ILLUS.) **$1,210**

Bell, white satin enameled w/pink florals & gold trim, original clapper, 5" h. **150**

Boudoir bottles w/original blown stoppers, decorated w/large shaded yellow roses, 9 1/4" h., pr. **145**

Bowl, 4 1/2 x 4 1/2", pillow-shaped, satin Diamond Quilted patt., creamy white ground decorated w/pink enameled florals & a yellow rim **275**

Bowl, 8 1/2" d., squatty melon-lobed body w/applied silver plate collar, the white body decorated w/bouquets of pink roses & blue forget-me-nots **165**

Box w/hinged cover, molded colorless round swirled form decorated in the Royal Flemish manner w/dancing flamingos, gilt-metal hinged rims, 7" d., 4" h. (wear, soiled lining) **3,450**

Box w/hinged cover, round, squatty bulbous base w/low domed cover joined by fancy gold-washed silver plate rim & hinge, the cover decorated w/a scene of a monk drinking a glass of red wine, shaded green ground on cover & base, artist-signed, original satin lining, 5 1/4" d., 3 1/4" h. **750**

Bride's basket, cased bowl w/pointed & ruffled rim, shaded rose interior, white exterior, ornate footed silver plate frame w/scrolling handle, 10 1/4" d. bowl, framed 12" w., 12 1/4" h. **550**

Bride's basket, pink shaded to white satin Hobnail patt., w/applied blue rim, on a tall footed Barbour silver plate frame w/large parrots on the handles, bowl, 9" d., 4 3/4" h., overall 13 1/2" d. **950**

Cameo bowl, 9" w., rounded body w/crimped & ruffled rim, white overlaid in blue & cameo cut w/grotesque figures & scrolling vines **495**

Celery tray w/original silver plate holder, acid-etched deep cranberry to clear floral design, patent dated Aug. 22, 1893, holder marked "Pairpoint," 2 pcs. **425**

Collars & cuffs box, cov., white opal wide short cylindrical box in the form of two collars w/a big bow in the front, the cover decorated w/Oriental poppies in shades of pink & orange w/a silver poppy finial w/gold trim, the sides of the base also w/Oriental poppies & gold trim, the bow at the bottom front in bright blue w/white polka dots & a buckle at the back, signed on the base "Patent applied for April 10, 1894," large **950**

Compote, open, 9 1/2" h., "Napoli," clear w/disk foot & tall slender stem supporting a low widely flaring ruffled bowl, enameled in the bowl w/blue, yellow, purple & red blossoms & green leaves, further leafage down the stem, traces of gilt outlining, unmarked **308**

Condiment set: salt & pepper shakers, cov. mustard pot & holder; robin's egg blue ground decorated w/daisies, silver plate holder w/swan-shaped feet & center ring handle signed "Wilcox," 4 pcs. **275**

Mt. Washington Cracker Jar

Cracker jar, cov., barrel-shaped, shaded pink & creamy white ground decorated w/delicate flowering branches, silver plate rim w/crimped edge, domed cover & arched bail swing handle, silver w/Pairpoint logo, slight wear to silver plate, 7" h. (ILLUS.)..................................... **345**

Cracker jar, cov., exterior decorated w/acorns & oak leaves on a pale pink shading to pale yellow ground, white interior, silver plate rim, cover & bail handle, cover marked "No. 4404/a".................. **900**

Melon-form Crown Milano Cracker Jar

Cracker jar, cov., melon-ribbed squatty white opal body decorated w/blackberries & green leaves, silver plate rim, domed cover & scroll-trimmed bail handle, silver marked w/Pairpoint logo, 5" h. (ILLUS.)...................................... **750**

Cracker jar, cov., Shell mold, decorated w/gold enameling w/touches of colored enamels, silver plate rim, cover & bail handle **475**

Creamer & cov. sugar bowl, "Albertine," deeply ribbed milk white body w/gold trim, silver plate cover marked "MW," creamer & sugar bowl signed w/Wreath & Crown, pr. **900**

Cruet w/original stopper, acid-cut white body, yellow throat, handle & stopper, decorated w/large leaves & blue berries ... **1,950**

Cruet w/original stopper, soft yellow shaded ground enameled w/blue & white flowers, satin finish **1,950**

Cruet w/original thorn stopper, applied frosted twig handle, apricot Diamond Quilted satin ground (chip on stopper) **450**

Dresser box, cov., round footed silver plate box w/a hinged lid inset w/a round opal glass disk h.p. w/delicate flower clusters, satin-lined, base w/the Pairpoint mark, 4 1/2" d., 1 3/4" h. (silver & satin worn) **275**

Dresser tray, free-form shape w/three turned-in scallops, h.p. purple irises & green leaves on a white satin ground, 8 x 8" **275**

Ewer, Colonial Ware line, wide squatty bulbous body tapering to a short cylindrical neck w/an arched spout, applied S-scroll reeded gilt shoulder handle, the sides decorated w/two bouquets of assorted garden flowers in pink, purple & yellow, encircled w/raised gold scrolls & con-

nected w/gold netting above an ivory white ground, glossy finish, 6" h. **650**

Flower bowl, raised satin Diamond Quilted patt., decorated w/a soft pink rim & enameled bouquets of yellow & white forget-me-nots, 4 x 4 1/2", 3 1/4" h.............. **350**

Flower frog, mushroom-shaped, the wide domed top in pale shaded blue satin enameled w/delicate colored florals, the top raised on a slender trumpet foot, 5" d., 3 1/4" h. **338**

Flower holder, footed mushroom shape, pale blue shading to white, decorated w/small white & yellow flowers & green leaves, 5" d., 3 1/2" h. **300-375**

Hatpin holder, mushroom-shaped, wide domed round top pierced w/holes & raised on a trumpet base, shaded pale blue ground enameled w/sprigs of blue & white forget-me-nots on the top, 5 1/2" d., 3 1/4" h. **339**

Jewel box w/hinged lid, squared form, the base w/rounded shoulders above relief-molded wreaths of roses & tied bows & garlands of roses in white against a pale green ground further decorated w/painted roses & baby asters, the conforming lid w/matching molded decoration & a white central medallion w/painted flowers, original "MTW" factory numbers on the base "3 2 12/26," ca. 1885, 7 1/2" w., 4 1/4" h. **1,250**

Rare Colonial Ware Lamp

Lamp, banquet-style, Colonial Ware, spherical ball shade on a metal ring & burner above a small squatty bulbous font w/ribbed scroll upturned handles above the tall slender shaft flaring to a wide squatty bulbous base, shiny opaque ground decorated down the side of the base w/a wide gilded ribbon of glass & h.p. on the shade w/a gilt lattice background at the lower section of the base, marked, all original, 38" h. (ILLUS.)... **12,650**

Mt. Washington Cameo Lamp

Lamp, table model, cameo-type, 10" d. open-topped domical shade in opal white overlaid in bright rose pink & acid-etched w/butterflies, ribbons & bouquets centering cameo classical portrait medallions, matching squatty bulbous base, silver plated burner, shoulder ring & round knob-footed base marked "Pairpoint Mfg. Co. 3013," electrified, needs rewiring, overall 17" h. (ILLUS.) **6,000**

Lamp, table model, 10" d. Mt. Washington Cameo shade in rose pink cut to white w/four beaded ovals w/a repeated portrait of woman wearing a Roman helmet, alternating w/floral & scrolled fern designs, resting on a reeded columnar metal base w/a triple pod leaf foot, overall 17 1/2" h. **750**

Mustard pot, cov., bulbous ribbed body, decorated w/florals, silver plate rim & cover **325**

Photo box, decorated overall w/gold scrolls & enameled blue forget-me-nots, satin finish, 3 3/4 x 5" **135**

Pitcher, 4 1/4" h., bulbous ribbed body in light blue shaded to white w/a satin finish, robin's egg blue interior **94**

Pitcher, 8 3/4" h., shaded pink mother-of-pearl satin Diamond Quilted patt., wide ovoid body tapering to a wide neck w/a tricorner rim w/crimping at the back & a wide smooth spout at the front, the sides enameled w/large white stylized flowers, applied clear reeded handle **880**

Powder box, cov., round, h.p. violets on base & cover **75**

Rare Mt. Washington Punch Bowl

Punch bowl on stand, decorated in the Royal Flemish manner, deep rounded bowl w/a flaring & notched rim, domed base, the bowl decorated w/three reserves of Palmer Cox Brownies in comic scenes involving a keg of ale, gilt scrolling trim, some gold loss, chip on base insert edge, 16" d., 13 1/2" h. (ILLUS.) **20,000**

Ring holder, saucer base supports a beaded ring-stick, satin white ground enameled w/blue forget-me-nots **85**

Rose bowl, bulbous base w/rim flaring to twelve protruding "fingers," white satin ground decorated w/lavender pansies & yellow rim, 4" d., 3" h. **375**

Rose bowl, crystal w/optic ribbing, the rim highlighted in gold, green ivy leaf decoration w/rust-colored stems w/petite pink & yellow blossoms **485**

Salt dip, individual, ribbed opal ground decorated w/a beaded gold rim & colored florals **110**

Salt & pepper shakers w/original lids, bulbous blue optic ribbed form enameled w/colorful florals, fitted in a marked Pairpoint silver plate footed stand w/central loop handle, 4 3/4" h., the set...................... **770**

Salt & pepper shakers w/original metal lids, fig-shaped, enameled daisy & forget-me-not decoration, pr. **350-400**

Salt & pepper shakers w/original metal lids, lobed tomato-shape, one w/a pink satin ground, the other w/a blue ground, each enamel-decorated w/a leaf & berry design, pr. **225**

Salt & pepper shakers w/original metal lids, molded acorn shape, h.p. floral decoration, pr. **138**

Set of Four Mt. Washington Shakers

Salt & pepper shakers w/original metal lids, lobed tomato-shape, each painted w/a pastel-colored floral band on a white satin ground, 2" h., set of 4 (ILLUS.) **400**

Salt & pepper shakers w/original metal lids, lobed tomato-shape, one shaded peach to creamy white, the other pale blue to creamy white, each enameled w/tiny green & blue florals, 2 1/2" d., 2" h., pr. (ILLUS. of one, top next page) **150-200**

Salt & pepper shakers w/original metal lids, egg-shaped, one deocrated w/fuschia blossoms & the other w/a band of ivy, 2 1/2" h., pr. (ILLUS. left & right, next page) **325**

Salt & pepper shakers w/original metal lids, cockle shell-shaped, one a Burmese color w/pale pink enameled flowers, the other in white opal painted w/a pastel pink floral bouquet, 2 3/4" l., pr. **2,200**

Salt & pepper shakers w/original tops, tapering five-lobed pear shape, delicate floral decoration on a white satin ground, pr. **150**

Salt & pepper shakers w/original two-piece metal tops, five-lobed apple-shaped body, matching decoration of pink & blue florals, pr. **225**

Mt. Washington Tomato-form Shaker

Salt, Pepper & Sugar Shakers

Salt shaker, lay-down egg-form, soft shaded colors on opal w/fine enameled florals **165**

Salt shaker w/original metal lid, fig-shaped, pale blue ground decorated w/green foliage & yellow flowers, 2 1/2" h. **220**

Salt shaker w/original metal lid, fig-shaped, cranberry enameled w/delicate flower blossoms, pointed metal lid, 2 1/2" w. **413**

Salt shaker w/original metal lid, ovoid lay-down form in mottled light tan deco-rated w/florals, figural silver plate chick head lid, rare, 2 3/4" l. **660**

Salt shaker w/original metal lid, figural cockle shell-form, decorated w/miniature yellow roses, 3" d. **1,760**

Salt shaker w/original top, egg-shaped, h.p. orchid decoration **150**

Salt shaker w/original top, egg-shaped, reclining-type, h.p. floral decoration on a white satin ground **100**

Salt shaker w/original top, egg-shaped, reclining-type w/a flat base, decorated w/pink apple blossoms on a white satin ground **150**

Salt shaker w/original top, figural cockle shell, decorated w/blue & yellow florals on a white satin ground **750**

Sugar shaker w/original metal lid, egg-shaped, clear cut glass in an overall fan design, 4 1/2" h. **1,045**

Sugar shaker w/original metal lid, lobed tomato-form opal body decorated w/enameled florals **440**

Sugar shaker w/original metal lid, melon-lobed tomato shape, pale green shoulder decorated w/pink & white enameled flowers, embossed floral lid, 2 1/2" h. **550**

Sugar shaker w/original metal lid, fig-shaped, shaded pale yellow to creamy opal, enameled w/dainty flowers & foli-age, 3 3/4" h. **2,310**

Sugar shaker w/original metal lid, fig-shaped, frosted clear Royal Flemish-style body decorated w/colorful pansies, 4" h. **2,000**

Sugar shaker w/original metal lid, figural cockle shell, the ribbed flattened body decorated w/a mottled wine red ground painted w/clumps of white enameled flowers w/colorful pastel leafy branches trimmed w/yellow highlights, 4" l. **5,720**

Sugar shaker w/original metal lid, egg-shaped, white satiny ground decorated w/a band of pink apple blossoms & green leaves, 4 1/4" h. (ILLUS. center w/salt & peppers) **375**

Scent bottle w/original stopper, milk white ground w/an overall decoration of color enameled florals, acid-etched on the base "Trademark of Mt. Washington Glass Co.," late 19th c., 9" h. **116**

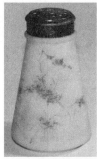

Tapering Cylindrical Sugar Shaker

Sugar shaker w/original metal lid, taper-ing cylindrical form, satin white ground decorated overall w/delicate stems of blue forget-me-nots, 4 3/4" h. (ILLUS.) **400**

Sugar shaker w/original metal top, squatty lobed tomato-shape, creamy ground enameled w/delicate blue & yel-low blossoms on leafy green stems, orig-inal embossed metal lid **258**

Sugar shaker w/original metal top, tomato-shaped, yellow ground w/enam-eled floral decoration **450**

Syrup pitcher w/original top, cannon ball-shaped, h.p. roses & foliage on a white opal ground, 5 3/4" h. **275**

Tazza, cornflower blue bowl w/engraved floral decoration, silver plate pedestal base w/three dolphin-shaped feet, signed **450**

Toothpick holder, bulbous melon-lobed body, decorated w/h.p. blue florals on a shaded yellow to white ground **150**

Toothpick holder, transfer-printed scene of three Brownies in a group on front & a Brownie dressed as an Indian w/hatchet on the reverse, light blue shaded to white (very minor flake on rim) **450**

Toothpick holder, fig-shaped, opaque satin w/salmon coloring & blue enameled floral sprays, 1 3/4" h. 950

Tumbler, cylindrical, Colonial Ware line w/a white glossy ground decorated around the body w/two raised gold bows suspending garlands of assorted flowers, crown & wreath mark on bottom, 3 3/4" h. 550

Fine Decorated Napoli Vase

Vase, 5" h., 6" d., "Napoli," globular w/widely flaring rim, colorless crystal dimpled bowl w/molded swirls, decorated w/gold floral tracery, green blossoms on rim, marked "Napoli 837" (ILLUS.)... **1,500**

Vase, 5 1/2" h., melon-ribbed body w/ruffled rim, apricot mother-of-pearl satin Raindrop patt., white lining.......................... 250

Rare Mt. Washington "Lava" Vase

Vase, 6" h., "Lava," wide ovoid body tapering to a trumpet neck, applied reeded black ring shoulder handles (ILLUS.)... **2,000-2,800**

Vase, 6" h., 5 3/4" d., footed squatty bulbous body tapering to a short cylindrical neck flaring to a four-fold rim, twenty-four swirling molded ribs in body, decorated w/blue & white forget-me-nots, signed.. **1,200**

Vase, 8" h., eight-ribbed body w/a flared rim, colored base w/green thistle decoration outlined in gold in the Verona manner 201

Vase, 11 1/2" h., decorated w/enameled spider mums & leaves & heavy gold branches, signed... 950

Vase, 13 1/2" h., pinched-form, white opal ground decorated w/enameled flowers in pink, gold & brown, marked at the base w/numbers & letter "P" 550

Vase, 14" h., ruffled rim, Delft blue h.p. windmill scene on white ground 375

MULLER FRÈRES

The Muller Brothers made acid-etched cameo and other fine glass at Luneville, France, starting in 1910 and until the outbreak of World War II in Europe.

Muller Freres Mark

Cameo lamp, table model, 19" d. wide domed umbrella-form shade on a bulbous nearly spherical matching base, both in grey overlaid in amber & forest green & cut w/a landscape of birch trees, simple four-arm iron mount, signed in cameo "MULLER FRES - LUNEVILLE," overall 19" h. **$25,300**

Cameo lamp, table model, a large 8" d. pointed mushroom shade on a three-arm wrought-iron mount above the slightly tapering cylindrical base w/a thick cushion foot, shade & base in creamy opalescent internally mottled w/ochre-yellow & blue, overlaid in deep crimson & midnight red & cut w/poppy blossoms & leafage, both signed "MULLER FRES - LUNEVILLE," ca. 1925, overall 14 1/2" h. **10,925**

Cameo vase, 7" h., 8 1/2" d., a cased dark blue short wide neck w/a jagged edge over the wide bulbous textured crystal body w/a central ridge, decorated w/a band of iridescent aqua swimming fish & a band of dark blue bubble designs around the base, signed in cameo **4,070**

Cameo vase, 8 1/4" h., fluogravure-style, footed ovoid body tapering to a short neck w/swelled ring below the flat upright rim, dark orange over white overlaid w/pale lavender, blackish green & white & cut & enameled w/a continuous landscape w/birch trees in the foreground, signed, ca. 1900.......................... **4,887**

Cameo vase, 10 1/2" h., ovoid form, grey infused w/creamy opalescence, overlaid in amber, moss green & charcoal, cut w/a mountainous landscape, signed in cameo **6,900**

Muller Fres. Blue Cameo Vase

Cameo vase, 11" h., bulbous ovoid body
w/a short cylindrical neck, grey internally
decorated w/silver foil inclusions, overlaid in turquoise & deep cobalt blue & cut
w/stylized large blossoms & leaves,
signed in cameo, ca. 1925 (ILLUS.).......... **3,450**

Cameo vase, 13 1/2" h., wide cylindrical
form rounded at the base & shoulder &
tapering to a low flat rim, grey shaded
lemon yellow & overlaid in orange &
brown & cut w/a continuous river landscape of leafy trees, signed in cameo
"MULLER FRES. - LUNEVILLE," pontil
label stamped "MADE IN FRANCE," &
vendor's label stamped "FORTU-
NATOR A. FASCE - Florida 425 - BUE-
NOS AIRES," ca. 1900.............................. **3,450**

Cameo vase, 17" h., ovoid body tapering to
a small neck w/flared rim, grey cased
over brilliant orange & encased by deep
brown, cut w/four ovoid reserves enclosing stylized flowerheads, signed in
cameo, ca. 1925.. **805**

Cameo vase, 17" h., wide gently flaring
cylindrical body w/an angled shoulder to
the low wide flat neck, dark orange
shaded to pale yellow mottled w/pale
green & overlaid in deep orangish red &
brown, cameo cut w/large roses on long
leafy stems, signed, ca. 1925................... **7,475**

Large Muller Fres. Floral Cameo Vase

Cameo vase, 18 1/2" h., ovoid body tapering to a flattened flaring rim, creamy
opalescent ground mottled w/ochre-yel-
low & blue, overlaid in crimson red &
deep umber & cut w/undulating poppy

blossoms & leaves, signed in cameo, ca.
1925 (ILLUS.)... **5,462**

Center bowl, wide low form w/incurved
sides, grey w/interior mottling in cobalt
blue, green, pink, amber & yellow,
signed on the side, 7 3/4" h....................... **476**

Rare Muller Frères Ewer

Ewer, squatty wide base w/an angled
shoulder sharply tapering to a tall neck
w/upright pointed & scallop-edged rim,
applied pale amber handle down the
neck, the sides w/a continuous carved &
enameled frieze in "fluogravure" of an
evening scene w/a deep red owl
perched on a branch before an impres-
sionistic wooded landscape in shades of
ochre, umber, chocolate brown, sapphire blue & opalescent olive green,
signed in cameo "Muller Croismare," ca.
1900, 10 5/8" h. (ILLUS.)........................ **11,500**

Lamp, table model, bullet-form shade of
grey glass molded w/a textured surface,
molded "Muller Fres - Luneville," on a
wrought-iron base composed of seven
scrolls on a square foot & surmounted
by four arms to support the shade, ca.
1925, overall 16" h. **1,725**

Muller Freres Table Lamp

Lamp, table model, molded & frosted grey
subtly shaded w/pale amber, the globular base molded in medium-relief
w/spread-winged swans & bands of berried foliage, mounted w/a silvered
wrought-iron three-arm mount supporting a domed shade molded in medium-
relief w/a star-form flower on a field of
overlapping petals, the shaped rim

w/sunbursts alternating w/stylized flowerheads, molded mark on shade,
chips, ca. 1935, 15" h. (ILLUS.) **2,300**
Vase, 11 1/4" h., tapering ovoid body
w/frosted surface in mottled cobalt blue,
orange & yellow, acid-stamped on lower
side "Muller Fres - Luneville" (annealing
fracture at rim) **633**

NAILSEA

*Nailsea was another glassmaking center in
England where a variety of wares similar to those
from Bristol, England were produced between 1788
and 1873. Today most collectors think of Nailsea
primarily as a glass featuring swirls and loopings,
usually white, on a clear or colored ground. This
style of glass decoration, however, was not
restricted to Nailsea and was produced in many
other glasshouses, including some in America.*

Fine Nailsea Bottle

Bottle, no stopper, cylindrical w/wide
angled shoulder to a short cylindrical
neck w/a flattened rim, clear w/white &
light pink looping, pontiled base, probably made for a cork closure, 19th c.,
6 1/4" h. (ILLUS.) **$385**
Flask, flattened ovoid form w/pointed base
& short cylindrical neck, clear w/pulled
white & pink looping, 8 3/4" l. **220**

Colorful Nailsea Flask

Flask, flattened ovoid form w/pointed base
& short ringed cylindrical neck, heavily
looped bands of red, white & blue, light
wear, 8 1/2" h. (ILLUS.) **303**

Flask, long flattened ovoid form w/narrow
flat base & short cylindrical neck, clear
w/tightly pulled white & pink looping,
7 3/4" l. **193**

Two Nailsea Rolling Pins

Rolling pin, cylindrical w/end knob handles, ruby ground w/fine bands of white
loopings, 19th c., 12" l. (ILLUS. top) **385**
Rolling pin, cylindrical w/long tapering
handles, clear w/red, white & blue loop-
ings, tooled ends, light wear, 14" l. **193**
Rolling pin, cylindrical w/short knob handles, clear w/deep blue & white loopings,
tooled ends, one w/polished pontil, other
w/cork, overall wear, 14 1/2" l. **204**
Rolling pin, cylindrical w/knob ends, clear
w/blue & red spattering on a white
ground, tooled ends, one w/a pontil,
other w/a cork, light overall wear, 15" l. **275**
Rolling pin, cylindrical w/knob end han-
dles, clear w/elongated cranberry &
white looping, 16 1/4" l. (ILLUS. bottom) **330**
Sugar bowl w/witch ball cover, bowl
w/applied clear foot supporting the
nearly spherical body w/wide galleried
rim, clear w/heavy white looping, fitted
w/a large clear white ball w/white loop-
ings, overall 8 1/2" h. **660**
Vase, 11 1/2" h., bulbous lower body w/a
tall cylindrical neck w/a widely rolled rim,
clear w/heavy white looping down the
sides, on an applied clear short pedestal
foot w/pontil, probably Pittsburgh (some
interior residue & cloudiness) **605**
Vase & witch ball, 11 1/4" h., free-blown
vase of trumpet form w/cushion foot,
clear w/white loopings, supporting a
round clear ball w/white loopings, 2 pcs. **660**

Nailsea Vase & Witch Ball

Vase & witch ball, white loopings in clear
vase w/a tall cylindrical bowl w/a wide
rolled rim & a swelled, ringed base
raised on an applied clear stem & disk
foot, topped by a large 5" d. witch ball in

clear w/white loopings, overall 14" h., 2
pcs. (ILLUS.) **2,640**

NAKARA

*Like Kelva, Nakara was made early in this cen-
tury by the C.F. Monroe Company. For details see
WAVE CREST.*

Box w/hinged cover, decorated w/h.p.
cupids on a blue ground, 3" d.................... **$425**

Small Nakara Box with Flowers

Box w/hinged cover, Hexagonal mold, the
top w/wide shaded pink angled panels
decorated w/large daisy-like blossoms
alternating w/tan panels w/white beading, the base w/a shaded pink ground
decorated w/large white blossoms,
signed, 3 1/4" w., 3" h. (ILLUS.) **375**

Nakara Box with Pansy Lid

Box w/hinged cover, molded Pansy lid,
green ground, 3 3/4" h. (ILLUS.) **765**
Box w/hinged cover, Hexagonal mold,
green ground w/pink roses on the top &
base, 4" w.. **425**
Box w/hinged cover, h.p. pink daisies dec-
oration on a blue ground, 4" d., 2 3/4" h....... **325**
Box w/hinged cover, green satin ground
w/portrait of woman on cover, raised
beading at border, original lining,
4 1/2" d.. **750**
Box w/hinged cover, Octagonal mold,
footed, green ground decorated w/large
pink rose, 4 1/2" w...................................... **550**
Box w/hinged cover, Octagonal mold,
plum ground w/Kate Greenaway tea
party scene, 4 1/2" w.................................. **750**
Box w/hinged cover, cov., Bishop's Hat
mold, blue ground w/florals, 5" w. **650**
Box w/hinged cover, oval, light green
w/pink roses & crown in center of lid,
5 1/2" l... **475**

Rare Nakara Portrait Box

Box w/hinged cover, Bishop's Hat mold,
the top decorated w/a large portrait
reserve featuring the bust of Queen Louise framed by a deep pink ground
w/scrolls & blossoms of white beading,
deep pink base w/matching white bead-
ing, 5 3/4" w., 4 1/4" h. (ILLUS.) **1,050**
Box w/hinged cover, Octagonal mold,
lemon yellow shaded to deep peach
ground decorated w/h.p. orchid-like blossoms in shades of orchid w/green foliage
& white beading, 6" w.................................. **550**
Box w/hinged cover, Octagonal mold, low
paneled base & conforming cover, each
half decorated w/purple iris on a yellow-
ish tan ground, 6" w. **990**
Box w/hinged cover, peach colored
ground, the cover decorated w/a color
scene of an 18th c. courting couple,
trimmed w/blue flowers, original lining,
marked, 6" d. (missing clasp) **1,370**

Nakara Box with Portrait Decoration

Box w/hinged cover, round, Burmese coloring w/18th century courting couple on
the cover, 6" d. (ILLUS.)............................. **1,250**
Box w/hinged cover, yellow shaded to
green ground decorated w/pink & white
flowers outlined in gold, white beading
on cover, 6" d. **875**
Box w/hinged cover, Octagonal mold,
shaded pale peach to brown ground
decorated w/h.p. yellow flowers w/pink
centers, 6 1/4" d., 4 1/2" h. **975**

Ornate Nakara Box

Box w/hinged cover, Crown mold, cover & sides w/a green ground w/swirled panels decorated w/pink roses, gold trim & enameled beading, gilt-metal base & scroll feet, clasp missing, 8" d., 6 1/4" h. (ILLUS.).. **2,500**

Box w/hinged cover, Rococo mold, decorated overall w/dainty beaded flowers, 8" d. **1,200**

Box w/hinged cover, shaded peach ground, the cover decorated w/two cupids, one w/a palette before an easel painting a lady's portrait, floral decoration around the base, original lining, 8" d. .. **2,315**

Box w/hinged cover, Crown mold, cover decorated w/five h.p. roses on an olive green ground, sides w/similar decoration, 8" d., 5" h. **1,750**

Cigar humidor, cov., blue mottled ground decorated w/h.p. pink flowers, "Cigars" in gold on the side **950**

Dresser box w/hinged cover, Bishop's Hat mold, blue ground finely decorated w/purple violets, original lining, wide gilt-metal rim fittings & base band w/pierced scroll feet, 4 3/4" w., 4 3/4" h. **798**

Dresser box w/hinged cover, Crown mold, shaded dark gold ground decorated w/h.p. large white & blue daisies, original lining & interior mirror, 8 1/2" w..... **2,090**

Dresser tray, squatty rounded tapering sides w/a decorative gilt-metal rim band & lacy tab handles, autumn green ground decorated w/a garland of pink mums highlighted w/white enamel, 6"d., 2 1/4" h. **248**

Ferner, cylindrical base below a bulbous shoulder, molded w/bands of leafy scrolls around the top & base, raised on a gilt-metal base w/scrolled feet (no metal liner) **650**

Fernery, deep wide cylindrical form w/rounded rims & a gilt-metal rim band, a dark green washed ground enameled w/large pink blossoms on scrolling stems trimmed w/white beading, marked, 8" d. **644**

Humidor, cov., decorated w/an owl sitting in a tree, metal lid..................................... **1,500**

Humidor, cov., base decorated w/h.p. enameled florals & "Tobacco" in gold, 7" w., 7" h. **750**

Humidor w/brass lid, wide bulbous baluster-form body w/a fitted domed metal lid w/wide knob, the shaded deep red to tan sides decorated w/a colorful bust portrait

of a Native American in headdress, 6" d., 5 1/2" h. **1,270**

Humidor w/hinged lid, flaring cylindrical body w/a swelled shoulder, a wide flattened domed cover, the side decorated w/a brown & white elk head & "B.P.O.E.," & "Tobacco" on the cover, shaded dark green to tan ground (ILLUS. below) **1,495**

"B.P.O.E." Tobacco Humidor

Humidor w/hinged lid, low wide tapering cylindrical base w/a wide low domed cover, the side decorated w/a color portrait of a Native American in full headdress w/h.p. trim & the word "Cigars" on the cover, brass holder for moistener inside cover, 6 1/2" d., 5 3/4" h. **750**

Pin tray, Bishop's Hat mold, yellow ground decorated w/delicate pink flowers, 4" w. **350**

Pin tray, decorated w/delicate roses, 4 1/2" d. **350**

Pin tray, Bishop's Hat mold, pink & white flowers on green ground, 5 1/2" w............... **450**

Small Nakara Ring Box

Ring box w/hinged lid, squared flat top w/notched corners, squatty rounded base w/corner notches, the lid w/a white diamond decorated w/a romantic couple in costume framed by pale blue w/small daisy-like flowers, the shoulder in creamy white & the base sides in pale blue, 2 1/2" h. (ILLUS.)................................. **950**

Salt shaker w/original metal top, concave bulb shape, decorated w/a transfer scene of Niagara Falls applied over a tan painted background, 2 5/8" h. **175**

Vase, 8" h., squatty bulbous base tapering to a tall cylindrical neck, h.p. florals &

white beaded decoration on a blue shaded to yellow ground, w/decorative footed ormolu base 375

Vase, 13 1/2" h., footed, burnt orange ground decorated w/purple irises **1,500**

Vase, 15 3/4" h., ovoid top tapering to a slightly flared base w/footring, pink & white flowers on a shaded green ground .. **1,900**

Tall Nakara Vase

Vase, 15 3/4" h., tall slender baluster-form body w/a wide flaring mouth, decorated w/large pink & white flowers on a shaded pale green ground (ILLUS.) **2,000**

NASH

A. Douglas Nash, a former employee of Louis Comfort Tiffany, purchased Tiffany's Corona Works in December 1928 and began his own operation there. For a brief period Nash produced some outstanding glasswares but the factory closed in March of 1931 and Nash then became associated with Libbey Glass of Toledo, Ohio. This quality glass is quite scarce.

Bowl, small, raised Maize patt. in gold iridescent w/blue highlights, signed **$175**

Bowl, 4 1/2" d., 4 1/2" h., blue ground w/silver mottling decorated w/red pulled-up stripes 175

Bowl, 8" d., Chintz patt., signed 165

Bowl, 8 3/4" d., footed low squatty round form w/upright optic ribbed fluted sides decorated w/a gold iridescent finish, signed "NASH" 303

Compote, open, 3 1/4 x 6 1/4", low, footed, scalloped top & ribbed body, overall gold iridescence, signed 550

Compote, open, 7 1/2" d., 4 1/2" h., Chintz patt., a domed wide foot & short pedestal supporting a deep rounded bowl w/a very wide, flattened rim, aquamarine transparent bowl & base w/the flat rim of red & greyish green controlled stripe decoration, base inscribed "Nash RD89" **950**

Console bowl, Chintz patt., violet & lime green, signed "501 - DD - NASH," 12" d. 330

Cordials, Chintz patt., red w/overall silver decoration, signed, set of 6 950

Goblet, round foot centered by a small compressed knop & a slender waisted stem supporting a tall tulip-form bowl w/slightly flaring rim, iridescent gold

w/orange, blue & violet highlights, signed "Nash," 7" h. 275

Nut bowl, ruffled rim, iridescent gold w/blue highlights, 3" d., 2 3/8" h 125

Vase, 5 1/2" h., Chintz patt., wide ovoid body w/a wide angled shoulder tapering to a short rolled neck, clear internally striped w/pastel orange alternating w/yellow Chintz decoration 275

Fine Nash Chintz Vase

Vase, 5 1/2" h., Chintz patt., wide-shouldered heavy ovoid body w/a short flaring neck, deep rose red w/alternating wide & narrow vertical silver lustre stripes, base signed "Nash RD 66" (ILLUS.) **1,000**

Vase, 5 1/2" h., wide bulbous ovoid body w/the wide rounded shoulder centered by a short rolled neck, brilliant red w/controlled blackish brown striped decoration, base signed 863

Vase, 7" h., 4" d., flared square shape, overall gold iridescence, signed 290

Vase, 8 1/2" h., Chintz patt., dark blue w/silvery iridescence 575

Vase, 9" h. "Polka Dot" style, gently swelled ovoid body tapering to a wide trumpet neck, deep opaque red molded w/sixteen prominent ribs, decorated by spaced white opal dots overall, base inscribed "Nash GD154" **1,093**

Vase, 11" h., Chintz patt., bulbous base surmounted by a cylindrical neck & short everted lip, red w/pale gold stripes, signed "NASH RD 86," ca. 1930 546

Vases, 4" h., ribbed & tapering ovoid body w/an everted lip & round foot, amber w/pink & blue iridescence, signed "Nash - 544," pr. 287

Small Iridescent Nash Vases

Vases, 4 1/4" h., tapering ovoid body w/indented panels around the base & interior ribbing on the short, flaring rim, applied to a disk foot, overall gold iridescence, signed "Nash 544," pr. (ILLUS.) **900**

OPALESCENT

Presently, this is one of the most popular areas of glass collecting. The opalescent effect was attained by adding bone ash chemicals to areas of an item while still hot and refiring the object at tremendous heat. Both pressed and mold-blown patterns are available to collectors and we distinguish the types in our listing below. Opalescent Glass from A to Z by the late William Heacock is the definitive reference book for collectors.

MOLD-BLOWN OPALESCENT PATTERNS

BIG WINDOWS
Lamp, kerosene finger-type, Swirl mold, cranberry **$995**
Lamp, stand-type, No. 1, Eason (rare)............. **635**

CHRYSANTHEMUM SWIRL
Creamer, cranberry **385**

Chrysanthemum Swirl Sugar Shaker

Sugar shaker w/original lid, blue (ILLUS.)... **340**
Sugar shaker w/original lid, cranberry........... **495**
Table set: butter dish, creamer & spooner; cranberry, 3 pcs. **2,195**

COIN SPOT
Lemonade set, ruffled pitcher & 4 tumblers, white, 5 pcs. **295**
Pitcher, clover leaf-crimp rim, cranberry **325**
Pitcher, tankard, three-tiered, cranberry **1,375**
Pitcher, triangular crimped rim, Windows mold, cranberry **395**
Pitcher, 8 1/2" h., blue, ovoid w/ruffled rim & applied clear blue handle........................... **105**
Sugar shaker w/original lid, nine-panel, Jefferson variant, cranberry **295**

Coin Spot Sugar Shaker

Sugar shaker w/original lid, ring-neck mold, blue (ILLUS.) **148**
Sugar shaker w/original lid, ring-neck mold, cranberry **220**

Coin Spot Syrup Pitcher

Syrup pitcher w/original metal lid, blue (ILLUS.)... **145**

COIN SPOT & SWIRL
Syrup w/original lid, blue **369**

CRISS CROSS
Creamer, white... **318**
Spooner, white satin **185**

DAISY & FERN
Cruet w/original stopper, Apple Blossom mold, blue **295**
Cruet w/original stopper, blue, swirled rib body, applied blue handle, facet-cut stopper, 6 3/4" h. **175-225**

Daisy & Fern Cruet

Cruet w/original stopper, Parian Swirl mold, cranberry (ILLUS.).............................. **723**
Pitcher, 8 3/4" h., bulbous body tapering to a flaring upright squared & ruffled neck, applied clear handle, cranberry **220**
Spooner, Parian Swirl mold, cranberry **175**
Sugar shaker w/original lid, blue **295**
Sugar shaker w/original lid, Parian Swirl mold, cranberry **355**
Tumbler, cranberry **98**

FERN
Cruet w/original stopper, blue **343**
Salt shaker w/original top, cranberry **195**

HOBNAIL, HOBBS'

Hobb's Hobnail Celery Vase

Celery vase, 9" h., bulbous cylindrical body w/a crimped & ruffled rim, cranberry (ILLUS.).. **248**
Pitcher, water, bulbous body w/square mouth, cranberry **440**
Pitcher, 8" h., bulbous body w/a squared mouth, canary **165**
Water set: pitcher & four tumblers; cranberry, applied clear handle on pitcher, bulbous w/squared mouth, pitcher 8" h., the set **605**

LATTICE (BUCKEYE)
Spooner, cranberry **165**

POINSETTIA
Syrup pitcher w/original metal lid, blue **900**

REVERSE SWIRL
Cruet w/original stopper, cranberry **375**

Reverse Swirl Sugar Shaker

Sugar shaker w/original lid, cranberry (ILLUS.) **490**
Syrup pitcher w/original lid, blue.................. **345**
Toothpick holder, cranberry **220**
Tumbler, cranberry **105**
Water bottle, cranberry satin **545**

RIBBED OPAL LATTICE
Cruet w/original stopper, cranberry **595**
Spooner, cranberry **185**
Sugar shaker w/original lid, cranberry **330**

Ribbed Opal Lattice Toothpick Holder

Toothpick holder, blue (ILLUS.)...................... **140**
Tumbler, cranberry **135**

SEAWEED
Bowl, master berry, cranberry **275**

SPANISH LACE

Spanish Lace Bowl

Bowl, w/upturned rim, canary, 7" d. (ILLUS.).. **100-125**
Butter dish, cov., canary................... **445**
Pickle castor, cov., cranberry cylindrical insert, ornate Meriden silver plate frame w/floral decoration, cover & tongs, overall 12 1/4" h. **440**
Pitcher, water, cranberry................................. **900**
Pitcher, water, 9 1/2" h., ruffled rim, blue........ **500**

Spanish Lace Opalescent Rose Bowl

Rose bowl, white (ILLUS.) **90**
Tumbler, canary **50**

STARS & STRIPES
Cruet w/original stopper, cranberry **575**

Stars & Stripes Tumbler

Tumbler, cranberry (ILLUS.) **450-475**

STRIPE
Celery vase, blue 145

Stripe Pitcher

Pitcher, ring-neck mold, cranberry (ILLUS.).. **1,500**
Tumbler, cranberry 60

SWIRL
Celery vase, blue 135

Swirl Sugar Shaker

Sugar shaker, blue (ILLUS.) **300-400**
Sugar shaker w/original lid, cranberry **488**

SWIRLING MAIZE
Tumbler, cranberry 105

TWIST, BLOWN
Sugar shaker w/original lid, blue 295

WIDE STRIPE
Cruet w/original stopper, blue 395

WINDOWS, SWIRL
Sugar shaker w/original lid, cranberry 635

PRESSED OPALESCENT PATTERNS

ARGONAUT SHELL
Butter dish, cov., white.................................. 243
Creamer & cov. sugar bowl, undecorated,
    white, no gold, pr... 225

Jelly compote, canary, enamel decorated 145
Sauce dish, canary 90

Argonaut Shell Spooner

Spooner, blue (ILLUS.) 150-175
Spooner, white 169
Toothpick holder, canary............................... 465

BEADED SHELL
Creamer, green 162

BEATTY HONEYCOMB
Sugar shaker w/original lid, blue 260
Tumbler, blue... 275

BEATTY RIB

Beatty Rib Celery Vase

Celery vase, blue (ILLUS.)...................... 250-275
Salt dip, white 42
Spooner, white.. 43
Toothpick holder, blue.............................. 75-100
Toothpick holder, white 30

CIRCLED SCROLL
Cruet w/original stopper, blue....................... 575
Sauce dish, blue 50

DIAMOND SPEARHEAD
Butter dish, cov., blue 235

Diamond Spearhead Butter Dish

Butter dish, cov., green (ILLUS.).............. 225-250
Celery dish, green 275
Creamer, miniature, cobalt blue 68
Cruet w/original stopper, canary................... 325
Jelly compote, canary 150
Pitcher, 5 3/8" h. 145
Pitcher, 6" h. 159
Sugar bowl, cov., canary 235
Syrup pitcher w/original top, canary............. 775
Toothpick holder, canary................................. 95

Toothpick holder, cobalt blue 200
Toothpick holder, green 70

DOUBLE GREEK KEY
Bowl, master berry, blue, 8 1/2". 75

EVERGLADES
Butter dish, cov., canary 345
Salt shaker w/original top, canary 195
Sugar bowl, cov., canary 200

Everglades Spooner & Butter Dish

Table set, blue, 4 pcs. (ILLUS. of part) 550-600
Tumbler, white 28

FLORA
Spooner, blue 100
Syrup pitcher w/original lid, white w/gold
    trim 285

FLUTED SCROLLS

Fluted Scrolls Creamer

Creamer, blue w/enameled florals (ILLUS.) 75
Creamer, canary 145
Pitcher, water, blue 350
Rose bowl, canary 105
Sugar bowl, cov., blue 130
Water set: pitcher & 5 tumblers, blue, the
    set 645

GONTERMAN SWIRL
Sugar bowl, cov., amber................................ 235

HONEYCOMB & CLOVER
Pitcher, green 325
Tumbler, blue 100
Tumbler, green 110

INTAGLIO
Compote, jelly, canary 70

INVERTED FAN & FEATHER
Card tray, canary 255
Creamer, blue 125-150
Spooner, blue 150-175

IRIS WITH MEANDER
Bowl, 9" d., footed, green................................. 40
Butter dish, cov., blue 275

Iris with Meander Creamer

Creamer, blue (ILLUS.) 125
Creamer, green 85
Sauce dish, canary 25
Sauce dishes, blue, set of 5 380
Spooner, white 50
Sugar bowl, cov., blue 180
Toothpick holder, blue.................................... 115

JEWEL & FAN
Pickle dish, green.. 99

JEWEL & FLOWER
Cruet w/original stopper, blue....................... 750
Cruet w/original stopper, canary................... 750

Jewel & Flower Creamer & Sugar Bowl

Table set, canary w/gold trim, 4 pcs.
    (ILLUS. of part)...................................... 775-800
Tumbler, blue... 96

JEWELED HEART
Tumbler, green 65

LUSTRE FLUTE
Butter dish, cov., blue 475

NORTHWOOD DRAPERY
Table set, w/gold.. 325

REGAL, NORTHWOOD'S
Butter dish, cov., green................................. 250
Sugar bowl, cov., green................................... 85

RIBBED SPIRAL
Butter dish, cov., white.................................. 275
Compote, jelly, blue 67
Compote, jelly, white...................................... 100
Creamer, white... 180
Spooner, blue 105
Sugar bowl, cov., white 225
Vase, swung-type, white, 14" h. 60

S-REPEAT
Tumbler, blue... 55

SUNBURST-ON-SHIELD
Butter dish, cov., blue 345

Blue Sunburst-on-Shield Cruet

Cruet w/original stopper, blue (ILLUS.) 450

SWAG WITH BRACKETS
Butter dish, cov., green 250
Compote, jelly, green.. 60

Swag with Brackets Creamer

Creamer, blue (ILLUS.) 105-115
Cruet, green 350
Pitcher, green 325
Sauce dishes, green, set of 6.......................... 275
Sugar bowl, cov., canary 115-125
Toothpick holder, white 50
Tumbler, canary 55

TOKYO
Bowl, master berry, green.................................. 75
Butter dish, cov., green 175

Tokyo Compote

Compote, jelly, blue (ILLUS.).............................. 50
Creamer, blue 95
Creamer, canary 79
Plate, footed, blue 69
Spooner, white... 65
Sugar bowl, cov., blue 160

WATER LILY & CATTAILS
Bowl, master berry, blue 65
Bowl, master berry, purple 95
Bowl, six-sided, purple 65
Butter dish, cov., white.................................... 230
Creamer, purple 140

Water Lily & Cattails Pitcher

Pitcher, water, purple (ILLUS.)................. **225-250**
Plate, purple 85
Sauce dish, small, purple 45
Vase, purple 79

WILD BOUQUET
Berry set, blue, enameled, 5 pcs. 375

Wild Bouquet Jelly Compote

Compote, jelly, blue (ILLUS.) 160
Creamer, green 140
Pitcher, water, blue 300
Sauce dish, blue 60

WREATH & SHELL
Bowl, master berry, 8 1/2" d., canary 110
Bowl, master berry, 8 1/2" d., white 45
Butter dish, cov., blue 275
Cracker jar, cov., canary, h.p. decoration........ 250
Creamer, blue 175
Creamer, decorated, canary 135
Spooner, canary 250
Spooner, white.. 72
Sugar bowl, cov., blue 275
Table set, blue, 4 pcs....................................... 695
Table set, canary, 4 pcs. 650
Toothpick holder, canary 310
Tumbler, footed, canary.................................. 375

L.G. WRIGHT COPIES

Wright Apothecary Jar

Daisy & Fern patt. apothecary jar, cov., cranberry (ILLUS.) **450**
Daisy & Fern patt. barber bottle, blue **275**

Wright Daisy & Fern Finger Bowl

Daisy & Fern patt. finger bowl, green (ILLUS.) **125**
Daisy & Fern patt. pitcher, reeded handle, canary **375**

Wright Dot & Mitre Milk Pitcher

Dot & Mitre pitcher, milk, cranberry (ILLUS.) **600**
Moon & Star patt. goblet, canary **75**
Panel Grape patt. sauce dish, blue **25**

Wright Stars & Stripes Cruet

Stars & Stripes patt. cruet, no stopper, cranberry (ILLUS.) **300**

MISCELLANEOUS PRESSED NOVELTIES

Basketweave Base Bowl

Basketweave Base bowl, open-edge, canary (ILLUS.) **25-30**
Beaded Drapes rose bowl, blue **57**
Bushel Basket, blue **140**

Cashews Bowl

Cashews bowl, ruffled, white (ILLUS.) **65**
Corn vase, blue **180**
Dahlia vase, blue **60**
Dew Drop candleholders, square, canary, pr. **60**
Dew Drop creamer & open sugar bowl, canary, pr. **40**

Frosted Leaf & Basketweave Spooner

Frosted Leaf & Basketweave spooner, blue (ILLUS.) **100**

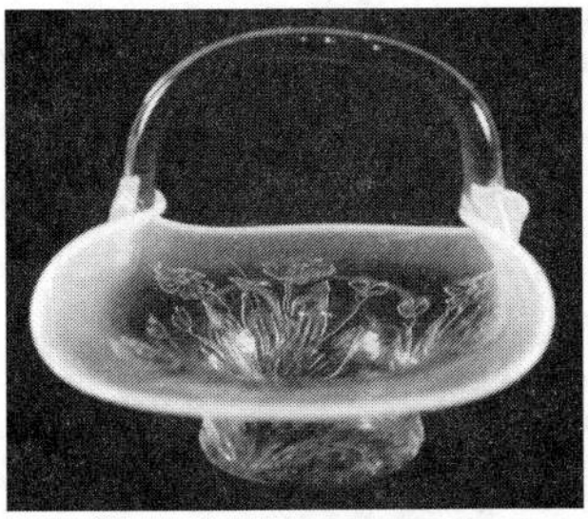

Dugan Intaglio Pattern Basket

Intaglio (Dugan's) basket, applied handle, white w/goofus decoration (ILLUS.) **60**
Jackson (Klondyke) creamer, blue, decorated **145**
Lace Edge vase, blue **30**
Lace Edge vase, green **35**
Northwood's Block celery vase, blue **55**

Peacocks on the Fence bowl, blue 300
Peacocks on the Fence bowl, ruffled,
green 145
Piasa Bird bowl, whimsey-type, blue 85
Piasa Bird rose bowl, blue.............................. 98
Pump & Trough, white, 2 pcs.......................... 195
Ruffles & Rings bowl, 9 1/2" d., green 38
Trailing Vine bowls, scalloped edges, var-
ious shapes, blue, each 110-150
Trailing Vine butter dish, cov., canary 225
Twist child's table set: creamer, cov.
sugar, cov. butter & spooner; canary, 4
pcs.. 450
Waffle & Vine compote, open, green.............. 500

OPALINE

Also called opal glass (once a name applied to milk-white glass), opaline is a fairly opaque glass with a color resembling the opal; however, pieces in such colors as blue, pink, green and others, also are referred to now as opaline glass. Many of the objects were decorated.

Powder box, cov., cranberry dots encircled
w/enameled foliage & gold trimmed cut
top & base, Bohemia, 4" d., 2 1/4" h. **$330**
Vase, 28 1/2" h., footed baluster-form w/tall
trumpet neck, the body & neck painted
w/a continuous scene of putti in various
pursuits among clouds, birds & beds of
flowers, the low domed round foot decorated w/rose-color leaf-tips & raised on a
square gilt-bronze base w/bracket feet,
France, late 19th c. 6,325

ORREFORS

This Swedish glasshouse, founded in 1898 for production of tablewares, has made decorative wares as well since 1915. By 1925, Orrefors had achieved an international reputation for its Graal glass, an engraved art glass developed by master glassblower Knut Berquist and artist-designers Simon Gate and Edward Hald. Ariel glass, recognized by a design of controlled air traps and the heavy Ravenna glass, usually tinted, were both developed in the 1930s. While all Orrefors glass is collectible, pieces signed by early designers and artists are now bringing high prices.

Orrefors Mark

$$\mathcal{O}r\,r\,e\,f\,o\,r\,s$$

Orrefors Mark

Bottle w/stopper, funnel-footed ovoid body
tapering to a very tall slender 'stick' neck
fitted w/a leaf-form stopper, pale smoky
amber, designed by Simon Gate, ca.
1925, unsigned, 15 3/8" h. **$230**
Bowl, 5" l., "Ravenna," small boat-form in
clear cased over dark blue tesserae
w/green interstices, inscribed "ORRE-
FORS - Ravenna 5115 - Sven Palmqvist," designed ca. 1948, executed
1971 862
Bowl, 6" d., 2 1/4" h., "Graal," a deep
rounded & gently flaring bowl w/flattened
rim raised on a thick disk foot, blue inter-

nally decorated w/colorless loops, foot
inscribed "Orrefors Graal 2109-E6
Edvard Hald," ca. 1940 1,380
Bowl, 11 3/4" l., "Kanterra," oblong form
w/upright pulled & ruffled sides, deep
burgundy cased over pale amber,
designed by Sven Palmqvist, ca. 1945,
inscribed "ORREFORS - pu 3023 - 1"........ 460
Bowl-vase, "Ariel," deep rounded thick-
walled vessel in clear infused w/vertical
bands of controlled air bubbles,
designed by Edvin Ohrstrom, inscribed
"Orrefors Sweden - Ariel - No. 520 - E.
Ohrstrom," ca. 1960s, 6 5/8" d., 3 1/4" h. 402

Cut Crystal Leopard Centerbowl

Centerbowl, cut crystal, caged animals
achieved by cut & faceted 'bars'
w/frosted spotted leopards behind peer-
ing through, raised upon applied dark
blue disk base inscribed "Orrefors 4688-
13 Gunnar Cyren," designed by Gunnar
Cyren, 8" d. (ILLUS.) 1,380
Charger, "Aqua Graal," broad round color-
less crystal form w/folded rim, internally
decorated w/concentric rings of aubergine windows & golden yellow swirls
all around a central dark core, designed
by Edward Hald, base signed "Aqua
Graal No. 481P - Edward Hald - Orrefors
'58," ca. 1958, 14 1/4" d. 805
Decanter, squared crystal bottle engraved
w/Romeo serenading on observe, Juliet
on balcony on reverse, optically as one,
case engraved "Orrefors No. 880,"
12 1/2" h... 345
Decanter w/stopper, domed rectangular
crystal form engraved on one side w/a
sailor playing accordion & on the other
w/a vignette of sailors on shore leave,
designed by Nils Landberg, signed on
the base "Orrefors Landberg 1938 C
IAD," 6" w., 10 1/4" h. (slight stopper
nick).. 1,150
Vase, 5" h., 8 1/2" l.,"Ravenna," small clear
round pedestal foot supporting a large
oblong boat-shaped bowl in clear w/an
internal layer of red over a layer of blue
containing windows w/a heavy blue rim
band, engraved "Orrefors Ravenna
nr1033 Sven Palmqvist" 2,200
Vase, 5 1/2" h., "Ariel," bubbled heavy flattened oval colorless vessel internally
decorated w/aubergine-amber spots in
symmetrically arranged progression,
base inscribed "Orrefors Ariel No.
341L/Ingeborg Lundin" 1,840

Vase, 5 1/2" h., "Edvin," heavy cylindrical form in turquoise blue overlaid in purple, cut w/a stylized gypsy palmist amid an open palm w/life lines, w/linear devices & stars in the background, designed by Edvin Ohrstrom, signed "Orrefors Sweden 1944 - Edvin - nr:89 - Edvin Ohrstrom," dated 1944 .... **20,700**

Orrefors Fish Graal Vase

Vase, 5 1/2" h., "Graal," heavy walled teardrop-shaped form, clear internally decorated w/fish among seaweed in brownish green, base signed "Orrefors Graal No. 95216 II Hald," designed by Edvard Hald, ca. 1940 (ILLUS.)................................. **920**

Vase, 5 3/4" h., fish "Graal," oval colorless body w/brown & green fish & water weeds in reflective illusion, base inscribed "Orrefors Sweden Graal No. 2770D Edward Hald," designed by Edward Hald.. **805**

Vase, 6" h., "Ariel," thick ovoid form enclosing a pair of stylized reclining odalisques within an interior, deep cobalt blue & aubergine, inscribed "ORREFORS - Sweden - ARIEL - 573 E - E. OHRSTROM," designed by Edvin Ohrstrom, ca. 1950 .... **17,250**

Vase, 6 7/8" h., "Ariel," cylindrical w/slightly flaring rim, internally decorated w/'Profiles' patt., deep purple & white stylized human profiles in a clear ground, designed by Ingeborg Lundin, signed "Orrefors Ariel No. 236 - E9 - Ingeborg Lundin" **6,325**

Vase, 7" h., clear flared cylindrical form, copper-wheel engraved decoration of a dancing female nude & a snake, designed by Simon Gate, incised "Orrefors Gate 128J. 03. XR" (scratches)............. **374**

Vase, 7 3/8" h., "Ariel," bottle-type, raised rim on oval colorless body internally decorated by alternating vertical aubergine & clear bubble stripes, inscribed on base "Orrefors Ariel Sweden 1851E/Edvin Ohrstrom"... **316**

Vase, 7 1/2" h., "Ariel," cylindrical w/slightly flaring rim, internally decorated w/'Profiles' patt., shaded moss green w/stylized human profiles in a clear ground, designed by Ingeborg Lundin, signed "Orrefors Ariel No. 556. G - Ingeborg Lundin" (ILLUS. top next column) **6,325**

Vase, 8 1/2" h., "Kraka," flattened teardrop form in deep cobalt blue shading to amber encompassing a fine network of tiny bubbles, further encased in a thick layer of clear glass, designed by Sven Palmqvist, designed ca. 1954, inscribed "ORREFORS - KRAKA - nr. 349 - Sven Palmqvist," retains retailer's label "A. B. SCHOU - NY OSTERGADE 1" **1,150**

Orrefors 'Profiles' Pattern Vase

Vase, 9" h., slender ovoid form w/a short ringed neck & flared rim flanked by pairs of small S-scroll applied handles, the clear body engraved w/a Bacchanalian tableaux of nude female dancers & musicians within fringed borders, signed by Simon Gate, Model G 234, dated 1925, engraved "Orrefors - Gate - 234.25. A.D."... **2,070**

Tall Engraved Orrefors Vase

Vase, 11 7/8" h., tall clear cylindrical form slightly incurved at the base, thick walls etched on the exterior w/a nude young woman standing in a garden & holding aloft a bunch of flowers, butterflies flitting around her, signed "Orrefors . Landberg. Expo. 3521...C3," early 20th c. (ILLUS.) .. **1,150**

Orrefors "Pearl Divers" Vase

Vase, 14 1/4" h., "Pearl Divers," tall slightly tapering cylindrical form w/optic banding, engraved w/a scene of nude male underwater divers, designed by Vicke Lindstrand, signed "Orrefors - Lindstrand - 1115 - B4 - KR," ca. 1932 (ILLUS.)......... **4,025**

Vase, 14 1/4" h., "Slipgraal," thick tall teardrop-form, clear enclosing deep burgundy spiraling threads, signed "ORREFORS - Sweden - S. Graal nr. 1218 L - Edward Hald," designed by Edward Hald, ca. 1953................................. **920**

Large Orrefors "Apple" Vase

Vase, 15 1/8" h., "The Apple," very large spherical form w/stem neck, overall rich green, designed by Ingeborg Lundin, inscribed "ORRESFORS - Expo. Nr. 32-57 - Ingeborg Lundin," ca. 1957 (ILLUS.).. **6,037**

Vases, 10" h., each colorless oval engraved w/two exotic angelfish, bubbles overall, base engraved "Orrefors LA 1916," the pair.. **345**

OVERSHOT

Popular since the mid-19th century, Overshot glass was produced by having a gather of molten glass rolled in finely crushed glass to produce a rough exterior finish. The piece was then blown to the desired size and shape. The finished piece has a frosted or iced finish and is sometimes referred to as "ice glass." Early producers referred to this glass as "Craquelle" and, although Overshot is sometimes lumped together with the glass collectors now call "crackle," that type was produced using a totally different technique.

Overshot Bride's Bowl

Bride's bowl, deep green shaded bowl w/heavy ruffled & crimped rim, bolted to a silver plate pedestal base w/flaring foot, 9" d., 6 1/2" h. (ILLUS.) **$195**

Pitcher bulbous, cranberry.............................. **350**

Cranberry Overshot Tankard Pitcher

Pitcher, cov., 9 1/4" h., 3 7/8" d., tankard-type, wide cylindrical cranberry body w/pinched spout & flat rim, applied clear reeded handle, flat hinged pewter cover w/thumbrest (ILLUS.) **$175**

PAIRPOINT

Originally organized in New Bedford, Massachusetts in 1880, as the Pairpoint Manufacturing Company, on land adjacent to the famed Mount Washington Glass Company, this company first manufactured silver and plated wares. In 1894, the two famous factories merged as the Pairpoint Corporation and enjoyed great success for more than forty years. The company was sold in 1939 to a group of local businessmen and eventually bought out by one of the group who turned the management over to Robert M. Gundersen. Subsequently, it operated as the Gundersen Glass Works until 1952 when, after Gundersen's death, the name was changed to Gundersen-Pairpoint. The factory closed in 1956. Subsequently, Robert Bryden took charge of this glassworks, at first producing glass for Pairpoint abroad and eventually, in 1970, beginning glass production in Sagamore, Massachusetts. Today the Pairpoint Crystal Glass Company is owned by Robert and June Bancroft. They continue to manufacture fine quality blown and pressed glass.

Atomizer, bulbous base tapering to a cylindrical neck, embossed swirl design, h.p. lily of the valley & scrolling decoration on white ground, signed "2341," 6" h. **$375**

Pairpoint Gravic Cut Bowl

Bowl, 4 x 12", 8" h. deep widely flaring sides w/two sides pulled up to make a basket form, Gravic cut w/a swirling design of flowers & leafy vines, unsigned (ILLUS.).. **275**

Box w/hinged cover, border of aqua & white scrolls surrounding vines of wild roses on cover, aqua base decorated w/wild roses, raised on a gilt-metal frame marked "Pairpoint," 4 1/4 x 6 3/4", 4" h. **750**

Candleholder-vase, Gravic cut w/an overall vining floral design, clear connecting ball between stem & foot, early 20th c., 12" h. **150**

Candlestick lamps, gold finish base w/pale green cut crystal standard, eight 6" clear crystal hanging prisms, 10" h., pr. **1,400**

Pairpoint Candlesticks & Vases

Candlesticks, dark amethyst cylindrical socket w/flattened rim above a slender baluster-form stem on a clear controlled-bubble connector on a wide amethyst foot, 20th c., 9" h., pr. (ILLUS. right)............. **345**

Candlesticks, emerald green standards & sockets raised on a clear controlled bubble ball stem & green foot, 12" h., pr. **275**

Castor set: two square cruets w/original square cut stoppers, one square mustard jar w/original silver plate top & circular handle & a silver plate holder w/ornate handle marked "Hartford," clear w/cut & etched overall floral designs, the set **175**

Center bowl, clear "controlled" bubble bowl w/applied ruby pedestal base, 12" d. **275**

Pairpoint Engraved Covered Compote

Compote, cov., 8 3/4" d., 13" h., clear deep rounded bowl on a knop stem & round foot, domed cover w/knop finial encasing a white rose & green leaves, the sides engraved w/a rosebush on trellis design, leafy floral bands on cover & foot, Sagamore (ILLUS.).......... **750**

Compote, cov., 9", ruby w/clear "controlled" bubble knob finial **225**

Compote, open, 5" h., ruby bowl w/clear "controlled" bubble knob pedestal base **135**

Compote, open, 7 1/2" d., 4" h., amethyst decorated w/engraved grape design.......... **225**

Compote, 12" d., 6 1/2" h., open, widely flaring bell-form bowl in black amethyst

raised on a clear bubble ball stem on a round black amethyst foot, unsigned **115**

Console set: candlesticks & vase; the disk-footed ovoid bulbous vase tapering to a short waisted neck w/a widely flaring flattened rim, the slender baluster-form disk-footed candlesticks w/a cylindrical socket w/flattened rim, all in cobalt blue cut & etched overall w/a grapevine design, ca. 1930, candlesticks 10 3/4" h., the set........ **1,495**

Rare Pairpoint Flambo Console Set

Console set: footed center bowl & pair tall candlesticks; Flambo color, deep tomato red bowl & candlestick stems & sockets, each on a clear "controlled bubble" stem knop on a black foot, decorated overall w/silver overlay, the set (ILLUS.) **3,500-5,000**

Console set: console bowl & pr. of candleholders; Vintage cut, green, 3 pcs.............. **750**

Cracker jar, cov., milk white w/h.p. blue Delft scenic decoration, silver plate rim, cover & handle, 5t 3/4" h. **550**

Dish, three-lobed sides forming three sections, green engraved w/the Colias patt., leaves, spider web & butterflies, early 20th c., 9" w. **225**

Dresser box w/hinged cover, round, the flattened radiating rib cover decorated w/colorful pansies framing a molded scroll center all within a gilt brass border, the low squatty bulbous pleated rib base decorated w/scattered floral sprigs, 6" d., 2" h. **475**

Pairpoint Ruby Ewer

Ewers, classic baluster-form w/clear applied ring foot supporting an ovoid ruby body tapering to a tall tricorner flaring neck, high arched applied clear handle, unsigned, 13 1/2" h., pr. (ILLUS. of one) **374**

Pitcher, 12" h., green body & foot w/clear applied handle & "controlled bubble" knop stem.. **155**

Plates, 8" d., Tavern line, clear w/galleon decoration, set of 12................................... **2,400**

Tumbler, Tavern line, barrel-shaped, clear w/h.p. black enameled galleon under full sail & rim trim **275**

Gundersen Gold Ruby Vases

Vase, chalice-form w/clear "controlled bubble" connector in pedestal base, rare Gold Ruby by Gundersen - Pairpoint (ILLUS. center)...................................... **300-400**

Vase, footed banjo-form w/taller slender flaring neck, rare Gold Ruby, Gundersen - Pairpoint (ILLUS. left)........................... **400-600**

Vase, footed fanned form w/applied clear swan rim handles, rare Gold Ruby by Gundersen - Pairpoint (ILLUS. right)..... **400-600**

Pairpoint Tavern Line Vase

Vase, 6" h., Tavern line (clear glass w/thousands of bubbles), ovoid body tapering to a short flaring neck, decorated in black & colors w/a sailing galleon on a wavy sea & enameled rings, signed "D1507" (ILLUS.)... **325**

Vase, 8 1/2" h., Tavern line, cylindrical form in bubbled colorless glass, decorated w/raised enameled vase of flowers, obscured mark on polished pontil, ca. 1920 (slight enamel wear)........................... **288**

Vase, 9" h., jack-in-the-pulpit-type, tall footed trumpet-form w/upturned pointed back top rim & downturned front rim, the exterior in opalescent white cased inside w/pink enameled near the center w/rings of small white blossoms, signed on outside of tip w/a "P" in a triangle **175**

Vase, 12" h., trumpet-shaped green body, clear "controlled bubble" ball connector & green foot.. **150**

Vase, 13" h., 6 1/2" d., cobalt blue trumpet-shaped body & pedestal foot w/clear "controlled bubble" ball connector............... **425**

Vases, 8" h., cornucopia-form, the deep amethyst cornucopia-shaped bowl raised on a clear "controlled bubble" ball connector to the amethyst foot, 20th c., pr. (ILLUS. left with candlesticks)................. **489**

Vases, 12" h., trumpet-form amethyst bowl w/Diamond Quilted patt., raised on a clear stem w/ringed sections centered by a large "controlled bubble" ball, applied amethyst foot, pr............................. **715**

PAPERWEIGHTS

Apsley Pellatt "Sulphide Medallion" weight, miniature, silhouette cameo of Prince Albert, inscribed "H. R. H. Prince Albert - Born August 26, 1819 - Married February 20, 1840," 1 15/16" d. **$468**

Ayotte (Rick) Paradisia Butterfly weight, bouquet of pale pink, yellow & white roses w/dark green leafy stems, signed "Rick Ayotte LE - 35 '98," 1998, 3 3/4" d...... **690**

Baccarat "Amber Flashed" weight, interior engraved w/a stag in the forest on an amber-flashed ground, 3" d......................... **385**

Baccarat Butterfly Garland Weight

Baccarat "Butterfly Garland" weight, the insect w/flattened millefiori wings, marbled in shades of orange, green, blue, yellow, purple & red, attached to an eggplant-purple body, w/a black head & antennae & turquoise eyes, floating over a star-cut ground inside a garland of emerald green, ruby & white cog/stardust canes alternating w/salmon, white & emerald green cog/star canes, 2 3/4" d. (ILLUS.)..................................... **7,150**

Baccarat "Butterfly" weight, insect w/flattened millefiori wings, marbled in shades of orange, green, blue, yellow & red, attached to an eggplant-purple body w/black head & antennae & turquoise eyes, insect floats over star-cut ground inside crystal dome w/six & one faceting, 2 13/16" d. **3,025**

Baccarat "Choufleur Carpet Ground" weight, w/complex canes in various colors, in a sea of twisted lilac & lemonade whorls, includes Gridel silhouette canes of two moths & a dog & a deer & a horse & a rooster & a goat & an elephant, w/millefiori flower portrait cane w/petals made from arrow canes & a center composed of a star cane, "B1848" signature/date cane, 3 1/8" d. **11,000**

Baccarat "Double Clematis" Weight

Baccarat "Double Clematis" weight, w/double tier of ridged robin's egg blue petals around a red & white stardust/bull's-eye cane center, on stalk w/pair of entwined buds & two types of green leaves, over star-cut ground, six & one faceting, 2 5/8" d. (ILLUS.) **1,980**

Baccarat "Double Overlay Interlaced Trefoil Garland Millefiori" weight, w/a trefoil of emerald green, cobalt blue, ruby & white arrow/six-pointed star canes interlocked w/a garland of white & lime green stardust/bull's-eye canes, around a central arrow/fortress cane encircled by a garland of salmon & white cog/star canes, pink over white double overlay cut w/a top facet & two rows of side facets, 3 1/8" d. **7,700**

Baccarat "Faceted Macédoine" weight, w/pieces of twists & filigree in blue & green & red amidst white lace, sides of the piece are cut w/geometric faceting, 2 7/8" d. **385**

Baccarat "Macédoine" weight, including several large bull's-eye canes w/pieces of twists & filigree in red & blue & green & yellow amidst white lace, 2 7/8" d. **468**

Baccarat "Pansy" weight, pansy w/deep purple upper petals & black-striped purple & yellow lower petals, around stardust/bull's-eye cane, on stalk w/yellow & purple bud & green leaves, in nineteenth-century flower language the pansy symbolized tender thoughts, 3 3/16" d. **1,045**

Baccarat Millefiori Lovebirds Weight

Baccarat "Patterned Millefiori" weight, w/large lovebirds silhouette cane sur-

rounded by patterned arrangement of complex canes in cobalt blue & white, including square clusters of canes on translucent green-over-white ground, seventeen other Gridel silhouette canes are composed about edge of weight, signature/date cane, acid etched w/Baccarat insignia, limited edition of 350, 1976, 3 3/8" d. (ILLUS.).............................. **660**

Baccarat "Patterned Moth & Shamrock Millefiori" weight, clear glass set w/a large central complex millefiori arrangement composed of seven shamrocks & ruby cogs, surrounded by ring of cobalt blue, ruby & white six-pointed star/arrow canes & a spaced garland of fourteen moth silhouettes, arrangement set on white lace ground, shamrock canes contain annealing cracks, an attribute commonly found in this design, 3" d. **3,850**

Baccarat "Rock" Weight

Baccarat "Rock" weight, miniature, also called mountains of the moon & sand dunes, sandy ground flecked w/green glass & mica, 1 7/8" d. (ILLUS.) **198**

Baccarat "Stardust Carpet Ground" weight, including a six-pointed star, arrow, whorl, cog, shamrock & trefoil canes, in coral, orange, yellow, plum, cadmium green, cobalt blue, ruby & turquoise, in a sea of red & white stardust canes, various silhouette canes including rare primrose portrait cane & signature date cane "B 1848," 3 1/8" d. **11,000**

Baccarat "Sulphide" weight, silhouette cameo of French King Louis Philippe, on translucent aqua ground, cut w/geometric faceting, 3 1/2" d. **825**

Baccarat "Wallflower Garland" weight, containing five white petals outlined in ruby, around a red, white & blue cog/six-pointed star cane center, on a stalk w/emerald green leaves, nestled on a white upset muslin ground inside a garland of cobalt blue, emerald green, white & ruby arrow/six-point star canes, 2 7/8" d. **1,100**

Bohemian "Scattered Millefiori" weight, w/star, cross, cog & bull's-eye canes, in pink, royal blue, ruby, turquoise & white, on a white lace ground decorated w/pieces of colored filigree, 2 3/4" d. **2,200**

Cape Cod Glass Works "Swirl" weight, alternating teal & white swirls, emanating from central pink & green Clichy-type rose, encircled by ring of blue complex cog canes, tiny signature placed in center of rose, 2 7/8" d. **220**

Charles Kaziun II "Ruby Crimp Rose" weight, tilted, featuring fifteen-petal crimp rose, cupped inside four green leaves, w/footed crystal pedestal, signed under flowers w/complex K signature cane surrounded by hearts, 3" d. **1,250**

Clichy "Chequer" weight, w/a pink & green rose & a purple & white rose amid large complex pastry mold, cog, six-pointed star & bull's-eye canes in pink, cadmium green, cherry, Naples yellow, lilac, black, thalo blue, turquoise & cobalt blue, divided by cables of white filigree, 3 1/4" d. **3,300**

Clichy "Close Concentric Millefiori" weight, w/central pink & green rose surrounded by concentric rows of complex canes, including row of ten white roses alternating w/pink pastry mold canes amidst rows of pastry mold canes, stardust/bull's-eye canes, & florets, in various colors, arrangement set inside turquoise & white stave basket, 2 5/16" d. **2,750**

Clichy "Close Packed Millefiori" Weight

Clichy "Close Packed Millefiori" weight, w/nine roses in various colors amidst six-pointed star canes, edelweiss canes, florets, bull's-eye canes, moss, stardust & cog canes in various colors, set in an alternating pink & white stave basket, 3 1/8" d. (ILLUS.) **5,225**

Clichy "Garland" weight, a pink central rose cane w/blue millefiori circlet & pink garlands, 2 3/8" d. **770**

Clichy "Rose Bud" weight, containing a large millefiori rose cupped in emerald green sepals, on a stalk w/emerald & sea green leaves, over a swirling white latticinio ground, 3" d. **9,900**

Clichy "Spaced Millefiori" weight, multicolored spaced millefiori canes on a turquoise ground, 2 3/8" d. **1,870**

Clichy "Spaced Millefiori" weight, opaque cobalt blue ground glass set w/a central pink & green rose amidst pastry mold, edelweiss, stardust, cog & bull's-eye canes, in pink & yellow & cherry & green & white, intriguing pastry mold cane is formed from pressed bull's-eye canes, 2 9/16" d. **2,090**

Clichy Swirl Weight

Clichy "Swirl" weight, alternating cobalt blue & white pinwheels radiating from a large central pink & green rose cane, 2 9/16" d. (ILLUS.) **7,150**

Clichy "Three-color Swirl" weight, w/alternating cobalt blue, teal green & white pinwheels radiating from a large central cadmium green, white & ruby pastry mold cane, 3 1/8" d. **1,430**

D'Albret "Sulphide" weight, front-view cameo of Albert Schweitzer renowned philosopher & musicologist, as sculpted by Gilbert Poillerat, on translucent dark purple ground w/diamond-cut base, six & one faceting, dated, limited edition of 1,000, 1969, 2 7/8" d. **154**

Edward Rithner "Candy Cane" Weight

Edward Rithner "Candy Cane" weight, w/striped pink & blue & white & aqua rods on spotted ruby ground, ruby ground of this piece is rarely found, minor bruise on underside of weight, 3 1/16" d. (ILLUS.) **248**

Footed Pinchbeck weight, w/armed men riding on horseback through wooded area towards young boy leading girl by the arm, copper-zinc alloy popular during the Victorian era for its resemblance to gold, 3 1/4" d. **660**

James Kontes "Pink Rose" weight, containing pair of pink blossoms w/upright yellow stamens on stalk w/three large buds & green leaves, flowers rest on bed of white lace placed on a translucent cobalt blue ground, signature cane, 3 1/8" d. **3,025**

Ken Rosenfeld "Rose Bouquet" weight, featuring furled ruby rose arranged w/three turquoise bell flowers w/green & yellow stamens & white bellflower w/pink & green stamens, on stem w/three white buds & yellow-striped green leaves over star-cut ground, five & one faceting, signature cane, 3 3/16" d. **1,100**

Rare New England Bouquet Weight

New England Glass Co. "Open Concentric Millefiori" weight, w/central running rabbit silhouette cane surrounded by a circlet of pink & white star canes & a circlet of complex pink, white & yellow cog canes on white double-swirl latticinio ground, dome decorated w/elaborate propeller cut encircled by a row of small circular facets & a row of large circular side facets divided by vertical printies, 2 5/8" d. (minor chip in the dome) **550**

New England Glass Co. "Pear" weight, the blown three-dimensional fruit w/a peach-colored blush on a round clear cookie base, a pink & yellow stem & a green glass stamp on the blossom end, 3" d. **1,320**

New England Glass Co. "Poinsettia" weight, the flower w/a double tier of pointed petals around a swirled matched center grows on a stalk w/a realistic furled ruby bud & spring green leaves, on a white double-swirl latticinio ground, 2 11/16" d. **1,045**

Orient & Flume "Hearts & Vines Surface Design" weight, w/reddish-orange hearts hanging from curling black & yellow vines on iridescent mottled caramel & yellow globe, signed & dated, 1976, 2 13/16" d. **358**

New England "Apple" Weight

New England Glass Co. "Apple" weight, the blown three-dimensional yellow fruit w/a rose peach blush on a round clear cookie base, w/a yellow stem & a green glass stamp on the blossom end, base 3" d. (ILLUS.) **1,045**

New England Glass Co. "Crown" weight, two-color ribbons in ruby, royal blue, yellow, emerald green & white interspersed w/white latticinio filigree spokes emanating from a mint green, white & ruby complex cog cane, 2 9/16" **1,650**

New England Glass Co. "Fruit Bouquet" weight, a formal arrangement containing five blushing pears & four ruby cherries nestled in a bed of green leaves on a white double-swirl latticinio basket, the blossom end of each fruit decorated w/green glass, 2 1/2" d. **605**

New England Glass "Fruit Bouquet" Weight

New England Glass Co. "Fruit Bouquet" weight, a formal arrangement containing five pears & four cherries, on a bed of green leaves in a white double-swirl latticinio basket, 2 13/16" d. (ILLUS.) **440**

New England Glass Co. "Magnum Floral Sheaf Upright Bouquet" weight, a dimensional portrayal containing a blue double clematis w/a blue & pink millefiori center & a yellow double clematis w/a white millefiori center crowning a bouquet w/variegated green leaves & clematis blossoms in amethyst, yellow, white & pink, a large ruby bud peeks from beneath green leaves on one side of arrangement, on a white double-swirl latticinio ground, 3 7/8" d. (ILLUS.) **10,450**

Parabelle Glass "Pink Clematis" Weight

Parabelle Glass "Pink Clematis Paneled Color Ground" weight, the flower w/green moss cane center, encircled by radiating buds & white clematis blossoms w/yellow moss centers, inside garland of complex cog canes in pink & white & yellow & royal blue, arrangement floats over an opaque pink & ruby panel ground inside a pink & ruby stave basket, limited edition of 10, 1993, 3" d. (ILLUS.) **715**

Paul Stankard "Bouquet" weight, w/Saint Anthony's fire, meadowreathe, forget-me-nots, chokeberry blossoms & bellflowers, signature cane, dated, 1978, 2 3/4" d. **1,980**

Paul Stankard "Faceted Saint Anthony's Fire" weight, flower w/pointed red petals & black-tipped yellow stamens, grown on stem w/trailing root system, pair of seeds sprout next to plant, five & one faceting, signature cane, 1976, 2 11/16" d. **1,320**

Paul Ysart "Ribbon Bouquet Garland" weight, featuring five flowers in pink & amethyst & Persian blue & baby blue & pistachio, w/opening blue bud, on stems tied w/looped pink ribbon & encircled by garland of complex fuchsia & white cog canes on black ground, signature cane placed in center of one of the flowers, signed, 3" d. **1,045**

Perthshire "Crown" weight, w/blue & red twisted ribbons alternating w/white filigree spokes projecting from complex millefiori cane, first special yearly collection weight produced at Perthshire, signed "P1969" in canes on the base, limited edition of 268, 1969, 3" d. **660**

Perthshire Paperweights "Golfer" Weight

Perthshire "Golfer" weight, w/central glass transfer of a golfer swinging a club on lace ground, encircled by triple garland of millefiori canes & spiral twists in pink & purple & red & blue, circular top facet, signature/date cane, Perthshire produced golfer designs over several years in edition sizes ranging from 250 to 450, edition size for this weight is not known, 1989, 3 1/8" d. (ILLUS.) **440**

Rick Ayotte "Golden-Back Oriole" weight, artist proof, black & yellow South American bird perched on jungle branch w/yellow & green leaves over opaque white ground, signed & dated, 1983, 3 1/8" d. **825**

Rosenfeld (Ken) "Apples & Blossom" weight, a spray of three red apples w/pink blossoms & two buds on clear, "R" signature cane, 1989, 2 3/4" d. **352**

Sandwich Glass Company "Red Poinsettia" weight, w/double tier of five pinkish-red petals around a red & white & green complex cog cane, on stalk w/green leaves over blue & white jasper ground, 3" d. **935**

St. Louis "Amber Ground Bouquet" weight, containing stalks of pink & blue clematis blossoms w/green & white stardust centers, over diamond-cut amber ground, six & one faceting, signature/date cane, limited edition of 450, 1979, 3" d. **550**

St. Louis "Carpet Ground" weight, a patterned arrangement containing five complex florets composed of lime green, white, Persian blue & pink, crimped cog/irregular leaf/quatrefoil canes, around a central floret w/powder blue, ruby, white & lime green cog & six-pointed star canes in a sea of pale pink & white crimped cog canes, 2 7/8" d. **9,350**

St. Louis "Nosegay" weight, miniature, w/three complex cog & star canes, in blue & salmon & ruby & white on stalk w/spring green leaves, over diamond-cut amber ground, circular top facet w/two rows of circular side facets, 1 5/8" d. (small chips to facets) **440**

St. Louis "Pansy & Camomile" Weight

St. Louis "Pansy & Camomile" weight, the pansy w/amethyst upper petals & black-striped amber lower petals around complex cob/six-pointed star cane, in amber & Persian blue & powder blue, w/millefiori cane at center of pansy, flower grows on stalk w/pink camomile blossom composed of recessed C-shaped petals, around pale yellow stamens, on stalk w/emerald green leaves, arranged on white double-swirl latticinio ground, rare, 3 1/8" d. (ILLUS.) **8,800**

St. Louis "Pompon" weight, the pink flower w/segmented C-shaped petals around an unusual millefiori center containing tiny ruby figure eight-shaped canes, on a stalk w/a ruby bud & variegated spring green leaves over a white double-swirl latticinio ground, 3 3/16" d. **4,125**

St. Louis "Three-color Crown" weight, containing ruby & cadmium green twists, alternating w/white latticinio spokes & ruby & cobalt blue twists, emanating from a central Persian blue, ruby & white cog/star cane, 2 13/16" d. **6,600**

St. Louis "Turnip" Weight

St. Louis "Turnip" weight, the five vegetables in pink, amethyst, amber & white w/emerald green tops in a central radiating arrangement in a white double-swirled latticinio funnel basket, 2 9/16" d. (ILLUS.) **1,320**

Saint Louis "Two-Color Crown" Weight

St. Louis "Two-Color Crown" weight, w/red & green twists interspersed w/white latticinio spokes projecting from central complex six-pointed star/bundled rod cane, in pink & white & green, 2 1/8" d. (ILLUS.) **1,650**

St. Louis "Upright Bouquet" weight, a white clematis w/a complex cog cane center tops a gathering of four lampwork blossoms in salmon, yellow, cobalt blue & white, on a bed of light green leaves w/a three-dimensional stem that extends down to a star-cut ground, inside a blue & white lace filigree torsade, six side facets, 2 3/4" d. **2,475**

Trabucco (Victor) "Rose" weight, a Chinese red rose w/four buds & green leaves, signed cane, 1987, 3" d. **413**

Val Saint Lambert "Pansy" weight, the flower w/two amethyst upper petals & three yellow-striped amethyst lower petals around a yellow center bloom on a stalk w/green & grey leaves, over an opaque black ground, the arrangement encircled by a pink & white spiral torsade, 3 1/2" d. **990**

William Manson "Green Aventurine Snake" weight, reptile w/black & yellow striped green aventurine coils, slithering over a sandy ground, five & one faceting, signed & dated, limited edition of 150, 3 1/8" d. **303**

William Manson "Ladybug" weight, plaque-type, featuring black-spotted red ladybug crawling on central white blossom w/yellow millefiori center & green leaves, inside a spaced garland of flowers, alternating between amethyst & turquoise w/yellow millefiori centers & green leaves, on dark translucent ruby ground, arrangement displayed in upright plaque w/tilted window facet, signature cane, signed & dated, limited edition of 50, 2 7/8" d. **440**

Yaffa Sikorsky-Todd & Jeffrey M. Todd "Wisteria" weight, featuring a tree w/vines of hanging purple millefiori blossoms & green leaves, in grassy field w/rocks & purple & white millefiori blossoms, signed & dated, 1995, 3 1/8" d. **468**

PATE DE VERRE

Pate de Verre, or "paste of glass," was molded by very few artisans. In the pate de verre technique, powdered glass is mixed with a liquid to make a paste which is then placed in a mold and baked at a high temperature. These articles have a finely-pitted or matte finish and are easily distinguished from blown glass. Duplicate pieces are possible with this technique.

Pate De Verre Marks

Book ends, figural, each upright back molded in full-relief w/two nude female musicians standing on either side of a fruit-filled bower, in shades of green, blue, beige, ochre & mauve, modeled by Henri Mercier, molded "AWALTER NANCY," & "h. mercier," ca. 1920s, 6" h., pr. **$5,175**

Pate-de-Verre Bowl & Bowl-Vase

Bowl, 3 1/8" h., "Ceres," footed squatty spherical form w/a wide flat mouth, triangular panels w/diamond lattice alternating w/triangular panels of wheat heads in shades of brown, gold & black, G. Argy-Rousseau, ca. 1926 (ILLUS. right) **5,175**

Bowl, 9 3/4" w., hexagonal, flat bottom & low angled sides, molded around the rim in low-relief w/festoons, the center molded w/a crab & seaweeds, shades of brown, yellow, ochre & bluish green, molded "A. WALTER - NANCY" & "Bergé - scp.," ca. 1920s **4,025**

Pate-de-Verre Bowl-Vase

Bowl-vase, deep ovoid form w/a wide flat mouth, shades of blue, turquoise, black & pale yellow, molded around the sides w/three stylized petals & scrolled handles, signed in the mold "G. Argy-Rousseau," ca. 1924, 4" h. (ILLUS.) **4,600**

Pate de Verre Bowl-Vase

Bowl-vase, deep rounded & gently flaring body in grey mottled & streaked w/green & turquoise, molded around the sides in low-relief w/a stylized wave design, the side handles molded as two leaping fish in full relief, molded "Décorchemont" w/a horseshoe, inscribed "D 69 H," 1903-09, 5 1/4" h. (ILLUS.) **11,500**

Bowl-vase, flared inverted bell-form w/rounded bottom, textured clear ground w/a band of stylized deep ruby leaping gazelles above a ruby & black base border & upright scrolled flowers, G. Argy-Rousseau, ca. 1928, 3 3/4" h. (ILLUS. left, w/bowl) **11,500**

Box, cov., low round shape, mottled pale yellow ground, the flattened cover centered by an orangish red molded grotesque mask framed by a ring of black & yellow leaf forms enclosed in a scalloped black ring w/small yellow stars between each scallop, the sides w/matching scalloped band, leaves & stars, cover molded "G. Argy-Rousseau," base molded "France," ca. 1923, 5 3/4" d., 3 3/8" h. **8,625**

Flower & Foliage Pate de Verre Box

Box, cov., round short cylindrical form, muted purple, molded on the flat cover w/a central red flower w/amber & purple leaves forming a border on the cover & around the sides, G. Argy-Rousseau, ca. 1923, 5 1/4" d. (ILLUS.) **4,313**

Box, cov., slightly swelled cylindrical sides w/a fitted domed cover, mottled frosted white & lavender, molded around the body w/large red roses on brown stems, a rose blossom on the cover, G. Argy-Rousseau, ca. 1920, 3" h. **5,750**

Pate de Verre Clock - Vide Poche

Clock case - vide poche, an upright square back w/rounded corners centered by the round clock dial w/Arabic numerals above a narrow rectangular dished front base, yellow shading to butterscotch ground molded w/green & rose budded stems up the sides w/a black bee at the center bottom, signed in the mold "A. Walter Nancy - H. Berge Sc.," designed by Henri Berge for A. Walter, 4 5/8" h. (ILLUS.) **3,450**

Unusual Pate de Verre Coupe

Coupe, round stepped foot tapering to cylindrical pedestal flaring into a deep rounded cup w/a wide flat rim, lemon yellow above mottled brown molded on the side w/a large insect, signed by Henri Bergé, molded "AWalter - Nancy - HBergé - sculp," ca. 1925, 6 1/2" h. **5,750**

Dish, round w/shallow incurved sides, greenish yellow frosted ground decorated on the interior w/a pair of large red fruits on brown stems w/green leaves, signed "Decorchement," 6 1/2" d. **2,750**

Dish, shallow rounded form in yellow, green & brown, molded in medium-relief w/a butterfly & in low-relief w/pine needles, signed in intaglio "AWALTER - NANCY," ca. 1920, 6 7/8" d. **2,070**

Inkstand, figural, double, a long rectangular platform w/wide rounded projecting central section, each end w/a raised buttressed square turret w/cross-molded lids on the inkwells, the center section molded w/a large model of a stag beetle, in shades of lemon yellow, ochre, brown & black, molded "A. Walter - Nancy" & "Bergé - SC," modeled by Henri Bergé, ca. 1920, 6" l. **5,175**

Lamp, the ovoid base in grey mottled w/purple & deep crimson, molded in low-relief w/large crimson flowers w/cascading stamens resembling tassels, high domed & pointed molded shade on an iron ring & three-arm support & the base on an iron round disk w/small ball feet, shade & base signed "G. Argy-Rousseau," ca, 1925, shade 7 1/8" d., 15 1/2" h. **40,250**

Lamp base, "The Garden of The Hesperides," ovoid body w/a mottled yellow & brown ground overlaid on the upper half w/a continuous scene of a stylized classical maiden in orange & black plucking yellow apples from brown trees, the lower half w/mottled black & brown band w/incised angular scrolls, patinated metal scroll-pierced footed base & domed cap for electric fitting, by G. Argy-Rousseau, 27 3/4" h. **5,175**

Model of a chick, modeled standing on a naturalistic base w/head cocked slightly to one side, in cobalt blue shaded w/green in the grass at its feet, inscribed "A. Walter - Nancy," ca. 1930, 4 1/8" h. **1,725**

Night light, "Dune Flowers," a spherical shade in shades of purple, magenta, cobalt blue, jade & raspberry molded w/swelled block bands under pendent half-round dark blossoms, signed "G Argy-Rousseau - France," set on a round hand-hammered wrought-iron ring w/curled upright bar supports above the thin disk foot, base signed "France 106," ca. 1925, 8 1/4" h. **5,750**

Paperweight, figural, molded in high-relief w/a beetle in cinnamon & black on a domed oval base in lime green speckled w/yellow, signed "A WALTER - NANCY" & "BERGÉ - SC.," modeled by Henri Bergé, ca. 1925, 3 1/4" l. **1,610**

Pen tray, figural, the edge molded w/an amber beetle on a blue ground, signed by Walter - Nancy, 9 1/2" l. **3,300**

Pendant, butterfly design, pierced square w/blue, green, reddish orange wings against colorless & clear ground, inscribed "GAR" in design, G. Argy-Rousseau, 2 1/8 x 2 1/4" **2,415**

Pendant, frosted clear disk decorated w/red flowers w/dark green & blue centers, Argy-Rousseau, 2" d. **1,265**

Pendant, round disk in yellow, orange, brown & black, molded in relief w/a scarab, signed in intaglio "AWALTER," ca. 1920, 1 3/4" d. **2,012**

Vase, 3 5/8" h., "Vase à décor de gazelles et de fleurs," gently flaring cup-form in frosted clear & mottled yellow cast around the base w/a dark orange band & around the sides w/a band of leaping orange gazelles & stylized brown stems

w/yellow blossoms, G. Argy-Rousseau, ca. 1928 .... **10,350**

Vase, 5 1/2" h., broad ovoid form w/a wide flat mouth, mottled frosted white ground molded around the upper half w/brown twigs & large reddish orange blossoms w/dark centers, G. Argy-Rousseau, ca. 1920 .... **7,475**

Vase, 6 3/4" h., tapering cylindrical form w/flaring lip & small foot, grey shaded w/amber & purple, molded w/flutes & vetruvian scrolls, impressed "Décorchemont," France, ca. 1925 .... **1,955**

Pate de Verre Vase with Figures

Vase, 9 3/8" h., wide ovoid body w/a short flared rim, molded in medium-relief w/a frieze of classical ladies picking apples above a lower border of square scrolls, in shades of grey, brown, russet, black & yellow, incised "G. Argy-Rousseau" & impressed "France," base drilled & cracked, 1926 (ILLUS.) **6,325**

Wolves in the Snow Vase

Vase, 9 1/2" h., "Les Loups dan la neige," simple ovoid body, boldly molded around the rim & lower half w/tiered undulating bands of white against a streaked white & purple ground molded w/a band of dark purple walking wolves, G. Argy-Rousseau, ca. 1926 (ILLUS.) **43,125**

Vase, 10 1/8" h., "Papyrus," simple ovoid form w/a flared rim, grey molded in low-relief w/papyrus fronds in turquoise & blue w/charcoal stems, between scalloped upper & lower borders in deep aubergine, molded "G. ARGY-ROUSEAU" & "GA085," ca. 1924 .... **11,500**

Vase, 10 1/4" h., "Vase à décor de dan-seuses grecques à robe longue," simple ovoid form w/flaring neck, the upper half molded w/panels w/deep reddish amber dancing Greek figures separated by dark brown geometric bands & herringbone-style bands in yellow & orangish brown, all on a mottled brownish yellow ground, G. Argy-Rousseau, ca. 1930 .... **23,000**

Veilleuse (night lamp), a domed grey glass shade molded in low-relief w/three butterflies w/outstretched wings, in rich shades of orange, crimson, white, purple & black, on a round iron disk base w/three small ball feet, shade molded "G. ARGY-ROUSSEAU - FRANCE," ca. 1924, 5 1/2" h. **10,350**

Pate de Verre Butterflies Veilleuse

Veilleuse (night light), "Papillons," large bulbous ovoid domed shade in grey molded in low-relief w/three stylized but-terflies lighting on blossoms in shades of crimson, black, purple & green, simple round wrought-iron footed base, shade by G. Argy-Rousseau, ca. 1924, 5 3/8" h. (ILLUS.) **12,650**

Vide poche (figural dish), oblong shallow dished form modeled in full-relief on one edge w/a lizard, in shades of lemon yel-low, green, orange & black, modeled by Henri Bergé, molded "A. WALTER - NANCY" & "Bergé - SC," ca. 1920, 6 3/4" l. **6,900**

Pate de Verre Vide Poche with Moth

Vide poche (figural dish), triangular, deep yellow mottled w/orange & molded at one corner with a large dark moth, A.

Walter, Nancy, ca. 1925, 6 3/8" w., 2" h. (ILLUS.) **4,945**

PEACH BLOW

Several types of glass lumped together by col-lectors as Peach Blow were produced by half a dozen glasshouses. Hobbs, Brockunier & Co., Wheeling, West Virginia, made Peach Blow as a plated ware that shaded from red at the top to yel-low at the bottom and is referred to as Wheeling Peach Blow. Mt. Washington Glass Works pro-duced an homogeneous Peach Blow shading from a rose color at the top to pale blue in the lower por-tion. The New England Glass Works' Peach Blow, called Wild Rose, shaded from rose at the top to white. Gunderson-Pairpoint Co. also reproduced some of the Mt. Washington Peach Blow in the early 1950s and some glass of a somewhat similar type was made by Steuben Glass Works, Thomas Webb & Sons and Stevens & Williams of England. New England Peach Blow is one-layered glass and the English is two-layered.

Another single layered shaded art glass was produced early in this century by the New Martins-ville Glass Mfg. Co. Originally called "Muranese," collectors today refer to it as "New Martinsville Peach Blow."

GUNDERSEN - PAIRPOINT

Bowl, footed, 5" d., 3 1/2" h. **$250**

Bowl, 9" d., satin finish **330**

Champagne, 4 1/4" d., 5 1/2" h. **350**

Compote, open, 4 1/2" d., 3" h., paper label **198**

Compote, open, 5 5/8" d., 2 3/4" h., the wide shallow flaring bowl raised on a short applied stem & wide disk foot, satin finish **143**

Compote, open, 6 1/2" d., 4 3/4" h. **350**

Compote, open, 7 1/2" h., bowl w/a softly flared rim raised on a swirled stem **275**

Compote, open, 10" d., 5" h., ruffled rim, signed **425**

Compote, open, 10" d., 7" h., pulled-up rim, signed **600**

Cup & saucer, glossy finish **250**

Gundersen Peach Blow Decanter

Decanter w/original stopper, footed ovoid body tapering to an arched spout, pink ball stopper, applied reeded white handle, satin finish (ILLUS.) **750-1,000**

Gunderson Peach Blow Decanters

Decanters w/original stoppers, footed tall ovoid body tapering to a small flared neck, tall oval stoppers, satin finish, mid-20th c., 12" h., pr. (ILLUS.) **575**

Nappy, triangular shape, w/applied milky white handle **175**

Vase, 4" h., wide rounded bottom below angled shoulder w/sides tapering to a quatreform neck, applied white reeded handles, ca. 1940 .... **460**

Vase, 7" h., lily-form **193**

Vase, cornucopia-type, 7" h., ruffled rim, satin finish **450**

Vase, 7 1/2" h., jack-in-the-pulpit shape, enameled decoration **375**

Vase, 9" h., lily-form **300**

MT. WASHINGTON

Peach Blow Creamer & Sugar Bowl

Creamer & open sugar bowl, lightly molded ribs, satin finish, applied satin handles, one of the items sold at the Libbey exhibit at the 1893 Columbian Exposition, sugar bowl bears faint trace of that decoration, 2 1/2" h., pr. (ILLUS.) **950**

Pitcher, 6" h., applied reed handle **400**

Tumbler, satin finish, 4" h. **2,000**

Vase, 7" h., glossy finish **1,500**

Vase, 7" h., satin finish **1,500**

NEW ENGLAND

Bowl, 5 1/4" d., 2 1/2" h., scalloped rim **300**

Bowl, 9 1/2" d. **250**

Bride's basket, the wide deep rounded bowl w/a widely flaring ruffled rim, set into an ornate silver plate frame w/high scroll-pierced legs below a plain base ring centered by a small embossed cylindrical ring holding the bowl, a wide curved upright handle trimmed along the top w/berries & leaf sprigs, frame marked by the Derby Silver Plate Co., bowl 10" d., overall 12 3/4" h.`` **840**

Celery vase, bulging cylindrical form w/piecrust crimped rim, 3 1/2" d. **650**

Creamer, 2 1/2" h. **225**

Creamer, squatty bulbous form w/lightly ribbed sides, applied white handle, 3 1/2" d., 2 3/4" h. **300-400**

Creamer, squatty bulbous lightly ribbed body tapering slightly to a wide flat rim w/pinched spout, applied handle, decorated w/leafy branches of asters, 2 1/2" h. **495**

Creamer & open sugar bowl, wide squatty bulbous lightly ribbed body w/flat rim & applied white handle, each inscribed "World's Fair 1893," satin finish, pr. **1,000**

Cuspidor, lady's, bulbous base narrowing in the middle then flaring to a wavy rim **750**

Peach Blow Darner & Pear

Darner, ball-shaped w/handle, deep rose pink shaded to white, glossy finish, 2 1/4" d., 6" l. (ILLUS., left) **135**

Dish, leaf-shaped w/applied handle, 6 1/2" d. **350**

Finger bowls, round w/upright crimped & ruffled sides, satin finish, 5 1/4" d., 2 1/2" h., pr. **385**

Model of a pear, deep pink shaded to white, glossy finish, 3" d., 5" l. (ILLUS., right) **135**

Pitcher, 4 1/2" h., squatty bulbous body w/tri-corner rim, satin finish, applied crystal reeded handle **865**

Rose bowl, bulbous, seven-crimp top, satin finish, 2 3/4" d., 2 5/8" h. **350**

Rose bowl, round w/crimped rim, satin finish, 3 1/2" h. **275**

New England Rose Bowl

Rose bowl, spherical, seven-crimp top, deep crushed raspberry color shading to off-white, satin finish, 2 7/8" d., 2 1/2" h. (ILLUS.) **350**

Sugar bowl, open, marked "World's Fair 1893," 2 1/2" h. **450**

Toothpick holder, cylindrical w/gently flaring squared rim **413**
Toothpick holder, cylindrical w/tricorner rim **413**

New England Peach Blow Tumbler

Tumbler, cylindrical, satin finish, 3 3/4" h. (ILLUS.) **425-475**
Tumbler, glossy finish, 4" h. **450**
Vase, square rim, two applied handles, glossy finish... **450**
Vase, 7" h., squatty bulbous base tapering to a tall slender 'stick' neck **650**
Vase, 7 3/4" h., jack-in-the-pulpit form w/very slender stem & round disk foot **495**
Vase, 8 1/4" h., lily-form.................................... **633**

New England Lily-form Vase

Vase, 9 1/2" h., lily-form w/a round foot & tricorner rolled rim, attributed to New England Glass Co. (ILLUS.) **850**
Whiskey tumbler, cylindrical, satin finish, 3 1/2" h. **330**

WEBB

Small Decorated Peach Blow Bowl

Bowl, 3 7/8" d., 2 5/8" h., small gilt footring below the wide squatty rounded body

w/a wide incurved rim, decorated around the sides w/heavy gold prunus blossoms on branches, gold pine needles, satin finish, glossy white interior (ILLUS.) **365**
Bowl, 4" d., 2 1/4" h., decorated w/gold prunus blossoms & pine needles & gold trim, white lining, satin finish **325**
Bowl, 4" d., 2 1/2" h., squatty bulbous shape, decorated w/heavy gold prunus & pine needles & a gold butterfly in flight, creamy white lining, satin finish................... **300**
Cologne bottle w/silver screw cap, spherical body decorated w/delicate gold enameled prunus blossoms & a flying butterfly, cased in white, hallmarked cap, Thomas Webb, England, 5" h. **748**
Cracker jar, cov., barrel-shaped, decorated w/daisies in light blue & white, matching glass cover w/metal finial, white interior, 7 3/4" h. **830**

Webb Peach Blow Finger Bowl

Finger bowl, three-lobed rim, gold prunus blossom decoration on three sides w/small butterfly in each corner, 4 1/2" d., 2 3/4" h. (ILLUS.) **325**
Finger bowl w/underplate, round bowl w/a tightly crimped rim, ruffled underplate, bowl shaded both inside & out w/creamy opaque layer between, underplate w/typical coloring on top, creamy color on bottom, glossy finish, decorated w/gold prunus flowers & butterflies, plate 6 1/4" d., bowl 4 1/4" d., 2 3/4" h., pr. **600**
Jar w/sterling silver cover, spherical squared body w/pinched-in sides, decorated w/a gilt floral sprig, hallmarked silver rim, inset cover & bail handle, 4 1/2" h. **173**
Pitcher, tankard, 9" h., signed........................ **385**
Pitcher, 11" h., bulbous body w/a tricorner mouth, applied clear frosted handle, trimmed in gold.. **193**
Rose bowl, miniature, decorated w/gold flowers & butterfly, 2 1/4" d. **425**

Webb Decorated Peach Blow Vases

Vase, 3 1/4" h., 2 3/4" d., baluster-form, decorated w/gold prunus & branches, creamy white lining (ILLUS. right) **400**

Vase, 3 1/4" h., 2 3/4" d., round short pedestal base below the bulbous nearly spherical body tapering to a short, wide rolled mouth, heavy gold decoration of flowers w/a butterfly on the reverse, gold rim trim, creamy white lining, satin finish...... **325**

Silver- and Gold-Decorated Vase

Vase, 6 1/2" h., 3 5/8" d., squatty bulbous body tapering to a cylindrical neck, decorated w/gold branches, prunus blossoms & a small butterfly, propeller mark **345**

Vase, 7 1/2" h., 3 5/8" d., bulbous body tapering to a tall 'stick' neck w/short flaring rim, decorated w/heavy gold florals & foliage, glossy finish **325**

Vase, 7 1/2" h., 4" d., squatty bulbous body tapering to a cylindrical neck, decorated w/heavy gold prunus blossoms, branches & pine needles, creamy white lining, glossy finish **325**

Vase, 8 1/4" h., pinch-sided bulbous body w/'stick' neck **300**

Vase, bottle-form, 10" h., footed squatty bulbous body w/the rounded shoulder centered by a tall slender slightly flaring 'stick' neck, the sides finely enamel-decorated w/a purple & rust butterfly & insect above clusters of white flowers & green leafy branches **1,650**

Vases, 5" h., 2" d., cylindrical, applied creamy blackthorn flowers, applied clear frosted leaves & clear frosted thorny base, creamy white lining, pr....................... **750**

Vases, 8 1/2" h., 4" d., tapering cylindrical body w/short neck, applied creamy white wafer foot, creamy white interior, pr. **395**

Vases, 10" h., bottle-form, bulbous base w/tall 'stick' neck, decorated w/applied raised flowers & pears in gold & silver, pr. **775**

WHEELING

Carafe, pyramidal body tapering to a slightly flaring cylindrical neck w/a molded ring around the base, 8" h. **935**

Claret jug w/stopper, large spherical body flattened on two sides, a slender cylindrical neck w/pinched spout, applied reeded amber handle & amber facet-cut stopper, 9" h. **1,430**

Creamer, globular w/tricorner top, applied amber handle, glossy finish, 4 1/4" h. (ILLUS. top next page) **785**

Creamer, tapering ovoid body w/a flared rim & pinched spout, satin finish, applied frosted pink handle, 5 1/2" h........................ **330**

Small Webb Decorated Vases

Vase, 3 3/8" h., 2 5/8" d., low pedestal base, globular body w/flared rim, decorated w/heavy gold florals & branch on front, reverse w/gold butterfly, creamy white lining, satin finish (ILLUS. right) **365**

Vase, 3 3/8" h., 2 5/8" d., pedestal footed squatty bulbous body w/short flaring rim, heavy gold florals & branches on front, gold butterfly on reverse, creamy white lining, satin finish.. **365**

Vase, 3 3/4" h., 2 3/4" d., ovoid body w/short flared neck, gold prunus blossom decoration, white lining, glossy finish.. **275**

Vase, 3 3/4" h., 3 1/4" d., ovoid form tapering to a short neck w/flaring rim, decorated w/silver flowers & heavy gold leaves, glossy finish (ILLUS. left with pedestal-based vase)............................ **325**

Vase, 5" h., 3 1/2" d., ovoid body tapering to a short cylindrical neck, heavy gold decoration of prunus blossoms, branches & bee in flight, creamy white lining.. **245**

Vase, 5" h., 3 1/2" d., ovoid body tapering to a short cylindrical neck, decorated w/enameled branches of white flowers, gold leaves, two birds on branches in brown, yellow & orange, white lining, glossy finish... **495**

Vase, 5" h., 3 1/2" d., ovoid body tapering to a short flared neck, enameled w/two-colored birds, white flowers & gold foliage, creamy white lining, propeller mark...... **495**

Vase, 5 1/8" h., 3 1/4" d., baluster-form, decorated w/gold & silver florals & leaves, creamy white interior (ILLUS. top next column).. **295**

Vase, 5 1/8" h., 3 1/4" d., ovoid body tapering to a cylindrical neck w/flaring rim, overall decoration of silver flowers & heavy gold leaves, creamy white lining, glossy finish.. **295**

Vase, 5 1/8" h., 3 1/4" d., ovoid body tapering to a small flared neck, decorated w/heavy gold leaves & silver flowers, creamy white lining (ILLUS. left with small vase) **295**

Wheeling Peach Blow Creamer

Wheeling Peach Blow Cruet

Cruet w/original facet-cut amber ball stopper, bulbous ovoid body tapering to a short neck w/high arched spout, dark reddish amber applied reeded handle, 7" h. (ILLUS.).. **1,200**

Flask, tooled lip, glossy finish, 4 1/2" widest, 7" h. **750**

Mustard jar, cov., footed spherical body, fitted w/a silver plate rim, hinged lid w/spoon hole & angular handle, glossy finish, 2 1/2" h... **476**

Pitcher, 4 1/4" h., wide ovoid body w/a flared quatreform neck, applied amber handle, late 19th c. **495**

Pitcher, 4 1/4" h., bulbous ovoid body tapering to a flaring tricorner rim, applied amber handle, glossy finish......................... **950**

Pitcher, 5 1/4" h., wide ovoid body w/a flared quatreform neck, applied amber handle, late 19th c. (interior bubbles, some staining) **374**

Pitcher, 6" h., footed squatty bulbous body w/a short squared flaring neck, molded Drape patt., applied clear reeded handle, glossy finish (four potstone blemishes).. **450**

Pitcher, 6 1/2" h., footed squatty bulbous body tapering to a flaring quatrefoil neck, mold-blown Drape patt., applied amber reeded handle (ILLUS. top next column) **460**

Pitcher, 7 1/4" h., bulbous body w/quatrefoil rim, applied amber handle, deep red shading to pale green, white lining, polished pontil (small factory imperfection bottom of handle) **795**

Salt & pepper shakers w/original lids, footed spherical bodies, cased w/exte-

rior shading from deep fuchsia to amber, 2 3/4" h., pr. **690**

Wheeling Peach Blow Drape Pitcher

Salt shaker w/original metal top, spherical footed shape, glossy finish, 2 3/4" h. **460**

Sugar bowl, open **445**

Wheeling Peach Blow Sugar Shaker

Sugar shaker w/original metal lid, cylindrical body tapering to neck fitted w/metal screw cap, glossy finish, 5 1/2" h. (ILLUS.)...................................... **316**

Syrup pitcher w/original hinged metal lid, footed tapering cylindrical body, applied amber handle, fine even coloring .. **3,520**

Toothpick holder, footring below a bulbed base ring below the cylindrical sides **1,265**

Tumbler, cylindrical, glossy finish, 3 3/4" h. **400-450**

Tumbler, cylindrical, molded Drape patt., 3 1/2" h. **275**

Tumblers, cylindrical, molded Drape patt., two w/satin & one w/glossy finish, 3 3/4" h., group of 3 .... **450**

Vase, baluster-form w/a short flaring neck, Shape No. 6 .... **400-500**

Vase, 3 1/2" h., miniature, spherical body w/a small short cylindrical neck, satin finish.. **440**

Vase, 3 3/4" h., 1 3/8" d., bulbous body tapering to a short cylindrical neck.............. **250**

Wheeling Peach Blow Vase

Vase, 6 1/4" h., bulbous ovoid body w/a wide rounded shoulder centered by a wide, short cylindrical neck, glossy finish (ILLUS.) **1,100**

Vase, 6 1/2" h., 6 1/2" d., bulbous, glossy finish **850**

Vase, 7" h., double-gourd form, a large & smaller spherical section below a small cylindrical neck w/flared rim, glossy finish **3,300**

Vase, 7 3/4" h., "Morgan Vase," slender ovoid shouldered body w/slender cylindrical ringed neck w/flared rim, glossy finish (no stand) **950**

Peach Blow "Morgan Vase"

Vase, 7 3/4" h., "Morgan Vase," slender ovoid shouldered body w/slender cylindrical ringed neck w/flared rim, glossy finish, set in original glossy amber gargoyle base, 2 pcs. (ILLUS.) **2,000**

Vase, 8" h., bottle-form, spherical body w/a tall slender 'stick' neck, satin finish **825**

Satin Peach Blow "Morgan Vase"

Vase, 8" h., "Morgan Vase," satin finish, in original glossy amber gargoyle base, 2 pcs. (ILLUS.) .... **2,200 - 2,800**

Vase, 8 1/4" h., bottle-form, footrim below the bulbous body tapering to a very slender tall 'stick' neck, glossy finish **750**

Vase, 8 1/2" h., a thin footring below the elongated teardrop-form body tapering to a tall 'stick' neck, glossy finish................. **633**

Vase, 8 1/2" h., ovoid body tapering to a slender 'stick' neck, satin finish **825**

Wheeling Peach Blow Bottle Vase

Vase, 9 1/4" h., bottle-form, bulbous base tapering to a slender 'stick' neck, glossy finish (ILLUS.) **985**

Vase, 10 5/8" h., bottle-shaped, spherical footed base tapering to a tall 'stick' neck **978**

Vase, 11" h., stick-type **1,200**

Wheeling Peach Blow Vase

Vase, 13 3/4" h., tall slender ovoid body w/a closed rim, satin finish, pinhead-size interior bubble (ILLUS.) **546**

PELOTON

Made in Bohemia, Germany and England in the late 19th century, this glassware is characterized by threads or filaments of glass rolled into the glass body of the objects in random patterns. Some of these wares were then further decorated.

Banquet lamp, kerosene-type, spherical Peloton font in white w/multicolored applied strands, raised on a slender spiraled brass standard set on a square stepped marble brass-trimmed foot, overall 17 1/2" h. **$495**

Toothpick holder, waisted cylindrical form w/molded ribbing, clear w/random white & colored threading **385**

Vase, 2 3/4" h., 3" d., miniature, ribbed body & pinched top, shaded pink to white w/multicolored threads **440**

Vase, 4" h., 4 3/4" d., white ribbed cased glass, bulbous base w/folded over tri-corner top, exterior w/pink, yellow, blue & white applied coconut strings **275**

Cylindrical Peloton Vase

Vase, 4 1/2" h., 4" d., cylindrical ribbed body w/a widely flaring ruffled & crimped rim, cased white overlaid w/pink, blue, yellow & white coconut strings (ILLUS.) **225**

PIGEON BLOOD

This name refers to the color of this glass, a deep blood-red. It was popular in the late 19th century and was featured in a number of mold-blown patterns.

Bowl, 8 1/2" d., Venecia patt., floral decoration **$125**

Celery vase Torquay patt. **145**

Jar, cov., handled, Torquay patt., quadruple plated fixture, 7 1/2" h. **879**

Pickle castor w/tongs, Torquay patt. insert in frame **395**

Pitcher, water, w/silver plated rim **450**

Toothpick holder, Bulging Loops patt. **175**

POMONA

First produced by the New England Glass Company under a patent received by Joseph Locke in 1885, Pomona has a frosted ground on clear glass decorated with mineral stains, most frequently amber-yellow, sometimes pale blue. Some pieces bore smooth etched floral decorations highlighted with staining. Two types of Pomona were made. The first Locke patent covered a technique whereby the piece was first covered with an acid resistant coating which was then needle-carved with thousands of minute criss-crossing lines. The piece was then dipped into acid which cut into the etched lines giving the finished piece a notable "brilliance."

A cheaper method, covered by a second Locke patent on June 15, 1886, was accomplished by rolling the glass piece in particles of acid-resistant material which were picked up by it. The glass was then etched by acid which attacked areas not protected by the resistant particles. A favorite design on Pomona was the cornflower.

Berry set: 8" d. master berry bowl & eight 4" d. sauce dishes; Inverted Thumbprint patt. w/turned-in scalloped amber rims, 2nd patent, 9 pcs. **$275**

Bowl, 4" d., crimped & folded rim, 2nd patent **60**

Bowl, 10" d., blue cornflower decoration, 2nd patent **250**

Bowl, 10" d., 4 1/4" h., upright crimped sides, pansy & blue butterfly design, 2nd patent **375**

Butter dish, cov., lid w/acanthus leaf decoration, 1st patent, 8" d., 4" h. **750**

Celery vase, ruffled rim, clear applied base, 1st patent, 6 1/4" h. **370**

Champagne, amber-stained rim, 2nd patent **325**

Rare Pomona Cracker Jar

Cracker jar, cov., large ovoid body w/a fitted domed cover w/an applied amber-stained crown finial w/clear ball knop, Acanthus Leaf patt., first patent (ILLUS.) **1,200-1,500**

Cracker jar, cov., bulbous ovoid body w/fitted domed cover w/clear ball finial, amber-stained etched acanthus leaf border trim, raised on applied amber wishbone feet & w/a band of amber wishbones around the cover finial, 1st patent, 10" h. (chip on base & finial trim) **385**

Pomona Creamer & Sugar Bowl

Creamer & open sugar bowl, squatty bulbous body w/Inverted Thumbprint patt., flaring ruffled amber rim & applied amber handles, 1st patent, pr. (ILLUS.) 600

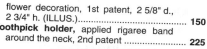

Pomona Cornflower Cruet

Cruet w/original bubble stopper, spherical body on applied crimped foot, applied handle, blue cornflower decoration, 2nd patent (ILLUS.) 700
Finger bowl, ruffled rim, 1st patent, 5 1/2" d., 1 3/4" h.. 220
Finger bowl & underplate, 3" d. bowl w/ruffled rim, 4 1/2" d. underplate; blue cornflower decoration, 2nd patent, 2 pcs...... 100
Finger bowls, amber-stained, 1st patent, 4 1/2" d., pr... 345
Goblets, 2nd patent, set of 6........................... 900
Mustard jar w/metal lid, second patent container w/scalloped border, topped w/a hinged silver plate lid, New England Glass Co., 2" d., 3 1/4" h. (mold imperfection in base, no spoon) 230
Pitcher, 7" h., blue cornflower decoration, 1st patent 750
Pitcher, tankard, 9" h., tall slender slightly tapering body w/a pinched rim spout & applied handle, Diamond Quilted patt. w/plain rim band etched w/acanthus leaves, 1st patent 650
Pitcher, tankard, 12 1/4" h., blue butterflies & gold grasses, 1st patent............................ 750
Punch cup, blue cornflower decoration, 1st patent 150-175
Punch cup, blue cornflower decoration, 2nd patent 125
Punch cup, blueberry decoration w/honey amber stain on rim, leaves & handle, 1st patent, 2 5/8" d., 2 3/4" h............................. 175

Pomona Punch Cup

Punch cup, rounded body w/amber-stained rim & applied handle, blue corn-

flower decoration, 1st patent, 2 5/8" d., 2 3/4" h. (ILLUS.)................................... 150
Toothpick holder, applied rigaree band around the neck, 2nd patent 225

Pomona Toothpick Holder

Toothpick holder, cylindrical base w/tricorner top, 1st patent (ILLUS.).................. 225-275
Tumbler, blueberry decoration, 2nd patent...... 200

Pomona Cornflower Tumbler

Tumbler, cylindrical, blue cornflower decoration, 2nd patent, 2 1/2" d., 3 1/2" h. (ILLUS.)... 145
Tumblers, cylindrical, decorated w/blue cornflowers, honey amber leaves & honey amber tops, 2nd patent, 2 1/2" d., 3 5/8" h., 4 pcs. 540
Vase, 3" h., 6" w., fan-shaped w/ruffled rim, blue cornflower decoration, 1st patent 275
Vase, 3 3/4" h., ovoid body w/ruffled top, on applied amber wishbone feet, 1st patent 200
Vase, 4 1/2" h., shouldered body w/applied rigaree collar below ruffled rim, Inverted Thumbprint patt., 1st patent 200
Vase, 5 1/2" h., ruffled rim, clear applied base, blue cornflower decoration, 1st patent 220

Unusual Pomona Vase-Planter

Vase, 5 1/2" h., 5 1/2" d., planter-form, cylindrical w/upright crimped rim, three applied peg feet, blue cornflower patt., 1st patent (ILLUS.) 546

Vase, 5 3/4" h., 4 1/2" d., crimped rim & ruffled foot, blue cornflower decoration, 2nd patent **500**

QUEZAL

In 1901, Martin Bach and Thomas Johnson, who had worked for Louis Tiffany, opened a competing glassworks in Brooklyn, New York. The Quezal Art Glass and Decorating Co. produced wares closely resembling those of Tiffany until the plant's closing in 1925.

Quezal

Quezal Mark

Bowl, 8" d., 4 1/2" h., deep rounded flat-rimmed bowl raised on a trumpet foot, orangish gold iridescent ground decorated on the exterior w/iridescent royal blue pulled swirls, signed (internal heat line in bottom above base) **$550**

Center bowl, deep flaring wide-ribbed bowl on a ribbed funnel base, blue shading to purple w/overall golden iridescence, signed, ca. 1900, 13 1/8" d........................ **1,200**

Compote, open, 5 1/4" d., 4 1/2" h., a disk foot & short ringed pedestal in bluish gold iridescence supporting a wide squatty bulbous bowl tapering below the wide flaring rim, bowl w/marigold iridescent exterior & gold iridescent interior, signed.. **550**

Decorative Quezal Compote

Compote, open, 5 1/2" h., wide squatty bulbous body tapering to a short flaring crimped & ruffled neck, raised on a tall widely flaring funnel foot, opal white decorated w/three broad green leaves interspersed w/gold tracery, iridescent gold interior, signed on base (ILLUS.) **2,500**

Cup & saucer, the cup in opalescent & amber iridescence w/a band of scrolled feathering, the saucer in overall amber iridescence, both signed, ca. 1900, saucer 4 1/8" d.. **805**

Decanter w/original pointed mushroom stopper, bulbous base tapering to a tall 'stick' neck w/flared rim, green & gold

double-hooked feather designs on green, gold iridescent neck & stopper, designed by Martin Bach, signed, 11 1/2" h. (ILLUS. below) **4,750**

Rare Quezal Decanter

Finger bowl, wide bulbous ovoid tapering body w/a flat mouth, the exterior decorated w/pulled green leaves w/iridescent gold tips on an almond brown ground, iridescent gold interior, signed, 4 3/4" d., 2 3/4" h. (internal line encircles base) **440**

Lamp, table model, two-light, the baluster-form body in cased white decorated w/feathered trailings in blue & iridescent silver & in iridescent gold, w/reeded & foliate-cast metal mounts, two curving arms fitted w/a pair of paneled opalescent floriform shades w/iridescent gold interiors & gold feathering on the exterior, each side signed, ca. 1925, overall 25 3/4" h.. **750**

Lamps, mantel-type, ten-ribbed tulip-form gold iridescent shade inverted on the gilt-metal ringed & knob short pedestal w/domed round foot w/electric switch, shades signed on rims, overall 9" h., pr. **575**

Plate, 6 1/2" d., gold iridescence w/purple highlights **225**

Taster, squared sides w/pinched dimples, gold iridescent interior & exterior, signed "Quezal" on base, 2 3/4" h. **175**

Bulbous Quezal Pulled-Feather Vase

Vase, bulbous ovoid body tapering to a short rolled neck, bold gold pulled-feather & scroll designs on a dark colored ground w/white around the shoulder & neck, gold iridescent interior (ILLUS.)... **2,800**

Vase, floriform, a decorated cushion foot supporting a slender stem to the widely

flaring ruffled top, iridescent gold ground
decorated w/white pulled-feather design... **2,750**
Vase, 3" h., miniature, slightly ribbed form
w/a bulbous base & flared neck, amber
w/strong overall gold iridescence, signed
in polished pontil "Quezal 866".................... **690**

Short and Tall Quezal Vases

Vase, 5 1/8" h., wide ovoid body tapering to
a tiny short neck, deep reddish amber
w/silvery blue & gold iridescence, overlaid w/silver depictions of flowers &
wispy foliage, signed "Quezal - D1150"
(ILLUS. left) **1,380**
Vase, 5 1/2" h., a thin cushion foot cen-
tered by a tall very slender cylindrical
body below the wide, shallow cupped
rim, overall gold iridescence w/rose &
blue highlights, inscribed mark.................... **413**

Quezal Floriform Vases

Vase, 4 1/4" h., floriform, cushion foot
below tapering to a slender ribbed body
w/a trefoil floriform lip, white w/green
trailings & pink & amber iridescence,
signed "Quezal - 167" centering a "T"
(ILLUS. right).. **920**
Vase, 4 1/2" h., ruffled rim, gold iridescent
pulled-feather decoration, signed................. **550**
Vase, 4 1/2" h., wide squatty bulbous body
tapering to a short cylindrical neck w/a
widely flaring rim, the neck in golden iridescence w/green pulled swirls around
the lower section over the creamy white
lower body w/dark gold pulled-feathers
around the bottom, signed & numbered
"487".. **3,245**
Vase, 4 1/2" h., wide squatty ovoid body
w/the wide shoulder centered by a short,
wide flaring neck, translucent amber
w/delicate green & gold feathers on a
thin opal surface, gold iridescent interior,
signed on base (surface bubbles in
feather area) **920**
Vase, 4 5/8" h., footed squatty bulbous
baluster-form w/flaring rim, cased dou-
ble-decorated opal body w/hooked &
pulled gold feathers below green hooked
elements w/medial gold band, gold iridescent surface above & within flared
rim, signed "Quezal 490" **2,070**
Vase, 5" h., lily-form, a thin round cushion
foot tapering to a tall slender waisted
body w/a widely flaring quatraform rim,
golden iridescent ground w/five subtle
green spiked feathers, large partial label
covers pontil reading "Art Quezal -
Brooklyn" **1,035**

Fine Pulled-Feather Quezal Vase

Vase, 6" h., bottle-form, spherical base
tapering to a tall slender 'stick' neck, yellow opal ground in iridescent gold w/a
pulled-feather band around the base
trimmed in dark green, signed on the
pontil (ILLUS.) **2,090**
Vase, 6" h., cushion foot w/a slender stem
on the trumpet-form body w/a 'jack-in-
the-pulpit' flattened rim, the back side
only slightly curved up, green body
w/overall iridescent blue exterior, signed
on the base **690**
Vase, 6 1/2" h., flaring top, gold iridescent
interior & white exterior w/gold iridescent
finish, signed **248**

Quezal Vase with Silver Overlay

Vase, 6 1/2" h., ovoid body w/a broad shoulder tapering to a short cyindrical neck w/a flaring crimped rim, amber w/gold iridescence, overlaid around the neck & shoulder w/silver Art Nouveau floral & vine designs, glass stressed at rim silver attachment, signed "Quezal - D 1193" (ILLUS.).. **1,035**

Vase, 7" h., trumpet-form body w/deeply ruffled rim raised on a cushion foot, opalescent decorated w/green & amber iridescent striated feathering & trailings, amber iridescent interior, inscribed "Quezal R 922," ca. 1920 .... **1,840**

Vase, 7 1/2" h., floriform, the opalescent sides decorated w/green striated feathering, the foot further decorated w/amber iridescent feathering, the interior in amber iridescence, inscribed "Quezal," ca. 1925...................................... **1,550**

Vase, 8 1/4" h., floriform, slender baluster-form body w/a trefoil lip & cushion foot, white w/green pulled-leaf decoration & gold trailings w/pink iridescence, very small internal crack under foot, signed "Quezal - 794" surrounding an O (ILLUS. left with small floriform vase)..................... **1,035**

Two Signed Quezal Vases

Vase, 8 1/4" h., gently flaring cylindrical shouldered body w/a tapering neck & swelled closed mouth, ambergris w/blue iridescence, signed on base (ILLUS. right) **690**

Vase, 8 1/2" h., simple ovoid body tapering to a short trumpet neck, amber w/gold iridescence decorated w/overall white pulled & hooked tracery design, base signed (interior in-the-making annealing line) **690**

Vase, 8 3/4" h., lily-type w/jack-in-the-pulpit upturned rim on a slender stem & cushion foot, stretched overall gold iridescence, signed "Quezal 176" (ILLUS. left) **1,150**

Decorative Quezal Vase

Vase, 9" h., ovoid body tapering to a slightly flared neck, green w/a raised gold iridescent neck decorated overall w/pulled leaves in gold lustre & brilliant iridescence, signed on pontil (ILLUS.) **4,600**

Vase, 9 3/8" h., slender footed ovoid body w/constricting neck & flaring lip, amber iridescence shading to yellow & violet, pontil signed, ca. 1920 .... **750**

Vase, 9 1/2" h., flared rounded base tapering gently to a tall cylindrical body w/a flat rim, amber w/golden crimson iridescence, signed "Quezal - D1203" (ILLUS. right with silver-decorated vase) **546**

Vase, 10 1/2" h., slender baluster-form, overall blue iridescence, signed **1,100**

Vase, 10 1/2" h., tall slender baluster-form w/short trumpet neck, overall blue iridescent finish, signed **1,375**

Fine Tall Quezal Vase

Vase, 12" h., slender baluster-form body w/a cushion foot & closed rim, rich opalescent cased over amber decorated w/pulled green leafage reserved against gold, applied w/six large iridescent drips in white, amber & blue, signed (ILLUS.).... **6,325**

Vase, 12 1/4" h., jack-in-the-pulpit form w/cushion foot, slender cylindrical body & wide rolled rim, purplish blue shading to golden iridescence, silver feathering on the foot extending into the body, signed.. **2,750**

Vase, 12 3/4" h., bulbous cushion foot tapering to a tall slightly flaring cylindrical body w/a widely flaring six-ruffle rim, overall gold iridescence, signed **1,568**

Vase, 12 3/4" h., tall baluster-form body swelled at the top & w/a short cylindrical neck, opalescent decorated w/pulled green & gold iridescent leafage & applied w/reeded gold medallions w/tendrils down the sides, unsigned, ca. 1910 .... **4,500**

Large Quezal Jack-in-the-Pulpit Vase

Vase, 15" h., jack-in-the-pulpit form w/cushion foot, slender cylindrical body & widely flaring gently ruffled rim, the exterior decorated w/green & gold pulled-feather decoration, iridescent gold interior, signed (ILLUS.) **5,500**

Vase, 16" h., jack-in-the-pulpit form, the broad undulating mouth w/crackled gold iridescence, issuing from a slender stem & bulbous cushion foot, elaborately decorated w/gold & green pulled-feather & swirled designs, signed "Quezal M 702" ... **6,500**

Quezal Candlestick-form Vases

Vases, 4 3/4" h., slender opal cylinder on an applied disk foot, green & gold pulled-feather design, gold iridescent interiors, each signed on base, accompanied by gold metal candlecup bobeche, pr. (ILLUS.) **690**

ROSE BOWLS

These decorative small bowls were widely popular in the late 19th and early 20th centuries. Produced in various types of glass, they are most common in satin glass or spatter glass. They are generally a spherical shape with an incurved crimped rim, but ovoid or egg-shaped examples were also popular.

Their name derives from their reported use, to hold dried rose petal potpourri or small fresh-cut roses.

Miniature Amethyst Rose Bowl

Amethyst, miniature, six-crimp rim, enameled w/white & rust blossoms & green leaves, 2" h. (ILLUS.) **$250**

Two Intaglio Engraved Rose Bowls

Amethyst, six-crimp rim, deep color w/intaglio floral engraving, attributed to Moser, ca. 1910, 2 1/2" h. (ILLUS. right) **300-350**

Two "Jewell" Glass Rose Bowls

Blue, eight-crimp rim, threaded body w/overall thumbprints, Stevens & Williams "Jewell" glass, 2 1/4" h. (ILLUS. right) **125-175**

Blue Stevens & Williams Rose Bowl

Blue, spherical w/six-crimp rim, box pleat style w/zipper bands on ribs, Stevens & Williams' "Jewell" line, etched English registry number on the bottom, 4" h. (ILLUS.) **125-165**

Reproduction Maize Rose Bowl

Cased, golden amber cased in white, Libbey's Maize patt. reproduced by L.G. Wright Glass Co., ca. 1970, 4 1/2" h. (ILLUS.).. **85-125**

Two Thomas Webb Satin Rose Bowls

Cased satin, eight-crimp rim, blue shaded to pale blue, decorated w/heavy gilt prunus blossoms, decorated by Jules Barbe for Thomas Webb & Sons, 2 1/4" h. (ILLUS. left) .... **250 TO 325**

Floral Embossed Rose Bowl

Cased satin, eight-crimp rim, dark green shaded to pale green, Floral Embossed patt., ca. 1890s, 3 1/2" h. (ILLUS.) **125-175**
Cased satin, eight-crimp rim, deep red shaded to soft orange, decorated w/heavy gold prunus blossoms, a butterfly on the reverse, decorated by Jules Barbe for Thomas Webb & Sons, 3" h. (ILLUS. right with blue bowl) **400-600**

Cabbage Pattern Satin Rose Bowl

Cased satin, eight-crimp rim, deep rose pink shaded to creamy white, Cabbage patt., white lining, 4 1/2" d., 4 1/2" h. (ILLUS.).. **165**

Souvenir Satin Rose Bowl

Cased satin, eight-crimp rim, peach shaded to creamy white, inscribed in yellow enamel "A Present from London," marked on base "Made in Bohemia," 3 1/2" h. (ILLUS.).................................... **125-175**

Mother-of-Pearl Satin Rose Bowl

Cased satin, eight-crimp rim, shaded blue mother-of-pearl Diamond Quilted patt., probably Webb, 3 3/4" h. (ILLUS.) **275-325**

Shell & Seaweed Pattern Rose Bowl

Cased satin, eight-crimp rim, Shell & Seaweed molded patt., deep pink shaded to pale pink, enameled around the top w/orange leaves & white blossoms, orange dots on the shells, ca. 1880s, 5" h. (ILLUS.)... **125-175**

Miniature Mother-of-Pearl Satin Bowl

Cased satin, Rainbow mother-of-pearl Diamond Quilted patt., miniature, six-crimp rim, 2 3/4" h. (ILLUS.).................................... **600**

Cased satin, shaded blue mother-of-pearl Ribbon patt., irregular ruffled rim, 3" h. **110**

Box-pleated Satin Rose Bowl

Cased satin, six-crimp box-pleated rim, brown shaded to creamy white, Stevens & Williams, 4 3/4" h. (ILLUS.)............... **200-250**

Plum Satin with Prunus Rose Bowl

Cased satin, six-crimp rim, miniature, plum shaded to light plum, heavy gilt prunus blossoms decoration, creamy lining, Thomas Webb, 3 1/2" d., 2 1/2" h. (ILLUS.) **245**

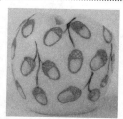

Satin Rose Bowl with Acorns

Creamy white, four-crimp rim, miniature, satin ground decorated overall w/orange acorns on green stems, 2 3/4" h. (ILLUS.).. **85-110**

Decorated Satin Rose Bowl

Creamy white, three-crimp rim, footed satin decorated w/light green & brown gingko branches, Thomas Webb, 2 3/4" h. (ILLUS.).................................. **225-275**

Miniature Rose Bowl with Daisies

Crown Milano, eight-crimp rim, miniature, pale blue shaded to creamy white, boldly enameled w/large yellow & purple daisies w/green leafy stems, 2 3/4" h. (ILLUS.).. **400**

Custard-colored Decorated Rose Bowl

Custard-colored, spherical w/eight-crimp rim, creamy ground, enameled w/a group of classical figures in shades of brown, raised scrolls in white w/nutmeg staining, 5" h. (ILLUS.) **175-200**

Miniature Green & Gilt Rose Bowl

Green, miniature, egg-shaped w/six-crimp rim, dark green decorated around the top w/a wide band of gold w/blue scrolls, gilt scrolls around the lower body, attributed to Moser, ca. 1885, 3" h. (ILLUS.).. **125-175**

Green, six-crimp rim, miniature, pale optic-ribbed form w/gilt decoration around the rim, 2" h. (ILLUS. top next page)............. **75-100**

Green shaded to clear, six-crimp rim, intaglio etched w/a large blossom, attributed to Moser, ca. 1910, 2" h. (ILLUS. left w/amethyst intaglio bowl) **250-300**

Olive green, eight-crimp rim, threaded body w/overall thumbprints, Stevens & Williams "Jewell" glass, 2 1/4" h. (ILLUS. left, w/blue "Jewell" bowl) **125-175**

Pale Green Decorated Rose Bowl

Satin glass, spherical melon-lobed form w/an eight-crimp rim, decorated w/enameled stylized flowers & scattered gold scrolls, 4 1/2" d., 3 1/2" h...................... **193**

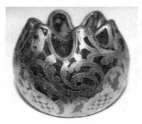

Rare Miniature Silver-Overlay Bowl

Silver-overlay, miniature, spherical w/six-crimp rim, dark blue overlaid w/elaborate silver scrolls & pierced lattice, probably German, signed "Bailey, Banks & Biddle, Phila.," 2" h. (ILLUS.) **200-250**

Spangled Glass Rose Bowl

Spangled, eight-crimp rim, reddish orange cased in white spatter w/silver mica flecks throughout, 3 1/2" h. (ILLUS.) **100-150**
Spangled, heavenly blue Vasa Murrhina overlay, white lining, six-crimp rim, loaded w/mica flakes on the outside, 3 3/8" d., 3 3/4" h... **95**

White Satin Souvenir Rose Bowl

White, eight-crimp rim, souvenir-type, satin ground decorated w/a black transfer of the U.S. Capitol, made in Austria, 4 1/2" d., 3 3/4" h. (ILLUS.) **100-150**

Yellowish Green Optic Ribbed Bowl

Yellowish green, eight-crimp rim, optic ribbed design, 5" h. (ILLUS.) **45-50**

ROYAL FLEMISH

This ware, made by Mt. Washington Glass Co., is characterized by very heavy enameled gold lines dividing the surface into separate areas or sections. The body, with a matte finish, is variously decorated.

Royal Flemish Cracker Jar

Cracker jar, cov., barrel-shaped, gold Roman Coin decoration on a ground of brown & tan random panels outlined in heavy gold lines, ornate silver plate rim, cover & bail handle, signed (ILLUS.)... **$1,800-2,200**
Cracker jar, cov., ovoid body, overall decoration of large Roman coins on stained panels divided by heavy gold lines, ornate silver plate cover, rim & bail handle, original paper label w/"Mt. W. G. Co. Royal Flemish," 8" h. **2,200**
Cracker jar, cov., tall barrel shape, angular panels in shades of tan & brown outlined in heavy gold & w/a large gold coin decoration, resilvered silver plate rim, domed cover & swing bail handle **2,035**

Rare & Unusual Royal Flemish Ewer

Ewer, slender ovoid body tapering to a slender cylindrical neck w/upright angled spout, high arched applied ropetwist handle, unusual flag staff decoration on segmented stained glass background, w/a fierce rampant lion above the company masthead double eagle emblem shield, 12 1/4" h. (ILLUS.) **2,990**

Lamp, kerosene table model, the bulbous cylindrical glass font decorated w/round gold portrait medallions separated by heavy gold banding from random pale colored panels, a scroll-embossed wide brass collar & domed foot w/four scroll feet, converted to electricity **358**

Pitcher, 8 5/8" h., bulbous body w/a low cylindrical neck w/angled rim, applied ropetwist handle, acid-finished, enameled w/two small fish swimming against a background of shells & marine plants in various shades of lavender puce, deep emerald green, Chinese red, chocolate brown & lemon yellow w/heavy gilt trim, reserved against a ground formed of irregular panels enameled in lavender & pale yellow between raised gold borders conjoined by raised balls, the neck enameled w/scrolling coral edged in gilt & reserved against a strawberry ground, original paper label (ILLUS. below) **9,000**

Rare Royal Flemish Pitcher

Vase, 4" h., gold enameled griffin & scrolling against an orangish amber stained glass window ground................................. **1,250**

Vase, 5 1/2" h., footed wide squatty bulbous body tapering sharply to a small flaring neck flanked by small applied leaf loop handles, decorated w/scattered bouquets of colorful pastel pansies trimmed w/raised gold sun rays & a gilt network of berried vines **2,200**

Vase, 6" h., double gourd-form, decorated w/colorful pansies & gold enameling on a frosted ground **1,500**

Rose-decorated Royal Flemish Vase

Vase, 9 1/2" h., footed ovoid body tapering to a ringed neck & high cupped rim, decorated overall w/trailing enameled roses in shades of pink & green, raised gold enamel outlines on a stylized trellis w/blue spiral accents, marked on base, slight gilt wear, ca. 1894 (ILLUS.) **3,335**

Fine Royal Flemish Vase

Vase, 10 1/4" h., 6 1/4" d., footed bulbous body w/short wide cylindrical neck w/leaf decoration & flared rim, heavy gold enamel lines separating areas in shades of green, yellow & maroon, large griffin & dragon opposite each other flanked w/large six-point stars, ring of applied glass separating the neck from the base (ILLUS.)...................................... **5,385**

Vase, 12" h., footed wide squatty bulbous base centered by a tall, slender swelled 'stick' neck w/flat rim, the body decorated w/raised gold sections w/subtle earth tones, three decorative medallions, the main one w/a griffin head, the other w/flowers, raised gold leafy vine w/wild berries & florals meander across the shoulder, the neck w/frosty leafy scrolls trimmed in raised gold on a wine red ground **3,575**

Royal Flemish Egyptian Scene Vase

Vase, 13" h., Egyptian scene, classic handled oval body decorated w/gilt enameled panels & medallions centering starstudded scene of camel w/ethnic costumed rider, body guard w/scimitar alongside, Mideastern scrolls & devices at reverse (ILLUS.) **13,800**

RUBINA CRYSTAL

This glass, sometimes spelled "Rubena," is a flashed ware, shading from ruby to clear. Some pieces are decorated, others are plain.

Bowl, 5 3/4" d., pressed Hobnail patt. w/upright crimped rim, frosted finish, probably Hobbs, ca. 1890 .... **$35**

Cracker jar, cov., slightly tapering cylindrical optic ribbed body w/enameled floral decoration, silver plate rim, cover & angled bail handle **385**

Salt shaker w/original lid, ring-neck mold **165**

Vase, 6 1/2" h., wide cylindrical form w/an upright ruffled upper half, enameled around the sides w/colorful pansies on green leafy stems, gold rim band, ground pontil, late 19th c. **316**

RUBINA VERDE

This decorative glass, popular in the late 19th and early 20th centuries, shades from ruby or deep cranberry to green or greenish-yellow.

Bowl, 4 1/2" d., 2 3/4" h., Inverted Thumbprint patt., attributed to Hobbs, Brocku-nier **$138**

Butter dish, cov., the domed mold-blown rubina verde cover in the Inverted Thumbprint patt. w/a large applied clear knop handle, on a matching clear pressed glass Daisy & Button patt. base, 7" d. **224**

Celery vase, Inverted Thumbprint patt. **165**

Cheese dish, cov., the domed mold-blown Coin Spot shaded cover sitting on a round pressed green Daisy & Button patt. base, overall 7" d. **275**

Decanter w/original stopper, spherical Inverted Thumbprint patt. body tapering to a cylindrical neck w/tricorner rim, applied yellow reeded handle & facet-cut stopper, 9 1/2" h. **385**

Finger bowl, Inverted Thumbprint patt. **95**

Pitcher, water, bulbous ovoid body tapering to a squared neck, Coin Spot patt., applied handle **242**

Pitcher, water, bulbous ovoid body w/flaring square mouth, Inverted Thumbprint patt., applied clear twisted & braided collar & handle, rosettes at base of handle, ground pontil **248**

Pitcher, 7 1/4" h., spherical w/cylindrical neck, Inverted Thumbprint patt., applied greenish yellow handle, attributed to Hobbs, Brockunier **275**

Fine Rubina Verde Pitcher

Pitcher, 8 1/2" h., spherical base w/a tall wide cylindrical neck w/flared & lightly scalloped rim w/pinched spout, optic ribbed design, appled angular reeded green handle, sand bruise on interior (ILLUS.) **385**

Punch cup, Inverted Thumbprint patt., ... **145**

Punch set: cov. footed punch bowl, ladle & six footed stems; the punch bowl in an Optic Rib patt. w/a deep ruby cover w/hollow ribbed pale green knop, the wide rounded bowl w/optic ribbing & shading from deep ruby to pale green & raised on a knopped pedestal & round foot, enamel-decorated around the cover & sides w/delicate white & colored floral sprigs, the matching saucer stems on knopped stems w/enamel decoration, Europe, late 19th - early 20th c., bowl 8" h., the set **1,035**

Vase, 12" h., jack-in-the-pulpit-form, the tall widely flaring blossom-form top in deep cranberry w/the wide rim pulled into long points, the back petal turned up, tapering to a slender stem w/the lower half in green on a green foot **275**

Rubina Verde Vases with Rigaree

Vases, optic-ribbed trumpet-form body w/scalloped rim & flaring cushion foot, applied clear rigaree wrapped around the sides, pr. (ILLUS.) **330**

SABINO

Ernest-Marius Sabino, a French Art Deco glassmaker, began production of art glass in the 1920s. He produced a wide range of items in frosted, colored, opalescent and clear glass in both blown and pressed glass. The Parisian shop closed during World War II and reopened in the 1960s. Earlier works included lamps, vases, figures and other items; after 1960 the production was primarily small birds and nudes. In the 1970s a line of limited edition plates was introduced. Pieces are marked with the name in the mold, an etched signature or both.

Sabino
France

Sabino Marks

Figure of a lady, "Nude with Draped Cloak," standing figure w/one arm extended straight out to the side, opalescent vaseline, original paper label reading "Sabino made in France," 7 3/4" h........ **$863**

Figure of Madonna, standing cloaked figure in clear opalescent, signed on the base "Sabino Paris," original paper label "Made in France," 5" h................................. **201**

Figure of young woman, "Idole," modeled as a young woman w/long hair seated on a cushion w/her legs crossed & her hands resting in her lap, wearing only a drapery around her waist, the cushion inscribed "Sabino France," ca. 1925, 6 1/8" h... **1,150**

Vase, 7" h., Bee patt., footed spherical body w/a small round short neck, opalescent press-molded design of raised bumblebees clustered on angular hon-

eycomb & floral latticework, engraved mark on base "Sabino Paris" **460**

Art Deco Sabino Wall Sconce

Wall sconces, long arched & gently curved piece in the form of a molded bouquet of flowers on a flared base, metal mounts inscribed "Sabino Paris - Made in France," ca. 1925, 17" w., pr. (ILLUS. of one) **1,380**

SATIN

Satin glass was a popular decorative glass developed in the late 19th century. Most pieces were composed of two layers of glass with the exterior layer usually in a shaded pastel color. The name derives from the soft matte finish, caused by exposure to acid fumes, which gave the surface a "satiny" feel. Mother-of-pearl satin glass was a specialized variety wherein air trapped between the layers of glass provided subtle surface patterns such as Herringbone and Diamond Quilted. A majority of satin glass was produced in England, Bohemia and America, but collectors should be aware that reproductions have been produced for many years.

Bowl, 3" d., ruffled rim, shaded pink mother-of-pearl Diamond Quilted patt. **$110**

Bowl, 5" d., 4" h., squatty round form tapering slightly to a wide triangular rim, lightly ribbed pink, attributed to Mt. Washington **1,210**

Bowl, 9 1/2" oval, shaded apricot mother-of-pearl Diamond Quilted patt., heavily enameled w/pears & stems w/gold trim **495**

Celery vase, cylindrical, shaded blue mother-of-pearl Diamond Quilted patt., 6 1/2" h. **165**

Cologne bottle & stopper, bulbous ovoid body tapering to a small neck w/a sterling silver rim & matching silver mushroom cover, Rainbow mother-of-pearl Diamond Quilted patt., some original gilt sprig decoration, 4 7/8" h. **715**

Creamer, blue mother-of-pearl Raindrop patt., bulbous base & wide cylindrical neck w/rim spout, applied reeded blue handle, 3 1/8" d., 4 1/2" h. (ILLUS. top next page) **195**

Mother-of-Pearl Satin Creamer

Rainbow Mother-of-Pearl Satin Ewer

Ewer, squatty bulbous base w/a wide shoulder centering a tall gently flaring neck w/a tricorner ruffled rim, Rainbow mother-of-pearl Herringbone patt., applied angular clear frosted handle, 10 1/2" h. (ILLUS.)........................... **1,500-2,000**

Rare Satin Creamer & Sugar Bowl

Creamer & open sugar bowl, each footed w/a melon-lobed body tapering to a upright crimped rim, nearly translucent opal to rose to blue mother-of-pearl Herringbone patt., applied frosted clear handle on creamer, sugar 3 1/2" h., creamer 5" h., pr. (ILLUS.) **5,060**

Creamer & open sugar bowl, footed bulbous form in blue mother-of-pearl Ribbon patt., the sugar w/a three-lobed form, the creamer w/one side pinched to form the spout, applied clear frosted handle & bases, creamer 2 1/8" h., sugar 2 3/8" h., pr. **325**

Cruet w/original stopper, shaded blue mother-of-pearl Raindrop patt., applied frosted reeded handle & stopper.................. **385**

Cruet w/original stopper, shaded pink mother-of-pearl Diamond Quilted patt., squatty bulbous body tapering to a slender neck & tricorner rim, decorated w/finely enameled blue forget-me-nots & white daisies & leaves, applied frosted clear reeded handle, clear frosted facet-cut stopper, 8" h. **990**

Cruet w/original stopper, shaded pink mother-of-pearl Herringbone patt., bulbous tapering to a tricorner rim, clear frosted stopper & applied handle, 5 1/4" h... **330**

Ewer, bulbous body tapering to a neck w/a ruffled top, shaded pink mother-of-pearl Diamond Quilted patt., applied pink thorn handle, 7" h. **220**

Decorated Pink Satin Jam Dish

Jam dish in holder, squatty bulbous bowl w/wide flat mouth in shaded pink decorated in enamels around the sides w/a black bird on a branch, blackberries & green leaves, in a footed silver plate holder w/swing bail handle, overall 4 1/2" d., 6" h. (ILLUS.) **245**

Mustard pot, cov., ovoid shaded pink mother-of-pearl Raindrop patt., silver plate rim, cover & bail handle, 3" h.............. **303**

Pitcher, 5" h., footed wide squatty round body tapering to a short cylindrical neck w/pinched rim spout, frosted clear applied squared handle, Rainbow mother-of-pearl Herringbone patt................ **660**

Pitcher, 8 1/2" h., bulbous ovoid body tapering to a short neck w/a crimped & ruffled rim at the back of the wide smooth spout, shaded pink mother-of-pearl Raindrop patt., applied frosted clear reeded handle **385**

Pitcher, 9" h., shaded golden brown to white mother-of-pearl Coin Dot patt., bulbous body w/pinched indentations around the sides, cylindrical neck, applied handle **330**

Vase, 5 3/4" h., ovoid body tapering to a short neck w/a widely flaring crimped rim w/two sides pulled up, shaded blue mother-of-pearl Herringbone patt., enameled w/large stylized orange & red blossoms on brown branches, signed by Webb **330**

Vase, 5 3/4" h., ovoid body tapering to a three-ringed lower neck tapering to a widely flaring tricorner rim, Rainbow mother-of-pearl Diamond Quilted patt. **413**

Decorated Blue Herringbone Vase

Vase, 6 1/2" h., 4" d., wide tapering ovoid body w/a wide shoulder centering a short trumpet neck, shaded blue mother-of-pearl Herringbone patt., decorated w/stripes of gilt leaf sprigs, white lining (ILLUS.) **225**

Vase, 7" h., bulbous teardrop body in deep pink mother-of-pearl Diamond Quilted patt., raised on three applied frosted clear leaf & tab feet, applied around the body w/frosted clear flowering leafy branches, attributed to Webb **275**

Double Gourd-form Satin Vase

Vase, 7 1/8" h., double gourd-form w/a spherical base tapering to a slender waist & swelled bulbous neck, shaded light blue mother-of-pearl Swirl patt., yellow interior, attributed to Stevens & Williams (ILLUS.) **316**

Vase, 7 1/2" h., 3 1/2" d., shaded blue ruffled, enameled cream & blue flowers, grey & white branches, rust colored but-

terfly, three frosted applied handles on each side, white inside **135**

Blue Diamond Quilted Satin Vase

Vase, 7 3/4" h., 4" d., simple ovoid form tapering to a cyindrical neck w/a widely flaring rolled three-lobe rim, blue mother-of-pearl Diamond Quilted patt., applied frosted clear rim (ILLUS.) **225**

Vase, 7 7/8" h., 6" d., rich blue mother-of-pearl Raindrop patt., melon sectioned, ruffled top, white lining, frosted top edging, unblemished satin **225**

Vase, 8 1/8" h. swelled bottom below the wide cylindrical body w/a tricorner flared rim, shaded orange to white mother-of-pearl Swirl patt. **220**

Vase, 10" h., spherical body below a tall slender 'stick' neck, shaded blue to white mother-of-pearl Diamond Quilted patt. **176**

Vase, 10 3/4" h., footed slender ovoid body w/a four-lobed crimped rim, shaded pink mother-of-pearl Diamond Quilted patt., ornately decorated w/enameled wildflowers in white, green & yellow w/large leafy stems, gilt trim, applied frosted clear rim band, polished pontil **201**

SCHNEIDER

This ware is made in France at Cristallerie Schneider, established in 1913 near Paris by Ernest and Charles Schneider. Some pieces of cameo were marked "Le Verre Francais" (which see) and others were signed "Charder."

Schneider Mark

Aquarium, jade in brown, white & yellow w/hints of lavender, signed, 6 1/2" h. **$468**

Bowl, 12" d., squatty bulbous form w/wide flared rim, red mottled w/purple & white, blown into a wrought-iron frame w/panels of scroll designs between top & base bands, apparently unsigned, ca. 1925 ...... **1,380**

Bowl, 12" d., 3 1/2" h., a wide flat bottom w/low rounded sides w/a wide flat rim, yellow shading to orangish red w/streaks of maroon, cased in clear, base inscribed "Schneider France - Ovington New York" **374**

Fine Schneider Cameo Ewer

Cameo ewer, bulbous cylindrical body tapering sharply to a tall slender neck w/a cupped rim & high arched spout, grey shading to lemon yellow, internally mottled & streaked w/amethyst, overlaid w/orange & cut w/arbutus berries & leaves, enameled in shades of brown & green, signed, ca. 1924, 10 3/4" h. (ILLUS.).. **5,750**

Schneider Poppy Cameo Vase

Cameo vase, 9" h., a dark purple round cushion foot & knopped stem supporting a wide bulbous ovoid body tapering to a molded mouth, deep golden yellow overlaid w/dark reddish orange & wheel-carved w/large stylized poppy blossoms w/angular spiraling stems, signed in intaglio, ca. 1925 (ILLUS.)........................ **5,750**

Large Schneider Centerpiece

Centerpiece, small ovoid center pedestal supporting a wide rounded & gently dished form, mottled blue, turquoise,

tangerine & burgundy, signed, ca. 1925, 15" d. (ILLUS.).. **1,495**
Lamp, table model, elongated baluster form on a wide spreading base, amethyst & blue w/deep purple or amethyst at the dropped footed base w/delicate random tangerine highlights, cased in clear subtly graduating into two-toned pale blue & a dense blue flame design, signed, adjustable, 18 3/4" h. **1,100**
Tazza, a wide shallow round flat-sided bowl in white w/a mottled amethyst & blue rim, raised on a slender double-bulbed amethyst stem & disk foot, foot signed, ca. 1920, 7 5/8" h............................ **863**
Vase, 3 5/8" h., miniature, "Aux Grappes de Raisins," ovoid body in clear cased in speckled yellow w/"marqueterie-sur-verre" decoration of stems around the neck & three clusters of red grapes, each centered by a black spot, engraved highlights, signed, ca. 1925 (rim polished down).. **575**
Vase, 7 1/2" h., a wide & deep rounded tapering bowl raised on a ringed short pedestal & low domed foot, deep plum internally decorated in the bowl w/stylized blossoms & leaves in shades of white, yellow, emerald & pea green, acid-stamped "Schneider" w/vase form, impressed "20," ca. 1925 .... **28,750**
Vase, 8" h., ribbed ovoid body, grey shading to lemon yellow, on a circular dark purple foot, signed "Schneider - FRANCE," ca. 1925 .... **1,265**
Vase, 8" h., tall double-gourd form, bubbled w/mottled yellow & mauve powder internal decoration & three applied oblong prunts in mauve, acid-etched mark, polished pontil, ca. 1925 .... **863**
Vase, 8 1/2" h., baluster-form w/ringed stem on cushion foot supporting a wide ovoid body w/a widely flaring neck, grey shaded mottled pale yellow & amethyst applied w/a medial band of black martelé glass w/yellow blossoms w/orange centers, signed in gilt enamel "Schneider - France," ca. 1925 .... **7,475**

Schneider Mottled Glass Vase

Vase, 11" h., triple gourd-form, white & purple mottled decorated w/dark purple vertical dashes & yellow dots, acid-etched "Schneider - France - Ovington," ca. 1925 (ILLUS.)................................. **920**

Vase, 11" h., trumpet-form, jade in brilliant tomato red w/dark purple inclusions............ **550**

Vase, 11 1/4" h., tapering ovoid body in clear shading to purple w/acid-etched & molded fluting on a deep purple circular foot, acid-etched mark, ca. 1925 .... **575**

Large Schneider Vase

Vase, 12" h., an aubergine disk foot & shoulder knopped stem supporting a tall ovoid internally decorated body in mottled rose red & yellow, the lower body w/a casing of deeper red & mottled grey, small aubergine loop handles at the flat rim, engraved signature (ILLUS.).............. **2,530**

Vase, 12" h., footed slightly flaring cylindrical form w/rounded base & shoulder w/a short widely flaring neck, swirled pink, red, white & clear enhanced w/Cluthra-like bubbles, etched "Schneider" on foot & "France" on base **978**

Shaded Clear Etched Schneider Vase

Vase, 14 1/4" h., swelled cylindrical form w/a flattened shoulder centering a cupped neck decorated w/three bosses alternating w/three etched squares & two rectangles, clear shading to tangerine at the base w/captive bubbles of various sizes, signed, ca. 1925 (ILLUS.)........ **1,725**

Schneider Vase with Applied Poppy

Vase, 15" h., cushion foot supporting a tall slender ovoid body w/a short flattened flaring neck, red internally shaded w/mottled amethyst at the base, overlaid w/a stylized orange poppy blossom w/an ideogram-form stem, the petals finely wheel-carved, signed in intaglio, ca. 1925 (ILLUS.)... **6,325**

Vase, 17" h., bulbous body tapering to a small mouth, burnt orange w/a mixture of darker veining throughout, signed............... **440**

SILVER DEPOSIT - SILVER OVERLAY

Silver Deposit and Silver Overlay have been made commercially since the last quarter of the 19th century. Silver is deposited on the glass by various means, most commonly by utilizing an electric current. The glass was very popular during the first three decades of this century, and some pieces are still being produced. During the late 1970s, silver commanded exceptionally high prices and this was reflected in a surge of interest in silver overlay glass, especially in pieces marked "Sterling" or "925" on the heavy silver overlay.

Silver Overlaid Round Box

Box, cov., black amethyst, low rounded body w/three interior compartments, the low domed cover w/repeating silver foliate & line designs, silver rim bands on base, fleur-de-lis finial on cover, 7" d., 4 1/2" h. (ILLUS.)...................................... **$230**

Cigar box, cov., rectangular, black amethyst glass, the cover w/silver overlay scene of goose in flight over lake, foliate silver border on cover & base, red enamel trim, acid-stamped marks of the Rockwell Silver Co., ca. 1925, 3 1/2 x 4 3/4", 1 7/8" h. (loss to enamel) **173**

Three Silver-Overlay Decanters

Decanter w/stopper, wide squatty bulbous clear form w/the wide shoulder centering a short cylindrical neck w/a high arched spout, flat-topped bubble stopper & applied silver-encased handle, the body & stopper overlaid w/ornate scrolled foliage designs, late 19th - early 20th c., 6 3/4" h. (ILLUS. right front) **748**

Decanter w/stopper, a wide domed form w/a flat base, short cylindrical neck w/spout & loop handle, clear decorated overall w/an elaborate silver overall vining floral design, monogrammed, 8 1/2" h. **715**

Decanter w/stopper, squared tapering clear body w/a narrow shoulder & short paneled neck w/flat rim, faceted clear stopper, decorated overall w/large silver overlay blossoms & scrolling leafy stems, late 19th - early 20th c., 9" h. (ILLUS. left front) **690**

Decanter w/stopper, bulbous teardrop-form w/fitted silver stopper, clear w/ornate silver oak leaf design centered by a scrolling silver monogram & a date on the collar, marked by Gorham Mfg. Co., Providence, Rhode Island, late 19th - early 20th c., 9 1/2" h. (ILLUS. center back) **863**

Silver Overlay Perfume Bottle

Perfume bottle w/original stopper, clear squatty tapering lobed form w/a short cylindrical neck & flattened rim, tall pointed & lobed stopper, decorated overall w/silver overlay scrolling design w/inscription dated 1913, 4 3/4" h. (ILLUS.) **305**

Perfume bottle w/stopper, squatty spherical teal green body centered by a short, small cylindrical neck w/flattened rim,

large mushroom stopper, decorated around the upper body & the stopper w/scrolling flower vines stamped "Sterling," 5 1/2" h. (stopper missing small piece of silver) **345**

Pitcher, 9 1/4" h., tankard-type, a swelled base tapering to a tall cylindrical body, clear completely encased in a silver overlay scrolling design of grapevines, silver-overlaid handle, marked "Sterling - 33" **825**

Vase, 3 5/8" h., simple shouldered ovoid body w/a short wide flared neck, mold-blown green iridized exterior w/overlaid scroll & floral silver decoration impressed "L Sterling," early 20th c. (design worn, crude) **633**

Vase, 8" h., fan-shaped, the widely flaring flattened black opaque top decorated w/silver overlay in a floral design within geometric panels, on a short baluster stem & disk foot w/silver rim band, maker's mark "Rockwell - no.1371B," ca. 1930 .... **259**

Vase, 8 3/4" h., wide tapering ovoid body w/a wide rounded shoulder centered by a cylindrical neck w/flared rim, amber iridized form overlaid on the front w/pendent berry & leaf silver decoration, leaf impressed "L Sterling," Austria, early 20th c. **1,380**

Vase, 10" h., slender baluster-form body in emerald green w/relief-blown oval sections through the ornate pierced sterling silver lattice design of lilies, leaves & vines, silver marked "G3223 - 925 fine" **825**

Ornate Silver Deposit Vase

Vase, 12 1/2" h., squatty wide base w/a wide shoulder centered by a gently flaring cylindrical body w/a bulbed shoulder below the short cylindrical neck, clear w/smoky iridescence & an overall silver deposit design of scrolling leafy stems & carnation blossoms, ca. 1920s (ILLUS.) **700**

Vase, 14" h., rose water sprinkler-form, a squatty bulbous base centered by a tall serpentine neck w/a pointed lip, cobalt blue w/silver iridescent butterfly decoration enhanced by elaborate overall silver overlay in scrolling foliate designs, apparently unsigned, recessed polished pontil, attributed to Loetz, Austria, early 20th c. (minor damage) **2,415**

SLAG

Marble and Agate glass are other names applied to this variegated glassware made from the middle until the close of the last century and now being reproduced. It is characterized by variegated streaks of color. Pink slag was made only in the Inverted Fan & Feather pattern and is rare.

Cruet w/original stopper, pink slag, Inverted Fan & Feather patt. **$1,638**
Sauce dish, pink slag, Inverted Fan & Feather patt., 4 1/2" d............................. **175**
Toothpick holder, pink slag, cylindrical footed form w/scalloped rim, Inverted Fan & Feather patt. **990**
Tumbler, pink slag, Inverted Fan & Feather patt., 4" h. **330**

SMITH BROTHERS

Originally established as a decorating depart-ment of the Mt. Washington Glass Company in the 1870s, the firm later was an independent business in New Bedford, Massachusetts. Beautifully deco-rated opal white glass was their hallmark but they also did glass cutting. Some examples carry their lion-in-the-shield mark.

Smith Brothers Mark

Bowl, 4" d., 2 1/2" h., squatty bulbous melon-lobed body w/a wide flat mouth, creamy beige ground enameled w/large blue pansies & green leaves, blue beaded rim band, white opal lining, lion trademark (minor rim bead damage) **$127**
Bowl, 5 1/4" d., 2 1/2" h., melon-ribbed body, decorated w/purple violets................. **100**
Bowl-vase, wide squatty bulbous body w/a wide short cylindrical neck, ivory ground decorated w/yellow daises & green stems, enameled dots around rim, stamped Lion trademark, 5 1/2" d., 3 3/4" h. (four rim dots missing) **220**
Box w/hinged lid, melon-ribbed body, white decorated w/h.p. pansies, 5 1/2" d...... **450**
Cracker jar, cov., barrel-shaped, creamy white ground decorated w/h.p. daisies, silver plate rim, cover & bail handle, signed.. **575**
Cracker jar, cov., melon-lobed body in almond decorated around the middle w/a raised gold floral design, silver plate rim & puffy cover w/embossed floral designs, bail handle, cover stamped "405," body inscribed "ROS (over) DTB"...... **303**
Cracker jar, cov., bulbous melon-lobed body in creamy white decorated w/enameled pink roses & raised gold leaves outlined in gold, ornate silver

plate rim, cover & bail handle w/looped lattice trim, bottom w/lion trademark, 7" h. (ILLUS.)... **1,045**

Smith Brothers Cracker Jar

Creamer & cov. sugar bowl, each w/a melon-lobed body in white satin deco-rated w/yellow-centered white daisy-like blossoms & green leaves, each mounted w/ornate silver plate rims w/spout & han-dle on creamer & lady's profile bust-dec-orated cover & a bail handle on the sugar, blanks by Mount Washington, 4" h., pr... **431**
Creamer & cov. sugar bowl, creamer w/ovoid body below the silver plate rim & low wide spout & loop rim handle, the squatty bulbous sugar bowl w/a match-ing silver plate rim, domed cover & flat bail handle, each body w/a satin ivory ground decorated w/gilt floral branches outlined w/raised gold, sugar 2 3/4" h., creamer 3 1/2" h., pr. **750**
Pitcher, 8" h., decorated w/gold floral branch on glossy white ground **198**

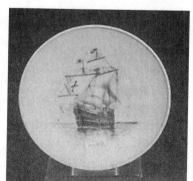

Smith Brothers Santa Maria Plate

Plate, 8" d., commemorative, satiny white ground decorated w/the ship Santa Maria, presumably commissioned by Libbey for the Chicago Columbian Exhi-bition of 1893, ship portrait signed "Copyrighted by A.E. Smith" (ILLUS.) **460**
Powder box, cov., enameled floral decora-tion w/beaded trim, lion mark **275**
Sugar bowl, cov., squatty bulbous body in opal decorated w/daisies & leaves, silver

plate rim, low domed cover & twisted bail handle, marked 413

Sugar shaker w/original metal lid, cylindrical finely ribbed body, decorated w/delicate daisy blossoms on a satin white ground, 5 3/4" h. 440

Sugar shaker w/original silver-gilt lid, ovoid melon-lobed body, satin ivory ground decorated w/gilt floral branches & raised gold outlines, 4 3/4" h. 550

Sweetmeat jar, cov., squatty bulbous melon-lobed form, creamy white enameled w/white & green lilies, resilvered Pairpoint rim w/flared spearpoint band, domed cover & swing bail handle, signed... 825

Vase, 3 3/4" h., acorn-shaped melon-ribbed body, decorated w/enameled florals & leaves w/enameled beading on rim 145

Vase, 4" h., spherical body w/a short cylindrical neck, beige ground decorated w/large orchid & yellow pansies & green leaves, beading around the neck, lion trademark 138

Vase, 4 1/2" h., bulbous cylindrical body w/three wide side dimples, the rounded shoulder centered by a short cylindrical neck w/flared rim, ivory ground decorated around the shoulder & down the corners w/long graceful leafy stems of daisies w/enameled highlights, enamel beaded rim, one side enameled in script "World's Fair 1893," marked 550

Decorated Smith Brothers Vase

Vase, 5" h., footed bulbous body deeply pinched-in on three sides, small short flared neck, creamy white satin ground enameled around the sides w/leaves & gingko tree branches in green, brown & rust w/gilt trim highlighted w/white dots, trademark on base (ILLUS.)........................ 173

Vase, 5 1/2" h., 2 1/2" d., melon-ribbed body, enameled daisies front & back, red rampant lion trademark on base 150

Smith Brothers Vase with Stork

Vase, 5 1/2" h., 3 3/4" d., narrow squatty base tapering to cylindrical sides, h.p. decoration of a stork standing amid grasses, pale pink background (ILLUS.)... 250-300

Smith Brothers Ring-style Vase

Vase, 6" h., 2 1/2" d., ring-type, cylindrical w/raised rings in white, pink ground enameled in color w/a stork standing among reeds, late 19th c. (ILLUS.) 150

Vase, 6 1/4" h., baluster-form, embossed rope decoration around rim, decorated w/delicate daisies & leaves & heavy gold trim, rampant lion mark 275

Rare Smith Brothers Canteen Vase

Vase, 8 1/2" h., double canteen-form, two flattened disk form vases conjoined & decorated w/lovely wisteria blossoms & vines on a creamy ground, signed (ILLUS.).. 2,000-2,500

Vase, 8 1/2" h., large ovoid melon-lobed body w/a squatty bulbed neck molded w/a repeating design of foliate, the body h.p. w/chrysanthemum blooms & leaves in shades of yellow, pink, brown & green on a cream ground, gold enamel trim, late 19th c. (wear to gold, mold imperfection in neck) **460**

Vase, 8 1/2" h., wide bulbous melon-lobed body w/the rounded shoulder centered by a short swelled neck molded w/stylized flowers tinted w/leaf color & gilt trim at the flat mouth, the body painted w/large lavender blue wisteria blossoms cascading from a greyish green leafy vine, gold outlining, original paper label **980**

Ornately Decorated Smith Bros. Vase

Vase, 8 1/2" h., wide ovoid double-bulbed lobed body, the bulbous gilt neck molded w/stylized florals, the body h.p. w/chrysanthemum blooms & leaves on a cream & green ground, Smith Brothers trademark on base, late 19th c. (ILLUS.) **1,150**

Vase, 8 3/4" h., decorated w/clusters of naturalistically colored wisteria blossoms clinging to the raised gold vine encircling the shoulder like a necklace **750**

Smith Bros. Vases with Birds

Vases, 4 1/4" h., 2 1/4" d., plain cylindrical body in white enamel-decorated in color w/a white & brown bird on a twig w/red berries & blue & green leaves, late 19th c., pr. (ILLUS.)...................................... **250-300**

Cylindrical Stork-decorated Vases

Vases, 4 1/4" h., 2 1/4" d., plain cylindrical form, h.p. w/facing standing storks in black, white & brown w/red legs & beaks, standing amid grasses, pale blue background, pr. (ILLUS.)....................... **250-300**

SPANGLED

Spangled glass incorporated particles of mica or metallic flakes and variegated colored glass particles imbedded in the transparent glass. Usually made of two layers, it might have either an opaque or transparent casing. The Vasa Murrhina Glass Company of Sandwich, Massachusetts, first patented the process for producing Spangled glass in 1884 and this factory is known to have produced great quantities of this ware. It was, however, also produced by numerous other American and English glasshouses. This type, along with Spatter, is often erroneously called "End of the Day."

A related decorative glass, Aventurine, features a fine speckled pattern resembling gold dust on a solid color ground. Also, see ART GLASS BASKETS and ROSE BOWLS.

Pitcher, 5 1/2" h., cased white w/silver mica flecks, h.p. w/gold flowers................... **$66**

Vase, 4 1/4" h., ruffled top, mottled white & tan spatter in cranberry w/overall mica flecks, gilt trim & neck decoration................. **176**

SPATTER

This variegated-color ware is similar to Spangled glass but does not contain metallic flakes. The various colors are applied on a clear, opaque white or colored body. Much of it was made in Europe and England. It is sometimes called "End Of Day."

Floral-decorated Spatter Cruet

Cruet w/stopper, squatty bulbous body tapering to a cylindrical neck w/arched spout, deep maroon, red & white spatter in clear, enameled w/a sprig of small blue flowers on green & yellow leafy stem, applied clear handle, facet-cut clear stopper, 3 1/2" d., 5 1/2" h. (ILLUS.) **$245**

Cruet w/stopper, melon-lobed body, shades of amber spatter, applied clear handle & facet-cut stopper, 6 3/4" h. **110**

Pitcher, water, bulbous Swirl patt. w/short cylindrical neck & applied reeded handles, cased overall pink, white & maroon spatter **385**

Pitcher, 8 1/4" h., water, spherical body w/square top & applied reeded handle, mottled wine red & white in clear **94**

Pitcher, 9" h., flat-sided, molded Swirl patt. in pinks, whites, yellows & greens, late 19th c. **55**

Decorated Spatter Vase

Vase, 7" h., 4 1/2" d., footed bulbous body w/a rounded shoulder centering a ringed trumpet neck, yellow cased w/white spatter, enamel-decorated w/a large flowering branch w/a bird in purple, white, green, brown & black, applied angled clear shoulder handles (ILLUS.)....... **165**

Water set: pitcher & one tumbler; bulbous pitcher w/a clover-form rim, decorated w/amber tones of spatter & enameled w/colorful spring blossoms, matching tumbler, pitcher 8 1/2" h., the set **110**

Water set: pitcher & six tumblers; bulbous pitcher w/squared mouth, Inverted Thumbprint patt. w/white & cranberry splashes in clear, applied clear handle, matching tumblers, pitcher 8 1/2" h., the set (one tumbler w/small chip) **193**

STEUBEN

Most of the Steuben glass listed below was made at the Steuben Glass Works, now a division of Corning Glass, between 1903 and about 1933. The factory was organized by T.G. Hawkes, noted glass designer, Frederick Carder, and others. Mr. Carder devised many types of glass and revived many old techniques.

Steuben Marks

ACID CUT-BACK

Steuben Acid Cut-back Lamp Base

Lamp base, baluster-form shouldered base w/an etched Alabaster surface overlaid in gold Aurene & acid-cut in the Newport patt., mounted in a two-socket gilt-metal fitting w/fleur-de-lis finial, wear to gilt, overall 30 1/2" h. (ILLUS.) **$3,450**

Vase, 7" h., Matsu patt., acid-etched sphere w/Ming trees & stylized clouds, Shape No. 6078 .... **690**

Vase, 8 3/4" h, round Alabaster foot below the wide bulbous body w/the shoulder centered by a wide low rolled neck, Green Jade cut to a textured Alabaster ground w/a scalloped green band around the neck & shoulder & a wide band of large stylized round blossoms on angular stems around the center **1,595**

Vase, 10" h., simple ovoid form w/a short cylindrical neck, Alabaster overlaid in Green Jade & cut w/a continuous scene of large birds perched in blossoming branches, Shape No. 3219 .... **825**

Vase, 12" h., bulbous ovoid lower body w/an angled shoulder tapering to a tall cylindrical neck, Oriental-style w/a dark green sculptured ground overlaid in black & cut w/grapevines w/grape clusters, pointed lappets around the rim, signed... **3,300**

Vase, 12" h., tall gently flaring cylindrical body w/a narrow angled shoulder centering the short, wide cylindrical neck, speckled pastel green Cintra in clear & white ground overlaid in Rose & acid-etched twice to shaded stylized blossoms & vertical geometric bars, Shape

No. 3279 (four chips on high blossom petals) **3,450**

Rare Acid Cut-Back Art Deco Vase

Vase, 12" h., 11 1/2" d., bulbous ovoid body w/a deep shoulder to the short flaring neck, double-etched, Mirror Black on Alabaster etched in the Shelton foliate Art Deco patt., Shape No. 2683 (ILLUS.).. **6,900**

ALABASTER

Centerpiece figure, figure of Kuan Yin, Buddhist goddess depicted in matching two-tier flower arranger, Shape No. 6637, 9" h. **439**

Compotes, 7" d., 3" h., open, wide shallow bowl w/Alabaster exterior raised on an applied slender Alabaster stem & round foot, bowl interior lined w/Green Jade, Shape No. 3234, pr. (slight variation in color) **489**

Lamp base, squatty bulbous base below a tall slender waisted neck in the white acid-etched glass body, overall design in the Grape patt., mounted on a silvered metal base, Shape No. 8006, ca. 1925, glass 14" h. **1,150**

Urn, cov., pedestal foot below the wide ovoid body tapering to a fitted domed cover, decorated around the bottom of the body w/a wide band of blue & iridescent gold leaf devices, similar design radiating from the center of the cover, acorn finial, 6 3/4" h. (small flake on finial) **1,925**

AQUAMARINE

Perfume bottle & stopper, footed tall slender swelled cylindrical body w/a short neck & flattened rim, tall pointed stopper, Shape No. 1988, 8" h. **330**

Vase, 6" h., "tree-trunk" form, three staggered thorny cylindrical holders on a round foot, inscribed "STEUBEN Aurene 2744," ca. 1910-20 .... **440**

AURENE

Atomizer w/original metal fittings, tall slender form, overall blue iridescence, signed "Aurene #5612," 7" h. **880**

Basket, tall waisted cylindrical form w/widely flaring ruffled rim joined w/a high arched applied handle, overall strong blue iridescence, coiled prunts at

tips of handles, Shape No. 5069, 7" h. (interior staining) **863**

Gold Aurene Small Bowl

Bowl, 4 3/4" d., 2 1/2" h., deep rounded sides w/flattened flaring rim, overall gold iridescence, ca. 1910 (ILLUS.) **550**

Bowl, 8" d., 4" h., gently flaring deep rounded sides w/a closed rim, overall gold iridescence, signed "Aurene #2687" **440**

Bowl, 10" d., slightly rounded tapering sides & an inverted lip, overall iridescent blue, w/original paper label & signed "AURENE 2637," ca. 1904 .... **920**

Bowl, 12" d., footed shallow form w/deep blue iridescent center & stretched rim, signed "Steuben Aurene #2586" **413**

Bowl, 12" d., 2 1/4" h., planter-form w/inward curved rim, reddish gold iridescent surface & interior, polished base inscribed "aurene 2879," Shape No. 2879 (wear scratches on base) **403**

Candlestick, disk foot below slender stem w/a swelled twist at the top below the tall cupped socket w/a flattened flared rim, fine overall blue iridescence, Shape No. 686, 8 1/4" h. (ILLUS. far right w/vase) **633**

Candlesticks, wide disk foot below the slender standard swelled & twisted near the top below the cylindrical candle socket w/flattened rim, overall gold iridescence, Shape No. 686, signed, 10" h., pr. **1,430**

Center bowl, round w/a wide flattened flanged rim w/eight pointed scallops, amber w/overall blue iridescence, Shape No. 158 (?), signed, 10" d., 3" h. (ILLUS. center w/vase) **1,035**

Console bowl, wide rounded form on three applied prunt feet, Shape No. 2586, signed, 10" d. **330**

Darning egg, spherical head on a tapering rounded handle, overall blue iridescence, 7" l. **308**

Finger bowl & underplate, cylindrical low bowl w/crimped & ruffled flared rim, w/matching underplate, overall gold iridescence, Shape No. 171, signed, 5" & 6 1/4" d., pr. (ILLUS. front left w/vase) **690**

Finger bowl & underplate, round bowl on matching wide underplate, overall gold iridescence, bowl signed "Steuben Aurene 2889," underplate signed "Steuben Aurene 2028," bowl 4 3/4" d., plate 8 1/4" d., the set **523**

Goblet, bell-form bowl raised on a slender stem w/a twist at the upper end, round disk foot, overall gold iridescence, Shape No. 2361 .... **385**

Goblets, tall bell-form bowls on slender twisted stems on a flattened disk foot, overall deep gold iridescence w/blue highlights, signed "Aurene" & numbered, 7" h., set of 6 .... **2,530**

Jar, cov., wide squatty bulbous body, the wide shoulder centered by a flattened domed cover, overall dark blue iridescence w/silver, blue & purple highlights, signed "Aurene #1616," 5" d., 3 1/2" h. **825**

Perfume atomizer, flaring base tapering sharply to a tall slender cylindrical body fitted w/gilt-metal attachment without the bulb, DeVilbiss, some interior stain, surface wear, Shape No. 6407, 7 1/2" h. (ILLUS. back right w/vase) **345**

Perfume bottle w/stopper, tapering cylindrical form w/rounded base, small flared neck & pointed mushroom stopper. overall blue iridescence, signed, Shape No. 2835, 3 1/4" h. **715**

Perfume bottle w/stopper, tapering paneled body w/a small trumpet neck holding a floral molded stopper, strong blue iridescence w/green & purple highlights on the blue ground, pontil signed "Aurene 2758," ca. 1920, 4 1/4" h. (light surface scratches) **863**

Potpourri jar, cov., fine bright gold iridescent surface on oval body, conforming cover w/three drilled fragrance holes & applied finial, Shape No. 2812, 5 3/4" h. **633**

Sherbet set: dished underplate w/wide flanged rim & stemmed dish w/bell-form bowl; twelve-ribbed underplate, overall strong purplish blue iridescence, Shape No. 2680, each piece signed, 4" & 6 1/4" d., the set (ILLUS. front right w/vase) **518**

Sherbets & underplates, rounded bowl on a short stem, matching round plate, overall deep gold iridescence, signed & numbered, pr. **550**

Tumbler, cylindrical w/slightly flaring rim, overall gold w/brilliant iridescence, signed "Steuben #2361," 4 1/2" h. **132**

Vase, 4" h., short waisted cylindrical body w/a widely flaring six-ruffled rim, overall gold iridescence on amber, stretched at rim, Shape No. 723 .... **316**

Vase, 4 1/4" h., millefiore-type, wide ovoid form w/the rounded shoulder centering a small cylindrical neck, ribbed green Aurene cased in white, the exterior decorated w/gold Aurene leaf & vine design & six gold-centered white millefiore "blossoms," inscribed on base "Aurene 550" **4,888**

Vase, 5" h., footed squatty bulbous ten-ribbed base continuing to widely flaring sides w/a ruffled rim, overall blue iridescence, Shape No. 2631, signed on base (ILLUS. back left w/vase) **1,093**

Vase, 5" h., ovoid body w/slightly everted lip & a cushion foot, grey w/amber, pink & blue iridescence, inscribed "Aurene," ca. 1920 .... **345**

Vase, 5" h., 5 1/2" d., classical form, overall gold iridescence, signed **440**

Vase, 5 1/2" h., ten-ribbed flared body w/extraordinary smooth & lustrous blue iridescent color, base inscribed "Steuben," Shape No. 913 (shade) **546**

Vase, 5 3/4" h., bottle-form, spherical body w/a tall slender 'stick' neck bulbed at the base & flared at the top, fine ribbing on the shoulder & up the neck, overall gold iridescence, Shape No. 240, signed **1,100**

Vase, 6 1/4" h., double-gourd form, the body composed of two squatty bulbous sections below the very wide flaring trumpet neck, spaced ribbing up the sides & neck, dark blue iridescence, signed **935**

Vase, 6 1/4" h., "tree-trunk" form, three staggered thorny cylindrical holders on a round foot, deep amber w/a golden crimson iridescence, inscribed "STEUBEN Aurene 2744," ca. 1910-20 .... **862**

Vase, 6 1/2" h., "tree-trunk" form, three staggered thorny cylindrical holders on a round foot, deep blue iridescence, inscribed "STEUBEN Aurene 2744," ca. 1910-20 .... **990**

Vase, 6 1/2" h., trumpet-form w/widely flaring six-ruffle rim, overall gold iridescence w/stretched effect at the rim, Shape No. 346, signed **880**

Vase, 7 3/4" h., stick-type, slender cylindrical body on a disk foot, overall blue iridescence, signed "Aurene" **259**

Vase, 8" h., ruffled trumpet-form w/strong golden iridescence stretched at rim, inscribed on base "Steuben Aurene 723," Shape No. 723 .... **748**

Peacock Feather Aurene Vase

Vase, 8" h., slightly waisted cylindrical form w/flaring neck, delicate blue peacock feathers pulled through a gold iridescent ground, signed "Aurene 261" (ILLUS.) **4,313**

Vase, 8 1/4" h., angular six-sided rim on flared brightly iridized oval raised on disk foot inscribed "Steuben Aurene 6241" on base, Shape No. 6241 .... **690**

Vase, 8 1/4" h., bulbous ovoid body w/a wide rounded shoulder centered by a wide short rolled neck, overall fine gold iridescence, Shape No. 2412, signed **825**

Aurene Acid-etched Vase

Vase, 8 3/8" h., bulbous ovoid body tapering to a short widely rolled neck, iridescent gold acid-cut w/a band of leafy vines laden w/grape clusters, the shoulder & base cut w/palm fronds, against a mirror black ground, ca. 1925 (ILLUS.) **4,025**

Vase, 8 3/8" h., jack-in-the-pulpit-form, iridescent amber glass decorated w/pulled silvery-blue feathering, inscribed "Aurene 751," Shape No. 751, ca. 1910 ... **4,312**

Vase, 8 1/2" h., double gourd-form, a bulbous base w/four deep 'dimples' tapering to a tall very slender swelled 'stick' neck, gold ground w/pale green loops from the top, gold, purple & green iridescent highlights, signed "Aurene #203B - F. Carder".. **1,430**

Vase, 8 1/2" h., stick-form, tall slender cylindrical body on a round disk foot, overall blue iridescence, signed "Aurene #2556" **440**

Grouping of Steuben Aurene Pieces

Vase, 9 1/2" h., 'stick'-type, a thin disk foot & a tall slender cylindrical shaft, fine overall blue iridescence, Shape No. 2556, signed on pontil (ILLUS. far left)........ **374**

Vase, 10" h., flaring foot below the tall swelled cylindrical body w/a narrow shoulder to the lower trumpet neck, overall blue iridescence, Shape No. 2908, signed **1,183**

Vase, 10" h., tall gently swelled cylindrical body w/a narrow angled shoulder & short cylindrical neck w/flared rim, blossom, heart & vine decorated in gold Aurene on an iridescent green body

cased in white, Shape No. 506, style D, signed "Aurene 506"................................. **5,175**

Vase, 10" h., 10" d., trumpet-form w/a footed slender stem below the wide bulbous shoulder below a wide squatty bulbous neck & wide flattened rim, overall blue iridescence, Shape No. 2684, signed... **1,980**

Feather-decorated Aurene Vase

Vase, 12" h., slender baluster-form w/cylindrical neck, organic green leaf forms pulled into Alabaster white decorated w/gold Aurene peacock feathers centering four gold hearts w/green peacock eyes, signed "Aurene - 535," short shallow scratch on side (ILLUS.) **3,910**

Vase, 12" h., 11" d., large wide ovoid shouldered form w/a short flaring neck, gold w/yellow, rose & platinum iridescent highlights, incised signature **1,650**

BRISTOL YELLOW

Center bowl, low ruffled rim enhanced by mirror black threads on the exterior, fleur-de-lis mark, 16" d., 4 1/2" h. **403**

Decanter w/stopper, gourd-form w/wide squatty bottom section connected by slender stem & four hollow buttresses to the matching upper section all w/swirled optic ribbing, the short small ruffled neck w/a solid teardrop stopper, 19" h................. **575**

Serving plate, round dished form w/wide flanged rim, radiating optic ribbing, Shape No. 3579, ca. 1925, 14 1/4" d., 2" h. (wear, scratches) **201**

CALCITE

Bowl, 2" h., round w/Calcite exterior & flared & scalloped rim, interior lined in gold Aurene.. **173**

Bowl, 10" d., wide low form w/flattened inverted rim, Calcite exterior & gold Aurene interior, ca. 1920 (light interior wear) **259**

Candlestick, flaring pedestal base supporting a cylindrical socket w/a domed & widely flaring rim lined in gold Aurene, signed, Shape No. 3581, 6 1/2" h. **385**

Ceiling light, a round bowl-form fixture w/deep flattened sides & a domed bottom, etched w/a classical foliate design radiating from the center, three sockets & three attached metal hanging hooks, 15 3/4" d. **690**

Vase, 8" h., trumpet-form w/a widely flaring six-lobed ruffled rim, iridescent gold Aurene interior... **495**

Vase, 8 1/4" h., gold Aurene on Calcite lily form, six scallop rim on trumpet-form w/iridized white calcite exterior, gold within, Shape No. 346 .... **575**

CELESTE BLUE

Celeste Blue Candlesticks & Bowl

Candlesticks, flaring foot supporting a slender baluster-form stem below a knop & petal-form bobeche & tall cupped sockets, ca. 1920-33, 11 1/2" h., set of 4 (ILLUS. of two, left) **2,300**

Center bowl, applied flared & optic-ribbed low foot supporting a wide swirled optic-ribbed bowl w/rolled rim, polished pontil, Shape No. 112, ca. 1925, 16 1/4" d., 4 1/4" h. (ILLUS. right).................................. **403**

Finger bowls & underplates, deep cylindrical bowl w/flared flattened rim, molded optic ribbed design on bowls & matching dished underplates, variation of Shape No. 2889, ca. 1925, bowl 5" d., underplate 6 1/2" d., eleven bowls & twelve underplates, the set (one bowl chipped) **518**

Plates, 8 1/2" d., luncheon, wide flat border engraved w/a band of leaves & dots, variant of the Kensington patt., set of 12 (one plate chipped) **546**

Stemware, footed, tall flaring bowls w/light optic ribbing on applied round foot, Shape No. 5192, eight juice glasses 4 1/2" h., seven iced tea glasses 6 1/4" h., the set **575**

Vase, 7" h., wide urn-form body w/narrow shoulder to the wide flaring neck, on a small disk foot, optic-ribbed design, recessed polished pontil signed "Steuben" w/fleur-de-lis mark **316**

Vase, 8 1/4" h., fan-shaped, internal air bubbles & applied glass threading near the rim, on a knopped stem & round foot, unsigned, ca. 1925...................................... **345**

CINTRA

Bowl, 7 1/4" d., 6" h., amethyst quartz-type, deep rounded cup-form w/undulating rim, mottled & crackled pink, blue & frosted colorless body w/three applied leafing branches connecting to the looped branch feet, Shape No. 6856, small chips (ILLUS.) **1,150**

CLUTHRA

Lamp base, large spherical glass body w/flared foot & rim set in a gilt-metal scrolled Oriental-style base & w/top electric fittings, the body in creamy white acid-etched to depict Art Deco-style flowers in a variant of the Moderne patt., ca. 1925, glass 12 1/2" h.................. **2,070**

Vase, 6 1/4" h., wide ovoid shouldered body w/a short wide flaring neck, mottled royal blue & white w/small trapped bubbles, polished pontil w/fleur-de-lis mark & "Steuben"... **1,035**

Vase, 9 3/4" h., bubbled white & green body w/a clear base **468**

Vase, 10 1/4" h., wide bulbous ovoid shouldered form w/a short small rolled neck, lime green w/overall white bubbled mottling, Shape No. 2683, signed **2,640**

Vase, 10 1/2" h., wide bulbous ovoid body tapering to a short wide rolled neck, creamy white & clear w/overall swirled & bubbled effect, Shape No. 2683.................. **920**

Large Rose Pink Cluthra Vase

Vase, 10 1/2" h., wide bulbous ovoid body tapering to a short wide rolled neck, rose, white & clear w/overall swirled & bubbled effect, Shape No. 2683, slightly irregular rim (ILLUS.)................................. **1,380**

Steuben Cluthra Wall Pocket

Wall pocket, half-round flared bowl of black & white Cluthra cut & mounted in a foliate gilt-metal framework, polished pontil, slight corrosion to metal, ca. 1930, 15 1/2" w., 8" h. (ILLUS.) **489**

CYPRIAN

Cyprian Candelabrum

Candelabrum, aquamarine tinted verre de soie w/Celeste blue accent rims on three-arm candleholder (2959), w/central pink, green, & blue decorative floral finial supported on brass connector, original conforming VDS candlecups, Shape No. 7382 variant, 19" h., one finial flower petal chipped (ILLUS.) **1,840**

GROTESQUE

Bowl, 6 3/4" h., three lined pillar-molded form, rounded base w/the high widely flaring clear sides pulled into four points, variation of Shape No. 7534...................... **230**

Vase, 5 1/2" h., 10" w., deep rounded form w/widely flaring upright randomly ruffled sides w/molded ribs, Ivrene (minor interior stain) **345**

Blue Jade Grotesque Vase

Vase, 6 1/2" h., 6 1/4 x 12 1/2", deep flaring oblong pillar-ribbed form w/deeply pulled & ruffled sides, dark Blue Jade, signed on pontil (ILLUS.) **3,335**

Vase, 9 1/4" h., upright floriform ruffled & ribbed bowl in amethyst shading to colorless, raised on an applied colorless disk foot, Steuben mark on the polished pontil, Shape No. 7090, ca. 1930 (light scratch) **518**

IVRENE

Bowl, 9 1/2" d., 4 3/4" h., footed wide squatty bulbous form w/four double-ribbed side panels curving up to the gently ruffled closed rim, Shape No. 7337, unmarked **431**

Bowl-vase, applied domed ribbed foot supporting the widely fanned ribbed bowl, Shape No. 7307, ca. 1930, 6 1/2" h. **431**

Candleholders, Grotesque line, iridescent white holders w/oval ribbed & folded bobeche cups, each inscribed on base "Steuben," Shape No. 7564, 4" l., 3 1/4" h. (one ruffle rough, as made)........... **431**

Candlestick, floriform, a round disk foot supports two ribbed stems, one taller

than the other, each supporting a petal-form drip pan centered by a tall cylindrical candle socket, Shape No. 7317, 10 1/2" h. **546**

Center bowl, Grotesque line, four-rib oval of lustrous opaque white w/manipulated undulating rim, Shape No. 7449, 12" l., 7" h. (base evened, minor chips)................. **345**

Center bowl, wide w/ruffled rim, Shape No. 7423, 12" d., 4 3/4" h................................... **248**

Console set, deep rounded bowl w/deeply ruffled flaring sides & a pair of cornucopia vases on trumpet bases, bowl signed, bowl 12" l., vases 6" h., 3 pcs....... **1,456**

Epergne, a wide round low domed foot supporting a tall slender central trumpet vase w/wide rim flanked by a pair of jack-in-the-pulpit vases w/high pointed pulled-up back edges attached to the central vase & rolled edges & front, Shape No. 7566, signed,12 1/4" h. **1,100**

Urns, classical form w/square stepped pedestal foot below the bulbous body w/tall upright curved loop handles & a tall wide trumpet neck, Shape No. 7468, 12" h., pr. **2,070**

Vase, 10" w., 8" h., twelve-ribbed white iridescent flared body w/six-ruffle top, base inscribed "Steuben," Shape No. 723 .... **345**

Ivrene Baluster-form Vase

Vase, 11 1/4" h., wide baluster-form body w/wide ribbing, lightly iridized finish, three applied aqua Cintra shoulder handles, thin brush line of opaque white around the shoulder, signed, Shape No. 7568 (ILLUS.)... **1,380**

Ivrene Jack-in-the-Pulpit Vase

Vase, 12 1/2" h., jack-in-the-pulpit-type, disk foot below the swirled trumpet-form body w/crimped & pulled-up rim (ILLUS.).. **1,200**

Vases, 5 1/2" h., ribbed morning glory-form bodies, Shape No. 813, pr. **220**

JADE

Center bowl, wide shallow round form w/incurved sides, Blue Jade, Shape No. 5019, 10" d. **440**

Center bowl, wide shallow round form w/incurved sides, Yellow Jade, Shape No. 5019, 10" d. **495**

Console bowl, wide round form, Mirror Black Jade, Shape No. 5019, 12" d. **220**

Lamp base, a slender ovoid Green Jade shape w/a bulbed slender neck w/flattened & ruffled rim issuing the electric socket shaft, the glass body applied w/Mirror Black double loop thin side handles, raised on a slender leaftip & beaded ring gilt-metal shape w/a tall flared leaf cluster on a ringed & beaded round foot w/small ball feet, fittings attributed to Crest Lamp Co., glass 9 1/2" h. **460**

Fine Yellow Jade & Aurene Lamp

Lamp base, baluster-form, the Yellow Jade body w/a speckled ground decorated w/an applied dripping shoulder band of iridescent blue Aurene, on a fitted gilt-metal base w/figural sphinx & paw feet, gilt-metal collar around the neck, ca. 1920, overall 27" h. (ILLUS.) **6,000**

Green Jade & Aurene Lamp Base

Lamp base, flattened round flask-form in Green Jade cameo-etched w/stylized

blossom forms below an applied gold Aurene dripping border incorporated into the acid-cut design, mounted on a scroll-pierced gilt-metal footed base & w/a pierced gilt-metal collar, possibly the Marlene patt., Shape No. 8492, glass 10" h. (ILLUS.).. **3,450**

Perfume bottle & stopper, footed tall slender swelled cylindrical body w/a short neck & flattened rim, tall pointed stopper, Green Jade w/Alabaster foot, Shape No. 1988, 8" h. **467**

Plates, 8 1/2" d., Green Jade, signed, set of 4 .... **230**

Sherbet set: serving dish & underplate; each in light Blue Jade, the dish w/a Flint White stemmed base, underplate 6" d., dish 4" d., 3 3/4" h., the set **575**

Vase, 6 1/4" h., bulbous ovoid form w/a wide rounded shoulder to a short widely rolled neck, Green Jade, Shape No. 2683 .... **805**

Vase, 7" h., 8" d., large spherical body w/a closed rim, Green Jade acid-etched overall w/a bold design of chrysanthemum blossoms & leafs, Shape No. 6078 .. **1,265**

Vase, 7 1/4" h., bulbous ovoid form w/closed rim & small cushion foot, Green Jade w/spiral ribbing, signed **575**

Rare Jade & Aurene Vase

Vase, 8" h., broad bulbous ovoid body w/a wide shoulder centered by a short cylindrical neck w/a flared & flattened rim, Yellow Jade body cameo-etched overall w/a blanket of flowers design, the neck & shoulder w/an applied dripping band of blue Aurene, Shape No. 7014 (ILLUS.) **9,775**

Vase, 8" h., fan-shaped, Green Jade fanned top on an Alabaster knopped stem & disk foot... **330**

Vase, 10 1/2" h., footed bulbous ovoid body w/flared neck, applied alabaster "M" handles, ca. 1929, Green Jade, polished pontil (light scratch) **1,093**

Vase, 10 1/2" h., upright rectangular Green Jade form acid-etched overall w/a large chrysanthemum & leafy stem design, Shape No. 6199 .... **1,093**

MATSU NOKE

Lemonade mug, optic ribbed colorless goblet-form w/Pomona Green Cintra rim, handle & three fan-shaped decorations, Shape No. 3329, 6" h. **230**

MILLEFIORE

Millefiore Vase

Vase, 5" h., style J   baluster-form gold Aurene internally decorated w/green hearts & vines interspersed w/clusters of white 'blossoms,' fine 'platinum' gold iridescence overall, Shape No. 573 (ILLUS.).. **2,760**

MOSS AGATE

Lamp base, a slender classic urn-form glass pedestal in swirled purple, blue & red Moss Agate mounted in a gilt-metal cupped base on a short pedestal & flaring ringed foot w/relief acanthus leaf design, metal fittings w/a purple jewel at the top, needs rewiring, Shape No. 8023, ca. 1930, glass 10 1/4" h. **2,415**

Lamp base, tall slender baluster-form glass shaft of swirled purple, red & blue, mounted in gilt-metal base lamp fittings w/an acanthus leaf socket above a short ringed pedestal & disk foot w/a band of acanthus leaf decoration, further electric fittings at the top w/a purple glass jewel finial, Shape No. 8023, glass 10" h. **2,645**

Vase, 6" h., gently swelled cylindrical form w/rounded shoulder centering a wide low flared neck, mottled green internally decorated by multicolored swirling powders in red, blue, white, brown, black & occasional metallic clusters, recessed polished pontil, possibly the work of Frederick Carder................................. **633**

ORIENTAL POPPY

Oriental Poppy Goblet

Goblet, tall bell-form bowl w/optic ribbing in fine opalescent pink, raised on an applied slender Pomona green stem & foot, 8 1/4" h. (ILLUS.)................................. **489**

Goblets, deep flaring bell-form bowls w/a swirled optic ribbed design in pink opal, raised on a slender opal stem & foot, 5 3/4" h., pr.................................... **575**

Lamp base, the glass shaft of ovoid form tapering to a compressed bulb at the base of the flaring ruffled trumpet neck in rib-molded satin pink opal, mounted in a gilt-metal decorative ring support on three slender legs w/hoof feet on a tripartite classical foot, complete w/lamp mounts, glass Shape No. 8490, glass 7" h., overall 10 3/4" h. **575**

Vase, 6" h., ovoid body tapering to a short widely flaring neck, pink w/sixteen integrated opal stripes, satin finish, Shape No. 650 (two potstone blemishes at side, small chip at rim) **690**

POMONA GREEN

Bowl, 10 1/2" d., 6" h., a deep flaring six-panel Pomona Green bowl w/a swirled optic rib design raised on a short flaring ribbed Topaz funnel foot, Shape No. 6241 .... **230**

Vase, 5 1/4" h., a four-pillared base, the body decorated w/airtrap designs, five top openings................................... **303**

Vase, 8" h., a disk foot below a knopped stem supporting a slender trumpet-form bowl w/a twisted rib design & a deeply pinched-in trefoil rim, Shape No. 6441 .... **230**

Vase, 9" h., shaded ribbed body, white lining, signed................................... **303**

ROSALINE

Perfume bottle & stopper, footed tall slender swelled cylindrical body w/a short neck & flattened rim, tall pointed Alabaster stopper & foot, Shape No. 1988, 8" h. **550**

Vase, 8 1/2" h., stick-form, tall slender cylindrical body on a round disk foot, pink body on an Alabaster disk foot, unsigned................................... **275**

SELENIUM RED

Centerpiece bowl, wide shallow round form w/incurved rim, Shape No. 3196, autographed "F. Carder - Steuben," 14" d., 6" h. (some use scratches) **403**

SILVERINA

Candleholders, a flaring domed base in mica-flecked light amethyst w/a controlled bubble design attached to a dark amethyst disk wafer to the cylindrical tall candle socket w/a flattened & widely flaring socket rim which matches the base, Shape No. 6637, 5" h., pr............................ **863**

SPANISH GREEN

Pitcher, 9" h., a raised disk foot below a short knopped stem supporting a bulbous ovoid optic ribbed body tapering to a short flared neck w/pinched spout, applied angled shoulder handle, Shape No. 6665, marked on base, ca. 1925 .... **460**

THREADED

Bowl, 4 1/2" d., 3" h., footed low clear form w/black threading, signed............................. 110

Cocktail set: six matching handled cups, fleur-de-lis on jug base; colorless crystal w/applied mirror black threads, stopper, jug monogrammed "H.W.N.," Shape No. 7056, 9 1/2" h., the set 403

Compote, 7" d., 7" h., open shallow flaring colorless bowl decorated w/a band of red threading, raised on a slender baluster-form stem & round foot, Shape No. 6886, base marked, ca. 1925...................... 316

Goblets, colored diamond-molded bowls w/Pomona blue threading on an applied Bristol Yellow foot, each stamped "Steuben," 5 3/4" h., set of 3 201

Plates, 8 1/2" d., luncheon, round colorless crystal w/applied Pomona Green concentric threads around the exterior rim, set of 6 230

Powder box, cov., round, diamond quilted clear body w/black threading, signed, 6 1/2" d. 440

TOPAZ

Candlestick, Shape No. 6384, 5 1/2" h. 105

Compote, 8 1/2" d., 8 1/4" h., open w/wide flat shallow bowl w/rib-molded design & low incurved rim in amber Topaz raised on a slender knopped Pomona Green stem on a double-cupped flaring ribbed Topaz foot, Shape No. 6044 431

Vase, 13" h., mounted, flared trumpet-form vessel w/rounded base inserted into black metal leaf design holder, Shape No. 7201 variant... 173

VERRE DE SOIE

Verre de Soie Basket

Basket, tall waisted cylindrical body w/a widely flaring ruffled rim, applied high arched handle w/a berry prunt at each end, iridized silky finish, Shape No. 5069, 10 3/4" h. (ILLUS.).............................. 920

Basket, tall waisted cylindrical body w/a widely flaring ruffled rim, applied high arched handle w/a berry prunt at each end, iridized silky finish, Shape No. 5069, 14 1/4" h. 805

Center bowl, wide flattened bottom on three applied prunt feet, the shallow sides incurved, Shape No. 2586 or 3198, 12" d., 2 3/4" h.. 230

Perfume bottle & stopper, squatty bulbous onion-form lobed body tapering to

a short neck w/flared rim, Celeste Blue flame stopper, Shape No. 1455, 4 3/4" h...... 523

Vase, 3 1/4" h., miniature, fluted top, Shape No. 1945.. 110

WISTERIA

Candlesticks, round disk foot & swelled stem supporting a cylindrical candle socket w/wide flattened rim, dichroic leaded glass, engraved Pillar patt., reverse-engraved dots on base, marked, Shape No. 7093, ca 1927, 8 1/4" h., pr..... 1,035

Finger bowls & underplates, footed flaring bell-form bowl engraved in the Pillar patt., reverse-engraved dots on bowl base, w/matching underplates, dichroic leaded glass, marked, Shape No. 1679, ca. 1927, underplate 7 1/4" d., bowl 4 3/4" d., 2 3/4" h., three bowls & four underplates, the set 748

Goblets, bell-shaped bowls on tapering rounded stems & round feet, in a dichroic leaded glass, the bowl engraved w/the Pillar patt., reverse-engraved dots on the foot, Shape No. 7182, ca. 1927, 9" h., set of 4 1,150

MISCELLANEOUS WARES

Large Steuben Crystal Bowl

Bowl, 9 1/4" d., deep crystal rounded vessel on a ring-form base applied w/six scroll feet, designed by John Dreves, 1942, signed (ILLUS.) 632

Bowls, 7 1/2" d., crystal, deep rounded center w/a wide flattened flanged rim, incised "S" on base, set of 12 (one w/rim chip) 546

Center bowl, crystal, broad conical form w/a deep well applied w/four swirled leaf forms, base engraved "Steuben," 10 3/4" d., 7" h. 316

Center bowl, crystal, shallow bowl supported by a hemisphere base on four scroll feet, polished pontil, John Dreves design, created in 1942, signed, 10 1/2" d., 4" h.. 288

Center bowl, crystal w/a pale rosa pink folded rim, round shallow rib-molded center surrounded by a wide matching flattened rim engraved w/elaborate florals, webbing & scrolled decoration, Shape No. 3579, fleur-de-lis mark, 16" d. (some wear scratches)................................. 345

Goblet, exhibition-type, "Lust," crystal, first in "The Seven Sins" series, engraved w/a woman watched by a man from behind a tree, designed by Sidney

Waugh, Shape No. 8212, inscribed on base "Steuben," 7 1/2" h. **1,380**

Goblet, toasting-type, bowl held aloft on a spiral-twist stem, designed by Golda Fishbein in 1958, base inscribed "Steuben," Shape No. 8202, 17 1/2" h. (light interior stain)..................................... **259**

Model of fish, crystal, stylized version of an angel fish, design by Frederick Carder & Sidney Waugh, both bases inscribed "Steuben," 10 1/2" h. (minor chips near one base)............................... **1,495**

Model of fox, seated w/tail wrapped, inscribed "Steuben" on base, Shape No. 8260, designed by Lloyd Atkins, ca. 1971, 8 3/4" h. **1,265**

Model of horse, stylized version of Clydesdale-type horse, rare form from 1930s, base inscribed "Steuben," Shape No. 7727, p. 282, designed by Sidney Waugh, 9 3/4" l., 7" h., ... **1,035**

Model of koala, seated, base inscribed "Steuben," Shape No. 8268, designed by Lloyd Atkins, 5 3/4" h......................... **1,093**

Model of wild dove, crystal, stylized bird w/turned head, designed by Bernard Wolff, Shape No. 8426, base inscribed "Steuben BXW," 9 1/4" l., 4 3/4" h. **316**

Models of gazelles or book ends, leaping Art Deco figures raised upon molded rectangular plinth in stylized curvilinear, bases inscribed "Steuben," Shape No. 7399, designed by Frederick Carder & Sidney Waugh, 7 1/2" l., 6 1/2" h., pr. **1,438**

Models of geese, gander & preening goose, Shape No. 8519, designed by Lloyd Atkins, 5 1/4" h., pr. **345**

Steuben Excalibur Paperweight

Paperweight, Excalibur, a faceted hand-polished solid crystal block embedded w/a removable sterling silver sword w/18k gold scabbard, designed by James Houston in 1963, signed, sword 8 1/2" l. (ILLUS.)..................................... **1,955**

Tableware: six 7" d. plates, six stemmed water goblets & six champagnes; crystal, Art Deco style, designed by Bolas Mankowski, w/engraved moon & star motif, bases inscribed "S" or "Steuben," c. 1934 .... **633**

Trillium bowl, crystal, tri-cornered bowl supported by a pinched trillium-shaped base, designed by Donald Pollard in 1958, signed, 10" d., 5" h. **316**

Vase, 7 3/8" h., "Wing"-style, colorless crystal w/tall trumpet-form bowl flanked near the bottom w/small applied clear 'wings' up the sides, raised on a thick tapering cylindrical solid foot, signed, No. SP919, ca. 1957 .... **316**

Vase, 12 1/2" h., Paul Revere patt., rare intricately engraved "W138," exhibition piece to commemorate the historic ride in three vignettes: Revere standing by his horse, lantern in North Church tower, British soldiers w/bayonet rifles, base inscribed "Steuben," designed by Sidney Waugh, case not available **3,450**

Steuben Heavy Cut Lion Vase

Vase, 12 1/2" h., 9" d., footed bulbous ovoid body tapering to a short trumpet neck, heavy cut smoky amber w/a relief design of walking lions around the center, a band of large diamond panels around the base & cut scrolls around the shoulder, Shape No. 6680 (ILLUS.) **2,750**

Vase, 12 1/2" h., 9 1/4" d., Mansion Vase, colorless crystal, large urn-form w/large flaring bell-form bowl flanked by large upright applied "M" handles, raised on a knop over a flaring square stepped base, designed by Frederick Carder in 1934, Shape No. 7389 (nick in base)................. **1,035**

Wines, crystal, the bowls raised on wide angular teardrop stems, designed by Sidney Waugh, Shape No. 7737, w/grey fitted Steuben box, 7 1/4" h., set of 11 .... **633**

STEVENS & WILLIAMS

This long-established English glasshouse has turned out a wide variety of artistic glasswares through the years. Fine satin glass pieces and items with applied decoration (sometimes referred to as "Matsu-No-Ke") are especially sought after today. The following represents a cross-section of its wares.

Basket, rounded blue cased in white body trimmed w/an amber band on the ruffled rim & an applied amber loop handle, applied w/an oak leaf in cranberry swirled in amber, white & cranberry spots on applied clear rosette, 10" h. (rough spot on leaf) **$165**

Tree-form Appliqued Bottle & Stopper

Bottle w/original stopper, footed tall tapering conical body w/greenish amber foot & body, the body applied w/tiers of crystal shells giving a Christmas tree effect, the tall matching stopper topped by an applied crystal figural peacock, 5" d., 11" h. (ILLUS.) **500**

Bowl, 4 1/4" w., round optic ribbed lower body below the four-scallop rim w/upturned sides, shaded blue to clear w/applied amber rigaree around the rim & around the center of the lower body **165**

Bowl, 7" d., a low rounded bulbed base supporting the wide squatty rounded bowl w/low incurved sides w/a crimped rim, mother-of-pearl satin design of delicate horizontal bands w/vertical stripes alternating amethyst & light violet, chartreuse lining.. **2,200**

Cameo vase, 4 1/2" h., tapering ovoid body w/a rounded shoulder centering a short trumpet neck, rose du Barry ground overlaid in white & cameo cut overall w/apple blossoms & leafy branches.......... **1,155**

Cracker jar, cov., cranberry w/a frost surface decorated w/a white overall arboresque design, hammered metal Moorish design rim, cover & bail handle, overall 8" h... **248**

Intaglio-cut Finger Bowl & Underplate

Finger bowl & underplate, crystal cased in dark green & intaglio-cut w/wide grapevines, seven grape clusters on the bowl & vines & leaves on the underplate, the round bowl w/tapering rounded sides, plate 6 1/2" d., bowl 4 3/4" d., 2 1/2" h., 2 pcs. (ILLUS.) **265**

Stevens & Williams Rose Bowl

Rose bowl, spherical w/a twelve-crimp rim, crackle ware, blue w/an overall white crackled design, 3 1/2" d., 3" h. (ILLUS.) **135**

Stevens & Williams Striped Tumbler

Tumbler, slightly flared cylindrical form, alternating wide vertical stripes of opaque white & chartreuse green & thin clear stripes, wide silver rim band, 3" d., 4 7/8" h. (ILLUS.)..................................... **100-125**

Vase, 4" h., 3 1/4" d., squared bulbous shape, round mouth, yellow inside, deep pink outside w/deeply cut intaglio designs in cream, glossy finish **210**

Vase, 4 7/8" h., slightly tapering cylindrical form w/upright crimped rim, blue satin cased in white, wrapped up & around the sides w/a frosted clear leaf & blossom vine, marked "R15353".................................. **688**

Vase, 5" h., shaded pink mother-of-pearl Swirl patt. **275**

Vase, 5 3/8" h., 5 1/4" d., wide bulbous ovoid body w/a wide shoulder to the short widely flaring neck w/a flattened rim, mother-of-pearl satin Pompeian Swirl patt. in pale greenish yellow shading to deep red, white interior (ILLUS. top next page) **750**

Vase, 7 1/2" h., spherical wide body centered by a tall slender cylindrical neck bulbed at the base, dark lavender mother-of-pearl satin Swirl patt. **853**

Rare Mother-of-Pearl Satin Vase

Stevens & Williams Appliqued Vase

Vase, 7 1/2" h., 4 1/2" d., footed ovoid body in opaque creamy white tapering to a flattened shaped rim applied w/a band of amber scallops, the body applied w/three large shaded green, amber & cranberry leaves curving up around the sides, deep rose interior (ILLUS.) **225**

Vase, 9 3/8" h., lavender mother-of-pearl satin Swirl patt., large ovoid body tapering to a tapering bulbed neck, white lining **825**

Vase, 10" h., footed, pink & white cased, decorated w/applied fruit, ruffled rim **290**

Vase, 10 1/2" h., slender baluster-form body w/a flaring cupped rim w/a flat edge, creamy satin ground finely decorated w/a tall branch of green leaves & soft pink blossoms & a large blue & rose perched bird, all trimmed w/gold, thin gold lancet bands around the rim & base (ILLUS. top next column) **425-450**

Vase, 12 1/2" h., bulbous ovoid base tapering to a tall slender cylindrical neck, deep orange mother-of-pearl satin Swirl patt. **952**

Decorated Stevens & Williams Vase

TIFFANY

This glassware, covering a wide diversity of types, was produced in glasshouses operated by Louis Comfort Tiffany, America's outstanding glass designer of the Art Nouveau period, from the last quarter of the 19th century until the early 1930s. Tiffany revived early techniques and devised many new ones.

Various Tiffany Marks & Labels

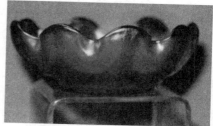

Tiffany Favrile Bonbon Dish

Bonbon dish, small round form w/upright sides & a deeply scalloped rim, overall gold iridescence, ca. 1903, 4" d., 1 1/2" h. (ILLUS.).................................. **$600**

Bowl, 4 1/2" d., 2 1/2" h., wide rounded body tapering slightly to a wide flat rim, decorated w/small pulled prunts around the lower body, overall peacock blue iridescence, signed **743**

Bowl, 5" d., 1 1/4" h., flared rim on a small round bowl w/optic-ribbed opalescence

shading to aqua blue, stretched iridescence at the interior rim, polished pontil,
base signed "1777 LCT Favrile".................. **575**

Bowl, 6" d., bi-color, gold-spotted opal
w/emerald green & blue border rim &
three applied reeded shell feet, button
pontil inscribed "L.C. Tiffany - Favrile" **920**

Bowl, 6" d., ten-ribbed deep form w/a white
opalescent exterior & deep cobalt blue
interior rim, base signed "L.C. Tiffany
Inc. Favrile" **978**

Bowl, 6" d., 2" h., ruffled rim on ten-ribbed
body, overall blue iridescence, inscribed
"L.C.T. Favrile".. **690**

Bowl-vase, paperweight-type, wide squatty
bulbous form w/the wide shoulder centered by a short wide cylindrical neck,
colorless internally decorated w/white
millefiori flowers among trailing green
hearts & pale aubergine vines, base
signed "L.C. Tiffany Favrile V149," 4" h. ... **3,450**

Candleholders, a clear disk foot & tapering
stem supporting a milky white opalescent socket shaded to stretched deep
pink on the wide flattened rim, signed
"L.C. Tiffany - #1927," 4" h., pr.................. **1,650**

Candlesticks, mushroom-shaped candle
cups of bright iridized pinkish rose above
an opal disk stem & conforming foot,
inscribed "L.C.T. Favrile 1846," 3 1/2" h.,
pr. **1,610**

Tiffany Spiral Candlestick

Candlesticks, tapering spirally-molded
stem on a cushion foot & supporting a
cupped ribbed socket, amber w/pink &
silvery blue iridescence, signed & w/orig-
inal paper label, 9" h., pr. (ILLUS.
of one) **1,610**

Candy dish, footed pointed leaf-shaped
dish w/incurved rolled sides & back,
applied finger handle w/thumbrest at the
back, overall gold iridescence, signed
"525274G LCT Favrile," 4" w., 5" l. **990**

Center bowl, ribbed rounded bowl w/wide
everted rim, amber w/pink iridescence,
signed "L.C. Tiffany - Favrile - 1925,"
11 1/2" d.. **1,380**

Compote, open, 5 1/4" d., 4 1/2" h., open,
the wide oval bowl w/a five-ruffled rim on
white opal decorated w/five green
pulled-feathers, gold iridized interior

w/stretched rim effect, iridized gold disk
foot, inscribed "L.C. Tiffany - Favrile
590E".. **1,495**

Compote, open, 5 1/4 x 7", 3 1/4" h., a
ribbed oval bowl in pale yellow w/applied
stem & disk foot, subtle stretch iridescence at rim, polished pontil, signed
"LCT Favrile 18930" **690**

Compote, open, 9" h., the shallow wide
dish tapered slightly to a wide flattened
rim, raised on a slender swelled stem on
a domed foot, iridescent amber, signed
"L.C. Tiffany - Favrile - 3919H," ca. 1913.. **1,955**

Compote, open, 9" d., 3" h., the rounded
bowl w/a widely flaring flattened rim,
raised on a wide short pedestal base,
blue w/strong blue lustre & stretched iridescence around the rim, base signed
"L.C. Tiffany Inc. Favrile X" (very light
center wear) **805**

Cordial, tall bell-shaped bowl on a tall slender stem & round foot, gold w/gold iridescent highlights, signed "LCT Favrile,"
5 1/2" h.. **275**

Tiffany Decanter for Cordial Set

Cordial set: decanter w/stopper & ten cordials; the globular decanter w/a tapering
base & a tall slender neck w/flared rim,
decorated around the shoulder w/twisted
points in the glass, fitted w/a bulbous
matching stopper, the cordials w/a bell-
form bowl on a baluster-form stem &
round foot, each in amber w/orange,
pink & blue iridescence, each signed
"L.C.T. - Favrile," cordials 3 7/8" h.,
decanter 10 3/4" h., the set (ILLUS. of
decanter) **4,600**

Cordials, disk foot & slender tall stem supporting a bell-form bowl, overall gold iridescence, signed, 4 1/2" h., pr.................... **476**

Cordials, ovoid small body w/a wide flared
rim, four pinched-in sides, overall golden
iridescence w/amethyst hues, each
signed & numbered, 2" h., set of 4 .... **660**

Decanter w/original stopper, footed bulbous ovoid body w/a wide rounded
shoulder centering a tall slender neck
w/flared rim, fitted w/double-knop bulbed
stopper, iridescent light gold, modeled
around the shoulder & down the sides
w/applied "pig tails," signed "L.C.T.
M9342," 10 1/2" h...................................... **1,265**

Finger bowls & underplates, round ruffled bowls w/prunt decoration, matching ruffled underplates, overall bluish gold iridescence, marked, set of 6 .... **3,465**

Flower frog, short cylindrical form w/an eight-loop rim, overall gold iridescence, signed "6 LC Tiffany Favrile," 3 1/2" d., 2 3/4" h. **330**

Flower frogs, cylindrical w/ribbed central section between the two rows of eight loop stem holders, overall gold iridescence, signed "3" h., pr................................... **460**

Goblet, tapering ovoid bowl w/a slightly everted lip, on a slender baluster-form stem & round foot, amber w/silvery pink iridescence, signed "L.C.T. - Favrile - L.C.T. 1267," 9 1/4" h. **1,035**

Goblets, wide cylindrical bowl w/rounded bottom, raised on a slender stem w/disk foot, each engraved around the rim w/a band of grape clusters & leaves, amber w/gold iridescence, signed "L.C.T. Favrile," 6 1/8" h., set of 8 .... **7,187**

Fine Tiffany Perfume Bottle

Perfume bottle w/stopper, footed bulbous spherical body w/a short cylindrical neck & flattened rim, in dark blue iridescence w/overall green heart-shaped leaves & vines, matching ball stopper, ca. 1912, 5 1/4" h. (ILLUS.) **2,900**

Roundel, round disk w/indented center, a large central blossom-form w/pulled & swirled white & gold threading within a pale gold stretched border band, overall light iridescence, experimental, signed "X2294" & w/original Tiffany Glass and Decorating Company paper label, early 20th c., 14" d. **2,875**

Salt dip, broad shouldered round form w/eight pulled prunts, blue w/strong blue iridescence, signed "L.C. T. Favrile X620," 2 1/8" d. **805**

Salt dip, bulbous squatty form w/heavy ribs & applied small prunts, tan to green overall iridescence, signed "LCT 02647"... **1,375**

Salt dip, round w/ruffled rim, overall blue iridescence, signed 2 1/2" d. **413**

Salt dip, squatty bulbous form w/incurved crimped rim, molded ribbing, overall bluish gold iridescence, signed "L.C.T.," 2 1/8" d., 1 1/8" h. **176**

Salt dips, raised & flared rims on faintly ribbed bodies, deep blue overall iridescence, each base signed "L.C.T. Favrile X355," 1 1/2" h., pr. (nicks).......................... **748**

Salt dips, ruffled rim on shallow bowl of amber w/overall gold iridescence, signed "L.C.T.," 3" d., pr... **489**

Tumbler, a bulbed base below gently flaring cylindrical sides, overall gold iridescent w/bluish highlights, signed, 3 3/4" h...... **248**

Tumblers, waisted cylindrical form w/applied threading around the middle, iridescent amber, all signed "L.C.T.," three numbered "5359" & three w/a "W" & number, ca. 1905, 4" h., set of 6............ **1,265**

Vase, 2 2/3" h., miniature, bulbous form w/a band of prunts & dimples, gold iridescence at the top w/caramel around the center, signed "LC Tiffany - #659"......... **385**

Vase, 4 1/4" h., floriform, a widely flaring five-lobed ruffled rim above the bulbous ovoid body tapering to a short stem & disk foot, gold w/gold stretched iridescence, signed "L.C. Tiffany - Favrile - 8651 D," ca. 1910................................... **1,265**

Vase, 4 1/4" h., ovoid tapering to a tiny flared neck, cased iridescent turquoise blue lined in white, signed "6467 N.L.C. Tiffany Favrile" **1,760**

Tiffany Floriform Vase

Vase, 4 3/4" h., floriform, a domed ribbed dark greenish amber foot below the swelled slender ovoid body tapering to a flattened mouth, tall green & gold pulled-feather designs on an opal ground w/overall iridescence (ILLUS.) **2,464**

Vase, 4 3/4" h., simple ovoid form tapering to a small trumpet neck, iridescent blue ground decorated around the shoulder & body w/silver pulled-feather designs, engraved "L.C.T. D2686" **3,220**

Vase, 5" h., bottle-form, spherical base w/a tall slender 'stick' neck, wavy gold iridescent peacock feather design on a bluish gold iridescent ground, signed "LCT 5177" **1,210**

Tiffany Internal Lustre Vase

Vase, 5" h., simple ovoid form w/widely flaring neck, eight-ribbed body in ambergris cased to transparent peacock blue exterior, the interior w/gold Favrile lustre, ribs in downward pulled silver dots, base signed "L.C. Tiffany - Favrile R812" (ILLUS.) **2,875**

Vase, 5 1/4" h., wide swelled ribbed cylindrical lower body w/a wide tapering shoulder w/a short neck & cupped rim, amber w/opalescent vertical stripes & pink & purple iridescent serpentine trailings, inscribed "L.C.T. - 10412" **1,495**

Vase, 5 1/2" h., floriform, a bulbous body in cobalt blue w/a wide flared & ruffled rim, stretch iridescence at the rim, strong blue lustre, short stem & applied disk foot, signed "L.C. Tiffany - Favrile 9041E" **978**

Vase, 5 1/2" h., footed bulbous base below a tall wide cylindrical neck, overall ruby red, signed "5949 N L.C. Tiffany Favrile" .. **4,070**

Vase, 5 3/4" h., "Cypriote," squatty wide bulbous base below a tapering swelled shoulder & small flat mouth, opaque green decorated w/an abstract petal & vine decoration in yellowish gold & red iridescence, remnants of Tiffany Favrile Glass and Decoration paper label, inscribed "M7155," ca. 1902 .... **3,737**

Vase, 6 1/4" h., flora-form, opal & crystal round foot below a short slender stem & a slender ovoid bowl w/green pulled feathers tapering to a tricorner opal rim, signed "1026G LC Tiffany Favrile" **3,300**

Vase, 7 1/4" h., paperweight-type, a broad ovoid body tapering to a short cylindrical neck, pale aqua decorated internally w/yellow, red & black millefiori flowers among trailing heart leaves & vines of deep green w/ochre swirls, base signed "L.C. Tiffany - Favrile 3527 P," also w/paper label, ca. 1920 .... **6,900**

Vase, 8" h., bud-type, tall slender waisted cylindrical form w/widely flaring base, cased opalescent & green w/gold iridescent feather decoration around the foot, signed "L.C. Tiffany - 6817K," ca. 1916 .... **1,265**

Vase, 8" h., waisted cylindrical lower body below a wide compressed bulbous upper body w/a band of dimples below the low rolled rim, grey w/overall silvery

blue & gold iridescence, "L.C. Tiffany Inc. Favrile 38-763," early 1900s **575**

Vase, 8 1/2" h., simple ovoid body tapering to a short neck w/rolled rim, experimental design in amber w/iridescent pulled-feather decoration, the feather tips reserved, late 19th - early 20th c **1,035**

Vase, 8 3/4" h., disk foot below a slender knopped stem continuing to a tall slender bulbed body w/a wide flat mouth, iridescent blue w/green trailings & heart-shaped leaves, engraved "3930 G L.C. Tiffany - Favrile" **3,680**

Vase, 9" h., a tall ten-ribbed tapering ovoid body w/a slightly flared scalloped rim, raised on a slender knobbed stem & ribbed slightly domed foot, blue w/strong blue iridescence, signed "L.C. Tiffany - Favrile - 1524-3333 P," ca. 1920 .... **2,415**

Vase, 10 1/4" h., stick-type, a conical bottom tapering sharply to a tall slightly flaring cylindrical neck, the upper body in dark gold iridescence w/a band of dark green pulled up pointed leaves around the base, signed "L.C. Tiffany - Favrile - 436J" **1,210**

Vase, 10 1/2" h., tall slender ovoid body w/a bulbed tall neck tapering to a small mouth, white opaque decorated w/feathering in gold at the collar, a gold zipper decoration running vertically from top to bottom, signed "LCT H1218" **3,575**

Vase, 11" h., squatty compressed lower body w/sharply angled shoulder tapering to a tall slender cylindrical neck, opalescent decorated w/pulled feathering in pale yellow & green highlighted w/silvery blue iridescence, inscribed "L.C.T. M7123," ca. 1904 .... **2,070**

Vase, 11 1/2" h., floriform, an iridescent amber base & extended slender stem w/green pulled-feather design against a clear ground, rising to a bulbous iridescent opal bowl, gold iridescent interior, signed "8194M LC Tiffany Favrile" **5,060**

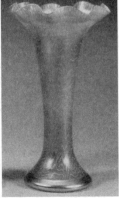

Tiffany Golden Damascene Vase

Vase, 12 1/2" h., flared foot tapering to a tall slender cylindrical body w/a widely flaring ruffled rim, amber w/overall golden iridized Damascene decoration, base inscribed "L.C. Tiffany - Favrile - 329-8242G" (ILLUS.)................................. **1,725**

Vase, 13" h., 5 " d., floriform, a disk foot below the tall slender swelled stem supporting a swelled ribbed bowl w/a wide flaring, ruffled & twisted rim, overall reddish gold iridescence, signed "165-D L.C. Tiffany - Favrile"................................. **4,950**

Vase, 13 3/4" h., glass & patinated bronze, trumpet-form, the flaring glass trumpet in pink & opalescent striped glass w/a scalloped rim, mounted in a bronze upright foliate mount above the flaring round ribbed foot, base impressed "Louis C. Tiffany Furnaces, Inc. - 158A" w/monogram, 1918-28.................................... **1,495**

Vase, 14 1/2" h., floriform on a shaped stem applied to a ribbed, domed foot, amber iridescent, inscribed "L.C.T. Favrile"... **1,495**

Vase, 16" h., trumpet-form, tall trumpet on a bulbed stem & domed ribbed foot, amber w/the upper section decorated w/heart & vine bands in green iridescence on a gold iridescent ground, inscribed "L.C. Tiffany - Favrile 9481K"..... **6,900**

Vase, 16 3/8" h., floriform, an upright bowl w/a crimped & ruffled rim, raised on a tall slender swelled stem on a domed optic-ribbed foot, pale green opalescent w/an amber foot, signed "L.C.T. R9652," ca. 1902 .... **9,200**

Vase, 18 7/8" h., jack-in-the-pulpit, form, wide ruffled rim turned up in the back & down in the front, raised on a very slender stem on a round cushion foot, overall gold iridescence, signed "L.C. Tiffany - Favrile 732C," ca. 1908.......................... **16,100**

Vase, 18 7/8" h., jack-in-the-pulpit-form, a thick cushion foot below the very tall slender stem topped by a widely flaring crimped & upturned rim, overall gold iridescence, signed "7793C L.C. Tiffany - Favrile"... **11,500**

Vase, 20 1/4" h., double-bulbed form w/an elongated neck of ambergris decorated w/blue iridescent pulled-feathers rising to red & gold lustre at the top base, signed "L.C.T. E550" & w/a paper label, ca. 1895 (rust-colored blemish to neck iridescence, inclusions in neck) **2,760**

Monumental Tiffany Vase in Stand

Vase, 21 1/4" h., tall slender baluster-form w/a short slightly flared neck, tall peacock feather design around the sides in dark blue & silvery iridescence against a feathered iridescent ground w/green & lavender highlights, fitted in a bronze support w/thin upright tabs on a disk base w/beaded rim band, signed "L.C.T. F1978" (ILLUS.) **25,300**

Vases, 20" h., conical base tapering sharply to a tall slender 'stick' neck, iridescent greenish blue band of upright pointed leaves around the base, overall iridescent gold necks, signed "L.C. Tiffany - Favrile," numbered "8929J" & "8934J," ca. 1915, pr. **3,737**

Fine Tiffany Wine Set

Wine set: decanter w/original stopper & six wine glasses; overall gold iridescence, the decanter w/a squatty bulbous base tapering sharply to a tall slender neck w/flared rim fitted w/a tall mushroom stopper, wine glasses w/tall cylindrical bowls on a tall slender stem, all engraved w/a grapevine design, the set (ILLUS. of part)............................. **3,000-4,000**

Wines, bell-shaped bowl raised on a knopped stem & spreading round foot, overall gold iridescence, signed, set of 11 .... **4,025**

Wines, deep stepped, flaring & gently ruffled bowl on a slender stem & round domed foot, pastel blue w/wide white opalescent bands, some signed, some w/paper label, set of 10 .... **3,450**

VAL ST. LAMBERT

This Belgian glassworks was founded in 1790. Items listed here represent a sampling of its numerous and varied lines.

Val St. Lambert Mark

Bowl-vase, bulbous body tapering slightly to a wide flaring & ruffled rim, finely decorated in blue & white monochrome w/a scene of two young Dutch boys blowing pipe smoke towards a puppy, frosted satin ground, smoke becomes visible when held to light, ground pontil, 6" h. **$224**

Cameo jar, cov., cylindrical w/fitted slightly domed cover, frosted clear layered in ruby red & intricately etched w/five scrolled cartouche panels, stylized foliate border on clear scrollwork ground, clear facet-cut knob finial, signed on base, 5 1/2" h. (rim nicks)............................. **316**

Perfume atomizer, cylindrical shouldered form w/gilt-metal top mount & atomizer, in clear layered in ruby red & acid-etched as wild roses & plants on a clear hatchwork ground, 5 3/4" h. (wear to mount finish, stress crack at metal, wear) **173**

Val St. Lambert Engraved Vase

Vase, 8 1/2" h., footed bulbous ovoid body tapering to a short flared neck, heavy colorless crystal enclosed w/a large single perfect rose on leafy stem at the center, base signed "VSG C. Graffart - Piece Unique 1949," attributed to Charles Graffart (ILLUS.) **347**

Vase, 14" h., tall slender swelled cylindrical form w/a flat mouth, mottled pink ground decorated w/an irregular dark green band near the top & tall dark green stylized stem & bud designs up the sides, original gold paper label (small flake on base) **660**

VENETIAN

Venetian glass has been made for six centuries on the island of Murano, where it continues to be produced. The skilled glass artisans developed numerous techniques, subsequently imitated elsewhere.

Heavy Barbini "Inciso" Bowl

Bowl, 9" d., 3 1/2" h., "inciso," round slightly irregular thick-walled sharply tapering body in clear, the interior in brilliant reddish orange, the exterior finely carved w/"inciso," unsigned, designed by Alfredo Barbini, ca. 1960 (ILLUS.) **$1,840**

Bowl, 10 3/4" l., "filigrano," footed deep rounded elongated leaf-form in clear internally decorated w/alternating pink, blue & white filigrano threading, unsigned Fratelli Toso **373**

Bowl, 5 1/2 x 12 1/2", 5 1/2" h., elongated form w/pulled handles, the interior decorated w/gold patches & glass fragments, Barovier and Toso Rugiadoso, ... **258**

Large Venetian Glass Bowl

Bowl, 14" l., the oblong bowl composed of caramel-colored tiles of glass delineated in black, designed by Ercole Barovier, inscribed "barovier & toso - murano," ca. 1956 (ILLUS.)....................... **1,265**

Bowl-vases, flat base w/rounded flaring cut & curled sides, cased w/coarse pink powder application, enhanced by gold foil on the exterior, 20th c., 4" h., pr. **345**

Candlesticks, each in pale pink w/gold foil inclusions w/lip wraps in deep cobalt blue, the knop applied w/multi-colored miniature fruit, slender baluster-form stem & flaring round gold foil foot, original paper label "VETRERIA ARTISTICA - BAROVIER & C. - MURANO," ca. 1925, 8 1/2" h., pr....................................... **488**

Decanter w/stopper, tall cylindrical form tapering to the rim, colorless w/pink latticino striped design on the body & the hollow ball-shaped stopper, mid-20th c., 18 1/2" h. **173**

Figures, jazz musicians, each seated w/the body in blue powders cased in clear "bullicante" glass, applied heads, hands & feet in clear w/foil inclusions, one holding banjo, the other an accordion, unsigned Barovier & Toso, ca. 1930, 6 1/2" h., pr. **2,875**

Figures of dancing man & woman, each a tall slender figure cased in deep red, he wearing tight pants in red threaded in white around the calves, his jacket trimmed w/clear rigaree, white face & arms, wearing a tall shaped red top hat, she wearing a long bell-form gown w/white threading around the bottom, red jacket w/applied clear rigaree, white arms & face, a large red picture hat, mid-20th c., 11 1/2" h., pr. **280**

Venetian Lamp with Encased Figure

Lamps, figural, each a freeform crystal upright slender block w/trapped bubble highlights encasing a figure of a stylized man or woman in black & white period costume w/gold foil trim, supported by an applied dome base, metal lamp fittings, mid-20th c., glass 18 1/2" h., pr. (ILLUS. of one) **978**

Lamps, table model, blown baluster-form body w/a thick metal base fitting & internal rod to upper electric fittings, the body decorated w/spiraling canes w/white latticino & copper powders, ca. 1950s, 7" d., 20" h., pr. (no shades, some wear to fittings) **121**

Model of a bird, free-blown elongated "J-form" stylized bird in bluish green w/millefiore eyes & three bands of murines around the body in blue & red, designed by Alessandro Pianon, ca, 1961, label reads "Vistosi," 12 1/4" h. **1,840**

Model of a bird, swan-like bird w/a clear applied long comb on head & pointed beak on a blue head & curved long neck shading to a red body w/raised ribbed wings, on a clear ribbed pedestal, paper label w/"Made in Italy - Murano," 11" h. **72**

Model of a bird, stylized slender J-form body w/a short beak & indentations applied w/glass disk eyes, teal green w/cobalt blue & dark red "murrine" decoration, mounted w/copper legs & feet, designed by Alessandro Pianon for Vistosi, ca. 1962, 11 3/4" h. **1,725**

Model of a bull, free-blown in orange & clear, signed "Seguso," 14" l. **805**

Model of a bull, "scavo," highly stylized model of the head down & back arched, tail sticking out, textured grey roughened surface, designed by Alfredo Barbini for Cenedese, ca. 1948, unsigned, 12" l., 7" h. (minor losses to horns & tip of tail) **977**

Model of a dove, large stylized bird in white latticino & pink twisted filigrano, applied clear beak & feet, original paper label w/"G.F. Murano made in Italy," ca. 1950s, 7" h. **173**

Deep Cranberry Venetian Duck

Model of a duck, free-blown bird standing w/head raised, large applied feet, deep cranberry red cased in heavy crystal, applied bill & feet w/gold inclusions, applied black bead eyes, 6" h. (ILLUS.) **100**

Model of a fish, large ovoid ribbed hollow body applied w/specks of white, yellow & green, raised on large wedge-form applied deep amethyst fins w/a serrated fin up the back & a large pointed amethyst mouth, applied yellow & black murrina eyes, attributed to Fratelli Toso, ca. 1930s, 8" h. **385**

Model of a polar bear, "scavo," highly stylized model of a bear w/arched back & pointed snout, grey w/roughened & spotted textured surface, designed by Alfredo Barbini, ca. 1952, unsigned, 10 1/2" l., 5 3/4" h. **862**

Model of a rooster, "mezza filigrana," blown deep U-form body w/the head held high & a long arched & fluted tail, the body & tail in clear internally decorated w/spiraling canes in white, red & copper colored inclusions, the crest, beak & base in clear w/gold foil inclusions, designed by Dino Martens, unsigned Aureliano Toso, ca. 1954, 9 3/4" h. **460**

Pitcher, 5 1/2" h., 'Floreale' style, ovoid body tapering to a tricorner rim, applied high looped green handle, the body of clear over green powders & opaque white w/inset murrina flowers, Fratelli Toso **660**

Reproduction Satin Glass Pitcher

Pitcher, 9" h., tankard-type, reproduction shaded blue mother-of-pearl satin in the

Diamond Quilted patt., tapering cylindrical body w/curled spout & applied frosted handle, mid-20th c. (ILLUS.) 90

Sculpture, in amber yellow & green, disk molded w/the surrealistic image of a face, designed by Max Ernst Elfo III, for Fucina degli Angeli Venezia, inscribed "Elfo 3/di Max Ernst 159/300," mounted on plexiglass, ca. 1966, 1 1/2" thick, 6 1/4" d. **1,265**

Sculpture, rectangular model of an aquarium, three thick fused sections of marine glass enclosing three whimsical exotic fish composed of red & yellow canes, swimming among emerald green seaweed, designed by Alfredo Barbini, probably for Cenedese, ca. 1950, 2 1/2 x 12 1/2", 8 1/2" h. **2,415**

Vase, 4 3/4" h., flared cylindrical form, clear, enhanced by gold dust, symmetrical trapped air bubbles & maroon pulled to create a plaid effect, 20th c. **173**

Vase, 4 3/4" h., handkerchief-type, folded upright ruffled form composed of opaque light blue, transparent blue, gold & clear in vertical stripes, paper foil label w/"Murano Glass Made in Italy," mid-20th c. **230**

Vase, 4 3/4" h., "scavo," wide squatty bulbous body tapering to a small short flared neck, pale orange w/a roughly textured surface, designed by Gino Cenedese, unsigned, ca. 1952 .... **1,035**

Vase, 5" h., Amberina coloration, original paper label "Murano - Seguso," 1950s **78**

Vase, 6 1/4" h., "zanfirico," footed slender ovoid body tapering to a small molded mouth, body w/vertical bands of "zanfirico" canes in orange & white latticino & blue & clear cane strips, applied clear foot & rim w/gold foil inclusions, unsigned Aureliano Toso, ca. 1940s **373**

Fine Venetian "Intarsio" Vase

Vase, 6 3/4" h., "intarsio," deep gently flaring bowl-form w/flat rim, composed of triangular inlays in bright red, amber, pale lavender & cobalt blue, alternating w/patches of clear bullicante glass, unsigned Barovier & Toso, designed by Ercole Barovier, original foil label "Made in Italy - For Gumps," ca. 1961-63 (ILLUS.) **7,187**

Vase, 6 3/4" h., "murrhine," slightly swelled cylindrical form composed of an overall pattern of pale amber & brown star "murrhines," a large & profuse cluster of pendent wisteria blossoms in shades of deep purple & cobalt blue, w/blossom centers in deep golden amber, w/a few leaves in deep emerald green, unsigned, possibly by Vittorio Zecchin for Artisti Barovier, ca. 1920 .... **9,775**

Vase, 7 1/4" h., raised & flattened rim on an ovoid body, black amethyst w/silver foil decoration cased in clear, polished pontil, mid-20th c. **288**

Vase, 7 1/4" h., "sommerso," swelled ovoid form w/a wide flat mouth, heavily molded w/swirled ribbing, thick clear sides over cranberry & purple, Archimede Seguso, ca. 1960, unsigned, original scalloped label reading "ARCHIMEDE SEGUSO - MURANO - MADE IN ITALY".. **1,265**

Vase, 8 1/8" h., "nerox," deeply waisted cylindrical form w/a wide flat rim, clear decorated w/patches of crimson & orange, designed by Ermanno Toso for Fratelli Toso, unsigned, ca. 1965 .... **460**

Vase, 8 3/4" h., "losanghe," swelled cylindrical form w/a wide flat rim, clear decorated w/a spiral grid of squares in white & caramel w/aubergine strips, Archimede Seguso, ca. 1956, unsigned ... **2,875**

Vase, 8 7/8" h., "tutti fruitti," flaring cylindrical form w/pinched rim, clear cased over a layer of multi-colored glass canes comprising latticino, millefiori, zamfirico, cane pieces & other broken pieces of glass, over a burst silver foil layer, further cased over deep turquoise blue, unsigned, remains of paper label of A.V.E.M., ca. 1955 .... **632**

Vase, 9 1/2" h., "Auriliano Toso Oriente," widely flaring trumpet-form body w/a pinched-in rim, clear infused w/patches of orange, black, teal, white, royal & light blue, crimson, plum, copper aventurine & latticino patches w/a large white star murrhina, designed by Dino Martens, ca. 1948 .... **9,775**

Vase, 10" h., "sommerso corroso," slender ovoid form on a thick cushion foot, foot & lower body in turquoise blue cased over emerald green above, acid-etched finish, attributed to Seguso Vetri D'Arte, ca. 1960, unsigned... **287**

Vase, 10 1/2" h., domed foot on a gently flaring cylindrical body w/a rounded bottom, bowl overlaid in gold foil & further decorated w/random applied dark spots, deep purple foot, unsigned Fratelli Toso, ca. 1950s **2,990**

Vase, 10 1/2" h., "scavo," blown & applied irregular bottle form w/applied figure of a nude woman carrying a basket of fruit, the reverse w/two fish, heavily textured glass, designed by Napoleone Martinuzzi for Cenedese, ca. 1953-58, unsigned... **3,450**

Vase, 10 1/2" h., "sommerso," thick slightly flared heavily swirl-ribbed squared form, pale amber cased over cranberry, Archimede Seguso, ca. 1960, unsigned **460**

Vase, 10 5/8" h., "piume," slender teardrop bottle-form w/ovoid body & tall slender neck, clear cased over peach, internally decorated in filigree feathers in white, black, periwinkle blue & yellow, Archimede Seguso, designed circa 1956.. **4,025**

Vase, 11 1/2" h., 'Gemmata' style, tall trumpet-form body, clear w/internal 'gems' created w/a double layer of chips w/red on the exterior & gold on the interior, engraved "barovier & toso Murano" **1,045**

Tall Fratelli Toso Vase

Vase, 11 1/2" h., tall flattened teardrop-form in emerald green overlaid w/gold foil, further decorated w/applied green glass drops, unsigned Fratelli Toso, ca. 1950s (ILLUS.) **1,495**

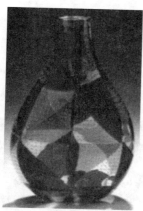

Venetian "Intarsio" Vase

Vase, 12" h., "intarsio," bulbous teardrop-form, composed of red & clear patches each enclosing tiny controlled bubbles, by Ercole Barovier for Barovier & Toso (ILLUS.) **4,025**

Cenedese "La Fornace" Vase

Vase, 12" h., 8" w., "La Fornace," thick cylindrical form cast in low-relief w/two glass artisans at work, in shades of tan, orange, red, green & blue, designed by Napoleone Martinuzzi, by Cenedese, 1953-58 (ILLUS.) **5,175**

Striped Seguso Studio Vase

Vase, 13 1/2" h., tapered ovoid heavy walled colorless form internally decorated w/transparent vertical stripes & an asymmetric opaque grey band about the body, signed "Desl. Seguso," 1975 (ILLUS.) **748**

Vase, 16 1/2" h., paperweight-style, tall slender slightly tapering form w/a lobed rim, thick clear sides changing to deep emerald green, internally decorated w/sea creatures including sea horses, jellyfish & brightly striped tropical fish, all in shades of green, red, yellow, white, black & blue, w/metallic foil inclusions, Vetreria Artistica Alfredo Barbini, unsigned, ca. 1950s **5,060**

Vase, 17 1/4" h., "Aureliano Toso Oriente," rose water sprinkler-form, bulbous base tapering to a tall slender undulating neck w/pointed tip, clear internally decorated w/random patches of black, red, yellow, white & light blue, also w/sections of aventurine inclusions, "zanfirico" threads & a large star "murrhina," designed by Dino Martens, ca. 1950s **4,600**

Vase, 17 3/4" h., "merletto," large tapering pear-form body w/a small short cylindrical neck, clear internally decorated w/white lace-like threading, Archimede Seguso, designed ca. 1954 (drilled).......... **2,300**

Rare Large Chalice-form Vase

Vase, 18 1/2" h., chalice-form, the large tall ovoid goblet-form body composed of fused murrine arranged as four golden amber iris blossoms on extended leafy blue stems w/red elements between & against sky blue starry background murrine, all raised on a clear knob w/applied blue prunts & rigaree above the flaring blue funnel foot, attributed to Artisti Barovier, ca. 1920s (ILLUS.).................. **28,750**

Vase, 19 1/16" h., 'Seguso vetri d'Arte,' tall gently flaring cylindrical sides, violet above a layer of crimson & a clear foot, designed by Falvio Poli, ca. 1951, unsigned.. **1,380**

VENINI

Founded by former lawyer Paolo Venini in 1925, this Venetian glasshouse soon developed a reputation for its fine quality decorative glass and tablewares. Several noted designers have worked for the firm over the years and their unique pieces in the modern spirit, made using traditional techniques, are increasingly popular with collectors today. The factory continues in operation.

Bottle w/original stopper, 'Morandiane' style, tall slender conical body w/flat rim & hollow ball stopper, composed of fine vertical canes of green, white & clear, acid-stamped mark "venini murano ITALIA," designed by Paolo Venini & Fulvio Bianconi, ca. 1950s, 14 1/2" h................... **$880**

Bowl, 14" h., free-blown wide form w/high upright sides & a flared rim, pale blue w/an applied deep blue rigaree band around the neck, pointed base pontil, designed by Napoleone Martinuzzi, ca. 1925, unsigned.. **460**

Chalice, free-blown pale blue w/a wide disk foot w/folded rim supporting an inverted baluster & knop stem below the tall gently flaring bowl w/a wide flattened, flaring rim, possibly designed by Vittorio Zecchin, ca. 1925, unsigned, 14" h. **632**

Clock, table model, in blue w/green inclusions, acid-stamped "Venini - Murano -

Made in Italy," ca. 1950s, 6 1/4 x 6 3/8", 6" h. **402**

Compote, 15 1/2" d., 5 3/4" h., pale blue, a flaring wide funnel pedestal foot w/folded rim supporting the wide bowl w/deep molded ribs in the cavetto below the very wide flattened rim, designed by Napoleone Martinuzzi, ca. 1925, unsigned........... **977**

Decanter w/stopper, "a canne," stylized female form, deeply waisted w/the flaring upper section w/a flat shoulder centered by a tall narrow cylindrical neck all in dark green, the neck fitted w/a dark blue tall teardrop stopper, the tall lower section composed of a "skirt" w/cane stripes in cobalt blue & emerald green, acid-stamped "VENINI - MURANO," designed by Gio Ponti, executed ca. 1955, 15" h. **4,025**

Decanter w/stopper, "sommerso inciso," tall slender slightly tapering triangular form w/a short neck & tall pointed & ribbed stopper, brilliant turquoise blue, acid-stamped "VENINI - MURANO - ITALIA," designed by Paolo Venini, ca. 1956, 14 3/4" h.. **575**

Venini Clown Figure

Figure of a clown "vurrina arlequino" style seated harlequin's body in blue & white amidst a lavender ground w/silver foil inclusions, applied lattimo glass hands & feet, the face a slice of murrina encompassing eyes, brows, nose & mouth, designed by Fulvio Bianconi, ca. 1950, unsigned, 8" h., 9 3/4" l. (ILLUS.)............ **25,300**

Venini "Pulegoso" Bird

Model of a bird, "Pulegoso," clear blown body w/applied tooled glass wings, pulled up at tail & beak, designed by Tyra Lundgren, ca. 1950s, acid-stamped "VENINI - MURANO - MADE IN ITALY," 6 3/4" h. (ILLUS.)... **862**

Model of a fish, shown lying flat, the body blown in lavender cased in clear, decorated w/applied canes in yellow & mustard yellow, applied turquoise eye, inscribed "venini - italia," designed by Ken Scott, ca. 1951, 19 1/2" l.................... **1,840**

Models of chickens, a hen & a rooster w/angled cornucopia-shaped bodies in opaque white w/polychrome applied bands, applied small black wings, white legs w/yellow feet, red combs & yellow beaks, designed by Fulvio Bianconi, acid-stamped "venini murano ITALIA," ca. 1950s, 7 1/2" h., pr. (rooster's first comb removed, possibly done at the factory) **2,860**

Venini Pitcher

Pitcher, 9 1/2" h., "a canne" swelled cylindrical body tapering to wide cylindrical neck w/arched spout, clear w/enclosed multi-colored canes in green, red, blue, yellow & lavender, designed by Gio Ponti, ca. 1952, acid-stamped "VENINI - MURANO" (ILLUS.)................................ **4,225**

Vase, 2 1/2" h., 'fazzoletto' handkerchief-form, upright pulled & ruffled sides in deep green, designed by Fulvio Bianconi, acid-stamped mark "venini murano ITALIA," ca. 1950s **121**

Vase, 3" h., 'fazzoletto' handkerchief-style, rounded flaring upright pulled & ruffled sides composed of orange & green 'zanfirico' canes, paper label & acid-stamped mark "venini murano ITALIA," designed by Fulvio Bianconi, ca. 1950s **121**

Vase, 5 1/2" h., 'soffiati' style, ovoid body tapering to a small neck w/flattened rim, light green w/six small applied opaque white loops around the lower body, acid-stamped "venini murano," ca. 1920s............ **358**

Vase, 5 1/2" h., "zanfirico fazzeletto," a handkerchief-style piece w/a rounded bottom & wide, upright folded & ruffled sides in clear enclosing vertical "zanfirico" canes in white & creamy yellow &

aubergine, acid-stamped "VENINI - MURANO - ITALIA," designed by Fulvio Bianconi, designed ca. 1949 .... **2,875**

Vase, 7 3/4" h., "latticino," swelled 'double-conical' form in clear decorated w/vertical white canes enclosing white threads, inscribed "venini - italia," designed by Paolo Venini, ca. 1955 .... **1,495**

Venini Cylindrical Vase

Vase, 8 1/4" h., "Pezzato," the cylindrical sides composed of patchwork squares in shades of aubergine, turquoise, smoky grey & clear, designed by Fulvio Bianconi, ca. 1950, acid-stamped "VENINI - MURANO- ITALIA" (ILLUS.) **7,475**

Vase, 9" h., "a canne," simple conical form w/angled rim, clear fused w/pale amber, blue, violet, teal & red stripes, acid-stamped "venini - murano - ITALIA," designed by Paolo Venini, ca. 1954 .... **2,875**

Venini Cylindrical Vase

Vase, 9 3/4" h., "a doppio incalmo," cylindrical body w/cobalt blue lower section, a middle band of "pettine murrhines" irregular white squares decoration w/red & blue lines, deep green upper section, designed by Riccardo Licata, ca. 1956, acid-stamped "VENINI - MURANO - ITALIA" (ILLUS.) **8,625**

Vase, 10" h., "pezzato" type, gently flaring rectangular sides in clear applied w/random patches of pink, blue & purple, designed by Fulvio Bianconi, acid-stamped "venini murano - ITALIA," ca. 1950 .... **6,900**

Vase, 10 1/2" h., "fazzoletto" (handkerchief) style, upright randomly pulled & ruffled sides composed of a vertical arrangement of pink & white "zanfirico" & "reticello" canes, acid-stamped "venini - murano - ITALIA," designed by Fulvio Bianconi, 1948 .... **3,450**

Vase, 10 1/2" h., "veronese," simple baluster-form w/short knopped pedestal & a small flared neck, brilliant ruby red, designed by Napoleone Martinuzzi, ca. 1925, unsigned... **690**

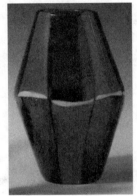

Venini "Pezzato" Vase

Vase, 10 3/4" h., "pezzato," flat flaring sides in a compressed cylindrical shape, green fused w/patches of red & white tesserae, designed by Fulvio Bianconi, ca. 1951 & inscribed "venini - italia" (ILLUS.) **5,750**

Vase, 11" h., figural, blown in the form of a nude female torso w/the arms stretched upwards, olive amber, designed by Fulvio Bianconi, ca. 1950, signed "venini - murano - ITALIA".................................. **6,325**

Vase, 14 1/4" h., "Tessuto," tall ovoid bottle form w/rounded shoulder to slender cylindrical neck, black & turquoise blue vertical fused canes, polished pontil w/foil label marked "Venini S.A. Murano," design attributed to Carlo Scarpa, mid-20th c., light abrasions **1,955**

Vases, 14 3/4" h., "Soffiati" style, ovoid baluster-form w/flaring neck & thin wafer connecting to a round disk foot, rich optic ribbed cobalt blue, designed by Napoleone Martinuzzi, ca. 1928, stamped "venini -murano," pr. **5,175**

VICTORIAN COLORED GLASS

There are, of course, many types of colored glassware of the Victorian era and we cover a great variety of these in our various glass categories. However, there are some pieces of pressed, mold-blown and free-blown Victorian colored glass which don't fit well into other specific listings, so we have chosen to include a selection of them here.

Gilt-decorated Sapphire Blue Bottle

Bottle w/original stopper, tall squared form w/incurved ribbed sides below the sharply tapering paneled shoulder & ringed neck w/flared rim, panel-cut mushroom stopper, sapphire blue, the body decorated w/scalloped gold grape clusters & leafy scrolls, 2 3/4" w., 8 1/8" h. (ILLUS.)...................................... **$160**

Blue Bottle with Enameled Bouquet

Bottle w/original stopper, footed bulbous cylindrical form w/a wide shoulder tapering to a cylindrical neck w/flared rim, sapphire blue decorated w/large white enamel floral bouquet, tapering amber bubble stopper w/white enamel dots, 3 1/2" d., 9 1/4" h. (ILLUS.) **135**

Bowl, 5 1/4" d., 3 1/4" h., deep cylindrical sides w/a widely ruffled rim, sapphire blue enameled around the sides w/colorful flowers & leaves in orange, blue, white, green & pink...................................... **110**

Decorated Blue Fanned Bowl

Bowl, 12" w., 8" h., deep form pulled up on two sides & fanned out, sapphire blue w/an applied crimped clear rim band & four applied clear peg feet, ornately enameled w/colorful banner & dotted blossoms (ILLUS.)... **275**

Box w/hinged lid, squatty bulbous round body in lime green decorated w/white enameled scrolls, the low domed matching cover decorated w/gold foliage & white scrolls, 6 1/4" d., 3 1/2" h. **195**

Enameled Blue Compote

Compote, open, 5 3/4" d., 7 1/8" h., deep rounded wide optic ribbed sapphire blue bowl raised on a hollow tapering stem & cushion foot, the exterior of the bowl delicately enameled w/small yellow & white flowers w/gold branches & leaves (ILLUS.).. **145**

Cruet w/stopper, optic ribbed ovoid body tapering to a tall cylindrical neck w/pinched spout, sapphire blue decorated around the shoulder w/yellow & white daisy-like blossoms & white stems & leaves, applied amber handle & amber teardrop stopper, 3" d., 8" h. **165**

Cruet w/stopper pressed Tree of Life patt., blue opaque **80**

Colorfully Decorated Blue Decanter

Decanter w/original stopper, footed cylindrical cobalt blue body rounded at the base & shoulder & tapering to a tall cylindrical neck w/pinched spout, applied blue handle & blue bubble stopper, the sides colorfully enameled w/scrolling gold stems w/green leaves & rust & white blossoms, gilt band trim, 4" d., 12" h. (ILLUS.).. **195**

Berry-decorated Blue Decanter

Decanter w/original stopper, footed ovoid sapphire blue body tapering to a tall slender cylindrical neck w/a tricorner rim, decorated down the sides w/an ornate thorny branch w/red berries, green & yellow leaves & pink blossoms, applied clear handle & tall pointed facet-cut clear stopper, 4 1/2" d., 13" h. (ILLUS.) **225**

Decanter w/original stopper, footed tall slender tapering melon-lobed body w/a tall slender cylindrical neck w/a flared rim, two lobes ornately enameled w/large white & yellow flowers & green leaves, clear applied foot, sapphire blue body & clear facet-cut stopper, 4 1/8" d., 14 1/2" h. **175**

Ruby Jar with Gold Filigree

Jar, cov., cylindrical deep ruby base w/a high domed cover w/knob finial, cover & base encased in lacy gold filigree metal on small ball feet, 3" d., 5 1/4" h. (ILLUS.).. **165**

Liqueur set: 9 1/2" h. decanter, four matching cups & a round tray w/flared rim; all in greenish amber, the decanter w/a footed bottle-form optic ribbed body w/a tricorner rim & applied amber handle & teardrop stopper, matching optic ribbed cups w/applied handles, decanter & cups enameled w/stylized blossoms & leaf sprigs, tray 8 1/2" d., decanter 9 1/2" h., the set (ILLUS.) **225**

Decorated Liqueur Set

Liqueur set: decanter w/stopper, six small cylindrical cups w/applied loop handles & a rectangular tray w/cut corners; all in lime green, the decanter w/an ovoid optic ribbed body w/a wide shoulder centered by a slender cylindrical neck w/arched rim spout, applied green handle & oblong bubble stopper, all decorated w/small white & gold dot enamel vine designs, tray 8 1/2 x 12", cups 1 3/4" h., decanter 7 3/4" h., the set **225**

Ornate Blue Covered Pitcher

Pitcher, cov., 6" h., 4" d., footed bulbous sapphire blue optic-ribbed body tapering to a wide cylindrical neck & applied blue handle fitted w/a hinged flat pewter cover w/thumbrest, the body ornately enameled w/gilt arches & scrolls alternating w/gold & white floral clusters, gilt script wording "Lamalou-les-Bains" (ILLUS.) **135**

Syrup pitcher w/original metal lid, Inverted Coin Spot patt., swirled base, blue, Central Glass Co. **138**

Vase, 8 1/4" h., 5 1/2" d., footed ovoid melon-lobed body tapering to a flaring lobed neck, deep amethyst enameled w/large branches of pink & cream blossoms & green leaves w/rust colored buds (ILLUS. top next column) **245**

Decorated Lobed & Enameled Vase

Ornate Fanned Vase

Vase, 11 1/4" h., 7 1/2" w., cylindrical sapphire blue body w/a widely flattened & fanned top, heavily enameled w/a gold banner trimmed w/pink & yellow flowers & sprays on the front & a small spray on the back, applied clear ruffled rim band & tall applied clear feet (ILLUS.) **245**

Whimsey, figural shoe thimble, blue **148**

WAVE CREST

Now much sought after, Wave Crest was produced by the C.F. Monroe Co., Meriden, Connecticut, in the late 19th and early 20th centuries from opaque white glass blown into molds.

It was then hand-decorated in enamels and metal trim was often added. Boudoir accessories such as jewel boxes, hair receivers, etc., were predominant.

WAVE CREST WARE

Wave Crest Mark

Ash receiver, squared body w/slight ribbing, floral decoration on a creamy white background, applied gilt-metal rim band, pierced handles, 5" d. **$495**

Bonbon, cov., Rococo mold, metal rim & twisted bail handle, 8" d. **925**

Bonbon w/silver bail handle, decorated w/a network of vines, leaves & blue flowers, deep lemon yellow at top shading to white, original label **595**

Bowl, 5 1/2" d., dresser-type, scroll-molded design w/floral decoration on a dark blue ground, marked **138**

Small Wave Crest Box

Box w/hinged lid, Egg Crate mold, lid decorated w/central floral decoration of pink & maroon flowers & green leaves on a shaded light green ground, 3" d., 2 1/2" h. (ILLUS.)....................................... **225**

Box w/hinged lid, Helmschmied Swirl mold, dainty flowers on the top, 3" d., 3" h. **248**

Box w/hinged lid, Hexagonal mold, applied pink ceramic flowers surrounded by green leaves on a light green ground, 4 1/2" d. **1,250**

Box w/hinged lid, Helmschmied Swirl mold, h.p. floral decoration on a creamy white ground, 4 1/2" d., 3" h. **425**

Box w/hinged lid, Egg Crate mold, decorated w/yellow & purple flowers, 5" sq.......... **430**

Box w/hinged lid, Embossed Rococo mold, decorated w/pink & white roses, original lining, 5" sq., 2 1/2" h. **425**

Box w/hinged lid, decorated w/pink blossoms on blue ground, metal base & feet, key lock, 5" sq., 6" h. **743**

Box w/hinged lid, Baroque Shell mold, scene of Niagara Falls bordered by white enamel dots & blue forget-me-nots, cream background, 5 1/4" d. **790**

Helmschmied Swirl Box

Box w/hinged lid, Helmschmied Swirl mold, lid decorated w/dainty pink & gold flowers & green leaves, shaded blue to white ground, unmarked, no lining, 5 1/2" d., 3 1/2" h. (ILLUS.) **400**

Box w/hinged lid, wide spiral panels on base & edge of lid, center of lid w/a large oval reserve decorated w/a row of dancing storks, panels alternating pink &

green w/dainty florals & scrolls, gilt-metal fittings, unsigned, 5 1/2" d., 3 1/2" h. **1,500**

Wave Crest "Collars & Cuffs" Box

Box w/hinged lid, Egg Crate mold, enameled floral decoration on lid & "Collars & Cuffs" on side, 6" w. (ILLUS.)............. **950-1,200**

Box w/hinged lid, Embossed Rococo mold, h.p. blue flowers on a pink ground, raised on an ornate gilt-metal footed base, 5" w., 6" l... **875**

Box w/hinged lid, Helmschmied Swirl mold, decorated w/delicate flowers on the lid & sides, 6" d., 5" h. **400**

Box w/hinged lid, Egg Crate mold, decorated w/two classical women, 6" d., 6" h. **950**

Large Egg Crate Wave Crest Box

Box w/hinged lid, Egg Crate mold, yellow lilies on a white ground w/light blue panels, all trimmed w/lavender & gold enamel, 6 3/4" w., 6 1/2" h. (ILLUS.)......... **1,750**

Box w/hinged lid, Egg Crate mold, decorated w/mauve to purple floral clusters, green ribbons w/enameled white dots & outlined in gold, 7" sq. **750**

Baroque Shell Wave Crest Box

Box w/hinged lid, Baroque Shell mold, top decorated w/blue, purple & grey flowers, green leaves & pink trim on a creamy white ground, 7" d., 4" h. (ILLUS.)............... 750

Scroll-molded Large Wave Crest Box

Box w/hinged lid, squared shape w/overall delicate molded scrolls highlighted w/pastel blue & pink blossoms & green leaves, delicately embossed metal fittings, unlined, unsigned, 7" w., 4" h. (ILLUS.).. 750

Box w/hinged lid, Helmschmied Swirl mold, lid w/h.p. peach, pink & white asters & moss green leaves, opaque white ground, ornate footed gilt-metal base, 7" d., 6 1/2" h.................................. **1,100**

Baroque Shell Box

Box w/hinged lid, Baroque Shell mold, decorated on top w/pink daisies bordered by sky blue & all outlined in lavender, 7 1/4" d. (ILLUS.) 765

Box w/hinged lid, Hexagonal mold w/embossed scrolling, top & sides decorated w/shaded pink florals & green foliage on a soft green ground, 8 1/2" w., 6" h. **1,500**

Broom holder, blue & lavender floral decoration on a creamy white ground, ornate gilt-metal frame **1,795**

Carafe, squatty bulbous round body centered by a tall reverse-swirl molded cylindrical neck in glossy white, the body w/a pale satin pink ground decorated in sepia brown monotone w/a scene of lakeside building & a distant bridge, the reverse side w/a lighthouse scene, 8 1/4" h. **1,073**

Card holder, upright rectangular form w/embossed frame design, gilt-metal rim, cloth lining, decorated w/delicate pink flowers & a blue border......................... 375

Card holder, upright rectangular form w/embossed frame design, gilt-metal rim, cloth lining, decorated w/h.p. blue flowers & pink border 425

Cigar box w/hinged lid, Egg Crate mold, the front panel marked "Cigars," the other sides & top decorated w/delicate rose strawflowers & stems, separate lid compartment for sponge, unmarked, 6 1/2" w. 770

Cigar holder, plain cylindrical body decorated w/h.p. florals, gilt-metal handled rim & scroll-footed base 550

Cigar humidor, cov., cylindrical, the white opal body molded w/florals & h.p. w/"Cigars" in pink on the side over blue enameled forget-me-nots, the domed cover decorated w/an Indian on horseback, gilt-metal hinged mounts, red flag mark on base 750

Cologne bottle w/atomizer, squatty bulbous body, h.p. yellow floral decoration & enameled white dots on a white opal ground, nickel plate atomizer dated "1889" w/rubber bulb 275

Wave Crest Cracker Jar

Cracker jar, cov., barrel-shaped w/a cream ground decorated w/soft pink, blue & yellow flowers & green leaves on brown branches, unmarked, replated silver plate rim, cover & bail handle, 5 1/4" d., 8 1/4" h. (ILLUS.)....................................... 295

Cracker jar, cov., Egg Crate mold, colorful floral decoration, silver plate rim, cover & twisted bail handle, 7 3/4" w., 5" h................ 450

Cracker jar, cov., Egg Crate mold, decorated w/large pink & yellow roses & yellow foliage on a creamy white ground, paper label intact...................................... 851

Cracker jar, cov., Egg Crate mold, pink floral decoration, silver plate rim, cover & bail handle, paper label mostly intact on the base **1,210**

Cracker jar, cov., raised florals & beading decoration, silver plate cover, rim & bail handle, unsigned 285

Cracker jar, cov., scroll-molded square form, decorated w/floral panels & pink trim, original label on the base, silver plate rim, cover & bail handle 550

Cracker jar, cov., Tulip mold, decorated w/pink apple blossoms front & back, cream shading to blue ground...................... 350

Cracker jar, cov., Helmschmied Swirl mold, decorated w/a pink floral bough & delicate grasses, alternating pale blue ground, embossed silver plate rim w/plain low domed cover w/knob finial & scrolled bail handle, 6 1/2" h. **633**

Wave Crest Cracker Jar

Cracker jar, cov., barrel-shaped, panels of yellow flowers w/pink centers & green leaves decorate a soft pink ground, resilvered rim, cover & bail handle, unmarked, 5 1/2" d., 7 1/4" h. (ILLUS.) **350**

Cracker jar, cov., barrel-shaped w/embossed scrolling, h.p. pink, blue & yellow pansies on a creamy white ground, resilvered cover, rim & bail handle, 5 3/4" d., 7 3/4" h. **295**

Cracker jar, cov., Egg Crate mold, decorated w/h.p. lavender, green & tan florals on a white shaded to pale blue ground, 5" d., 9" h. **650**

Wave Crest Cracker Jar

Cracker jar w/metal lid, smooth tapering cylindrical body decorated w/a large white & purple iris & green leaves on a cream ground bordered by scrolled panels of pale tan, silver plate rim & twisted bail handle, unmarked (ILLUS.) **450**

Creamer, Helmschmied Swirl mold, mushroom garden decoration **75**

Creamer, Helmschmied Swirl mold, decorated w/blue forget-me-nots, 3 1/4" h. **116**

Creamer & cov. sugar bowl, decorated w/h.p. cupids & whimsical scrolling, creamer w/gilt-metal lipped rim & handle, sugar bowl w/gilt-metal rim, cover & bail handle, pr. **100**

Creamer & cov. sugar bowl, Helmschmied Swirl mold, lower portion in solid beige separated by enamel beading from the upper section w/pink roses, pr. **630**

Deck of cards holder, turquoise ground w/enameled large pink rosebud, white dotting on the front & back & similar decoration on both sides **450**

Dish, round w/applied brass collar, decorated w/pansies, signed, 5 1/2" d. **110**

Wave Crest Dresser Box

Dresser box, short radiating molded ribs on the cover & around the base, cover decorated w/pink & blue florals, giltmetal fittings, red banner mark, 4 1/4" d., 3 1/4" h. (ILLUS.) **325**

Dresser box w/hinged cover, Helmschmied Swirl mold, decorated w/a wide central pale blue band decorated w/white daisies & green leafy stems, outlined in delicate gilt scrolls on a white ground, unlined, unmarked, 7 1/4" d. **403**

Dresser box w/hinged cover, ornate scroll-molded body decorated in light green w/dainty pink roses, 7 3/4" d. **440**

Dresser box w/hinged cover, round, the cover molded in bold-relief w/a large single zinnia blossom in pink & white w/a yellow center & dark green border, squatty bulbous dark green base w/four molded blossoms, marked, 4 1/2" d., 2 1/2" h. **990**

Dresser box w/hinged cover, Baroque Shell mold, round, the flattened cover & body w/a satin almond ground, the cover center decorated w/a mauve & pink daisy bouquet, pale enamel-dotted ground bordered w/enameled plum scrolls, 7" d., 4" h. **770**

Ewer, ovoid egg-shaped body decorated w/large pink wild rose blossoms & green leafy stems, an attached ormolu neck & handle, the spiral-twist neck topped by a high wide spout, the scrolled handle topped by a winged putto head, signed, 6 1/2" h. **990**

Ewers, bulbous rounded melon-lobed body decorated w/yellow florals, top fitted w/tall metal arching forked spout & a large S-scroll handle, raised on tapering pedestal above a flaring scroll-molded cast-metal footed base w/grotesque masks at each corner, pr. **500**

Ferner, Egg Crate mold, decorated w/light pink spider mums, no liner, 7" sq. **375**

Ferner, Egg Crate mold, decorated w/yellow wild roses, metal twisted rope rim, 7" sq. **650**

Ferner, low cylindrical body on a narrow footed ring base w/gilt-metal rim insert, light overall scrolling w/h.p. green & brown fern leaves on a shaded yellow ground **650**

Glove box w/hinged cover, pink w/blue floral decoration, 4 x 8 1/2"........................ **1,200**

Handkerchief box w/hinged cover, rectangular low domed cover w/rounded corners & sides molded w/a border of scrolls centering a wild rose decoration, the matching low rounded base raised on an ormolu frame w/scrolled legs, signed, 6 x 9 1/2" **1,155**

Humidor w/hinged metal cover, cylindrical body w/scroll-embossed domed cover, floral decoration on a blue & cream ground, "Tobacco" across the front, 5 1/4" h.............................. **750**

Humidor w/original brass cover, bulbous tapering cylindrical body decorated w/enameled house & bridge scene, cover w/finial & tapering base **750**

Wave Crest Humidor

Humidor w/original brass cover & finial, cream & brown bulbous cylindrical body decorated w/three bulldog heads & "Three Guardsmen," unmarked, 5 1/8" d., 6 1/2" h. (ILLUS.) **525**

Jardiniere, bulbous body tapering to a short cylindrical rim, body decorated w/h.p. mums & foliage, gold lacy trim on the rim, 9" d., 8" h................................ **600-800**

Jardiniere, bulbous nearly spherical body w/a wide short cylindrical neck, the sides molded w/delicate scroll-bordered cartouches decorated w/h.p. flowers, all on a pink ground, raised on a gilt-metal base w/scroll feet, 6 1/2" h. **895**

Jewelry box w/hinged cover, piecrust edge around top, relief-molded florals on sides, h.p. flowers on top, back & front **525**

Key box w/original key, Petticoat & Mushroom mold, nicely decorated, 7 1/2" d. **900**

Letter receiver, Egg Crate mold, ormolu trim, floral decoration **425**

Match holder, decorated w/flowers & beading on the top & bottom, on four gilt-metal ornate feet **195**

Match holder, low plain cylindrical form w/a gilt-metal rim, floral decoration, originally part of a cigar set, unmarked **165**

Match holder, bulbous ovoid milk white holder tapering slightly to a wide, short cylindrical neck, decorated w/a blue daisy bouquet against a pale pink & blue ground, set upon an ornate gilt-metal footed base, marked, 2 3/4" h. **605**

Mirror tray, embossed scrolls, decorated w/dainty blue flowers on a creamy white ground, ornate gilt-metal frame, 5 1/4" d... **1,200**

Photo receiver, Egg Crate mold, the body decorated w/clusters of pink & blue flowers & light green foliage on a creamy white ground, ornate gilt-metal rim.............. **425**

Photo receiver, Egg Crate mold, upright rectangular form, floral decoration on a creamy white ground w/gilt-metal rim **475**

Salt & pepper shakers w/original metal tops, cylindrical base below a bulbous shoulder, house decoration, pr. **250**

Salt & pepper shakers w/original tops, Helmschmied Swirl mold, opaque white ground decorated w/delicate white flowers w/yellow centers & green foliage, pr. **485**

Salt & pepper shakers w/original tops, hexagonal, Embossed Rococo mold, decorated w/h.p. florals, pr.......................... **145**

Salt shaker w/original metal top, Scroll Wave mold, pink to white ground w/blue flowers.. **75**

Salt shaker w/original top, embossed beaded foot, squatty bulbous body tapering to a cylindrical neck w/embossed beaded ring below the lid, decorated w/embossed scrolling & enameled w/two red-headed birds sitting side-by-side among yellow & brown foliage, 2 1/4" h.. **75**

Salt shaker w/original top, jug-shaped, blue shading to white w/a transfer of a pointer dog in foliage, 2" h. **95**

Spooner w/silver plate rim & loop handles, cylindrical paneled rib shape, decorated w/floral transfer **285**

Sugar bowl, cov., Helmschmied Swirl mold, decorated w/flowers & three mushrooms on each side, silver plate cover & two-handled rim, unsigned............. **175**

Sugar shaker w/original top, Helmschmied Swirl mold, alternating panels of blue scrolls & yellow flowers **650**

Syrup pitcher w/original hinged top, paneled cylindrical body w/tapering shoulder, lacy transfer decoration & h.p. pink daisy-like flowers.. **165**

Syrup pitcher w/original hinged top, Ribbed Skirt mold, h.p. blue florals, tall **165**

Tobacco box w/hinged cover, Egg Crate mold, white ground decorated w/green clover, unmarked, 5" w. **750**

Toothbrush jar, cov., tall cylindrical body w/original silver plate cover, floral decoration **525**

Toothpick holder, cylindrical w/molded designs & decorated w/florals, signed, 1 1/2" h.. **138**

Toothpick holder, h.p. yellow daisies, footed gilt-metal frame, signed.................... **275**

Vase, short cylindrical neck above an ovoid body w/scrolled trim, reserve decoration w/blue florals, pale yellow ground, fitted w/a gilt-metal rim w/small scroll handles & floral flower holder, set into a gilt-metal scrolling branch-form pedestal base, small **375**

Vase, bud, 5" h., cylindrical, tapering at base, beaded metal rim & footed metal base, decorated w/blue flowers on a creamy ground **320**

Vase, 6 1/2" h., footed, cylindrical body, embossed scrolling, beaded rim, decorated w/pink flowers **325**

Vase, 9" h., 1 1/4" rim d., squatty bulbous body tapering to a tall cylindrical neck, decorated w/shaded pink to burgundy mums, deep green enameled swags & a deep green enameled rim w/white dotting, footed gilt-metal base **750**

Vase, 9" h., pink shading to burgundy w/h.p. floral decoration & raised gold beading **2,200**

Large Fine Wave Crest Vase

Vase, 11 1/2" h., large ovoid body w/a wide flat mouth, fitted w/a gilt-metal rim band, ornate scrolling handles & a footed base, decorated w/scattered Wedgwood blue cartouches painted w/white daisies against a white ground w/clusters of small pink blossoms on slender leafy stems, signed (ILLUS.) **1,500-2,000**

Vase, 12 1/4" h., footed tapering bulbous body, Rococo mold w/gilt-metal fittings, daisies on a shaded rust background, olive green flare around the bottom **1,850**

Rare Wave Crest Whisk Broom Holder

Whisk broom holder, cylindrical body w/pointed ribbing decorated w/a large gilt scroll-trimmed cartouche of pink & purple rose buds & green leafy stems & white dotting, very pale blue ground, mounted w/a brass base & rim ring & ornate pierced & scrolling backplate (ILLUS.) **1,750**

WEBB

This glass is made by Thomas Webb & Sons of Stourbridge, one of England's most prolific glasshouses. Numerous types of glass, including cameo, *have been produced by this firm through the years. The company also produced various types of novelty and "art" glass during the late Victorian period. Also see BURMESE, ROSE BOWLS, and SATIN & MOTHER-OF-PEARL.*

Rare Webb Gem Cameo Bowl-Vase

Cameo bowl-vase, footed wide squatty bulbous form tapering to a wide upright rim band, white cut to blue, the neck w/band enclosing reserves of an exotic bird perched on flowering branches alternating w/scale-form panels w/quatrefoils, the body cut w/a continous exotic scene of small birds flying amid delicate leafy branches & large flowering plants, Gem Cameo, 9" d., 7" h. (ILLUS.) **$28,000**

Cameo cologne bottle w/stopper, flat-bottomed domed cylindrical form w/a small cylindrical neck & ball stopper, white cut to ruby red, the sides divided into three arched panels each featuring a different flower bloom, a band of small daisies around the neck & a narrow ribbed band around the stopper, acid-stamped mark "Thomas Webb and Sons Gem Cameo," 5" h. **4,510**

Cameo rose bowl, wide bulbous body tapering to flat mouth, translucent ruby w/white overlay carved & etched elaborately w/brambles & thorny rosa rugosa bushes, butterfly & caterpillar at reverse, stamped on base for retailer "Theodore B. Starr, New York," 6" h. **2,875**

Cameo vase, 3 1/4" h., miniature, double-gourd form w/a bulbous squatty lower body below a bulbous cupped neck, bright crimson red overlaid in white & cameo etched w/a passion flower design w/pendant leafy vines above & on the reverse, late "Webb" on base **690**

Cameo vase, 5 1/2" h., footed ovoid body w/a cupped neck, white cut to dark blue, the sides decorated w/large leaves, buds & a flower w/a butterfly on the reverse, the cupped neck cut w/delicate elaborate geometric bands **4,950**

Cameo vase, 6" h., footed ovoid body w/the rounded shoulder centered by a short cylindrical neck, white cut to a

frosted deep raisin amber ground & decorated w/sunflowers on leafy stems & a
butterfly, white bands around the neck &
foot **4,125**

Tricolor Water Lily Vase

Cameo vase, 7 1/2" h., tricolor water lily
vase, complex oval body composed of
transparent ice blue overlaid at top quarter in stippled ruby red w/white layer
below etched and carved as pond lilies &
leaf pads upon the clear blue water
background, base borders center
"Webb" medallion, possible restoration
at center base (ILLUS.) **20,700**

Cameo vase, 8" h., flared urn-form body,
red mother-of-pearl satin Diamond
Quilted patt. overlaid in opaque white &
cameo-etched w/an iris & wildflowers,
base marked "Webb".................................... **575**

Cameo vase, 9 3/4" h., three-layer, footed
wide ovoid body tapering slightly to a
wide short cylindrical neck, citron yellow
overlaid in bright red & opal white,
cameo etched & carved to depict perfect
poppy blossoms on leafy stems w/wild
grasses at the sides, stepped & angular
borders, case marked "Thos. Webb &
Sons. Cameo" **4,600**

Cameo vase, 10" h., bud-type, footed slender ovoid body tapering to a tall slender
'stick' neck, light blue overlaid in white &
cut w/morning glories & a butterfly
between banded borders, ca. 1890,
unsigned... **2,415**

Tall Webb Cameo Vase

Cameo vase, 18 1/2" h., bottle-form, bulbous base tapering to a tall slender
'stick' neck, yellowish amber overlaid in
white, finely carved w/a little bird
perched in a flowering prunus branch
continuing up around the body w/a variety of flowering plants, unsigned, ca.
1900 (ILLUS.) **9,775**

Cameo vases, 5" h., footed bulbous ovoid
body tapering to a short wide cylindrical
neck, yellow overlaid in white, one cut
w/a pendent branch of bleeding hearts,
the other w/a vine of trumpet-form flowers, each cut w/a butterfly between double band borders, impressed "THOMAS
WEBB & SONS - CAMEO," ca. 1890, pr... **1,380**

Cameo vases, 5" h., ovoid footed body
w/short neck, yellow overlaid in white,
one cut w/a pendent branch of bleeding
hearts, the other w/a vine of trumpet-
form flowers, each w/a butterfly & dou-
ble-band borders, impressed mark, ca.
1890, pr. **2,070**

Perfume container, cameo, lay-down type,
model of a duck head, cameo cut white
over yellow forming the bill, fine detail-
ing, 9" l. **7,700**

Vase, 5 3/4" h., Rainbow mother-of-pearl
satin Dewdrop patt., alternating stripes
of pink & blue, decorated overall
w/dainty gilt flowers & leaves, registry
mark **440**

Ornate Webb Moroccan Ware Vase

Vase, 7 7/8" h., 6 1/8" d., Moroccan Ware,
bulbous four-lobed body w/a flaring
squared neck, elaborately enameled
overall w/pink oblong reserves w/fine
colored florals & central diamond framed
w/light blue floral vine-decorated bands
& a pink band around the base & rim of
the neck w/a pink quatrefoil on each side
of the neck (ILLUS.) **595**

Vase, 8" h., Bronze Ware, tall ovoid body
tapering to a trumpet-form neck, overall
dark greenish bronze iridescent finish.......... **165**

Vase, 12 1/4" h., footed simple ovoid body
tapering to a short flaring neck, colorless
body w/etched overall surface & raised
enamel-painted iris flowers around a
frosted Mallard duck poised for flight,
base inscribed "Thomas Webb & Corbett
Ltd. - Stourbridge, England," late 19th c. **690**

Glossary of Selected Glass Terms

Acid (or satin) finish— A matte finish on glassware which is achieved by exposing the piece to acid fumes during the finishing process. More rarely the finish is obtained by the use of a mechanical grinding wheel.

Applied— A handle or other portion of a vessel which consists of a separate piece of molten glass attached by hand to the object. Most often used with free-blown or mold-blown pieces but also used with early pressed glass.

Appliqued glass— A type of decorative glass which features hand-applied three-dimensional trim, often in the form of fruit or flowering vines. This glass trim is applied in the semi-molton state while the main object is still extremely hot so that the appliqué becomes an intregral part of the piece.

Art Glass— An umbrella term that refers to all types of decorative glasswares but most specifically to the expensive, specially patented lines produced during the late 19th century. Notable types of Art Glass include Amberina, Burmese and Peach Blow, among many others.

Butter pat (or chip)— A very small dish, often round or square, used on Victorian tables to hold an individual pat of butter. Most often

produced as part of china table services, only a few types were produced in glasswares, most notably in cut glass.

Cameo glass— A glass composed of two or more layers of glass, most often of contrasting colors, which are then carved through the surface with decorative designs. This ancient Roman technique was revived by the English in the late 19th century and English examples usually feature a white outer surface cut through to expose a single color background. English cameo often featured classical and botanical designs whereas the slightly later French cameo often featured more abstract naturalistic and landscape designs in more than two colors. Cameo carving can be done either by hand or with the use of acid, the hand-carved examples bringing higher prices.

Cased glass— Glassware which is composed of two or more layers of colored glass. The inner layer may be blown into outer layers while the glass is still hot or a piece in one color may be dipped into the molten glass of another color while it is hot. Cameo glass (see above) and Victorian satin glass are also often cased.

Console set— A three-piece tableware set generally composed of a pair of candlesticks and a wide, low-sided center bowl. These sets in pressed and mold-blown glassware were especially popular in the 1920s and 1930s.

Cracker jar— Also sometimes referred to as a 'bisquit jar,' these are decorative Victorian counterparts of the modern cookie jar. Produced in various chinawares as well as Art glass, they are often rounded barrel-shaped pieces fitted with a silver plate rim, cover and bail handle.

Crimping— A method of decorating the rims of bowls and vases. The glassworker used a special hand tool to manipulate the nearly-molten pressed or blown glass and form a ribbon-like design.

Crosshatching— A term generally used in discussing Brilliant Period cut glass. It refers to a cut design of parallel or crossed fine lines.

Crystal— A generic term generally used today when referring to thin, fine quality glass stemware produced since the early 20th century. Derived from the Italian term *cristallo* referring to delicate, clear Venetian blown glass produced since the 14th century.

Enameled decoration— A form of decoration used on many types of Victorian Art glass. White or colored enamel paints were generally hand-painted on a finished piece of glass which was then refired to bake-on the enamel decoration.

Epergne— A French term used to describe a special decorative vessel popular in the 19th century. It generally consists of one or more tall, slender trumpet-form vases centering a wide, shallow bowl base. The bowl base could also be raised on a pedestal foot. It sometimes refers to a piece with a figural pedestal base supporting several small bowls or suspending several small baskets. Also made from silver or other metals.

Etching— A method of decorating a piece of glass. The two main types are *acid etching* and *needle etching*. In acid etching a piece is covered with an acid-resistant protective layer and then scratched with a design which is then exposed to hydrofluoric acid or acid fumes, thus leaving a frosted design when the protective layer is removed. Needle etching is a 20th century technique where a hand-held or mechanized needle is used to draw a fine-lined design on a piece. Ornate repetative designs were possible with this mechanized needle.

Fire-polishing— A process used to finish mold-blown and pressed glass where a piece is reheated just enough to smooth out the mold seams without distorting the overall pattern.

Flashing— A form of decoration popular on various types of Victorian glass wherein a glass piece of one color is, while still very hot, dipped into molten glass of another color to form a very thin outer layer. Quite often this thin outer layer was then engraved with a naturalistic design cut through to the base color. A similar effect could be obtained by applying a color stain (often in ruby red or amber) and this staining was especially popular on late 19th century pattern glass whereas flashing was reserved for generally more expensive lines of glassware.

Handkerchief vase— A form of vase most often seen in 20th century Venetian glass where the sides of the piece are pulled straight up and randomly pleated to resemble a large handkerchief.

Iridescence— A type of shiny, metallic finish popular on late 19th and early 20th century glassware from makers such as Tiffany, Loetz and Steuben. The effect is achieved by spraying the still-hot piece with metallic oxides which deposit the shiny surface. Early 20th century Carnival glass utilized this finish on less expensive, mass-produced lines of pressed and mold-blown glass.

Jack-in-the-pulpit vase— A form of vase with the rim manipulated to resemble the wildflower of this name. Generally the back edge is curled up while the front edge is curled downward. Many types of late 19th century decorative glass featured vases in this form.

Knop— Another term for 'knob,' usually referring to a finial on a lid or a bulbous section on the stem of a goblet or wine glass.

Millefiori— An Italian term meaning "thousand flowers," in glass it refers to a design produced by combining small multicolored disks (or 'canes') of glass to form an overall design or to decorate the interior of a paperweight.

Mold-blown— A method of glass production where a blob of molten glass (called a "gather") is blown into a patterned mold and then removed and further blown and manipulated to form an object such as a bottle.

Novelty— A pressed or blown glass object generally made in the form of some larger item like a hatchet, boat or animal. They were extremely popular in the late 19th century and many were meant to be used as match holders, toothpick holders and small dresser boxes.

Opal— Pronounced o-pál, this was the term used by 19th century glassmen to describe the solid white glass today known as milk glass.

Piedouche— A French term referring to a paperweight which is raised on a low, applied clear foot.

Pontil mark— The scar left on the base of a free-blown, mold-blown and some early pressed glass by the pontil or punty rod. The hot glass object was attached at the base to the pontil rod so the glassworker could more easily handle it during the final shaping and finishing. When snapped off the pontil a round scar remained which, on finer quality pieces, was polished smooth.

Rigaree— Applied ribbon-like crimped decoration which highlights some types of Victorian Art glass. It is a form of *appliqued* (which see) decoration.

Rose bowl— A decorative small spherical or egg-shaped bowl, generally with a scalloped or crimped incurved rim, which was designed to hold rose petal potpourri or small rose blossoms. It was widely popular in the late 19th century and was produced in many pressed glass patterns as well as more expensive Art glass wares such as satin glass.

Scalloping— A decorative treatment used on the rims of plates, bowls, vases and similar objects. It was generally produced during the molding of the object and gave the rim a wavy or ruffled form.

Serrated— A form of notching on the rims of glass objects which resembles the edge of a saw blade. Sometimes reffered to as a *sawtooth* edge, it is quite often found on cut glass pieces.

Sickness— A term referring to cloudy staining found in pressed or blown glass pieces, especially bottles, decanters and vases. It is caused when a liquid is allowed to stand in a piece for a long period of time causing a chemical deterioration of the interior surface. Generally it is nearly impossible to remove completely.

Spall— A shallow rounded flake on a glass object, generally near the rim of a piece.

Stemware— A general term for any form of drinking vessel raised on a slender pedestal or stemmed base.

Teardrop— A deliberately placed inclusion in a piece of glass which is formed by a bubble of air. They are sometimes used to highlight the stopper of a bottle or decanter or in the stems of goblets, wines and other stemware.

Vesica— A cut glass term referring to a cut design in the form of a pointed oval.

Water set— A tableware set popular in all types of 19th and early 20th century glassware. It usually consisted of a large pitcher and a set of six matching tumblers or goblets.

Whimsey— A glass or ceramic novelty item. Generally in Victorian glass it is a free-blown or mold-blown object, often made by a glassworker as a special present and not part of regular glass production. Glass shoes, pipes and canes are examples of whimseys.

Appendix I
Glass Collectors' Clubs

Art & Decorative Glasswares

American Cut Glass Association
P.O. Box 482
Ramona, CA 92065-0482

Antique & Art Glass Salt Shaker
  Collectors' Society
2832 Rapidan Trail
Maitland, FL 32751-5013

Czechoslovakian Collectors Guild
  International
P.O. Box 901395
Kansas City, MO 64190-1395

Mount Washington Art Glass Society
P.O. Box 24094
Fort Worth, TX 76124-1094

Paperweight Collectors' Association
P.O. Box 40
Barker, TX 77413-0040

Vaseline Glass Collectors, Inc.
P.O. Box 125
Russellville, MO 65074

Wave Crest Collectors Club
P.O. Box 2013
Santa Barbara, CA 93120

The Whimsey Club
Lon Knickerbocker
2 Hessler Ct.
Dansville, NY 14437

Other Types of Glass

AKRO AGATE

Akro Agate Collector's Club, Inc.
Roger Hardy
97 Milford St.
Clarksburg, WV 26301

CAMBRIDGE

National Cambridge Collectors
P.O. Box 416
Cambridge, OH 43725-0416

CANDLEWICK

National Candlewick Collector's Club
6534 South Ave.
Holland, MI 43528

CARNIVAL

American Carnival Glass Association
9621 Springwater Lane
Miamisburg, OH 45342

Heart of America Carnival Glass
4305 W. 78th St.
Prairie Village, KS 66208

International Carnival Glass Association
P.O. Box 306
Mentone, IN 46539-0306

New England Carnival Glass Club
% Eva Backer, Membership
12 Sherwood Rd.
West Hartford, CT 06117-2738

DEPRESSION

National Depression Glass Association
P.O. Box 8264
Wichita, KS 67209-0264

20-30-40's Society, Inc.
P.O. Box 856
LaGrange, IL 60525-0856

Western Reserve Depression Glass Club
5168 Lake Vista Dr.
Solon, OH 44139

Canadian Depression Glass Association
119 Wexford Road
Brampton, Ontario CANADA L6Z 2T5

DUNCAN & MILLER

National Duncan Glass Society
P.O. Box 965
Washington, PA 15301

FENTON

Fenton Art Glass Collectors of America
P.O. Box 384
Williamstown, WV 26187

National Fenton Glass Society
P.O. Box 4008
Marietta, OH 45750-4008

FINDLAY

Collectors of Findlay Glass
P.O. Box 256
Findlay, OH 45839-0256

FOSTORIA
The Fostoria Glass Society of America
P.O. Box 826
Moundsville, WV 26041-0826

GREENTOWN
National Greentown Glass Association
P.O. Box 107
Greentown, IN 46936-0107

HEISEY
Heisey Collectors of America
169 W. Church St.
Newark, OH 43055

IMPERIAL
National Imperial Glass Collector's
    Society
P.O. Box 534
Bellaire, OH 43906

MILK GLASS
National Milk Glass Collectors Society
% Helen Storey
46 Almond Dr.
Hershey, PA 17033-1759

MORGANTOWN
Old Morgantown Glass Collectors' Guild
P.O. Box 894
Morgantown, WV 26507-0894

Morgantown Collectors of America, Inc.
% Jerry Gallagher
420 1st Ave. N.W.
Plainview, MN 55964-1213

PATTERN
Early American Pattern Glass Society
P.O. Box 266
Colesburg, IA 52035

PHOENIX & CONSOLIDATED
Phoenix & Consolidated Glass
    Collectors
41 River View Dr.
Essex Junction, VT 05452

STRETCH GLASS
Stretch Glass Society
P.O. Box 901
Hampshire, IL 60140

TIFFIN
Tiffin Glass Collectors' Club
P.O. Box 554
Tiffin, OH 44883-0554

WESTMORELAND
National Westmoreland Glass
    Collectors' Club
P.O. Box 100
Grapeville, PA 15634

Westmoreland Glass Society
1144 42nd Ave.
Vero Beach, FL 32960

Special Glass Clubs

Marble Collectors' Society of America
P.O. Box 222
Trumbull, CT 06611-0222

National Marble Club of America
440 Eaton Rd.
Drexel Hill, PA 19026-1205

National Reamer Collectors Association
% Deborah Gillham
47 Midline Ct.
Gaithersburg, MD 20878-1996

National Toothpick Holder
    Collectors' Society
P.O. Box 417
Safety Harbor, FL 34695-0417

International Perfume Bottle Association
3314 Shamrock Rd.
Tampa, FL 33629

General Glass Clubs

Art Glass Discussion Group
405 Lafayette Ave.
Cincinnati, OH 45220

Historical Glass Museum
1157 N. Orange, Box 921
Redlands, CA 92373

Glass Research Society of New Jersey
1501 Glasstown Rd.
Millville, NJ 08332-1566

National American Glass Club
P.O. Box 8489
Silver Spring, MD 20907

Appendix II
Museum Collections of American Glass

Many local and regional museums around the country have displays with some pressed glass included. The following are especially noteworthy.

New England

Connecticut: Wadsworth Atheneum, Hartford.

Maine: Jones Gallery of Glass and Ceramics (June - October), Sebago; Portland Museum of Art, Portland.

Massachusetts: Old Sturbridge Village, Sturbridge; Sandwich Glass Museum (April - November), Sandwich.

New Hampshire: The Currier Gallery of Art, Manchester.

Vermont: Bennington Museum (March - November), Bennington.

Mid-Atlantic

Delaware: Henry Francis du Pont Winterthur Museum, Winterthur.

New Jersey: Museum of American Glass, Wheaton Village, Millville.

New York: Corning Museum of Glass, Corning; Cooper-Hewitt Museum, The Smithsonian Institution's National Museum of Design (by appointment), New York; Metropolitan Museum of Art, New York; New-York Historical Society, New York.

Pennsylvania: Historical Society of Western Pennsylvania, Pittsburgh; Philadelphia Museum of Art, Philadelphia; Westmoreland Glass Museum, Port Vue.

Southeast

Florida: Lightner Museum, Saint Augustine; Morse Gallery of Art (Tiffany glass), Winter Park.

Louisiana: New Orleans Museum of Art, New Orleans.

Tennessee: Houston Antique Museum, Chattanooga.

Virginia: Chrysler Museum of Norfolk, Norfolk.

Washington, D.C.: National Museum of American History, Smithsonian Institution.

West Virginia: The Huntington Galleries, Inc., Huntington; Oglebay Institute - Mansion Museum, Wheeling; West Virginia Museum of American Glass, Weston.

Midwest

Indiana: Greentown Glass Museum, Greentown; Indiana Glass Museum, Dunkirk.

Michigan: Henry Ford Museum, Dearborn.

Minnesota: A.M. Chisholm Museum, Duluth.

Ohio: Cambridge Glass Museum, Cambridge; Milan Historical Museum, Milan; National Heisey Glass Museum, Newark; Toledo Museum of Art, Toledo.

Wisconsin: John Nelson Bergstrom Art Center and Mahler Glass Museum, Neenah.

Southwest and West

California: Los Angeles County Museum of Art, Los Angeles; Wine Museum of San Francisco and M.H. de Young Museum, San Francisco.

Texas: Mills Collection, Texas Christian University, Fort Worth, MSC Forsyth Center Galleries, Texas A & M University, College Station.

Selected Bibliography

ART GLASS - GENERAL

Grover, Ray and Lee. *Art Glass Nouveau.* Rutland, Vermont: Charles E. Tuttle Company, 1968.

Grover, Ray and Lee. *Carved & Decorated European Art Glass.* Rutland, Vermont: Charles E. Tuttle Company, 1970.

Lee, Ruth Webb. *Victorian Glass, Specialties of the Nineteenth Century.* Rutland, Vermont: Charles E. Tuttle Company, 1985.

Pullin, Anne Geffken, *Glass Signatures, Trademarks and Trade Names from the seventeenth to the twentieth century.* Radnor, Pennsylvania: Wallace-Homestead Book Company, 1986.

Revi, Albert Christian. *Nineteenth Century Glass - Its Genesis and Development.* New York, New York: Thomas Nelson, Inc., 1971.

BOHEMIAN GLASS

Truitt, Robert and Deborah. *Collectible Bohemian Glass, 1880-1940.* Kensington, Maryland: B & D Glass, 1995.

CHOCOLATE GLASS

Measell, James. *Greentown Glass - The Indiana Tumbler & Goblet Company.* Grand Rapids, Michigan: The Grand Rapids Public Museum, 1979.

CUSTARD GLASS

Heacock, William. *Encyclopedia of Victorian Colored Pattern Glass, Book 4, Custard Glass from A to Z.* Marietta, Ohio: Antique Publications, 1976.

_____. *Fenton Glass - The First Twenty-five Years.* Marietta, Ohio: O-Val Advertising Corp., 1978.

Heacock, William and James Measell and Berry Wiggins. *Harry Northwood - The Early Years - 1881-1900.* Marietta, Ohio: Antique Publications, 1990.

_____. *Harry Northwood - The Wheeling Years - 1901-1925.* Marietta, Ohio: Antique Publications, 1991.

CUT GLASS

Boggess, Bill and Louise. *American Brilliant Cut Glass.* New York, New York: Crown Publishers, 1977.

_____. *Collecting American Brilliant Cut Glass, 1876-1916.* West Chester, Pennsylvania: Schiffer Publishing, Ltd., 1992.

Farrar, Estelle Sinclaire, and Jane Shadel Spillman. *The Complete Cut & Engraved Glass of Corning.* New York, New York: Crown Publishers and The Corning Museum of Glass, 1979.

Pearson, J. Michael and Dorothy T. *American Cut Glass For the Discriminating Collector.* New York, New York: Vantage Press, 1965

Pearson, J. Michael. *Encyclopedia of American Cut and Engraved Glass (1880-1917) Volumes I, II and III.* Miami Beach, Florida: self-published, 1975, 1977 & 1978.

Revi, Albert Christian. *American Cut and Engraved Glass.* New York, New York: Thomas Nelson, Inc., 1972.

Spillman, Jane Shadel. *The American Cut Glass Industry - T.G. Hawkes and his Competitors.* Wappingers' Falls, New York: Antique Collectors' Club and The Corning Museum of Glass, 1996.

Wiener, Herbert, and Freda Lipkowitz. *Rarities in American Cut Glass.* Houston, Texas: The Collectors House of Books Publishing Co., 1975.

ENGLISH GLASS

Grover, Ray and Lee. *English Cameo Glass.* New York, New York: Crown Publishers, 1980.

Hadjemin, Charles R. *British Glass - 1800-1914.* Woodbridge, England: The Antique Collectors' Club, 1991.

Manley, Cyril. *Decorative Victorian Glass.* New York, New York: Van Nostrand Reinhold Company, 1981.

Wakefield, Hugh. *Nineteenth Century British Glass.* London, England: Faber and Faber, Ltd., 1982.

FRENCH GLASS

Garner, Phillippe. *Emile Gallé.* New York, New York: Rizzoli International Publications, Inc., 1976.

McClinton, Katharine Morrison. *Introduction to Lalique Glass.* Des Moines, Iowa: Wallace-Homestead Book Company, 1978.

Percy, Christopher Vane. *The Glass of Lalique, a collector's guide.* New York, New York: Charles Scribner's Sons, 1983.

LIBBEY GLASS

Fauster, Carl U. *Libbey Glass Since 1818 - Pictorial History & Collectors' Guide.* Toledo, Ohio: Len Beach Press, 1979.

MARY GREGORY

Truitt, R. & D. *Mary Gregory Glassware, 1880-1990.* Kensington, Maryland: self-published, 1992.

MOSER GLASS

Charon, Mural K. *Ludwig (Ludvik) Moser - King of Glass.* Hillsdale, Michigan: Charon/Ferguson, Division of Ferguson Communications, Publishers, 1984.

OPALESCENT GLASS

Heacock, William. *Encyclopdia of Victorian Colored Pattern Glass, Book II, Opalescent Glass from A to Z.* Marietta, Ohio: Antique Publications, 1975.

_____. *Fenton Glass - The First Twenty-five Years.* Marietta, Ohio: O-Val Advertising Corp., 1978.

Heacock, William, and William Gamble. *Encyclopedia of Victorian Colored Glass, Book 9, Cranberry Opalescent from A to Z.* Marietta, Ohio: Antique Publications, 1987.

Heacock, William and James Measell and Berry Wiggins. *Harry Northwood - The Early Years - 1881-1900.* Marietta, Ohio: Antique Publications, 1990.

_____. *Harry Northwood - The Wheeling Years - 1901-1925.* Marietta, Ohio: Antique Publications, 1991.

PAIRPOINT GLASS

Avila, George C. *The Pairpoint Glass Story.* New Bedford, Massachusetts: The New Bedford Glass Society, 1978.

Padgett Leonard E. *Pairpoint Glass.* Des Moines, Iowa: Wallace-Homestead Book Company, 1979.

PAPERWEIGHTS

Flemming, Monika and Peter Pommerencke. *Paperweights of the World.* Atglen, Pennsylvania: Schiffer Publishing, Ltd., 1993.

Hollister, Paul. *Glass Paperweights of the New-York Historical Society.* New York, New York: Clarkson N. Potter, Inc., 1974.

STEUBEN GLASS

Dimitroff, Thomas P. *Frederick Carder and Steuben Glass - American Classics.* Atglen, Pennsylvania: Schiffer Publishing, Ltd., 1998.

Gardner, Paul V. *The Glass of Frederick Carder.* New York, New York: Crown Publishers, Inc., 1971.

TIFFANY GLASS

Koch, Robert. *Louis C. Tiffany's Glass - Bronzes - Lamps, A Complete Collector's Guide.* New York, New York: Crown Publishers, 1971.

_____. *Louis C. Tiffany - Rebel in Glass.* New York, Crown Publishers, 1964.

McKean, Hugh F. *The "Lost" Treasures of Louis Comfort Tiffany.* New York, New York: Doubleday & Company, 1980.

WAVE CREST

Cohen, Wilfred R. *Wave Crest - The Glass of C.F. Monroe.* Paducah, Kentucky: Collector Books, 1987.

Grimmer, Elsa H. *Wave Crest Ware - An Illustrated Guide to the Victorian World of C.F. Monroe.* Des Moines, Iowa: Wallace-Homestead Book Company, 1979.

INDEX